Trade Unions in Western Europe

Trade unions in most of Europe are on the defensive: in recent decades they have lost membership, sometimes drastically; their collective bargaining power has declined, as has their influence on government; and in many countries, their public respect is much diminished.

This book explores the challenges facing trade unions and their responses in ten west European countries: Britain, Ireland, Sweden, Denmark, Germany, Austria, the Netherlands, Belgium, France, and Italy. Based on a substantial number of interviews with key union representatives and academic experts in each country, together with the collection of a large amount of union documentation and background material, the book gives an account of how trade unionism has evolved in each country, the main recent challenges that unions have faced, and their responses. The book engages with the debates of the past two decades on union modernization and revitalization, and more generally with theories of institutional change and the literature on varieties of capitalism.

Some observers ask whether unions remain relevant socio-economic actors, but challenging times can stimulate new thinking, and hence provide new opportunities. This book aims to show why trade unions are (still) important subjects for scientific analysis: first, as a means of collective 'voice' allowing employees to challenge management control and bringing a measure of balance to the employment relationship; second, as a form of 'countervailing power' to the socio-economic dominance of capital; and third, their potential as a 'sword of justice' to defend the weak, vulnerable and disadvantaged, express a set of values in opposition to the dominant political economy, and offer aspirations for a different—and better—form of society.

Rebecca Gumbrell-McCormick is a Senior Lecturer in Management at Birkbeck College, University of London.

Richard Hyman is Emeritus Professor of Industrial Relations at the London School of Economics.

Trade Unions in Western Europe

Hard Times, Hard Choices

Rebecca Gumbrell-McCormick
and
Richard Hyman

UNIVERSITY PRESS

UNIVERSITY PRESS

Great Clarendon Street, Oxford, OX2 6DP,
United Kingdom

Oxford University Press is a department of the University of Oxford.
It furthers the University's objective of excellence in research, scholarship,
and education by publishing worldwide. Oxford is a registered trade mark of
Oxford University Press in the UK and in certain other countries

© Rebecca Gumbrell-McCormick and Richard Hyman 2013

The moral rights of the authors have been asserted

First published 2013
First published in paperback 2018

All rights reserved. No part of this publication may be reproduced, stored in
a retrieval system, or transmitted, in any form or by any means, without the
prior permission in writing of Oxford University Press, or as expressly permitted
by law, by licence or under terms agreed with the appropriate reprographics
rights organization. Enquiries concerning reproduction outside the scope of the
above should be sent to the Rights Department, Oxford University Press, at the
address above

You must not circulate this work in any other form
and you must impose this same condition on any acquirer

Published in the United States of America by Oxford University Press
198 Madison Avenue, New York, NY 10016, United States of America

British Library Cataloguing in Publication Data

Data available

Library of Congress Cataloging in Publication Data

Data available

ISBN 978–0–19–964441–4 (Hbk.)
ISBN 978–0–19–881678–2 (Pbk.)

Links to third party websites are provided by Oxford in good faith and
for information only. Oxford disclaims any responsibility for the materials
contained in any third party website referenced in this work.

To the memory of Georges Debunne (1918–2008) and
Jack Jones (1913–2009), inspirational European trade unionists

Preface

For several decades, trade unions in Europe have been on the defensive. They have lost membership, sometimes drastically. Their collective bargaining power has declined, as has their influence on government and, in some countries, their public respect. Unions in western Europe achieved their greatest socio-economic status half a century ago, in the context of large-scale industrial production ('Fordism') and the rise of the Keynesian welfare state. Leading employers were 'national champions', and national governments self-evidently shaped social and economic policy; it seemed obvious that unions were a crucial actor in a triangular relationship.

Today the landscape has changed irrevocably. Governments profess their inability to resist the dictates of global economic forces; major companies are almost universally transnational in ownership and in their production strategies; trade unions are often disoriented. Many show obvious uncertainty as to their role in the 21st century, giving rise to internal conflicts. Some observers ask whether unions remain relevant socio-economic actors. But hard times can stimulate new thinking and hence provide new opportunities; the challenge is to review unions' purposes and priorities and to devise new ways of achieving these. This can involve hard choices: not all objectives can receive priority, particularly when resources are scarcer. In our view, participation in the search for effective responses is a key task for socially responsible researchers.

Why do we insist that trade unions are (still) important subjects for scientific analysis? First, unions provide a collective 'voice' through which employees can counter unilateral, and potentially autocratic, management control (Freeman and Medoff 1984); they bring a measure of democracy to the employment relationship. Second, they constitute a form of 'countervailing power' to the socio-economic dominance of capital (Galbraith 1952); this function is even more important, if also far more difficult to perform, in an era of multinational corporations (MNCs) and the financialization of the global economy. Third, unions are, at least potentially, a 'sword of justice' (Flanders 1970): they have historically fought to defend the weak, vulnerable, and disadvantaged, have expressed a set of values—or 'moral economy' (Thompson 1971)—in opposition to the dominant dehumanizing political economy, and have offered aspirations for a different—and better—form of society.

Preface

This book is the main outcome of a research project for which we received funding between 2006 and 2009 from the Danish Social Research Council (*Forskningsrådet for Samfund og Erhverv*), enabling us to undertake our fieldwork. The original aim was to address trade union responses to globalization. It soon became obvious that this definition was both too broad and too narrow. Too broad, in that globalization is a portmanteau concept with no agreed definition: it can be stretched to encompass virtually every major social and economic trend. Too narrow, in that unions face many challenges—the difficulty of recruiting younger workers, to give just one example—which it would be far-fetched to attribute primarily to globalization. Our research developed in line with the unfolding global financial and economic crisis: this was inevitably the main preoccupation of many participants in our fieldwork, becoming a dominant background theme to the research. Since we focused on different countries at different phases of the crisis, comparative analysis became particularly challenging.

Our study includes larger and smaller countries from each of the four commonly identified varieties of west European capitalism: in the Nordic case, Sweden and Denmark; the 'central' group of Germany, Austria, the Netherlands, and Belgium; in 'southern' Europe, France, and Italy; and the 'liberal market economies' of Britain and Ireland. It would have been valuable to include countries from Central and Eastern Europe (CEE), but the limitations of our linguistic abilities precluded this: we strongly believe that serious comparative research requires the capacity at least to read the languages of the countries covered.

In each country we recorded interviews with key officials at confederal level and in sectoral unions—normally including metalworking and public services—and in some cases at regional as well as national levels. This provided a range of perspectives, but certainly not a full picture. Normally the interviews were in the relevant national language. We also interviewed academic experts and other informed observers. Beyond this, we accumulated a large volume of primary documentation as well as digesting a mass of secondary literature. Studying trade unions, which are elaborate social organizations with often opaque internal political dynamics, in ten countries at a time of economic turmoil has involved issues of some analytical complexity. To return to the initial conception of our project, economic internationalization has clearly been a source of many of the key challenges facing trade unions, but change in industrial relations 'is not so much driven by the juggernaut of global product markets but is the result of a complex interaction of markets, institutions and actors' (Kelly 2012: 354). In the book that follows we have attempted to do justice to this complexity, while also seeking to identify broad general trends and processes.

We are very grateful to the *Forskningsråd* for its financial support, and to our colleague Steen Scheuer, now at Syddansk Universitet, who was the main award holder. Without the cooperation of our interview partners who willingly gave of their time, often when themselves under great pressure—we recall one general secretary who had to interrupt our conversation in order to take a call from the prime minister—this study would have been impossible, and we offer our profound gratitude. We also record special thanks to Stefania Marino, who provided major assistance with our research in Italy and compensated for limitations in our command of the language. Finally, we thank Heiner Dribbusch, Roland Erne, Janine Goetschy, John Kelly, Salvo Leonardi, Guglielmo Meardi, Steen Scheuer, and Kurt Vandaele, who made valuable comments on a draft of this book. The usual disclaimers apply.

We commence with two introductory chapters, the first mapping the trade union landscape in the ten countries and the second presenting an overview of key challenges and responses. The next five chapters are arranged thematically, each examining union initiatives in a key policy area. We make no attempt to present detailed conclusions to each chapter, for the separate sections stand on their own. We end, not with an overview of the book as a whole—an impossible task—but by returning to these themes by exploring ways in which unions can integrate strategic action with democratic involvement.

Our hope is that this work will be of value, not only to scholars but more importantly to trade unionists themselves, as they struggle to find solutions to immense challenges. Hard times, hard choices; but strategic initiative is still possible.

Contents

List of Figures   xiii
List of Tables   xv
List of Abbreviations   xvii

1. Mapping the Terrain: Varieties of Industrial Relations and Trade Unionism   1
2. Hard Times: Challenges and Responses   29
3. Renewing Power Resources: Recruitment, Representation, and Mobilization   52
4. Restructuring Trade Unionism: Mergers and Organizational Redesign   81
5. Bargaining in Adversity: Decentralization, Social Partnership, and the Crisis   102
6. Unions and Politics: Parties, Alliances, and the Battle of Ideas   132
7. Beyond National Boundaries: Unions, Europe, and the World   158
8. Hard Choices: Reconciling Strategy and Democracy   191

Afterword to the Paperback Edition   207
References   233
Index   263

List of Figures

8.1 Strategic unionism: A stylized framework for comparison 195
8.2 The 'magic triangle' 198

List of Tables

1.1	Labour market indicators, 2011	4
1.2	Trade union density and collective bargaining coverage, 1980 and 2010	5
2.1	Labour market insecurity, age 15–24 (2011)	34
3.1	Disaggregated union density statistics (%)	54
5.1	Strike days per 1,000 workers, annual averages	105
5.2	Dimensions of the crisis	123
6.1	'Left' seats in most recent national and European elections	139
A.1	Labour market insecurity, 2010 and 2016 (%)	211
A.2	Trade union density and collective bargaining coverage, 2010 and 2015	211
A.3	Trade union density by age group, 2015	212
A.4	Strike days per 1000 workers, annual averages	221
A.5	'Left' seats in most recent national and European elections	223

List of Abbreviations

AbvaKabo	[public services union, Netherlands]
ABVV	Algemeen Belgisch Vakverbond
AC	Akademikernes Centralorganisation
ACLVB	Algemene Centrale der Liberale Vakbonden van België
ACV	Algemeen Christelijk Vakverbond
ACW	Algemeen Christelijk Werknemersverbond
AK	Bundesarbeitskammer or Arbeiterkammer
ATTAC	Association pour la taxation des transactions pour l'aide aux citoyens
BASTUN	Baltic Sea Trade Union Network
CDA	Christlich-Demokratische Arbeitnehmerschaft
CDU	Christlich Demokratische Union
CD&V	Christen-Democratisch en Vlaams
CEE	Central and Eastern Europe
CFDT	Confédération française démocratique du travail
CFTC	Confédération française des travailleurs chrétiens
CFE-CGC	Confédération générale des cadres
CGB	Christlicher Gewerkschaftsbund Deutschlands
CGIL	Confederazione generale italiana del lavoro
CGSLB	Centrale Générale des Syndicats Libéraux de Belgique
CGT	Confédération générale du travail
CISC	Confédération internationale des syndicats chrétiens
CISL	Confederazione italiana sindacati lavoratori
CME	coordinated market economy
CNV	Christelijk Nationaal Vakverbond
CPE	contrat première embauche
CSC	Confédération des Syndicats Chrétiens
CSR	corporate social responsibility
DBB	dbb beamtenbund und tarifunion
DGB	Deutscher Gewerkschaftsbund
ECJ	European Court of Justice
EEA	European Economic Area

List of Abbreviations

EEC	European Economic Community
EFA	European framework agreement
EMCEF	European Mine, Chemical and Energy Workers' Federation (now IndustriALL)
EMF	European Metalworkers' Federation (now IndustriALL)
EMU	Economic and Monetary Union
ESF	European Social Forum
ETUC	European Trade Union Confederation
ETUF	European Trade Union Federation
ETUI	European Trade Union Institute
EU	European Union
EWC	European works council
FeLSA-CISL	Federazione lavoratori somministrati autonomi atipici
FES	Friedrich-Ebert-Stiftung
3F	Fagligt Fælles Forbund
FGTB	Fédération Générale du Travail de Belgique
FIOM	Federazione impiegati operai metallurgici
FNV	Federatie Nederlandse Vakbeweging
FO	CGT-Force ouvrière
FOA	[Danish union of public employees]
FPÖ	Freiheitliche Partei Österreichs
FTF	[Danish white-collar confederation]
GEW	[Gewerkschaft Erziehung und Wissenschaft]
GMB	[British general union]
GPA	Gewerkschaft der Privatangestellten
GUF	Global Union Federation
HK	[Danish retail and clerical union]
HTF	[Swedish retail and commercial union]
ICFTU	International Confederation of Free Trade Unions
ICTU	Irish Congress of Trade Unions
IFA	international framework agreement
IG BAU	Industriegewerkschaft Bauen-Agrar-Umwelt
IG BCE	Industriegewerkschaft Bergbau, Chemie, Energie
IG Metall	Industriegewerkschaft Metall
ILO	International Labour Organization
IMF	International Monetary Fund
IndustriALL	*see* EMF
ITUC	International Trade Union Confederation
IWW	Industrial Workers of the World
KAD	Kvindeligt Arbejderforbund i Danmark
KriFa	Kristelig Fagbevægelse
LGBT	lesbian, gay, bisexual, and transgender

List of Abbreviations

LME	liberal market economy
LO (Sweden)	Landsorganisationen i Sverige
LO (Denmark)	Landsorganisationen i Danmark
Mandate	[Irish union of retail, bar, and administrative workers]
MBL	Medbestämmandelagen
MEDEF	Mouvement des Entreprises de France
MHP	Vakcentrale voor Middengroepen en Hoger Personeel
MNC	multinational corporation
MOC	Mouvement ouvrier chrétien
NFS	Nordens Fackliga Samorganisation
NGG	Gewerkschaft Nahrung-Genuss-Gaststätten
NGO	non-governmental organization
NIdiL	Nuove indentità di lavoro
NKV	Nederlands Katholiek Vakverbond
NVV	Nederlands Verbond van Vakverenigingen
ÖGB	Österreichischer Gewerkschaftsbund
ÖTV	Gewerkschaft Öffentliche Dienste, Transport und Verkehr
ÖVP	Österreichische Volkspartei
PCF	Parti communiste français
PCI	Partito comunista italiano
PCS	Public and Commercial Services Union
PD	Partito democratico
PS (Belgium)	Parti Socialiste
PS (France)	Parti socialiste
PSI	Partito socialista italiano
PvdA	Partij van de Arbeid
PWD	Posted workers directive
QMV	qualified majority voting
RILU	Red International of Labour Unions
RMT	National Union of Rail, Maritime and Transport Workers
RSU	rappresentanza sindacale unitaria
SACO	Sveriges Akademikers Centralorganisation
SAF	Svenska Arbetsgivareföreningen
SAP	Sveriges socialdemokratiska arbetareparti
SEA	Single European Act
SER	Sociaal-Economische Raad
SF	Socialistisk Folkeparti
SiD	Specialarbejderforbundet i Danmark
SIF	Svenska industritjänstemannaförbundet
SIPTU	Services, Industrial, Professional and Technical Union
SMART	specific, measurable, achievable, realistic, time-based (of goals)

List of Abbreviations

SMIC	salaire minimum interprofessionnel de croissance
SMT	senior management team
SN	Svenskt Näringsliv
SP	Socialistische Partij
SPD	Sozialdemokratische Partei Deutschlands
SPÖ	Sozialdemokratische Partei Österreichs
SUD	Union syndicale solidaires
STvdA	Stichting van de Arbeid
TCE	Treaty establishing a Constitution for Europe
TCO	Tjänstemännens Centralorganisation
TGWU	Transport and General Workers' Union (now Unite)
TIB	Forbundet Træ-Industri-Byg
TUC	Trades Union Congress
UCATT	Union of Construction, Allied Trades and Technicians
UIL	Unione italiana del lavoro
UK	United Kingdom
UMF	Union Modernisation Fund
UNI	Union Network International
Unionen	[merger of Swedish SIF and HTF unions]
Unison	[British public service trade union]
Unite	*see* TGWU
USA	United States of America
USDAW	Union of Shop, Distributive and Allied Workers
VENRO	[umbrella body of development NGOs]
ver.di	Vereinte Dienstleistungsgewerkschaft
WCL	World Confederation of Labour
WFTU	World Federation of Trade Unions
WKÖ	Wirtschaftskammer Österreich

Note: references in square brackets are for organizations which now use only initials, not a full title, or have adopted a name that is not an abbreviated title.

1

Mapping the Terrain: Varieties of Industrial Relations and Trade Unionism

What is a trade union? More than a century ago, when Sidney and Beatrice Webb wrote their pioneering *History of Trade Unionism*, they offered the following definition (Webb and Webb 1894: 1): 'a trade union, as we understand the term, is a continuous association of wage-earners for the purpose of maintaining or improving the conditions of their employment'. In their subsequent analytical study, *Industrial Democracy* (Webb and Webb 1897), they described trade union functions as comprising 'mutual insurance' (by which they meant providing financial benefits when members faced adversity); collective bargaining (a term which they themselves invented); and 'legal enactment' (pressure for favourable government action).

These conceptions were limited by time and place. When they published a revised *History* in 1920 they referred to 'the conditions of their working lives', not just 'employment': a recognition that unions were concerned with the position of workers within society, not only in relation to their particular employer. They might also have noted that the growth in white-collar unionism made the reference to 'wage-earners' unduly narrow. Yet a more fundamental issue is that their much-quoted definition frames trade union purposes in terms of the defence of primarily economic interests, whereas the notion of 'industrial democracy' implied that unions were, at least potentially, vehicles of social and political transformation. In their book with that title, indeed, they distinguished two trade union 'devices' which they termed 'restriction of numbers' and 'the common rule': the first defending the market position of relatively advantaged groups of workers against encroachment by others less favourably placed; the second pursuing improvements from which all could benefit.

How far unions pursue narrow economic interests on the one hand, a broader social agenda on the other, changes over time and differs significantly between (as well as within) countries. To an important extent, such differences connect to contrasting understandings of trade unions and their primary objectives and modes of action. Do they recruit only employees, or also the self-employed, the unemployed, pensioners? Do they represent only their members, or the interests of a broader constituency? Is the agenda they pursue exclusively employment related, or does it encompass broader social and political issues? Do they rely primarily on peaceful bargaining (whether with employers or with governments), with strike action the very last resort, or do they often resort to mobilization and militancy, understanding trade unionism as a social movement rather than simply an organization?

Trade unions have been described as 'intermediary organizations' (Müller-Jentsch 1985), since their main task as collective actors is to deploy workers' collective resources in interaction with those who exert power over them. This means that it is impossible to understand unions in isolation. They are embedded in four main types of relationship. First, with their own members and constituents, giving rise to issues of democracy and accountability. Second, with employers, raising issues of recognition, and of the distribution but also production of profit. Third, with governments, involving issues of the economic and juridical framework of industrial relations, the representative status of unions in policy-making—what Ewing (2005) terms their 'public administration function'—and the 'social wage' constituted by public welfare provision. Fourth, with 'civil society' (or 'public opinion'), which has become increasingly important as unions' intrinsic resources diminish and they seek external legitimacy and alliances with other non-governmental organizations (NGOs). We may note that the first relationship generates a 'logic of membership', which implies responsiveness to members' expectations; the second and third, a 'logic of influence', whereby action is adapted to the expectations of unions' interlocutors in order to deliver results (Schmitter and Streeck 1981); the fourth, however, transcends this division.

In this book we explore these four patterns of relationship in ten countries. Some scholars question whether nations are (still) the appropriate unit of analysis when examining the actors and processes of industrial relations (Katz and Darbishire 2000); and we will certainly consider some of the key variations within each country. But it is also important to stress that individual countries (or groups of countries) possess distinctive configurations of institutions which establish the terrain of trade union organization and action. As Meardi insists (2011: 339), 'if nations are not the beginning and the end of culture, they are not dead or irrelevant either...Law, political traditions and language are particularly important factors that operate mostly at the national level.' For example, labour law in many countries precisely defines the legitimate actors in industrial relations, the status of collective agreements, the legality of strikes, the mechanisms for remedying disputes.

The functioning of works councils or committees, firmly established in most of the countries we examine, follows nationally specific rules which help define the degree to which they are complementary to trade unions. Some 'state traditions' (Crouch 1993) assign unions an accepted role in the formulation of public policy. In many cases, the processes of 'industrial relations' as understood in the anglophone world and of social policy are closely intertwined, giving unions a key role in the administration of the welfare state. The organization and preferences of employers differ significantly across countries, with major implications for the character and coverage of collective bargaining (Clegg 1976). The institutional shape of trade unionism itself reflects often long processes of historical evolution which are often path dependent and resistant to change; so, for example, ideological divisions which have lost much of their former resonance may still leave a powerful institutional heritage in conflicts between rival confederations which to the outsider possess little practical logic.

Certainly institutions can change, not least in the sphere of industrial relations: this is the theme of a large and growing literature (Crouch 2005; Streeck 2009; Thelen 2004). However much some of the discussion of 'globalization' may exaggerate, the intensification of cross-national competitive forces, the internationalization of financial capital, and the strategic priorities of MNCs have indeed stress-tested national industrial relations systems. The policies of the European Union (EU), themselves among the drivers of economic internationalization, have also had a direct influence on national labour law and labour market institutions. To acknowledge such trends, however, is not to accept that homogenization has proceeded so far that national distinctiveness has vanished. When we survey European trade unions, national specificity remains striking.

It has become common to distinguish between different 'varieties of capitalism' according to how far, and through what mechanisms, markets—including labour markets—are socially and politically regulated. Hall and Soskice (2001), in their pioneering exposition of the thesis, drew a dichotomy between 'liberal' and 'coordinated' market economies (LMEs and CMEs). Subsequent studies (Amable 2003; Hancké et al. 2007; Schmidt 2002) have criticized this binary schema and developed more elaborate classifications, taking into account in particular the role of the state in managing the economy and structuring the labour market. An analogous debate has followed the effort of Esping-Andersen (1990) to outline 'three worlds' of welfare provision: a privatized 'liberal' model, an egalitarian 'Social-democratic' model, and a state-led but inegalitarian 'social insurance' model. Here too, critics have argued the need to distinguish additional models. In both respects, attention to national socio-economic context is crucial for any comparative analysis of trade unionism. As Hoffmann and Hoffmann insist (2009: 389), the impact on unions of similar external challenges is very different, 'depending on their own organisational structures and political culture and on the particular variety of capitalism and welfare state model in which they are embedded'.

It has also long been argued that small countries, particularly when highly exposed to world markets, exhibit particularly strongly organized industrial relations (Katzenstein 1985), and that unions are likely to be tightly integrated into national policy-making institutions. Accordingly, our study includes larger and smaller countries and encompasses each of the four commonly identified varieties of capitalism in western Europe: Sweden and Denmark, with Social-democratic traditions, exceptionally high union density, and elaborate egalitarian welfare regimes; Germany, Austria, Belgium, and the Netherlands, with institutionalized 'social partnership'; France and Italy, with a history of strong Communist parties linked to adversarial and weakly institutionalized industrial relations; and the LMEs of Britain and Ireland. These four groupings are widely adopted as broad classifications of industrial relations regimes in western Europe (Ebbinghaus and Visser 1999; Visser 2009). We outline some of the characteristics of each country, pointing to the complexities affecting any attempt at classification, and indicate ways in which traditional models have been changing. Some basic labour market indicators are presented in Table 1.1. We list the countries in the order of the summaries above.

We link these accounts to the literature on 'varieties of unionism', showing how traditional union identities have reflected national contexts but are also

Table 1.1. Labour market indicators, 2011

	Population (million)	Employment rate 20–64 (%)	Female rate (%)	Fixed-term contracts (%)	Part-time (%)	Unemployment rate (%)
SE	9.3	80	77	16	26	7.5
DK	5.5	76	72	9	26	7.6
DE	82.0	76	71	15	26	5.9
AT	8.4	75	70	10	27	4.2
NL	16.5	77	71	18	49*	4.4
BE	10.8	67	62	9	25	7.2
FR	62.5	69	65	15	18	9.6
IT	60.0	61	50	13	16	8.4
UK	61.6	74	68	6	27	8.0
IE	4.5	64	60	10	24	14.4

* In NL, part-time status is defined as working under 35 hours a week; elsewhere, it is based on employees' self-definition.

Source: Eurostat.

Table 1.2. Trade union density and collective bargaining coverage, 1980 and 2010

	Union density		Bargaining coverage	
	1980	2010	1980	2010
SE	78	69	85	91
DK	79	68	72	80
DE	35	19	78	62
AT	57	28	95	99
NL	35	19	79	82
BE	54	52	97	96
FR	18	8	85	90
IT	48	33	85	80
UK	51	27	70	33
IE	64	37	64	44

Source: ICTWSS database for 2008–9, based on national sources (Visser 2011).

subject to transformation. As an indicator of two key features of different national models, Table 1.2 presents data for membership density and collective bargaining coverage in each country, showing clear cross-national differences and also significant changes over time. Four points emerge clearly. First, density varies remarkably across countries, the differences even more striking if compared to the far more uniform proportion of voters supporting 'left' parties, usually regarded as partners within a broader labour movement. Second, density has declined universally in the past three decades, but far more severely in some countries than others. In general, unions where membership levels were initially high have proved more resilient, thus disparities have increased over time. Third, while there are clear differences in bargaining coverage, they are less dramatic; and some countries with very low union density have high coverage. Finally, coverage levels have fallen far less than union density, and indeed in some countries are today higher than thirty years ago. Overall, as Checchi and Visser (2005) argue, the relative positions of different countries tend to persist: collective regulation seems path dependent.

Below we present a brief initial outline of our ten countries, focusing on the social, economic, and political context and the characteristics of each movement in the period of its greatest strength and influence. As part of this discussion we first review some of the explanations for these distinctive national patterns. In the following chapter we survey the key challenges and changes which have threatened each of the national models, and present an initial overview of different attempts at 'revitalization'.

Models of Trade Unionism

In any cross-national comparison one can use the telescope or the microscope. The first reveals broad contours rather than fine details, and from a sufficient distance one mountain may resemble many others. On this basis, comparativists create classifications of country groups, proposing a parsimonious catalogue of types rather than insisting on the uniqueness of each national case (which would make comparative analysis virtually impossible). But there is always a trade-off between parsimony and accuracy. Through a microscope, the differences between seemingly similar cases become all too apparent. In the 19th century, Darwin distinguished 'lumpers' (who worked with broad, encompassing categories of phenomena) from 'splitters' (who emphasized the differences between cases). In the following discussion we lump our ten cases into the four groups outlined above, but in splitting mode outline key differences within each category.

Before turning to national cases, we address some key issues which recur in the scholarly analysis of comparative trade unionism. The *first* concerns union membership and density. Approaches tend to be either longitudinal (examining growth and decline) or cross-sectional (addressing cross-national or intra-national variation—for example between manual and white-collar occupations, public and private sectors, male and female employees). There is a fashion for econometric analysis of national membership data. However, such analysis does not always take adequate account of the limits of national statistics, since these typically derive from unions' own declarations, which may be exaggerated, particularly in countries with rival union organizations seeking to assert their own representativeness. More elusively, the very meaning of union membership can vary cross-nationally. One reason why density in Sweden was until recently 80 per cent, as against only 8 per cent in France, is that to become a formal union member in France has traditionally implied a commitment to active participation and engagement, whereas in most other countries a far more passive affiliation is the norm. As Müller-Jentsch insists (1985: 22), 'union density tells us nothing about the quality of the ties between the organization and its membership'.

Explanatory approaches are of several types. Traditionally, the most influential were economic in focus, treating changes in the levels of employment or unemployment, or movements in prices and wages, as key causes of fluctuations in union density. Such approaches address longitudinal changes rather than cross-sectional differences; and they fail to explain trends in the Nordic countries and Belgium, which are often counter-cyclical. This can be explained by the key union role in the administration of unemployment benefits (at least until recently), creating a particular incentive to membership in times of rising unemployment (Ebbinghaus et al. 2011; Van Rie et al.

2011). Hence institutional factors are also important. These are addressed by many theories of cross-national differences in unionization, which highlight the effects of government policy and the legal framework, and more general institutional supports for 'union security' (Western 1997). Clegg (1976) has stressed the impact of specifically industrial relations determinants, such as employer policies and the structure of collective bargaining. Several writers (Ebbinghaus et al. 2011; Fazekas 2011; Hancké 1993) have identified strong mechanisms of workplace representation as an important institutional influence on density. Recent research has also highlighted social attitudes and the importance of 'social custom' (Visser 2002).

A *second* issue is that all union movements display structural demarcations based on principles (explicit or implicit) of inclusion and exclusion. Familiar differentiations are those based on ideology (common in southern Europe and much of the global South); on industrial or sectoral boundaries (which in recent decades has often resulted in conflicts between public and private sector unions); and on occupational status (with divisions between craft and general unions, or manual, white-collar, and professional associations). The different national structural patterns, and the changes which have been occurring in recent decades, are themes of Chapter 4.

Some explanations of cross-national variation in structural patterns emphasize historical origin. For example, countries which industrialized early were more likely to contain self-confident craft groups which formed exclusive occupational unions; conversely, an influential Socialist movement inspired multi-occupational industrial unionism. Employers' organization and policies have also been important: strong sectoral employers' associations encouraged the formation of integrated counterparts on the union side. Legal regulation of union recognition (certification) and rules on 'representativeness' have in some countries created obstacles to small occupational unions and incentives for more encompassing organizations. Finally, powerful, centralized union confederations may be able to regulate inter-union demarcations among their affiliates.

A *third*, and complex, array of issues concerns union government and democracy. There is great diversity in the formal decision-making structures both within and between countries, to some extent reflecting diverse understandings of the *meaning* of union democracy. There is, however, a problematic relationship between formal decision-making structures and the complex and elusive dynamics of real intra-union politics. Famously (or notoriously), Michels (1915) argued that trade unions and Socialist parties were subject to an 'iron law of oligarchy'. Most members lacked the knowledge or motivation to engage actively in the democratic processes of union policy-making; officials had the skills and the personal interests to dominate the decision-making and electoral processes, creating a vicious circle. In Chapters 4 and

8 we examine this argument, and the differences in both formal and real democracy between and within countries.

A *fourth* issue is how to assess the outcomes of trade union action. There are many possible measures of union achievements. One is the share of wages and salaries in the national income (the division between labour and capital). On this index, unions in most countries have been losing effectiveness, since the wage share in national income has almost universally declined in recent decades. Another measure is the union 'mark-up': the extent to which wages in firms covered by union organization and/or collective agreements exceed those without. This has varied substantially across countries, being greatest where company bargaining is the most important level of pay determination, far less significant where multi-employer bargaining prevails and agreements are legally extended across whole sectors of the economy. A third, almost contrary, measure is the degree of equalization in wages and conditions of employment. In many countries, union understandings of 'solidarity' have implied the minimization of differences in rewards based on sector, occupation, gender, or employment status; and they seem to have been successful in reducing such differentials. In some countries, unions may measure their achievements less in terms of collective bargaining outcomes than by the significance of the 'social wage', including benefits from the state. More insubstantial but perhaps no less important is the union role in securing employee rights at work and effective 'voice' over key decisions which affect their employment, which usually requires strong workplace representatives. As we will see (particularly in Chapters 5 and 8), trade union preferences—and success in achieving these—differ radically across countries.

Is a universal theory possible? Price and Bain (1983) contrast phases of institutional stability (when econometric models fit) and phases of crisis and innovation (which they term 'paradigm breaks') when other factors are more important. But we must also ask how much unions themselves can influence their fate. Golden and Pontusson (1992) have stressed the importance of 'strategic choice'; Martin and Ross (1999) write of unions as 'strategic actors'. Research increasingly explores how opportunity structures, even if overall unfavourable, nevertheless offer space for positive outcomes. Such strategic choices are a major focus of this book.

The Nordic Countries: Sweden and Denmark

It is common to refer to a 'Nordic model' of trade unionism and industrial relations, a concept which must be used with caution. As noted above, there is a danger of exaggerating cross-national similarities and neglecting differences. Danes do not like being regarded as surrogate Swedes, and vice versa; and as we will see, the structure of trade unionism in the two countries differs substantially. But in addition, to speak of 'models' risks placing undue emphasis on the coherence and stability of institutional configurations which in reality contain internal tensions and are subject to constant evolution.

However, to deploy the telescope rather than the microscope, some common 'Nordic' features are evident. The most obvious is the exceptionally high level of union membership, particularly in the two countries on which we focus, and the resilience of high density when unions in most other countries were declining numerically—though in recent years, as we discuss in the next chapter, this has changed. Unions are structured sectorally and occupationally, with separate confederations representing manual, white-collar, and professional employees. Strong union organization is matched on the employers' side, and both types of confederation possess considerable centralized authority. This reciprocal strength has encouraged conflict containment, with formal peak agreements dating back to 1899 in Denmark and 1938 in Sweden. In both countries, unions are strongly committed to 'voluntary' regulation of employment conditions through collective bargaining rather than statutory enactment; this has also extended to the institutions of workplace representation, through trade union stewards rather than mandatory works councils. For a long period there were institutionalized links between unions (or at least those of manual workers) and Social-democratic parties, based on collective affiliation, and for decades these parties dominated national politics. In Sweden the Social democrats were in government in 1932–76, 1982–91, and 1994–2006; in Denmark, for twenty years between 1947 and 1973, sixteen years between 1975 and 2001, and again since 2011. (They have been even more dominant in Norway, though much weaker in Finland.) The years of union strength and Social-democratic government were associated with the creation of an exceptionally developed welfare state, economic equality, and 'negotiated labour markets' (Dølvik 2008); and even the increasing frequency of right-wing governments has not involved frontal attacks on the Social-democratic settlement (Dølvik et al. 2011). For decades there was a virtuous circle between high union density and the welfare regime: as noted above, the Nordic countries have long possessed systems of unemployment insurance which are state regulated but largely administered by the unions (often known as the Ghent system, after the Belgian town where this principle originated) (Lind 2007; Scruggs 2002). Most workers have traditionally joined an insurance scheme and a union at the same time (as is also the case in Belgium).

In *Sweden*, the industrial relations framework was established by legislation in 1928 which imposed a peace obligation during the currency of agreements, with fines for illegal strikers, and created a Labour Court to adjudicate disputes over the application of agreements. Modern industrial relations derives from the 'historic compromise' in 1938 between a strongly organized, initially militant labour movement and concentrated, assertive private capital within a relatively small, export-dependent economy. This facilitated a positive-sum economic strategy. Sweden under the Social Democrats (*Sveriges socialdemokratiska arbetareparti*, SAP) was one of the first countries to develop a 'Keynesian welfare state' or socially regulated market economy. This included a Ghent-type unemployment insurance system, established in 1935. Partly because of the expansion of the welfare state, there have long been high rates of labour market participation, with minimal differences between men and women. However, there is marked gender segregation: manufacturing is male-dominated, services (especially public) largely female.

Partly as a result of the Ghent system, union density rose steadily, reaching a peak of over 85 per cent in the 1990s (Kjellberg 1998). There are three main confederations. The largest, LO (*Landsorganisationen i Sverige*), was founded in 1898 as an explicitly Socialist body. Its constitution provides central discipline over affiliated industrial unions (currently fourteen), themselves with strong authority over branches and members. But unions also have active local branches, workplace 'clubs', and shop stewards. LO organizes only blue-collar workers, having historically viewed white-collar workers as politically beyond the pale. With the shift in the labour force away from manual work, its membership (today roughly 1.5 million) is now under half the total number of Swedish trade unionists. The second confederation, TCO (*Tjänstemännens Centralorganisation*), was formed in the 1930s and has a general white-collar membership totalling 1.2 million. The third, SACO (*Sveriges Akademikers Centralorganisation*), established in the 1940s, has over 0.6 million members and mainly recruits graduates, particularly in the public sector. There are also some minor independent unions.

The Swedish economy has long been dominated by a number of large, often family-owned, firms, with tight collective organization. Sectoral employers' associations formed a powerful confederation, *Svenska Arbetsgivareföreningen* (SAF) in 1902, taking a very assertive role in structuring industrial relations institutions and practices. It also long acted as a dominant representative of 'bourgeois' political interests in the context of rather fragmented conservative political parties. In 2001 it merged with *Sveriges Industriförbund* (Federation of Swedish Industries) to form *Svenskt Näringsliv* (SN, Confederation of Swedish Enterprise).

A pattern of coordinated relations between strong unions and employers, institutionalized in 1938, was further elaborated in the 1950s with the adoption of the 'Rehn–Meidner model' (named after two LO economists who devised its principles). This model embraced the principle of 'solidarity wages': pay should be relatively equal across firms in the same sector, irrespective of company profitability. The rate should be high enough to force struggling firms to rationalize (or go under); more profitable firms would be able to expand, increasing overall Swedish productivity and hence competitiveness in export markets. This implied some plant closures with job losses, but the costs of restructuring were mitigated by active labour market policy (retraining, income support, selective job creation programmes) and generous unemployment benefits, under the auspices of the tripartite *Arbetsmarknadsstyrelsen* (Labour Market Board). There was close integration between LO and SAP leaderships, with a functional alignment between government socio-economic policy and unions' collective bargaining strategies. The 'Swedish model' was acceptable to employers because there was little interference with their rights of ownership or investment policy, beyond taxation to fund the growing welfare state. In the 'golden age' of the Swedish model (1950s and 1960s), labour conflict was rare; rapid economic growth combined with export success; inflation was low and unemployment was minimal; there was an exceptional degree of equality.

In subsequent decades, the Swedish model came under increasing pressures, many of which we discuss further in later chapters. Economic success was threatened by 'regime competition'. Major Swedish companies became increasingly transnational, and to maximize competitiveness their investment became concentrated in countries with lower wages and less rigorous regulatory frameworks. The long electoral hegemony of the SAP began to erode. LO made a strategic shift in the 1970s away from voluntarism and towards more legal regulation. Focal issues were the adoption of the Codetermination Act (MBL) in 1976 and the abortive demand for compulsory wage-earner funds. Cooperation collapsed, and in 1992 SAF withdrew from almost all tripartite bodies. Employers for their part pressed for increased pay differentials to encourage skill formation, challenging the principle of solidarity, and demanded greater company-level autonomy to facilitate work reorganization. Organizationally, the ability of LO to sustain a cohesive approach to wage bargaining was undermined by the rapid rise of public sector unions with a distinctive agenda and the growth of TCO and SACO. Underlying growing inter-union divisions was a question of gender inequality: 'solidaristic' wage policy applied primarily within, rather than between, sectors, and the Swedish labour market, as noted above, is marked by considerable gender segregation.

By the early 1990s, it was widely assumed that the Swedish model of industrial relations was disintegrating. The breakdown of peak-level LO–SAF bargaining brought pressures for further decentralization to company level, threatening a complete collapse of coordinated industrial relations. Yet a new institutionalization of conflict occurred. The 'shadow of the law' created strong pressures to re-regulate: the two sides were impelled to seek institutionalized compromises in order to avoid government compulsion. Stronger mediation procedures –a halfway house between voluntarism and state direction—sustained relative industrial peace. Cross-sectoral coordination of pay bargaining in manufacturing created a functional substitute for peak-level agreement. And despite a growth of company bargaining over 'qualitative' issues, sectoral bargaining remained robust. Unionization remained exceptionally high. Hence a 'new Swedish model' seemed to have emerged, sustaining many of the features of the old—indeed Anxo and Niklasson (2006) argued that it was now closer to the original than in the 1970s and 1980s. The key question, to which we return, is whether recent changes have more radically eroded the basis for strong and effective Swedish trade unionism.

In *Denmark* there are many parallels, with an institutional framework set even earlier than in Sweden. The main confederations of unions (LO) and of employers (*Dansk Arbejdsgiverforening*) were both formed in 1898 and engaged in a bitter conflict followed by the 1899 'September compromise', establishing a centralized system of collective bargaining (Scheuer 1998). Legislation subsequently recognized the new framework and created a system of labour courts. Though the Danish industrial relations actors are strongly committed to the principle of 'voluntarism', in contrast to Sweden there is a long tradition of government intervention should centralized negotiations break down (Due et al. 1994: 132–42).

Denmark has far fewer large firms than Sweden, and has also been affected by far longer membership of the EU (1973 as against 1994). There is a highly developed welfare state, but its features have been distinctive. Employment protection legislation is weaker than in most European countries, but labour market flexibility was long counterbalanced by particularly generous unemployment benefits and (as in Sweden) by active labour market policies—a combination often described as a 'golden triangle' (Madsen 2003).

Because of the strong small-firm craft tradition, Danish trade union structure is in some respects closer to that of the anglophone countries than to its Nordic counterparts. It does indeed have an occupation-based division between three main confederations, similar to that in Sweden: LO has traditionally organized primarily manual workers, but also includes lower-level white-collar grades; it has 1.3 million members in eighteen affiliated unions. FTF (which no longer uses a full title but calls itself the organization for professionals) was formed in 1952, and has some 360,000 members, predominantly in the public sector. AC (*Akademikernes Centralorganisation*) was established in 1972 and has 137,000 members. There are a number of unions outside these three confederations, with a total membership of 350,000. Thus LO in Denmark remains far more dominant than its Swedish counterpart, largely because it has been more willing and able to recruit beyond manual occupations. The main distinctive feature of trade unionism in Denmark is the importance of craft organization: most notably the large *Dansk Metal*, but with many far smaller craft unions. The counterpart of exclusive craft organization was the rise of a general union catering for less skilled workers, and—virtually unique to Denmark—a union of women industrial workers. These two amalgamated in 2005 to create 3F (*Fagligt Fælles Forbund*), the largest LO affiliate, with members covering the bulk of the economy.

The 'Central' Countries: Germany, Austria, the Netherlands, and Belgium

If we apply the microscope, the four countries which we discuss in this section are very diverse; but using the telescope we can identify commonalities which justify treating them as a group. In all four, society was divided in the late 19th and much of the 20th century between rival ideological (political and/or religious) identities, with trade unions forming part of a network of institutions within each 'family'. This resulted in a history of union fragmentation, still present in Belgium and the Netherlands. Until recently, Social-democratic and Christian-democratic parties dominated the political scene; but because of the many smaller parties (encouraged by proportional representation), coalition government has been the norm for much of the post-war period (often uniting the two main parties). Because of party–union links, the trade union movement has always been closely associated with political power. Traditions of 'social partnership' have involved both strongly institutionalized relationships with employers and an accepted role in public policy. All four countries have elaborate but rather inegalitarian welfare states ('conservative', in the Esping-Andersen typology). All possess 'dual' systems of workplace representation through works councils.

As a result of state-sponsored industrialization in the late 19th century, *Germany* has many very large firms (as in Sweden); but there is also an extensive small-firm sector or *Mittelstand* (as in Denmark). There is a strong tradition of collective organization, particularly among employers. Employer solidarity, more than union strength (for union density is below the west European average), explains the persistence of organized industrial relations.

From the 1950s, it was common to speak of a German 'economic miracle': despite the devastation of the war and the loss of much former territory, Germany soon became the strongest west European economy. Corporate governance contributed to this success story: firms traditionally had close links with institutional investors ('patient capital') with a long-term commitment to company success, and a place on the supervisory board; but industrial relations also seemed important. For example, manufacturing exports concentrated on high-skill, high-value-added products. The German workforce has far more apprentice-trained workers (roughly 30 per cent) than most other European countries. This is facilitated by the distinctive vocational training system, which is statutorily based but involves a high degree of both inter-employer and employer–union cooperation. What Streeck (1992) termed 'diversified quality production' owed a great deal to the 'functional flexibility' of the workforce. Streeck argued that employment protection legislation and the codetermination rights of works councils made it difficult to dismiss workers, but for this reason workers felt secure and were willing to cooperate in productivity improvements.

The institutional framework of industrial relations has long historical origins but was recast after the war. The status of the key actors is specified in detail by law: the *Tarifvertragsgesetz* (first adopted in 1949) gives the right to bargain collectively exclusively to employers, their associations, and trade unions (without defining what constitutes a trade union, recently a source of dissension), and prescribes the binding character of collective agreements. But the content of agreements is the responsibility of the bargaining parties themselves: there is strong commitment to the principle of *Tarifautonomie* (roughly equivalent to 'free collective bargaining'). Disputes over the interpretation of agreements may be referred for adjudication in special labour courts. Legislation also establishes the institutions of codetermination (*Mitbestimmung*): works councils (*Betriebsräte*) at company or establishment level, and employee representation on the supervisory boards of larger companies. Councils are required in all but the smallest firms (though in practice they are often absent from smaller workplaces), have detailed sets of rights to information, consultation, and (on a limited set of issues) codetermination (which gives them a virtual veto power), but are obliged to cooperate with management and may not engage in conflictual action. In theory there is a clear distinction between collective bargaining and codetermination, but reality is far more complex.

The German welfare state dates back to Bismarck in the 19th century, and involves an insurance-based system with wide-ranging benefits (covering health, pensions, and unemployment) related to income. Unlike the other three countries in this group, Germany has no formal institutions of peak-level tripartite consultation, but in practice the ideology of 'social partnership' has implied that the management and adaptation of the system should be based on agreement between government, unions, and employers (Müller-Jentsch 2011). Trade unions, formerly divided along political and religious lines, were reconstituted after the war on a unitary basis. In consequence they have no formal political affiliations; but in practice, their closest relations are with the SPD (*Sozialdemokratische Partei Deutschlands*), though Christian democrats usually hold a minority of leadership positions (Jacobi et al. 1998: 200). The SDP has never achieved the dominance of its Nordic counterparts, and has been the largest parliamentary party in only twenty of the years of the *Bundesrepublik*.

The DGB (*Deutscher Gewerkschaftsbund*) was formed in 1949 with fifteen industrial unions (following several mergers, now eight). Today 70 per cent of members are in two unions, *IG Metall* and the conglomerate services union *ver.di*. Membership is just over six million, as against almost twelve million at the peak after German unification in 1990. A smaller confederation, the DBB (*dbb beamtenbund und tarifunion*), has 1.2 million members, mainly among *Beamte* (tenured civil servants), as against just under half a million organized by DGB unions. *Beamte* have no right to collective bargaining or to strike. There are also a number of non-affiliated, mainly professional unions (hospital doctors, train drivers, airline pilots) which have become increasingly assertive, and a tiny religious-based confederation, the CGB (*Christlicher Gewerkschaftsbund*).

The DGB does not itself engage in collective bargaining; that is the task of its affiliates. Its role is to seek to generate a consistent set of policies on social, political, and economic issues (Hartmann and Lau 1980); to represent these to governments and parliamentarians at federal, *Land*, and local levels; and to influence public opinion. It assists member unions in local campaigns, and propagates trade unionism in colleges and universities. One of its major functions is to provide legal advice and representation on employment issues (*Rechtsschutz*) to union members, for which it maintains a large specialist staff.

Collective bargaining may take place at either multi-employer level or with individual firms. Traditionally, multi-employer bargaining has predominated, since most large firms have been members of employers' associations. Unions have strongly supported the principle of the sector-wide agreement (*Flächentarifvertrag*), as traditionally have most employers, though this has been changing. There is a tradition of 'pattern bargaining', with one sectoral agreement (usually in metalworking) setting the trend for the whole economy, though this is less true today. High export dependence creates strong incentives towards relatively consensual industrial relations: despite often militant rhetoric, unions have always been sensitive to the demands of competitiveness, and wage increases have usually been at, or even below, the growth in productivity.

While *Austria* shares some institutional characteristics with its far larger northern neighbour, in many respects its system of industrial relations is 'exceptional' (Traxler 1998: 239). The law underwrites a particularly strong bias towards collectivism. Particularly notable is the statutory underpinning of the *Kammer* system, once far more widespread in Europe (Crouch 1993): workers are obliged to join the Chamber of Labour (*Bundesarbeitskammer*, AK) and employers the Chamber of Business (*Wirtschaftskammer Österreich*,

WKÖ). The AK is not a trade union and does not engage in collective bargaining, but works closely with the unions, its 500 staff undertaking research and education and helping draft policy for the trade union movement, as well as providing advice services to workers, which in most countries are trade union functions. By contrast, Austrian employers have historically been relatively weak and fragmented (Traxler 1998: 252), and it is not the main employers' confederation which engages in collective bargaining but the WKÖ and its sectoral chambers.

Because membership of the WKÖ is compulsory, collective bargaining covers virtually the whole of the labour force. Another remarkable feature of labour law is that only associations have the right to conclude collective agreements; individual employers may not do so (Traxler and Pernicka 2007: 211). However, as in Germany, employers may negotiate agreements on some issues, with a different legal status, with their works councils. There is a diverse range of collective agreements, commonly negotiated separately for manual and white-collar workers, for different sectors and sub-sectors and for large and small firms. Though there is a tradition of pattern bargaining, as in Germany, this diversification offers individual firms the opportunity to engage in 'agreement shopping', affiliating to the sectoral organization which negotiates terms best suited to their own interests.

In Austria there is a far more intimate overlap between politics and industrial relations than in Germany. In part this reflects the strength of Social democracy: the *Sozialdemokratische Partei Österreichs* (SPÖ) has been the largest party in parliament for most of the post-war period, and in government for all but seven years, usually in coalition with the Christian-democratic *Österreichische Volkspartei* (ÖVP). Union leaders have historically played a major role in party politics, mainly in the SPÖ but also in the ÖVP, often sitting in parliament. Since 1957 an institutionalized system of social partnership has existed: the *Paritätische Kommission* comprises representatives of government, the WKÖ, the Chamber of Agriculture, the AK, and the *Österreichische Gewerkschaftsbund* (ÖGB). It has no statutory basis, and formally only an advisory capacity; but plays a major role in policy-making, particularly since coalition governments need consensus for their programmes. It has subcommittees dealing with wages, prices, social and economic policy, and international issues.

Historically, the ÖGB has been exceptional in its centralization: constitutionally it controls the finances and the appointment of officials in its affiliates. It is also unique in covering all trade union members in Austria. It was created with fourteen sectoral affiliates, though this number has been halved by mergers. Although in theory committed to the principle of industrial unionism, in order to sustain a unified confederation it accepted the existence of a cross-sectoral union for white-collar workers in the private sector, the *Gewerkschaft der Privatangestellten* (GPA), which for some four decades has been its largest affiliate. Austrian unions are also unique in formally recognizing internal political factions, which nominate separate lists of candidates for works council elections and achieve representation on union governing bodies in proportion to the seats won.

In *the Netherlands*, institutionalized 'corporatist' concertation is also an established element in industrial relations. It has long been common to refer to the '*polder* model': *polders* are land below sea level protected by dikes which must be maintained in good repair, a distinctive feature of Dutch topography. This physical imperative to cooperate had its parallel in the post-war era, with the need to rebuild the ravaged Dutch economy after Nazi occupation. The *Stichting van de Arbeid* (STvdA, Foundation of Labour), a joint body representing employers and employees, was founded in 1945, and accepted by government 'as its top advisory body in matters of socio-economic policy-making' (Visser 1992: 324). As part of the same 'historic compromise', the two sides of industry endorsed 'management's right to manage' and 'free collective bargaining' (Visser 1995: 89–90). The tripartite *Sociaal-Economische Raad* (SER, Social and Economic Council) was established by law in 1950. As in Austria, 'social partnership' involved a high degree of centralization within the representative bodies on both sides of industry. Though centralized regulation of pay bargaining disintegrated in the 1960s, it was renewed two decades later, as we discuss in Chapter 5.

In a small, open economy, with large transnational firms highly dependent on export markets, socio-economic consensus was founded on wage moderation but a generous social wage: 'by international standards, The Netherlands has one of the most developed welfare states' (Visser 1992: 324). There was strong government regulation of wage bargaining until the 1980s, and subsequent agreements have often been reached under the shadow of the law. One important means of government pressure is the mandatory extension of collective agreements to all firms in a sector, a mechanism which may be withheld if a settlement is considered excessive. In the same spirit of consensus, works councils (*ondernemingsraden*) were established by law in 1950, for the specific purpose of contributing 'to the best functioning of the enterprise' (Visser 1995: 89). They were not designed as organs of representation or voice for the workforce, but as a channel of communication. Though their powers have been extended by subsequent legislative changes, their role remains less important than in Germany or Austria (Gumbrell-McCormick and Hyman 2010: 292–4).

A distinctive feature of both Dutch and Belgian societies is *verzuiling* or 'pillarization', with competing ideological identities embodied in a network of institutions such as unions, political parties, insurance schemes, and social organizations. Paradoxically, such fragmentation could enhance social cohesion by moderating purely class divisions and creating a need, and possibility, for negotiated compromise (Visser 1998a: 283). One consequence of diluted class identity has been the relative weakness of the *Partij van de Arbeid* (PvdA, Labour Party): it has headed the government (always in coalition with the right) for only twelve years in the past half century, and has been a minority member of government for eight more years.

For much of the 20th century, trade unionism reflected the pillar structure, though this effect has been moderated over time. The *Nederlands Verbond van Vakverenigingen* (NVV) represented the Socialist pillar, the *Nederlands Katholiek Vakverbond* (NKV) the Catholic, and the *Christelijk Nationaal Vakverbond* (CNV) the Protestant. But as religious identities weakened, the Catholic pillar lost adherents and the NKV agreed in the 1970s to merge with the NVV, resulting in the formation of the *Federatie Nederlandse Vakbeweging* (FNV) in 1981. The CNV, which had been involved in the initial merger discussions, withdrew from the process and managed to attract some dissident NKV unions into its ranks. In addition, a separate confederation competes to represent white-collar staff, the *Vakcentrale voor Middengroepen en Hoger Personeel* (MHP). These organizations claim respectively 1.4 million, 330,000, and 160,000 members. Though FNV has nineteen affiliates, the conglomerate unions for the public and private sectors (*AbvaKabo* and *Bondgenoten*) together constitute 60 per cent of total membership, creating issues of internal democracy which have brought FNV to the point of collapse, as we discuss later. A notable feature of the Dutch system is the agency fee of roughly €20 (popularly known as the *vakbondstientje*) paid by employers on behalf of every worker covered by a collective agreement, unionized or not, and used for training worker representatives.

In *Belgium*, as in the Netherlands, national reconstruction after wartime occupation created pressures towards institutions of social partnership. Shortly before liberation, the leading employer and trade union organizations negotiated a 'social pact' through which 'workers were given some social benefits if the unions were willing to leave the capitalist enterprise structure and its economic decision-making alone' (Hancké and Wijgaerts 1989: 194). The agreement was elaborated in subsequent legislation and 'led to a multitude of legal and voluntary arrangements, bilateral and trilateral, at almost every level of activity', resulting in 'one of the most formalized participation structures in Europe' (Vilrokx and Van Leemput 1992: 362). At the peak was the Central Economic Council (known in the two national languages as *Centrale Raad voor het Bedrijfsleven* or *Conseil centrale de l'économie*), an advisory body comprising equal numbers of employer and union representatives along with independent experts. At enterprise level, the works council (*ondernemingsraad* or *conseil d'entreprise*) was assigned primarily information and consultation functions; the 'social elections' held every four years provide a measure of support for the rival unions and are often vigorously contested. The councils operate in parallel with the workplace union delegation (*syndicale delegatie* or *délégation syndicale*), which is nominated by trade union members and/or officials and recognized by the employer for collective negotiation and individual representation.

Like the Netherlands, Belgium is a small, export-oriented country with a highly coordinated market economy (Faniel 2012: 20). The cleavage structure entailed by pillarization is cross-cut, and in recent years has been increasingly compounded by tensions between Dutch-speaking Flanders and French-speaking Wallonia, and these divisions have left their mark on industrial relations. Belgian cleavages, like the Dutch, have reinforced the need for strong concertative institutions. One example is the tradition of biennial cross-industry collective agreements, which often provide the material for subsequent legislative enactment, as well as setting the framework for bargaining at sectoral and company levels.

Pillarization has proved more resilient in Belgium than in the Netherlands. The two main confederations historically represented the Socialist and Catholic pillars, each with its own related parties and institutions for social insurance. But uniquely in Europe, for the past four decades the largest organization has been the *Algemeen Christelijk Vakverbond/Confédération des Syndicats Chrétiens* (ACV/CSC) with some 1.7 million members in seven sectoral federations; somewhat surprisingly, it overtook its Socialist rival in a period of weakening religious attachments and declining electoral support for the Christian-democratic party (Arcq and Aussems 2002); and it propagates a less strongly religious message than the Dutch CNV. The Socialist *Algemeen Belgisch Vakverbond/Fédération Générale du Travail de Belgique* (ABVV/FGTB) has some 1.4 million members, also in seven sectoral federations. Also virtually unique is the survival of a separate liberal confederation, the *Algemene Centrale der Liberale Vakbonden van België/Centrale Générale des Syndicats Libéraux de Belgique* (ACLVB/CGSLB) with 270,000 members (Faniel and Vandaele 2011; Faniel et al. 2011). Internally, the regional (Dutch- and French-language) union organizations have become increasingly separate; there are also separate federations within each union for white-collar workers. This causes considerable complexity in employee representation in national bargaining.

As 'the homeland of the Ghent system' (Vandaele 2006), Belgium has a framework for unemployment insurance which in effect privileges the three confederations and creates incentives for union membership, at least for workers at risk of unemployment (Faniel 2012). This has resulted, as Table 1.2 indicates, in union density not far short of Nordic levels, and in exceptional stability of membership over the past three decades.

The 'Southern' Countries: France and Italy

Can one speak of a 'southern model' of trade unionism and industrial relations? Yes, if we keep in mind the reservations noted previously. It is possible to construct a stereotype, representing a number of contextual features common (at least historically) to France, Italy, Spain, and Portugal (Greece is similar in some but not all respects). These include relatively late industrialization, a large agricultural sector, and a high proportion of self-employment, with many small employers, often violently anti-union. Historically, the Catholic church was a major obstacle to modernization, resulting in sharp lay–clerical cleavages; perhaps linked to this, in most cases there were strong Communist parties for much of the 20th century, resulting in sharply polarized politics and a division (and hence weakening) of the left. Trade unions have been ideologically divided, collective bargaining in most cases has been underdeveloped and there is a tradition of extensive state regulation of employment conditions. Despite an elaborate framework of representative institutions, their practical impact on employment regulation often seems weak. Many observers perceive a self-sustaining dynamic of highly politicized industrial relations; but others argue that there are signs of significant change, or emphasize the diversity within this group of countries. France and Italy are good cases to consider: up to the late 1960s the similarities in their industrial relations systems were notable; now there are marked contrasts. In both countries, the leading unions were once Communist dominated, and the shift to a more autonomous and more moderate position has involved open and acrimonious internal conflicts: one reason why these unions receive primary attention in our analysis.

The post-war evolution of industrial relations in *France* was shaped by the interaction of an inflexible power structure and economic modernization from above; but for several decades, governments have attempted to overcome the rigidities inherent in the traditional institutional structures and to encourage employers to take greater initiative. This has been reciprocated in major companies by more proactive, 'modern' management, with enthusiasm for US-style 'human resource management' (Hancké 2002). The main organization of larger employers, reconstructed in 1998 as *Mouvement des Entreprises de France* (MEDEF), exerts a powerful political influence in favour of liberalization. For the bulk of the post-war period, the political right has held power, since 1958 within a strong presidential system. At company level there is a tradition of authoritarian management and rigid occupational hierarchies: Taylorism, with its rigid division of labour, was more enthusiastically embraced in France than in the rest of Europe. The almost revolutionary upsurge of industrial and social protest in 1968 had little long-term impact on employment relations, in part because the main oppositional force, the

Parti communiste français (PCF) preferred to stabilize a social order in which it (and the main trade union which it dominated) enjoyed an established role. However, one outcome was an expansion of the welfare state, and today the unions (together with employers) play an important role in the administration of its complex institutional apparatus—a source of significant resources (Andolfatto and Labbé 2000).

At workplace level, the law defines a complex network of committees and delegates, with limited powers but symbolic importance. *Délégués du personnel* deal with individual grievances; *comités d'entreprise* have powers (unlike German works councils) limited to workplace consultation and the administration of social and welfare facilities, for which they receive a budget from the company; *sections syndicales* are entitled to facilities as union representatives. *Délégués* and *comités* are elected by proportional representation; election results are taken very seriously by the rival unions because they offer evidence of relative strength.

Collective bargaining can take place at economy-wide, sectoral, and/or company level. Until very recently, any of five 'representative' unions could sign a valid company agreement, even if it had few members. The sector was long the main level of collective bargaining, but company bargaining has increased considerably in the past three decades. On paper, there is 90 per cent collective bargaining coverage, despite the collapse of union membership. What does this tell us about the practical importance of collective agreements? Many sectoral agreements merely replicate what is already prescribed by law (some even specify minimum wages *below* the statutory level). Key contentious questions are how far, and how, company agreements should be able to 'derogate' from the terms of sectoral agreements; and whether there should be alternative arrangements for workplace bargaining where no union representatives exist. Some argue that the growth in company bargaining is actually a means by which managements evade the effect of higher-level regulation, leading to 'managerial unilateralism' (Goyer and Hancké 2004) and 'deregulation of the labour market' (Jenkins 2000).

French unionism comprises a multiplicity of rival confederations with component industrial federations and regional or departmental sections. They possess complex political and ideological identities, often with internal divisions; all three main confederations declare themselves Socialist. For half a century until changes in 2008, five were formally recognized as 'representative', regardless of their numbers, giving membership in national consultative machinery and bargaining rights at every level. These are the *Confédération générale du travail* (CGT), long closely linked with the PCF, though the ties have formally disappeared; the *Confédération française démocratique du travail* (CFDT), created in 1968 by the secularized majority of the Christian confederation; the CGT-*Force ouvrière* (FO), which broke away from the CGT in 1948 but claims to be the true representative of its original traditions; the *Confédération française des travailleurs chrétiens* (CFTC), concentrated in a few strongly Catholic regions; and the *Confédération générale des cadres* (CFE-CGC), which competes with the other confederations to represent engineers, technicians, supervisors, sales, and other white-collar staff. Other confederations include the *Union nationale des syndicats autonomes*, a federation of 'independent' unions, in particular in education; the *Fédération syndicale unitaire*, consisting of mainly leftist unions which broke away from, or were expelled by, the former; and SUD (*Union syndicale solidaires*), a group of independent leftist unions, largely breakaways from CFDT.

Membership figures are notoriously difficult to verify in France, but it is agreed that unions' combined density has fallen continuously for several decades, and is now the lowest in western Europe. The CGT has traditionally been regarded as the largest, though this is contested by the CFDT (Goetschy 1998). The main strength of all unions is in the public sector. The meaning of union membership has differed from that in most other countries, implying a willingness to engage actively in the work of recruitment and representation. With declining numbers, it has become increasingly common for one activist to hold a number of representative positions (*cumul des mandats*). Since the law provides for a specified amount of paid release from work for elected representatives, those holding a multiplicity of positions may become full-time unionists, and there has thus developed a large 'trade union elite' (Guillaume 2011) at workplace level: what has been termed 'virtual unionism' given the paucity of members, particularly in the private sector (Howell 2009).

In many respects, *Italy* paralleled France in its historical background to industrial relations. The early post-war decades were marked by social and economic backwardness; the political hegemony of the right; authoritarian employers; weak, politicized, and fragmented unions. As in France, we can identify an interaction of politics and economic modernization, but the dynamics have been very different. During the Cold War there was a succession of centre-right governments, dominated by the Christian democrats. The Communists (*Partito comunista italiano*, PCI) were the second largest party, with a peak of a third of the popular vote, but excluded from government after 1948. There was an 'opening to left' in the 1960s, when the Socialists were admitted to the ruling coalition; and in the 1970s the PCI adopted the 'historic compromise', supporting the existing constitutional order in return for enhanced status in policy-making. In the early 1990s, a succession of corruption scandals led to the collapse of the ruling parties, while the PCI dissolved. This resulted in a new polarization between a restructured right led by Berlusconi, and a centre left led by ex-Communists.

Early post-war industrialization was driven by the substantial state-owned sector and by large private employers such as Fiat. Economic growth was at first based on unilaterally imposed wage restraint, extensive migration from the rural south to the industrial north, a rigid division of labour, and work intensification. This resulted in social dislocation, which in turn fuelled an explosion of grassroots militancy, culminating in the 'hot autumn' of 1969. In contrast to France in 1968, mass industrial militancy had long-term effects. A new system of workplace union representative structures emerged, and was codified by the *Statuto dei lavoratori* (Workers' Statute) of 1970. This created a trade union-based workplace representative institution with considerable legal rights but without a clear organizational definition. A revised system was introduced following a peak-level agreement in 1993, giving a clearer structure to representation by what is now called the *rappresentanza sindacale unitaria* (RSU). Workplace representation is union based, and representatives enjoy the extensive legal powers specified in the 1970 Statute. The powers of the RSU have made it difficult for employers to impose change unilaterally, leading to the development of 'microcorporatism' (Regini 1995) in company-level and regional industrial relations from the 1980s: modernization has tended to be negotiated rather than unilaterally imposed (as in France), though a more aggressive and authoritarian management approach has become increasingly evident.

As in France there are rival trade union confederations, but the pattern is less complex. The largest, the *Confederazione generale italiana del lavoro* (CGIL), was created at the end of the war as a unitary organization but soon split. It was long controlled by the PCI with a left-Socialist minority, but from the 1970s became increasingly autonomous. Numerically it is more clearly dominant than the CGT in France, accounting for roughly the same total membership as the other two confederations combined (Regalia and Regini 1998). Second is the *Confederazione italiana dei sindacati lavoratori* (CISL), traditionally led by Christian democrats but with no formal religious identity. Considerably smaller is the *Unione italiana del lavoro* (UIL), formed by right-wing Socialists and republicans. A variety of other confederations and 'autonomous' unions also exist, but their influence is relatively small, except among some strategically important groups of public service workers.

The weak and politically divided movement obtained a major boost after the 'hot autumn', with a rapid rise in membership and self-confidence, and growing cooperation (often tense) between the three main confederations. Unstable governments with little popular legitimacy felt obliged to negotiate with the unions over significant social and economic policy moves. This strengthened unions' public status, but also made them co-responsible for at times unpopular reforms. In the 1980s and 1990s, unions lost employed membership, so that today half the total in the main confederations is actually retired. (This reflects union efforts to retain and represent pensioners, but also strong union involvement in administering the occupational pensions system.) Over the same period, the main unions have at times faced serious challenges from 'autonomous' rivals. Nevertheless, they retain a high degree of popular legitimacy. 'Union exclusion' is not a realistic option for most large employers, though 'divide-and-rule' tactics remain common and have recently intensified.

Collective bargaining involves a reasonably effective 'articulation' between economy-wide, sectoral, local, and company levels, reconfigured by several peak-level agreements in the last two decades. At least in the major areas of union organization (the public sector and large private firms), there is a far more serious bargaining culture than in France. Legal regulation is less comprehensive, and in recent decades there has been a shift towards much stronger 'voluntarism'. A new principle of 'negotiated legislation' developed from the 1980s: more flexible statutory regulation is normally agreed in peak-level tripartite bargaining before being approved by parliament. But the agenda of both collective bargaining with employers and 'political exchange' with governments (Pizzorno 1978) has posed serious challenges to many of the gains of the hot autumn and the years of union strength which followed. The most sensitive and symbolic was the *scala mobile*, the system of wage indexation which had distinct egalitarian effects; during the 1980s and 1990s it was reduced and eventually abolished. We pursue some of the issues in the next chapter.

The Anglophone Countries: Britain and Ireland

It is reasonable to discuss Britain and Ireland together as 'anglophone' countries (although Irish is the 'official' language of the latter, it is spoken by only a minority of the population). Properly one should distinguish between (Great) Britain, which comprises only the mainland (England, Scotland, and Wales), and the United Kingdom (UK), which includes Northern Ireland; but for simplicity we follow common practice in using the terms interchangeably. Ireland was part of the UK until gaining independence in a series of stages after 1922, becoming separated from the 'six counties' of Northern Ireland—a source of persistent and at times bloody tension. Its past colonial status left Ireland with the legal and other institutional features of British industrial relations. Though these have altered over time, both countries can be regarded as LMEs, very open to foreign trade and investment, and with 'voluntarist' industrial relations systems.

The character of *British* industrial relations and trade unionism has long been distinctive. Britain was the home of capitalist industrialization, and this 'first-mover advantage' together with military power resulted in global economic hegemony for much of the 19th century when the main elements of industrial relations were formed. Employers, subject to only limited competitive pressures, perceived little need for external support and displayed only weak collective solidarity: a trait very evident in more recent times. Imperialism brought economic growth from which many workers could also benefit, facilitating a long and 'spontaneous' evolution of pragmatic industrial relations processes and institutions.

In contrast to the revolutionary crises in many other European countries, in Britain the rising entrepreneurial class achieved economic autonomy and political rights peacefully and incrementally, and did not need to mobilize the working class as fellow contestants of the traditional order (a mobilization which in many European countries then resulted in autonomous working-class assertiveness). The transition from feudalism to capitalism involved the *negative* principle of detachment of the (relatively weak and undeveloped) state from economic life: the doctrine of *laissez-faire*. This was carried over into industrial relations, running with the grain of a common law system within which the freedom of (individual) contract was paramount. This legal framework created a bias against collective regulation of employment conditions, making trade union organization and action for many decades unlawful. The distinctive British route to legalization of trade unionism and collective bargaining was through negative 'immunities' rather than positive rights: creating a system known as 'voluntarism' or 'collective *laissez-faire*'. Collective agreements are not legally binding contracts, unions are not 'agents' of their members, and there are no extension mechanisms to generalize agreements across whole sectors. Nor (until the recent application of minimal European provisions) has there been a legally prescribed system of workplace representation. Until the late 20th century, the role of statute law in defining substantive conditions of employment (pay, working hours) was extremely limited and the legal basis of employment protection was likewise extremely weak; job security largely depended on scarce skills or collective strength. Britain also differs from most of continental Europe in that collective bargaining is detached from the welfare regime and labour market policy.

British trade unionism evolved slowly within this distinctive socio-economic and legal framework. In one respect it is a unitary movement, with a single confederation, the Trades Union Congress (TUC)—formed in 1868—representing almost all significant unions. But in other respects it is remarkably fragmented. From the 1890s (when official labour statistics were first compiled) to the 1940s there were over 1,000 union organizations; and though numbers have been reduced substantially through a series of merger waves, there are still 170 (of which 54 are affiliated to the TUC). Most are very small; conversely, there are fourteen very large unions with over 100,000 members each, accounting for 85 per cent of the total. The earliest unions emerged as small societies of skilled workers; later, 'industrial' unions (which, however, rarely covered every category of worker in their sector) were created in the major 19th-century industries; 'general' unions arose for lower-skilled workers excluded from the craft unions; in the 20th century there was a substantial growth of white-collar and public sector unionism. Mergers, and the efforts of old unions to expand into new areas of recruitment, have created an immensely complex map of trade unionism in which no 'pure' models exist.

Traditionally there has been a profound ambiguity at the heart of British trade union ideology and practice. For over a century, most main unions (though not the TUC itself) have espoused Socialist objectives and are collectively affiliated to the Labour Party. Though the Party has never been Social-democratic in the continental sense, its policies have been comparable and it was in part responsible for the construction of a welfare state significantly different from the 'liberal' model which Esping-Andersen (1990) bases primarily on the USA. Yet 'voluntarism' has shaped trade union identity, with 'free collective bargaining' a pivotal principle. This meant, for example, that throughout the 20th century most unions opposed the idea of a statutory minimum wage. Effective collective organization, ideally resting on a strong network of workplace representatives (shop stewards), was considered the best source of improved standards and job protection. Cooperation with management was viewed with suspicion, though pragmatic accommodation was in reality the rule. In their years of greatest membership—the 1960s and 1970s—British unions could be described as both militant and moderate. Militant in that strike action was often used in the early stages of negotiation rather than as a last resort, at least in major union strongholds in manufacturing. But modest in that struggles were often defensive, or involved efforts to maintain a group's position in the earnings hierarchy rather than to change that hierarchy itself.

Over a long period, 'voluntarism' delivered results (Heery 2010: 550–1). However, the effectiveness of a system of industrial relations based on 'free collective bargaining' rested on important preconditions: a favourable employment structure; acquiescent employers; and an 'abstentionist' state. As we discuss in the next chapter, the erosion of all these foundations has posed major challenges. Rapid occupational and sectoral changes, the rise of more sophisticated and aggressive managements, and above all the systematic anti-union offensive of the Conservative government elected in 1979 confronted British unions with an existential challenge.

Industrial relations and trade unionism in *Ireland* are marked both by the formative period of incorporation in the UK, and by the struggle against British rule. From the British tradition stemmed a fragmented union structure deriving from craft origins; tense and antagonistic relations between unions and employers; and a suspicion of company-level cooperation (von Prondzynski 1998). But in contrast to Britain, nationalism overrode class politics. The two leading parties, *Fianna Fáil* and *Fine Gael*, have their origins in divisions in the republican movement in the 1920s and are both on the political right; for most of the post-war era the Irish Labour Party achieved only around 10 per cent of the popular vote, with a peak of just under 20 per cent, though on several occasions it has been a junior partner in government. Nationalism (and a strong strand of Catholic conservatism), together with the country's small population (the lowest of our ten countries), contributed to a centralized, highly institutionalized, and quasi-corporatist system of industrial relations. Notably, the Labour Court (actually a tripartite mediation body) has played a key role since its creation in 1946; while the series of formal 'social partnership' agreements, first signed in 1987, marked a very different path from that taken in Britain.

Ireland was long an impoverished, highly agricultural economy, with unemployment leading to large-scale emigration. Rapid economic advance from the 1950s—the 'Celtic tiger' phenomenon—was based to an important extent on government pursuit of foreign inward investment, particularly from US-based (often fervently anti-union) multinationals in high-technology sectors. Low corporate taxation and a minimal welfare state were concomitants of this approach. Liberalization of financial markets, and an artificial housing boom, made this model of economic modernization extremely vulnerable.

Trade union structure has many parallels with that in Britain, with the same range of cross-cutting occupational, sectoral, and conglomerate organizations. As in Britain, a single confederation, the Irish Congress of Trade Unions (ICTU), encompasses most significant unions (indeed it is more representative than its British counterpart). Following mergers, a single union, the Services, Industrial, Professional and Technical Union (SIPTU), occupies a dominant position. A distinctive complexity is that the ICTU covers both the Republic and Northern Ireland, and many of its affiliates do not recruit in the Republic. Of those that do, some have members only in the Republic, some organize in both parts of the island, while some are UK-based. The presence of British-based unions was once a source of considerable tension, and indeed provoked a split in the predecessor of the ICTU, but these historical frictions seem to have been largely resolved.

Conclusions

In this chapter we have outlined some of the key features of trade union organization and its context in each of ten countries. Patterns of recruitment and representation differ substantially, to an important extent in line with national institutional differences; these are certainly associated with contrasting 'varieties of capitalism', but no neat classification is possible (Thelen 2012). Different organizational forms are linked to differences in union identities, in understandings of trade unions' mission in society, and in assessments of their key historical achievements. As Locke and Thelen argue (1995), these factors colour the threats and opportunities that unions encounter in hard times, shape their perceptions of the significance of the challenges that confront them, and hence inform their responses. These are themes we explore in the next chapter.

2

Hard Times: Challenges and Responses

In the past quarter century, trade unions across Europe have faced severe challenges which, in the view of some observers, threaten their viability. These include a decline in the large-scale manufacturing industries in which unions long had a major stronghold; Visser (2012) writes of the eclipse of the 'industrial union' model which once shaped most national movements. This shift has been followed by budgetary pressures and the drive to privatization in unions' other main stronghold, public services, and the growth of diverse forms of 'atypical' employment. Linked to these changes are a political drift to the right and, some argue, the rise of individualism in place of the collectivism on which unions are founded. Associated with all these challenges, though in complex ways, is the process of 'globalization', which weakens trade union capacity to regulate work and employment within the national boundaries in which they are embedded. One outcome has been a loss of membership density over the last three decades: in some countries by roughly half, though in others the decline has been far less dramatic, as Table 1.2 indicates.

Falling membership means depleted financial resources. In some countries, it has also been linked to a decline in collective bargaining coverage; this is not the general rule, as we showed in the last chapter, mainly because of multi-employer bargaining, often buttressed by legal provisions for the extension of agreements to all firms in a sector. But if unions' power is reduced, the efficacy of these bargaining institutions cannot be taken for granted; as Thelen argues (2012: 141), their force can be eroded by 'processes that unfold beneath the veneer of formal institutional stability'. Hence almost universally, the content of sectoral agreements is being hollowed out as decision-making shifts towards the individual company, creating problems of coordination and of solidaristic union strategy. Membership decline may also mean weaker political influence and an erosion of social legitimacy. Below we review these challenges, together with the distinctive forms they assume in each of the ten countries, before surveying in broad terms the varieties of union responses, signalling issues for more detailed discussion in the following chapters. First, however, we address key analytical issues which must underlie any serious discussion of the challenges facing trade unions and their possible repertoire of responses: the sources of union power and the challenge of constructing solidarity out of diversity.

Conceptualizing Trade Union Power

'Union power and influence [are] secured in different ways in different national systems' (Frege and Kelly 2004: 40); but from the extensive literature on trade union power resources it is possible to identify four widely recognized forms. The first is *structural* (Silver 2003: 13–16; Wright 2000: 962), deriving from the location of those workers organized in a specific union. They may possess scarce skills or competences, making them valuable to the employer and difficult to replace, giving the union 'marketplace bargaining power'; or they may occupy a strategic position within the production process, such that disruptive action will impose serious costs on the employer, creating 'workplace bargaining power'. Workers who possess both types of structural power (in the past, for example, skilled typographers in the newspaper industry) may establish particularly strong trade unionism.

The second type of power is *associational*: the simple fact of having members provides a union with resources, not least financial. However, association and organization are not synonyms: the former may merely involve passive membership of a union by individuals primarily concerned to obtain personal benefits or protections, without necessarily entailing any interrelationship amongst them. It may thus reflect what Offe and Wiesenthal (1985) term 'willingness to pay', without a 'willingness to act'.

Hence we must distinguish a third category, which is *organizational* power. As we will see later, this distinction underlies many of the debates about union revitalization, which insist that membership recruitment alone does not equate to organization (though it may be an essential precondition). 'Unity is strength' has long been a trade union motto: but membership itself does not guarantee unity. Constructing organizational power resources is, in part, a process of cultivating and synthesizing the 'social capital' of the members (Ebbinghaus et al. 2008; Jarley 2005) so that they identify themselves as part of a collectivity and support its purpose and its policies. As Lévesque and Murray insist (2003: 16), organizational power also requires effective processes of internal democracy, together with 'a culture favouring discussion between rank and file and officials and educational work to ensure that policies are well understood and reflect the conditions experienced on the ground'.

A fourth type of power is *institutional*. As discussed in more detail in the previous chapter, associational and organizational strength may be bolstered by employer solidarity, legislative supports, the powers of statutory works councils, the administration of social welfare, or a status in structures of tripartite peak-level consultation. These institutional supports may well be a product of the prior acquisition of other power resources, but may then provide a substitute if structural, associational, and organizational power resources dwindle (Dörre et al. 2009: 37–9; Frege and Kelly 2003: 8). As we examine later, institutional power may prove precarious in the long run but may induce complacency within unions which face serious threats to their continuing effectiveness (Hassel 2007). Unions may face a choice between defending their institutional status or recovering their representational capacity by more innovative policy initiatives (Dufour and Hege 2011).

A corollary of the weakening of what are traditionally recognized as key supports for trade unionism is the need for complementary power resources which are not necessarily new but which have been insufficiently appreciated in the past (Lévesque and Murray 2003). Such power resources are key themes of the chapters which follow. The first may be described as *moral*—or in more contemporary vocabulary, *discursive* or *communicative* (Munck 2000; Urban 2012; Webster et al. 2008), involving a conception of social and societal change and a vocabulary which makes this conception persuasive. To employ the term presented in the previous chapter, unions need to act as a 'sword of justice', to demonstrate that a better society is their mission and identity and to convince that this is a possible and desirable goal. As Webster et al. put it (2008: 220–1), this must involve 'a vision of an active democratic society', but also a demonstration—as the Webbs insisted over a century ago—that trade unions are themselves democratic organizations and propagators of democracy.

Another power resource may be termed *collaborative* (or *coalitional*). If unions have a declining capacity to achieve their goals through their own resources, they need allies. This requires cooperative relationships with other groups, movements, and organizations which have goals and interests in common but also differ from unions in their structure, constituency, and agenda. Achieving synergies is a necessary but difficult task, as we discuss in a later chapter.

A final type of resource may be termed *strategic* or *logistical*. If resources are scarce, they must be deployed smartly. There is a distinction to be made between resources and resourcefulness (Ganz 2000): if unions can make more effective use of limited resources than seemingly stronger adversaries, they may still prevail. This indeed is the lesson of labour history, when workers and their unions have at times succeeded against the odds. With strategic skill, threats may be turned into opportunities. This is another theme that we pursue later in our book.

Diversity and Solidarity

Historically, most unions were built on pre-existing solidarities: they gave institutional form to a prior consciousness of collective interests and collective identity. Forging unity in union was often an uphill struggle; but collectivism had firm supports. In some cases (notably craft unionism) the principles of collective identity had an institutional foundation predating capitalist employment relationships. In others, the displacement of traditional norms of moral economy by the ruthless logic of wage slavery fired spontaneous collective resistance to exploitation (Thompson 1968). In more settled times, when the capital–labour relation attained a largely unquestioned normality, collective experience at work was often complemented by domestic life in close-knit communities and by shared recreational, cultural, and sometimes religious pursuits; the union was an institution embedded in an encompassing social landscape. Later still, within a 'Fordist' production regime, the employer often functioned (wittingly or unwittingly) as a recruiting agent; the union was an extension of the company community.

Trade unions have always had two faces (Flanders 1970): as a 'sword of justice', fighting for all those oppressed and underprivileged; but also as a 'vested interest', defending the particular interests of the relatively advantaged groups with market power who in most countries have disproportionately filled the ranks of union membership and leadership (an issue to which we will return). This tension, it should be added, was historically mediated by differences in union ideologies and identities both within and between countries.

Most traditional unions in Europe were founded on what has often been termed the 'normal' employment relationship. Those whose situation seemed most evidently appropriate for collective organization and representation, and certainly as the most favourable support for union recruitment and retention, were employed full time on more or less permanent contractual terms. Of course there were exceptions: dockers or building workers, for example, might be hired by the day or even by the hour; but such workers had other bases of collective identity and community. Most early unions also arose in occupations with workplace power, where collective withdrawal of labour could have a persuasive impact: the stereotypical trade unionist possessed 'industrial muscle'. He (in trade union iconography it was almost always a 'he') was identified above all else with his work, and this identification was carried over into his allegiance to his union.

In most countries where unions first emerged, this core constituency could be regarded as (almost) a popular majority. Even if the manual industrial working class was in few countries numerically dominant, it was the most visible and could plausibly be regarded as the face of modern society. Even if union membership largely excluded workers who were female, insecure, or transitory, unions' pretensions to represent a general working-class interest were rarely questioned.

Yet the 'traditional' worker with a standard employment contract—working full time, with the reasonable expectation of continued employment until retirement—is a declining species. With high unemployment, market power has diminished and insecurity is the new normality. There has been a substantial growth of diverse forms of 'atypical' employment, all adapted to the needs of employers for a 'flexible' workforce. Manual workers are now outnumbered by a diversity of white-collar occupations; partly as a corollary, there has been an increasing feminization of work, and in many countries a high proportion of the female labour force works part-time. How can trade union organizations which were traditionally based on male manual workers with a 'normal' employment relationship recruit, and represent effectively, very different categories of worker (Carrieri 2008)? If they still rely primarily on their traditional 'core membership reserves' (Crouch 2000a: 71), they suffer declining membership and face increasing marginalization. If they succeed in extending their boundaries of organization, the consequence may be internal conflict over priorities and the loss of capacity to constitute an integrated movement.

In parallel with these changes in the world of work, unions also face more diffuse but perhaps more extensive social and generational changes. There is a stereotype of the traditional proletarian status which emphasizes a common work situation, an integrated and homogeneous local community, and a limited repertoire of shared cultural and social pursuits. The cohesive working-class communities in which 'modern' mass trade unionism had its strongest roots have largely disappeared; in contemporary society the spatial location and social organization of work, residence, consumption, and sociability have become highly differentiated. Employees may live a considerable distance from fellow workers, possess a largely 'privatized' domestic life or a circle of friends unconnected with work, and pursue cultural or recreational interests quite different from those of other employees in the same workplace (even if they still have a single, stable workplace). This disjuncture between work and community (or indeed the destruction of community in much of its traditional meaning) has eliminated many of the localized networks which strengthened the supports of union membership. Different types of collectivism—in the trade union, at the workplace, and in everyday life more generally—have become increasingly separated (McBride and Martínez Lucio 2011; Pocock 2011). Class boundaries have become fuzzier, and there seems less willingness than in the past to submerge particular interests within a more broadly defined class identity. 'Solidarity is our core business,' the leader of the Dutch FNV told us; but this was once easier to achieve with a homogeneous workforce. Referring to the cleaners' strike described in the next chapter, she added, '[a]t the low end of the labour market the emancipation task is perhaps bigger than ever...but if you don't have familiarity with those cleaning ladies who are wearing black, with long overcoats and headscarves, it's difficult to organize that form of solidarity'. The union succeeded by presenting the strikers 'as hard-working people who try to make something of their lives...but it's not as easy, you have to use different words, different tactics, different strategies to organize solidarity'.

In many European countries it has also become common to argue that one of the key problems confronting trade unions has been a sociocultural transformation whereby traditional working-class values of collectivism have given way to more individualistic orientations. In one sense this argument is trite and simplistic. As D'Art and Turner demonstrate (2008), popular support for unions is actually increasing. It is important to add that collectivism has never represented an *alternative* to individual interests and individual identities: trade unionism traditionally provided a pooling of resources allowing workers more effectively to defend and advance their personal interests. While union members have always been conscious of common occupational or employment interests, this never negated their individual circumstances and projects. Trade unions have rarely been able to rely on a spontaneous urge to collectivism: to integrate diversity into an organization with a common set of objectives has been a task to accomplish, with no guarantee of success.

Difficulties in building collective organization are particularly evident with workers in their twenties and younger, who virtually everywhere are far less unionized than their parents. Commonly, indeed, the median union member is aged around 50, and will have retired in little more than a decade. Partly this is because new entrants to the labour market are particularly liable to be unemployed, or else forced into precarious employment in sectors where unions are weak, as Table 2.1 shows and as we discuss in Chapter 3. But some suggest that there has been a generational change in social attitudes, making

Table 2.1. Labour market insecurity, age 15–24 (2011)

	Unemployment rate (%)	Fixed-term contracts (%)
SE	22.9	57.3
DK	14.2	22.1
DE	8.6	56.0
AT	8.3	37.2
NL	7.6	47.7
BE	18.7	34.3
FR	22.9	55.1
IT	29.1	49.9
UK	21.1	13.5
IE	29.4	33.8

Source: Eurostat.

younger workers less susceptible to the appeal of trade unionism (Ebbinghaus 2002). A different way of presenting the same problem is to suggest that unions are widely perceived as tired, archaic bureaucracies, largely irrelevant to the major issues of the contemporary world. Certainly it is clear that if unions are to appeal to the Facebook and YouTube generation, their image, language, and modes of communication must be very different from what is traditional, even if the underlying message of solidarity remains the same.

National Industrial Relations Systems, Globalization, and Neoliberalism

Trade unions—even those embracing ideals of internationalism, as most indeed do—are embedded in national societies. Their world views have always been coloured by national cultural assumptions (or sometimes prejudices); and crucially, their regulatory capacity has been conditioned by their adversaries and interlocutors—employers and political authorities—who likewise operated on a primarily national terrain. The industrial relations systems of which unions became components and ultimately defenders were nationally bounded and nationally distinctive.

National industrial relations systems founded on the triangular relationship of unions, employers, and governments have been destabilized by a series of external challenges, usually identified as 'globalization'. In part this involves the intensification of cross-national competition, as new economic powers make inroads in product markets once dominated by a small number of European and North American economies. Another aspect is the internationalization of production chains within MNCs; such companies are detached from the regulatory frameworks of national industrial relations systems and have become increasingly assertive in redefining the industrial relations agenda, whether through policies of union exclusion or by clawing back (in 'concession bargaining') many of the gains won by organized labour in earlier decades. Faced with the threat (and reality) of production shifts to lower-wage locations (notably the CEE countries which joined the EU in 2004 and 2007), and the outsourcing of key activities to low-wage suppliers within the home country, unions have few resources with which to respond.

The visible hand of MNCs interacts with the increasingly coercive invisible hand of finance capital. The last three decades have seen the liberalization and deregulation of international capital and currency markets; the acceleration of transactions through advances in information and telecommunications technologies; the rise of hedge funds, private equity, and leveraged buy-outs; and the breakdown of the American-dominated post-war system of international monetary stabilization. The resulting volatile capital flows translate into disruptive instability in the physical economy. Peters (2011) has argued that financialization and 'shareholder value' capitalism have undermined good jobs and trade union capacity. The EU, long regarded by many trade unionists as a protection against these trends and a defence for the social regulation of employment, has from the turn of the century shown an increasing commitment to advancing further liberalization of trade, capital mobility, and financial transactions.

In much of Europe in the post-war decades, systematic economic planning linked to Keynesian demand management was broadly accepted—even by conservative parties—as the recipe for growth and full employment. In most countries, key public services such as posts and railways were brought into public ownership if they were not already part of the state system. In some countries—France and Italy in particular—strategic manufacturing industries and banks were nationalized. Governments also accepted a duty to protect the vulnerable through an expanding system of public welfare. Typically, this provided fertile ground for institutionalized industrial relations and the growth of union membership. Trade unions could also engage, in effect, in collective bargaining at the level of the state, agreeing to refrain from exploiting their advantageous labour market position in return for an appropriate share in growing prosperity.

The material and ideological foundations of this benign environment have been undermined. Socio-demographic changes have played a significant role. Rising educational standards are linked to higher costs of schools and universities and a rise in the average age of entry into the labour force. At the other end of the age scale, life expectancy is higher while most workers retire earlier than in the past, putting pressure on pensions systems and also on health services. The ratio of working to dependent population has thus fallen, reducing the income tax base, while corporate taxation is squeezed by the threat of capital mobility. Almost universally, this has been reflected in government efforts to raise the retirement age, increase individual contributions, and (in many cases) reduce the level of benefits; and in more general efforts to limit public expenditure. This has inevitably posed a major challenge for unions.

In broader economic policy terms, as governments (even when notionally of the left) perceive a greatly reduced room for manœuvre in shaping macroeconomic policy, they have typically abandoned Keynesian principles and embraced policies of 'deregulation' in support of supply-side flexibility in labour markets. Either from ideological conviction or as a short-term remedy for budgetary stringency, most governments have also adopted privatization programmes. More generally, with the rise of neoliberalism the dominant policy view is now that less, not more, state intervention is needed to restore competitiveness in a globalized, post-Fordist world. Many see the collapse of the Soviet empire, which appeared to present an alternative economic model, as reinforcing such trends. While the extent of such challenges varies substantially cross-nationally, universally the foundations of the Fordist industrial relations compromise—and the status of unions as its ambiguous beneficiaries—are significantly weakened. While mainstream politicians of both left and right—and their counterparts at EU level—still profess belief in a 'European social model', social protection is increasingly subordinated to market 'freedoms'.

All these challenges have been compounded—throughout the period when we undertook our research—by a succession of crises: the global financial crisis, the drastic (though uneven) impact on production and employment across Europe, the sovereign debt crisis (partly a result of bailing out failed banks), and the severe austerity measures imposed by the EU, the international financial institutions, and most national governments.

Varieties of Challenges

Writing a quarter of a century ago, Müller-Jentsch (1988: 177–8) identified three 'crises' besetting trade unions. The first was a 'crisis of interest aggregation', the product of a more heterogeneous labour force and growing employer pressures for flexibility and decentralization. The second was a 'crisis of workers' loyalty towards their unions', stemming from sophisticated management efforts to strengthen commitment to the employing organization. The third was a 'crisis of union representation', caused by the expansion of highly qualified occupational groups disinclined to organize collectively. More recent observers have offered similar diagnoses. But while the changing world of work, the impact of globalization, and the rise of neoliberalism have affected the environment of trade unionism in all our countries, they have done so in different ways and to different degrees. These differences are closely related to diverse threats to nationally specific constellations of trade union power resources.

Nordic unions have traditionally enjoyed exceptional levels of associational and organizational power (high membership density together with trade unions which combine centralized cohesion and vigorous workplace organization), as well as considerable institutional power derived in part from their privileged relationship with governments dominated by Social democrats. But Social-democratic hegemony has been increasingly eroded. In Sweden, the party's vote fell from over 50 per cent in 1968 to just over 30 per cent in 2010, and prospects for a return to office are uncertain. In Denmark's fragmented party system the Social democrats never achieved the same proportion of the popular vote but were by far the largest party, scoring over 40 per cent in the 1960s and over 36 per cent as recently as 1998. This fell to just under 25 per cent in 2011—though the party succeeded in forming a minority coalition government, which, however, seems precarious.

The increasing dominance of right-wing parties—together, as in many other countries, with a shift by Social democrats towards neoliberal economic policies (Notermans 1993; Piazza 2001)—has posed major challenges to the unions. The most important has been a weakening of the Ghent system in both countries (Dølvik et al. 2011; Kjellberg 2009, 2011b; Lind 2009). In Sweden—where unemployment levels have risen considerably, particularly for young workers, who also have the highest rate of temporary employment—insurance contributions were increased dramatically (roughly fourfold) in 2007, while tax allowances were abolished. The following year, contributions were linked more closely to the rate of unemployment for members of each fund, meaning that the most vulnerable workers were hardest hit, while benefit levels were reduced. Since unemployment insurance is voluntary, the result has been a substantial decline in membership of the union-controlled funds and a corresponding decline in union membership. LO suffered worst: it lost 16 per cent of its membership between 2007 and 2010. Membership has also declined in some TCO unions, but SACO has increased membership as well as overall density over the same period. Overall, union density fell by 10 percentage points between 2000 and 2010 (Kjellberg 2011a).

In Denmark, the government in 2001 ended the trade union monopoly of unemployment insurance, and allowed funds to compete across sectoral and occupational boundaries. Two years later, contribution rates were doubled, followed by a reduction in tax allowances. In 2009, the duration of unemployment benefits was cut from four to two years. As in Sweden, membership in the insurance funds dropped, though less severely. Here too, LO has fared worst, losing 22 per cent of its membership between 2000 and 2011. But more generally, some observers identify a significant shift of attitudes, particularly among younger workers, away from trade union membership (Ibsen et al. 2012). A distinctive development has been the rise of a previously insignificant Christian union (*Kristelig Fagbevægelse* or *KriFa*), which has no collective bargaining power but offers cut-price membership; it now claims over 100,000 members and almost twice this number in its unemployment insurance fund, and has signed a few collective agreements which undercut the established union rates.

As we described in the previous chapter, a key principle of Nordic trade unionism has been that the main conditions of employment are regulated by collective bargaining rather than by law; so, for example, there is no minimum wage legislation. This creates vulnerability to EU rules on free movement of labour and freedom of establishment, signalled by the judgments of the European Court of Justice (ECJ) which we discuss further in Chapter 7. These ruled that the EU directive covering workers 'posted' from one member state to another 'cannot be interpreted as allowing the host Member State to make the provision of services in its territory conditional on the observance of terms and employment which go beyond the mandatory rules for minimum protection'. Since collective agreements are not universally binding by law, this prohibits unions from taking industrial action to enforce their terms on non-compliant foreign service providers. This 'ruling has struck at the very heart of the so-called Swedish model for setting wages and conditions' (Woolfson et al. 2010), and has similar implications for Denmark.

We mentioned above that pensions have been a focus of contention for unions in many countries. In Denmark this has taken a distinctive form in respect of the early retirement scheme (*efterløn*), which since the late 1970s allowed workers in physically demanding jobs to retire from the age of 60 on relatively generous terms. This was a target of the cost-cutting measures pursued by the right-wing government elected in 2001; and the radical changes which it announced shortly before the 2011 election have been implemented by its Social-democrat-led successor (even though it contested these when in opposition). This has obviously created serious problems for the trade unions, in particular LO, since it has traditionally been close to the Social democrats and its members are most affected by the changes.

Unions in our 'central' group of countries face a somewhat different set of challenges. Hoffmann and Hoffmann (2009: 398–400) identify two main threats to the traditional security of trade unionism which create 'a precarious phase of transformation'. First, the 'Rhineland' CME model depended crucially on the role of 'patient capital': banks and other institutional investors were committed to a long-term relationship with major companies, protecting employers from short-term market pressures. Germany was here the archetype, as we noted in the previous chapter. While all four countries have always been integrated into international product markets, they were relatively insulated from the volatility of global financial markets. This has changed significantly, with an incremental shift towards Anglo-American principles of 'shareholder value' and the encroachment of associated financial instruments and institutions (facilitated, and in part driven, by EU competition rules). A dramatic illustration is the spread in Germany of hostile takeovers, previously virtually unknown: symptomatic was the takeover of Mannesmann by Vodafone in 2000. Such changes expose employees to previously unknown levels of instability and insecurity, posing major problems for trade unions.

Second, as described in the previous chapter, unions in all four countries have long enjoyed strong institutional supports which made them less dependent on associational and organizational power resources. As Table 1.2 showed, while union density in Austria and Belgium was over 50 per cent in 1980, in Germany and the Netherlands it was only 35 per cent. Since then, density in the last two countries has fallen to around 20 per cent, while in

Austria it has halved; only Belgian unions, buttressed by the Ghent system, have withstood the trend. But institutional supports may induce dangerous complacency: without adequate associational and organizational power resources, unions may lose representative legitimacy and find their institutional power resources undermined (Bispinck et al. 2010). As Rehder (2008), Streeck (2009), and Thelen (2012) have demonstrated, it is possible for the form of institutions—such as German codetermination—to remain intact but for their practical effect to atrophy. German unions present an extreme case of a more general problem: disproportionately comprising a core of relatively secure, male manual workers in traditional manufacturing (as well as the public sector), whose own security is threatened by the growth of a more diversified and often precarious workforce outside the ranks of trade unionism. Most unions in the 'central' countries have responded rather belatedly to these challenges, as we discuss in the next chapter.

In addition to these two general challenges, there are others specific to each country. Any discussion of Germany must refer to east–west unification in 1990. First, incorporating a virtually bankrupt state into the former West Germany imposed enormous costs, effectively ending the post-war 'economic miracle'. Second, unions initially secured mass membership in the east but these gains were rapidly lost as unemployment mounted, resulting in an extended apparatus (offices, representative structures, officials) which membership subscriptions could not sustain. Third, harmonization of wages and conditions within unified Germany was not achieved; and the existence of a new low-wage area placed major strains on the cherished principle of uniform collectively agreed standards. This has been one reason for an increasing fragmentation and decentralization of collective bargaining, for an erosion of membership in employers' associations (whose own encompassing character traditionally compensated for the relative numerical weakness of the unions), and hence the declining coverage of collective agreements. As Table 1.2 shows, this has fallen considerably over the past three decades, in contrast to the stability in the other three countries in this group, all of which have much stronger mechanisms for the extension of collective agreements. A related threat is the large number of 'works-council-free' firms, since councils have long operated as an extended arm of the unions (Gumbrell-McCormick and Hyman 2006; Hassel 1999). Also important has been the dramatic shift to a two-tier labour market (Palier and Thelen 2010), in marked contrast to the traditional German image of employment security. Though youth unemployment rates are low, a majority of workers aged 15–24 are on temporary contracts—the second highest rate in any of our countries (see Table 2.1).

In Austria, union density has been declining for half a century. White-collar workers are only half as likely to be unionized as manual, hence unions have lost out with the changing composition of employment. They may also have suffered from the negative face of institutionalized social partnership. As indicated in the previous chapter, government for most of the post-war period has involved coalitions between the SPÖ and the conservative ÖVP, which for a time shared over 90 per cent of the popular vote. This consensual model was challenged from the 1990s by the rise of minority parties, and in particular the far-right *Freiheitliche Partei Österreichs* (FPÖ), which split in 2005. The combined vote of the two main parties fell to 55 per cent in 2008, while the SPÖ, which in the 1970s had won more than half the popular vote, achieved under 30 per cent (though still emerging as the largest party). The unions, closely integrated into the political establishment, have suffered a loss of popular legitimacy, which may have compounded the decline in membership (Stern 2010: 1–2). Problems were accentuated in 2006 by a scandal surrounding the large union-owned bank, BAWAG, which collapsed as a result of speculative investments and internal corruption; the ÖGB president, Fritz Verzetnitsch, was forced to resign his post and his parliamentary seat. The FPÖ, as well as tapping broader anti-establishment sentiments, has campaigned on a virulently anti-immigrant platform; and faced with the prospect of a considerable influx of CEE workers after EU enlargement in 2004 and 2007, the ÖGB demanded the most restrictive conditions of any European trade union for the regulation of 'free movement', as we discuss in Chapter 7.

The Netherlands has also seen challenges to the post-war consensus model, causing serious problems for the unions. In a multiparty system the PvdA, to which the FNV has long been closely linked, achieved first or second place in every post-war general election until a decade ago, usually achieving around 30 per cent of the popular vote. In 2002, however, it scored only 15 per cent and was pushed into fourth place, behind two conservative parties and a far-right anti-immigrant party (its rise parallel to that of the FPÖ in Austria). The PvdA is also challenged from the left by the *Socialistische Partij* (SP), which for a time topped the opinion polls (though faring less well in the September 2012 elections) and has achieved significant influence within a number of FNV affiliates.

The sense that Dutch unions, like their Austrian counterparts, had become part of the establishment precipitated in 2011 the most serious crisis in any of the movements included in our study. Following lengthy discussions over government plans to raise the retirement age, the FNV—which had previously resisted the demands though the smaller confederations were ready to negotiate a compromise—eventually accepted a phased increase to 67 and a reduction in benefits for early retirement. This was endorsed by most of its affiliates but the two largest, *AbvaKabo* and *Bondgenoten*—together accounting for the majority of its membership—were opposed. The outcome was a decision by the affiliates to replace the FNV by a new organization (*De Nieuwe*

Vakbeweging) under new leadership, though its structure remains far from clear at the time of writing.

If the dynamics of national social partnership pose one major challenge for Dutch unions, another is the relationship between the workplace and trade unionism. Works councils possess fewer powers than in Germany or Austria, and are less integrated with union structures. As a government-established study argued (van het Kaar and Smit 2006), their effectiveness is likely to be further reduced: on the one hand by internationalization of ownership, which means that strategic decisions are increasingly taken outside the Netherlands; on the other by decentralization of decision-making within companies, including mechanisms for direct employee participation. Such problems are certainly not unique to the Netherlands, but it is particularly difficult for Dutch unions to respond effectively.

Within the 'central' group, Belgian unions probably face the fewest nationally specific threats. As we have seen, membership density is stable and is now far higher than in the other three countries. Trade unions are among the few national institutions which remain relatively well integrated, at a time when conflicts between the Dutch- and French-speaking communities seem to be tearing the country apart (for most of 2010 and 2011 it was impossible to form a government). Given the increasingly precarious position of national governments, unions hold a powerful position as policy brokers; perhaps paradoxically, the division of the trade union movement between rival 'pillars' actually enhances its channels of influence within the political sphere. And in contrast to the Netherlands, workplace organization seems more effectively integrated within trade union structures (Mok 1985).

Our two 'southern' countries face specific but distinct challenges. In France, as we saw in the previous chapter, unions have the lowest density in western Europe. Traditionally, membership implied a far more active commitment than in other countries; and unions measured their support, first by votes received in elections to works committees and second by willingness to follow calls to strike action. But the number of strikes has fallen dramatically in recent decades, at least in the private sector—though other forms of 'unorganized' conflict remain widespread (Béroud et al. 2007, 2008; Giraud 2006), while workplace elections are marked by high abstention rates (over a third of the constituency) and the election of many non-union nominees (roughly a quarter) (Gumbrell-McCormick and Hyman 2006). Unions have increasingly depended for their effectiveness, first, on their implantation within the extensive public sector, which once employed almost a quarter of the labour force, and allowed generous time off work for union workplace representatives; second, on their ability to mobilize to secure government regulation of the labour market, social benefits, and working conditions.

This industrial relations model has been challenged in three main ways. First, governments since the mid 1980s have implemented large-scale privatizations: employment in nationalized enterprises, then over two million, has fallen by over two-thirds. Second, sectoral agreements have lost much of their effect, giving way to company bargaining; and managements (including those in newly privatized enterprises) have adopted more sophisticated and assertive human resource strategies, often bypassing the formal institutions of trade unions and works committees (Bunel and Thuderoz 1999). Some argue that the whole structure of collective representation has become a façade. As Goyer and Hancké put it (2004: 176), 'the organizational weakness of unions within companies meant that managerial unilateralism became the norm for corporate decision-making'. Third, governments have distanced themselves from the regulation of industrial relations, attempting to devolve responsibility to the 'social partners' (Howell 2009; Schmidt 2002). Given trade unions' diminished power resources, this in effect means enhancing the autonomy of management.

An additional challenge is increasing labour market segmentation, with the rapid growth of a 'precarious generation' (Mabrouki 2004): roughly half those aged under 25 are either unemployed or on temporary contracts. A further threat to the three smaller confederations (FO, CFTC, and CGC) whose representative status was hitherto unchallengeable is the agreement reached in 2008 between their two larger rivals (CGT and CFDT) and the employers, and then given legal backing. This specifies that a union must win at least 10 per cent of votes in works committee elections to be eligible to negotiate at company level, and 8 per cent at sectoral; and also imposes thresholds of representativeness before an agreement can be considered legally valid. This may force smaller unions either to merge or to be sidelined.

In Italy, the growth of a 'precarious generation' is even more marked than in France: as Table 2.1 shows, almost 30 per cent of young workers are unemployed and almost 40 per cent of those in work are on temporary contracts. This poses special problems for Italian unions, given their exceptional age profile (half their members being pensioners): unions risk being regarded by younger workers as organizations of the elderly, primarily committed to defending their distinctive interests (Molina and Rhodes 2007). This profile has also affected unions' role in negotiating the highly contentious reforms of the pensions system, as discussed in a later chapter.

Three more general problems may be noted. The first has been the policies of the Berlusconi governments, in office with only a two-year break between 2001 and 2011 and pursuing labour market deregulation, weakening some of the rights contained in the 1970 Workers' Statute, restructuring the system of collective bargaining, and reducing welfare benefits. Berlusconi was successful in splitting the trade union movement between CGIL (itself internally divided) and its rivals, who were more ready to compromise. Some of the same problems continued under the 'technocratic' Monti government which took office at the end of 2011, and are unlikely to be resolved by the chaotic outcome of the elections in February 2013. Hence the relative inter-confederal unity which had prevailed for much of the 1980s and 1990s has been ruptured (Negrelli and Pulignano 2008).

Second, as in France, there has been a move towards more aggressive managerialism. This is symbolized above all by developments in Fiat, Italy's largest private employer, which now defines itself as a global rather than an Italian firm and in 2011 withdrew from the employers' confederation *Confindustria*. It has demanded radical alterations in working conditions, together with pay reductions and job cuts, under threat of withdrawing production from Italy, and has derecognized CGIL, which refused to accept the changes.

Third, the economic and financial crisis has had a particularly severe impact in Italy, with threats to continuing membership of the eurozone leading to a radical programme of cuts in public expenditure. Moreover, the EU institutions insisted on the removal of statutory employment protections and a weakening of national pay bargaining. As Meardi has commented (2012c), the European Commission and the European Central Bank achieved in a few months what 'employers and rightwing government had not even dared to ask. Labour resistance, which had previously had some success, is now in a weaker position when fighting a more elusive opponent, uninterested in local political exchange and unaffected by general strikes.' Again, the main unions have been divided over their response.

In the anglophone countries, unions have traditionally enjoyed only limited institutional supports and are thus particularly dependent on their own internal power resources. In the UK, density has almost halved since 1980 and—because of the virtual absence of sectoral bargaining and the lack of extension mechanisms—collective bargaining coverage has fallen even more sharply (Marginson 2012). The number of workplace union representatives (shop stewards), on whom most unions depended heavily for the work of recruitment and representation, fell by over two-thirds between 1984 and 2004 (Charlwood and Forth 2009: 81). In the private sector, where union recognition still exists it encourages a form of 'de facto enterprise unionism' (Howell 2005: 132).

One crucial challenge is sustained government hostility. The Conservative governments between 1979 and 1997 introduced a radical legislative programme designed to make effective trade union organization and action extremely difficult; 'New Labour' in office until 2010 pursued ambivalent policies designed to encourage only 'supply side trade unionism' which served the interests of employer competitiveness (Ewing 2005; Smith 2009).

Both governments also imposed extensive privatization. Many managements have utilized the new legal regime to exclude union representation, or at least to minimize the scope of collective bargaining. As in other countries, the proportion of precarious jobs seems to be increasing: though paradoxically, Table 1.1 shows that the proportion of fixed-term contracts in the UK is lower than in any of the other countries, perhaps since 'permanent' workers enjoy far less job security than elsewhere. Most recently, the savage austerity measures imposed since 2010 by the Conservative-Liberal government threaten many areas of public services and public employment. Given the structural complexity of British trade unionism, formulating a coherent response has been extremely difficult.

In Ireland, the public status of trade unions was boosted by a quarter century of peak-level partnership agreements. Yet at company level, 'employer opposition to trade unions appears to have increased during the period of social partnership' (D'Art and Turner 2011: 166). Critics argued that 'social partnership...demobilises workplace unionism by ensnaring it in a web of procedural agreements and detailed productivity concessions that have been dictated from above' (Allen 2009: 60). Demands for effective statutory support for union recognition as compensation for wage restraint proved unsuccessful; and indeed, the lack of legislative constraints on management autonomy has been one of the government's selling points in attracting overseas investment. Hence 'unions have only a small presence in the foreign-owned sector' (Donaghey and Teague 2007: 23).

Since 2008 all other challenges have been overwhelmed by the impact of the global financial crisis, which brutally exposed the fragility of Ireland's growth model based on cheap credit, speculative banking, and an artificial housing boom. Having committed some €50 billion to cover bank losses, the Irish government was the first to impose a massive austerity programme, with a major impact on jobs, wages, and pensions in the public sector. The threat was intensified under the terms of the EU/IMF 'bailout' of November 2010. This crisis tested social partnership to destruction, but also created serious divisions between public and private sector unions.

'Contextualized Comparisons' of the Challenges to Trade Unions

Not only do the principal challenges facing unions differ from country to country; their impact is also mediated by distinctive institutional contexts and by the strategies, power resources, and interrelationships of the key actors—governments, employers, and, of course, unions themselves. Nor should any of these be treated as unitary actors. Governments are traditionally cross-party coalitions in all ten countries except the UK, though here too a coalition is currently in office. Regardless of party there are other sources of division within governments, most notably between those responsible for economic policy on the one hand, social and employment policy on the other. Employer interests (and often collective representative structures) differ between large and small firms, those in manufacturing and in services, export-oriented companies and those catering primarily for domestic markets. Such differences have their parallels in trade union movements, cross-cut and reinforced in countries marked by ideological pluralism. The scope for strategic conflict and disarray is considerable.

Beyond such considerations, the very *meaning* of analogous challenges can differ radically between countries. Locke and Thelen (1995: 342–3) give the example of employer demands for greater employment flexibility. In the USA, a system of clearly defined work rules and job classifications was historically a major trade union achievement, a bulwark against arbitrary and discriminatory action by managements, which thus 'defined and anchored the moral order of shop floor relations... and the unions' role in that order'. Employer demands for work reorganization represented a major threat whereas in Germany, for example, they had no such implications. Similarly, pressure by Swedish employers for increased wage differentials, including the introduction of discretionary pay, challenged traditional union policies of wage solidarity whereas neither American nor German unions felt similarly threatened. In similar ways, demands in Italy in the 1980s for the abolition of the *scala mobile* were an attack on the symbolic achievements of the years of mobilization a decade earlier. Thus 'traditional union identities', linked closely to past struggles and past victories, helped define the key 'sticking points' for unions in each country.

The logic of this argument is that as well as identifying objective challenges, we must also explore how these are perceived and interpreted: in the language of mobilization theory, the ways in which they are *framed* (Kelly 1998). As Frege and Kelly argue (2003: 14–15), such framing processes reflect traditional identities and shape not only perceptions of challenges but also assessments of appropriate responses. Trade unions possess traditional repertoires of action, and the line of least resistance is to apply these to new situations where they may not necessarily prove effective. It may require an existential shock before new strategic initiatives are embraced, and radical policy shifts commonly provoke severe inter- and intra-union conflict.

Strategic Innovation and 'Revitalization'

Many researchers have explored the degree of innovation in union responses to recent challenges. Writing over a decade ago, Waddington (2000: 318) identified three main emergent approaches. The first was increased articulation and coordination of activities, involving stronger vertical linkages between workplace and national unionism and between members and leaders; and more effective horizontal cooperation between different unions. The second entailed constructing a new agenda which could attract previously under-represented groups of workers without alienating existing members. The third involved 'the development of coherent international activities and policies'. Frege and Kelly (2003: 9) expand this catalogue, identifying 'six major strategies': adopting an 'organizing model'; restructuring (mergers or internal reorganization, or both); developing partnerships, with employers or with governments; new forms of political action; coalition building; and reinforced international links to counter the challenges of globalization. Their list frames our brief discussion below. Behrens et al. (2004) have also specified four 'dimensions' of revitalization, with a focus first on membership (increasing density, reshaping its composition, increasing membership engagement with the union); second, unions' economic functions (developing new forms of bargaining and leverage); third, political (new forms of electoral involvement, new efforts to influence legislation, a changed role in public administration); fourth, institutional reform (organizational restructuring). These 'dimensions' overlap with the 'strategies' identified by other authors, but as Frege and Kelly (2004) comment, there is no linear relationship between them.

One response to membership decline has been the proliferation of individual services (for example, cut-price banking, insurance, travel) as selective incentives to membership. Olson (1965) argued that individual workers can obtain the benefits of collective agreements without becoming union members ('free-riding'), but that if unions offer 'private goods' they provide a stronger incentive to membership. While often presented as a (post-)modern adaptation to more individualistic and consumerist worker orientations, such services have affinities with the portfolio of individual benefits which early craft trade unions offered to their members. There is little evidence, however, that they have contributed significantly to membership recruitment and retention. What does appear more effective, however, is enhanced advice on career contingencies and representation in the case of employment-related grievances and problems (Leisink 1997; Waddington 2000).

A very different response is the rediscovery (or reinvention) of the principles of active recruitment and representation, particularly of groups of workers (women, ethnic minorities, new labour market entrants, those on 'atypical' contracts—categories which in practice often overlap) who are traditionally under-represented among union memberships. Pioneered in North America, further developed in Australia, and latterly adapted in Europe, the struggle for an 'organizing culture' involves building a cadre of recruiters (both paid and volunteer) with whom the target groups can identify, and giving their specific concerns a higher priority on the union agenda. In the abstract this can appear straightforward; in practice there are many difficulties. Active organizing is expensive, both in simple balance-sheet terms and in its demands on the time and energies of those involved. Crucially, there are hard choices to be made between an emphasis on new areas of recruitment on the one hand, and effective representation of existing members (including new recruits) on the other. Again in theory, the dilemma may be resolved by 'empowering' members to constitute the front line of their own self-representation; again in reality, the effort to construct and sustain a structure of workplace activism can be a thankless labour of Sisyphus. The vicious circle of membership loss, declining efficacy, and demoralization is not readily transformed into a virtuous circle of recruitment, representation, and empowerment. We discuss these issues in the next chapter.

Organizationally, hard times have also precipitated a wave of union mergers (Chaison 1996; Streeck and Visser 1997). While at times rationalized as a proactive strategy to facilitate recruitment in new growth sectors, more typically these have been defensive reactions to membership loss and the shrinkage of traditional recruitment bases. Often the pattern of amalgamations has owed more to inter- and intra-union politics than to any clear labour market rationale. Certainly this has at times brought advantages from economies of scale (or at least counteracted the diseconomies of membership decline), but often also has generated structurally complex conglomerates riven with barely concealed internal tensions. These are themes we examine in Chapter 4, together with internal structural changes within unions.

In some countries a widespread response to hard times has been the pursuit of 'partnership'. This can be directed at different levels. In Britain (there are analogies here to the idea of 'mutual gains' in North America) an important focus has been the company. Here, the emphasis has been on a joint interest of employer and employees in workplace competitiveness and survival: expressed in union agreement to changes in the production regime (reduced numbers of employees, more flexible working-time arrangements, interchangeability of jobs) in return for management commitment to (more or less bounded) guarantees of continued operation. Such deals have become quite widespread: for example, in the German notion of *Standortsicherung* (safeguarding the production location). Sometimes the shift to partnership may be a primarily opportunistic response to the erosion of traditional power resources: if unions no longer have the capacity to fight effectively against employers, cooperation may seem the only alternative. Another spur to partnership may be a view that workers themselves perceive no fundamental conflict of interests with their employer and reject the traditional image of unions as militant and obstructive. One problem, however, is the risk of creating a form of company unionism when intensified competition implies that not all companies will compete successfully, however much their workforces agree to abandon previously sacrosanct conditions of employment. The role of unions as national organizations defending minimum standards across a far broader constituency is thereby threatened. In addition, there is an evident tension between partnership approaches and the 'organizing model', which typically focuses on employees' grievances, attributing responsibility to the employer and mobilizing for redress (Kelly 1998). In Britain, the TUC has endeavoured to manage this tension by distinguishing between 'good' and 'bad' employers: it is possible to pursue partnership with the former while mobilizing against the latter. But in reality, employers cannot be so neatly demarcated into these two contrasting types.

'Partnership' is also a factor at macro level. In much of Europe, the theme of 'social partnership' has long been regarded as both an ideal and a reality of national industrial relations, involving institutionalized cooperative relationships between confederations of unions and employers, and in some cases also governments. Even in some countries without such traditions, a notable feature of the 1990s was an emergence of 'social pacts' involving trade union cooperation, not simply as in previous decades in wage restraint but also in concessions to relax the restrictions on employers contained in labour law regimes, and to 'reform' state welfare provision, in return for (typically imprecise) commitments to employment-creating policies on the part of governments and employers (Fajertag and Pochet 1997). Here too there is a collective actor problem: unions (and to a large extent also governments) address the problem of intensified competitiveness at national level; MNCs are happy to accept the concessions but as a precedent for more ambitious demands in other jurisdictions. In Europe, this process has notoriously been described as 'social dumping'. Economic crises from 2008–9 had contradictory effects, on the one hand stimulating efforts to find consensual solutions, on the other placing existing institutions of social partnership under severe strain. These themes are part of our focus in Chapter 5.

'Revitalization along the political dimension implies that unions improve the effectiveness of their efforts to influence the policy-making process, either through traditional or innovative methods' (Behrens et al. 2004: 22). In all our countries, unions have traditionally been closely linked to political parties, primarily Social democratic but in some cases Christian democratic or Communist. The effectiveness of such linkages has generally declined, forcing unions to redefine or even abandon them. The shift to neoliberalism has also meant that established methods of intervention in the policy process yield diminishing returns, and indeed in some cases the very legitimacy of such intervention has become suspect. One response has been for unions to raise their profile by engaging in 'contentious politics' (Tarrow 1998), contesting oppression, inequality, and discrimination, and campaigning for rights. This can also involve cooperation, often uneasy, with other social movements and NGOs, most of which have never acquired the respectability gained by trade unions. Potentially, such 'social movement unionism' (Fairbrother and Yates 2003) redefines unions as outsiders in a terrain where until recently the role of insiders was comforting and rewarding. We discuss such developments further in Chapter 6.

As we argued above, trade unions are rooted in nationally specific economies, societies, and polities. However, most have long expressed their commitment to international solidarity, and international trade union organizations have existed since the 19th century. Globalization has led to a restructuring of international linkages, and in many cases a revision of their objectives and methods. The increasing impact of the EU, and its geographical extension to encompass twenty-seven member states, has also made European regional organization a key feature of trade union activity. In times of financial stringency, this can result in a competition for resources between global and European activities. We explore some of these themes in Chapter 7.

Are these different approaches to revitalization complementary or contradictory? As we have indicated, there are at least unresolved tensions; more generally, they require investment of resources, so in hard times there are inevitably hard choices to be made. And even compatible policies can be made truly complementary only if consciously and purposefully integrated. But unions are primarily reactive organizations, responding to the actions of employers and governments rather than shaping the agenda on which they operate. Certainly unions seem to possess greater strategic capacity in some countries than in others; and more generally, there have been clear efforts across the board in recent years to formulate more coherent, integrated, and proactive policy interventions. These issues frame our concluding chapter.

Conclusions

In this chapter we have identified the main trade union power resources, 'old' and 'new'; and we have explored how changes in the world of work, in the relationship between national economies and the global level, and in political environments have weakened some traditional resources, encouraging a search for alternatives. We have summarized the key challenges facing unions in each of the ten countries, noting that because of different histories and identities, objectively similar challenges may have very different implications. All European unions face hard times, but for some they are harder than for others. Their responses are to some extent path dependent, reflecting traditional identities and repertoires of action; but there are many signs of innovation. Finally we have surveyed the main routes to union 'revitalization', outlining the agenda for the remainder of this book.

3

Renewing Power Resources: Recruitment, Representation, and Mobilization

As we have seen, union density varies radically across countries, from under 8 per cent in France to (until recently) over 80 per cent in Sweden. Membership in Britain has fallen drastically and almost continuously for the past three decades. In many other countries the decline began later and has been less severe, but the trend is now universal. The composition of union membership often reflects the structure of the labour force several decades ago. In most cases, as we saw in the previous chapter, density is far below average for younger age groups; in many countries, half the present membership will retire within roughly a decade, while in Italy half are already pensioners. How have European unions responded?

In this chapter we examine recruitment, representation, and mobilization. These three processes are intertwined. The 'organizing model' developed in North America assumes a close connection between recruitment and mobilization: in order to turn associational into organizational power, the process of recruiting new members should also develop new activists and encourage activism at local and national levels. The recruitment of categories which in most countries have been seriously under-represented—beginning with women—also needs to go hand-in-hand with better representation of their distinctive interests, which can then become a recruiting and organizing tool.

Representation is a concept with at least two meanings. In one sense, an individual is representative of a constituency by sharing the same demographic characteristics: an important debate within many trade unions is whether a middle-aged white male can effectively represent a workforce which is predominantly young, female, or of ethnic minority background. But representation can also mean to defend and advance the interests of a constituency, whether or not those who form the group take part in a union's representative structures or are even union members (Briskin 1999: 155). For example, unions may attempt to represent the interests of transitory migrant workers but regard these as 'unorganizable'. Recruitment and representation build a capacity for mobilization, which may itself be both the goal of recruitment and a means to achieve it.

Our primary focus is on recruitment, which develops associational power, and on the more ambitious effort to build *organizational* power resources. We then discuss, less extensively, the issue of representation, including the development of structural provisions to improve the involvement of under-represented groups of workers such as women, ethnic minorities, and younger workers. Finally, we turn briefly to innovative approaches to mobilization.

Union Membership and Density

In Chapter 1 we presented the contrasting patterns of membership density in the ten countries (summarized in Table 1.2), and in Chapter 2 we outlined the general trend of membership decline between 1980 and 2010. Density has fallen by over 20 percentage points in Austria, Ireland, and the UK; the greatest stability has been in Belgium and the Nordic countries, in all of which a Ghent system has provided institutional support for trade union membership. The ranking of the ten countries has altered little; in general, those with high density rates have fared best, so that cross-national differences have widened. In assessing the reasons for these trends, Visser (2006: 46) has suggested common structural factors but also continued national particularities, many of which we summarized in the previous chapter.

In this section we briefly disaggregate some of the national patterns, considering variations in terms of gender, ethnic origin, age, and type of employment contract. This is not easy, because of limits to the available data. Unions do not systematically provide a breakdown of their membership in this way; the main sources are surveys which are not primarily concerned with trade union analysis. The ICTWSS database (Visser 2011) gives details for some of these categories for some countries, but not all. The other main source is the European Social Survey, undertaken in various years, but here too the coverage for some of the categories is incomplete, and where the aggregate level of trade union density is low—notably in France—any breakdown is very unreliable. Table 3.1 assembles what information is available, though the reliability of some figures is questionable.

These data reveal complex cross-national variations. In a number of countries, the unionization rate is lower for women than for men: most dramatically in Germany, where it is only half. But in the two Nordic countries the female rate is higher than the male, and this is also the case in Britain and (for one of the two data points) in France. Any crude gender breakdown may be misleading, for three reasons. First, public services, with a high female

Table 3.1. Disaggregated union density statistics (%)

	SE	DK	DE	AT	NL	BE	FR	IT	UK	IE
Female	74	73	13	21	17	46	8	20	30	35
Male	68	69	25	37	25	57	9	32	25	32
Part-time	69	76	18	25	24	46	14	28	22	37
Full-time	80	87	24	33	33	44	14	28	28	42
Fixed-term	60	76	11	28	15	39	9	15	10	37
Permanent	81	86	24	31	32	45	15	30	29	42
Foreign-born	70	54	18	13	16	33			9	15
Native-born	78	72	20	34	22	51			28	37
Under 25	*36*	*28*			*8*				*9*	*14*
16–34	*62*	*71*	*15*	*19*	*15*	*40*	*4*	*20*	*15*	*29*
35–54	*83*	*89*	*22*	*33*	*34*	*46*	*16*	*28*	*30*	*44*
55–64	*84*	*91*	*29*	*41*	*47*	*53*	*23*	*30*	*35*	*51*

Source: Gorodzeisky and Richards 2013 for foreign- and native-born workers, derived from European Social Surveys 2002–8; remaining data based on Ebbinghaus et al. 2008, derived from European Social Survey 2002. Note, however, that the survey figures for Italy are far below those generally accepted; we have therefore (arbitrarily!) adjusted these upwards by 50 per cent.

Figures in italics from ICTWSS database for 2008–9, based on national sources (Visser 2011).

employment ratio, are almost everywhere more unionized than the private sector; disaggregated by sector, women's unionization rates in most countries would look worse. Second, manual occupations are usually predominantly male, and white-collar occupations female; and manual workers are often significantly more unionized (though there is no such differential in the Nordic countries). Third, women are much more likely to be employed part-time, and in most countries (see below) part-timers are less unionized than full-time employees. This almost certainly explains much of the gender differential in the Netherlands, because of the exceptionally high proportion of part-time employment there.

Table 3.1 indicates the differential in unionization between full-time and part-time employees, who are less unionized in all countries except Belgium, Italy, and France (in the latter two countries, the figures may reflect unreliable data). There is likewise a gap between density for permanent and fixed-term workers, though this is quite narrow in Austria, Belgium, and Ireland. Foreign-born workers have a lower density rate than native-born workers in the eight countries for which we have data; arguably this is attributable primarily to their greater probability of filling low-paid, precarious jobs. There is no breakdown for France and Italy, though Feltrin (2009) documents a sustained increase in union membership among foreign-born workers in Italy. Germany is also an exception—perhaps because at the time of the survey, before 'free movement' was allowed for CEE migrants, most foreign-born workers were long settled in the country. (More generally, the significance of being 'foreign-born' differs considerably across countries.) Union density among younger workers is universally lower than for older workers. In the five countries for which we have data covering those aged under 25, the gap is dramatic: unionization is usually well under half the overall average. By all accounts, a similar picture exists in the remaining countries. In some cases, unions have established separate structures and forms of activity for young workers, as we discuss below; but in others there has traditionally been reluctance to create youth structures which might engage in 'embarrassing' actions or be 'captured by political extremists'.

All these observations indicate that unions in each of our countries face serious challenges, even though there is much that remains unexplained when we examine the contrasting national patterns of unionization. The workforce is becoming increasingly feminized and is shifting from old union strongholds to sectors and occupations with much weaker union traditions; the old 'normal' employment contract is being displaced by 'atypical' (though now, increasingly typical) forms; the old generation of (relatively) strongly unionized workers is giving way to those who are much less likely to be union members; free movement of labour within the enlarged EU presents national unions with additional problems. In what ways have they attempted to reverse the downward trend?

Our discussion includes separate sections on recruitment, representation, and mobilization, even though as we have noted all three are closely linked, and we end by offering a more integrated overview of responses to membership decline. We focus in particular on women, young workers, migrants, and ethnic minorities.

Recruitment Strategies and the 'Organizing Model'

If unions are declining in membership, then by definition they are failing to recruit new members as fast as they are losing old ones: to reverse the trend they must improve either recruitment or retention, or both. Some two decades ago, certain US unions saw the answer in the 'organizing model', often contrasted starkly with the dominant 'servicing model' of North American trade unionism. In the latter, a bureaucratic apparatus of union professionals provided benefits to members through collective bargaining and representation over individual grievances; members were treated as largely passive recipients of these services. But if the union in hard times could no longer deliver evident results, they were likely to abandon their membership. The aim of the alternative model was to engage members collectively in developing their own representative capacities, so that much of the day-to-day work of representation and bargaining could be undertaken from below, with the union apparatus providing background support. This was intended both to save resources and to increase the attractiveness of the union to actual and potential members. Organizing, in the face of hostile employers with a large repertoire of 'union-busting' tactics, required careful 'mapping' of the characteristics of target workers and the vulnerabilities of their employers, the 'framing' of their grievances in ways which would build collective solidarity, and aggressive one-to-one recruitment drives.

Trade unions in our ten countries have responded to falling density to various degrees and in a variety of ways. Some have remained complacent but most are now taking seriously the challenges of recruitment, representation, and mobilization. In some but by no means all countries, the 'organizing model' has been accepted, at least in part. In this section we explore some of the variations in acceptance, or rejection, of a turn to organizing. There are good reasons to expect significant contrasts. First, as we have seen, the actual extent of membership decline—or declining density, for actual numbers of members may be rising but less fast than the labour force—varies substantially across countries. Second, as we argued in discussing 'contextualized comparisons', objectively similar challenges may have different meanings according to national context; 'membership loss...has different meanings in different national systems' (Frege and Kelly 2003: 20). Third, national traditions and national institutions give rise to different 'repertoires of action' (Tarrow 1998); hence particular remedies (especially if drawn from the USA, with its distinctive industrial relations system) may seem inappropriate in most European countries (Brinkmann et al. 2008; Heery and Adler 2004; Rehder 2008). Finally, the meaning of the organizing model is itself often unclear, ambiguous, and contested (de Turberville 2004; Fairbrother and Yates 2003; Simms 2012). Is it simply a toolkit which can be applied selectively, or does it require an integrated approach with a radical rethinking of broader trade union objectives and ways of operating? Can organizing be reduced to recruitment, or does it require a much wider range of activities in order to progress from associational to organizational power? As Dörre et al. argue (2009: 35), 'the problem of trade union renewal strategies is not the adoption of single organizing practices, but instead their conjunction and consolidation in a coherent concept of associated power'. Are servicing and organizing really alternatives, or do effective recruitment and retention require both? We explore some of these issues below.

We pay particular attention to recruitment efforts among the growing numbers of workers on precarious contracts (who are disproportionately composed of women, migrants and ethnic minorities, and young people). Responses to the challenge of 'atypical' work have taken many forms, involving organizing and recruitment, revisions to internal structures, and new industrial, political, and societal policies and actions. First, though, unions have to decide to act on behalf of precarious workers. They have naturally opposed the deterioration in job security, pay rates, and terms and conditions of employment that has accompanied more precarious forms of work, and have concentrated on opposing initiatives by employers or governments to expand temporary and agency work and contracting-out—particularly, of course, when such moves are linked to reductions in existing staff. However, opposition to precarious work has also meant, in practice if not by design, that many unions have excluded precarious workers, for example by limiting membership to those working over a specific number of hours or with a particular contract of employment. *IG Metall*, for instance, traditionally refused to organize temporary agency workers on the grounds that this would give their status 'legitimacy'. A similar position was common in Italy and the UK. In Belgium, public sector unions often restricted recruitment to those with the official status of 'public servants' (*ambtenaren* or *fonctionnaires*) whilst excluding those on fixed-term contracts.

Conversely, some unions have tacitly accepted the outsourcing of risk as a means of enhancing the security of their core members (Palier and Thelen 2010), creating a conflict of interests between 'protected' and precarious groups. More generally, 'most European unions have a rather strong institutional position...[and thus] the incentive to organize new groups of workers is relatively weak' (Kloosterboer 2008: 120–1). Even when not formally excluding such workers, in the past few unions have actively recruited them because of the difficulty and expense, while failing to address their specific concerns in services, collective bargaining, and proposals for legislation. Devoting more time and resources to atypical workers was seen as reducing attention to 'traditional' members. However, unions have gradually come to understand that the increase in atypical forms of work would undermine their power resources and weaken their capacity to act, unless precarious workers become members. Recruitment and organizing of such workers have therefore become a priority for many unions and confederations (Gumbrell-McCormick 2011). Such a change in priorities can be understood as 'a process of frame extension' whereby divisions within the labour force are perceived in a new light, allowing 'a redefinition of interests that are deemed legitimate and worthy of representation' (Heery and Conley 2007: 6).

While precarious workers are often in low-skilled occupations, there are also specific problems in organizing highly skilled self-employed workers, especially where these are separated from other workers for the same company or supply chain, such as technicians in research and development. These workers may have no experience of or affinity to trade unionism, so unions have to present themselves in a more 'modern' and instrumental way, showing how they can be of practical help but also instil a spirit of solidarity. Many such workers may believe that unions are not necessary for them to achieve their career objectives; however, that attitude appears to be changing in the increasingly insecure economic climate. Many initiatives to organize these workers involve the use of information technology and its possibilities for networking and web-based services, sometimes creating a distinctive style of 'freelance unionism' (Heery et al. 2004), a theme we consider further in the next chapter.

Varieties of Approaches to Organizing

In both Nordic countries, any turn to organizing has been relatively recent and limited. Traditionally, exceptional membership density was reinforced through the Ghent system—so that, in contrast to virtually every other country, membership tended to increase in times of rising unemployment. Moreover, the very fact that family members, friends, and fellow workers were usually trade unionists meant that joining a union was 'normal': high membership was sustained by social custom (Visser 2002). Hence unions had reasons for complacency. But in the past decade, as we saw in the previous chapter, changes in the unemployment benefit regime in both countries have been followed by a rapid loss of membership. In Sweden, the recent decline has hit the LO unions especially hard, as a result of the vicious circle whereby workers with the greatest risk of job loss, and in most cases the lowest wages, have now been obliged to pay the highest rates for unemployment insurance and so have often ceased their membership in the funds and the unions (Kjellberg 2009: 491, 495). For example, *Hotell- och restaurangfacket* (the Hotel and Restaurant Workers' Union) lost one-third of its members in 2007–8 alone (Kjellberg 2009: 497). Accordingly, unions in both countries have become increasingly aware of the need to take action against the decline in membership, realizing, as a Danish official told us, that 'over the past years we have forgotten how to organize'.

As noted above, women now have a higher union density than men in both Denmark and Sweden, largely because of their concentration in the well-organized public sector but also as a result of many early initiatives aimed at recruiting and representing them. An LO study (Larsson 2009) reported a membership density of 74 per cent for Swedish women in its recruitment area, compared to 69 per cent for men. However, young women had a lower density rate than young men. Blue-collar unions have a relatively high membership among foreign-born workers employed in lower-paid manual jobs in the private sector; but with the decline of such jobs, density for these workers has gone down disproportionately (Kjellberg 2011a: 84–5). More generally, young workers are particularly likely to be in precarious employment and thus are severely affected by the changes in unemployment insurance, and union membership has fallen sharply, as Table 3.1 indicates (Kjellberg 2009:

494–7). Even in more stable employment contexts, 3F in Denmark discovered that only half of all apprentices in its recruitment areas were unionized. However, one of our TCO interviewees showed survey evidence indicating that young workers continue to express strong support for trade unions in principle, even if they are less likely to be members.

For these reasons, organizing efforts in both countries have tended to focus on young workers, and to some extent on foreign-born or ethnic minority workers. For example, *Dansk Metal* organizes in schools, while the clerical and commercial union HK offers free membership to students in vocational training schools, and 3F has introduced a much publicized scheme for trainees at one krone (about €0.1) a day. As in many countries, the Danish teachers' union offers trainee teachers free membership, and as a result claims almost 100 per cent density. Several Swedish unions have carried out similar initiatives, including SACO, which recruits in higher education establishments and among students with summer jobs. Targeted recruitment has led in some cases to specific structures, for example a 'club' of young workers in *Unionen*. TCO's initiative for internal trade union change (*Facketförändras.nu*) is largely aimed at young workers and has led to specific policies for representing their interests, for example on fixed-term work.

Despite these efforts, however, unions in both countries face the structural problem that more and more young people are in precarious forms of employment, and for this reason are more difficult to organize once they are in the workplace. A study by LO Sweden found density among manual workers aged 16–24 at 40 per cent, roughly half the rate of those in older age groups (Larsson 2009). It also appears that unions representing blue-collar workers and those in small workplaces face special difficulties in recruiting young workers. There are conflicting views on the extent to which young people fail to join because trade unions do not appeal to them or are perceived as being for older people; but there is evidence that 'younger people do not, as did earlier generations, take union membership for granted [and] are more likely to question the ways the unions work' (Hansen 2004: 134). In particular, they are unlikely to become active if this requires election to a formal position in the union. Ethnic minority workers are even more difficult to recruit than young workers (there is naturally some overlap between the two groups), but as with young workers one of the main reasons is that foreign-born workers tend to change jobs frequently. Unions in both countries have made significant attempts to recruit foreign-born and minority ethnic workers, for example by providing information and recruitment materials in foreign languages.

Unions in the 'central' group of countries, as we have seen in the previous chapters, possess strong institutional supports; however, density has fallen dramatically in Austria and Germany, and all four countries face problems with an ageing membership and under-representation of women, atypical, and ethnic minority workers.

Though German unions are often regarded as particularly strong, membership density has fallen from a post-unification peak of 36 per cent in 1991 to just under 19 per cent today. As Table 1.2 shows, this ranks above only France among the ten countries we examine. Unions are particularly weak in the expanding private services sector, where a vicious circle exists: most workers do not think unions can be effective, so do not unionize (Dribbusch 2003). Density in Austria has fallen by just over half during the past three decades, albeit from a significantly higher starting point. Even though there has been a shift away from manufacturing to private and public sector services in both countries, women remain seriously under-represented among union members. In Germany they are only half as likely as men to be unionized—the largest gender gap in any of the countries—while in Austria they are only two-thirds as likely to be members. Union density is also significantly lower among young workers and migrant workers in both countries. For example, the age profile of *IG Metall* has changed dramatically from three decades ago, when workers between 16 and 20 were the largest cohort; 'after the mid 1980s, the wave of young entrants petered out' (Hassel 2007: 185). While there has been some decline in the number of new jobs in the metal industry, most of this fall has to do with the failure to recruit young workers—half of whom, in Germany as a whole, are today employed on temporary contracts.

Unions in both countries have attempted to address these disparities, with varying degrees of success (Pernicka and Aust 2007). In Germany, *ver.di* pioneered an 'organizing model', studying American practice but adapting this to the German context. Particular targets have included the retail sector (Annesley 2006), call centres (Holtgrewe and Doellgast 2012), church workers, and other services with low union membership. These campaigns have not necessarily led to significant success in recruitment, unlike 'infill' recruitment in more traditional sectors such as airlines and postal services. Overall, membership has fallen from 2.8 million in 2001, the year *ver.di* was created, to under 2.1 million today, provoking a search for more radical initiatives. *IG Metall* has also drawn explicitly on US experience in adopting a 'membership-oriented offensive strategy' for organizing (Wetzel et al. 2008), appointing specialist organizers to target sectors with a growth potential such as wind power and motor repair. Hence 'the question is no longer if, but how the German unions are learning from the Anglo-Saxon examples' (Dörre et al. 2009: 52). In Austria, the GPA has become probably the most active union in terms of recruitment and organizing, like *ver.di* with a particular focus on the retail sector and call centres. The union staged a series of successful actions aimed at organizing these workers (Stern 2010: 43) and at publicizing employers' exploitation of *freie Dienstnehmer* (self-employed) contracts for workers in call centres. These actions may have contributed to gains in membership and have led to improvements in the status of many of these workers through collective bargaining and legal representation. The GPA has also formed an *Interessengemeinschaft* (interest group) for freelance workers, called *work@flex*; by 2009 this had recruited 9,000 members. Few other Austrian unions have devoted substantial resources to precarious workers, because the potential gains are considered too low to justify the costs.

German and Austrian unions have attempted to present a woman-friendly image, in many cases making changes to internal representation structures, which we discuss below. Young workers have also become an explicit target, for example in *IG Metall* which has launched campaigns addressing young people with precarious contracts. At the union's 2011 congress its president, Berthold Huber, made youth policies the first item in his address, declaring that '*IG Metall* with over 200,000 young members is the biggest youth organization in Germany'. Temporary agency work, which has grown very rapidly in German metalworking, has been a major theme since 2008, with a campaign for equal pay and for transition to permanent employment. Another campaign, launched in 2009, was *Operation Übernahme*, in response to the declining opportunities for apprentices to secure permanent jobs at the end of their training. The demand for them to be 'taken on' into permanent employment was a key issue in the 2012 bargaining round, and achieved at least partial success. As a result, young workers' membership seems to have stabilized or even increased (Dobbert 2010). In Austria there appears to be less difficulty in recruiting young male workers, who are well integrated into the vocational and apprenticeship systems, but there is now more focus on recruiting young people, particularly women, who go through higher education and tend to have a much lower membership density.

German unions have also made efforts to recruit workers with migrant or ethnic minority backgrounds, and have been active in anti-racist campaigns. *IG Metall* launched a four-monthly magazine, *IGMigration*, in 2007, while *ver.di* has set up a Migration Unit to encourage the integration of migrants in the union, and has opened advice centres in Hamburg and Berlin aimed specifically at migrants, including undocumented workers. The construction union IG BAU, organizing in a sector with particularly high levels of labour migration, even attempted to establish a European Migrant Workers' Union—though with little success (Greer et al. 2013). There has been much less focus on migrant workers in Austria, perhaps reflecting the sensitivity of challenging head-on the right-wing populism which many union members support. Until 2006, foreign workers were not able to stand for election to works councils or the *Arbeiterkammer*; and only in 2010 did the ÖGB make 'Migration and Integration' a key theme, since taken up by a number of affiliates. For example, the GPA has now adopted a clearly progressive policy commitment (GPA-djp 2012). Recently there have also been efforts to cooperate with Hungarian unions in organizing cross-border migrant workers (Hammer 2010).

Union density in the Netherlands has fallen somewhat less drastically than in Germany and Austria, but from a lower base three decades ago, to fractionally above the German level today. Belgium, by contrast, stands out for its membership stability, a resilience at least partly linked to its 'de facto' Ghent system where unions continue to dominate the administration of unemployment funds even though these are now state-run and compulsory. Belgian unions also have a higher level of youth membership than in most other countries (Arcq and Aussems 2002), partly because of their role in administering the unemployment funds at a time of high youth unemployment (Vandaele 2006), and partly as a result of the strong presence of unions at the workplace. The unemployment funds do not extend to public sector workers, who in any case tend to have a higher level of employment security, which may explain the continuing higher density of manual private sector workers.

In both these countries, female density is lower than for men. In the 1980s, the Dutch level was among the lowest in any of our countries, but membership increased dramatically in the 1990s; 'women rescued Dutch unions' (Visser 2007: 110). There is a notably lower density for fixed-term workers in the Netherlands, whereas in Belgium the gap is small. However, the growth of precarious work may create problems for membership and recruitment over a longer period (Faniel 2012: 21). In both countries, there is a significant gap between unionization of native-born and foreign-born workers.

Recruitment has become an important priority for Dutch unions, while (understandably) much less so in Belgium. Much of the focus has been on recruitment of young and precarious workers, many of whom are foreign-born. Organizing efforts among young workers have led to the creation of *FNV Jong*, initially an internal grouping but now a separate union, as well as to the creation of *CNV Jongeren* (van der Meer et al. 2009). The multi-industrial *FNV Bondgenoten* has devoted substantial resources to organizing low-paid service workers. One high-profile campaign, discussed further below, was for improved pay and conditions for the largely foreign-born contract cleaners on the Dutch railways and at Schiphol airport. Other organizing campaigns have focused on agricultural and food-processing workers, many of them seasonal CEE migrants and often undocumented. The US-inspired 'organizing model' was one explicit point of reference. These campaigns may not have led to sustained higher membership among the largely low-paid and precarious workforce: some fear, with good reason, that they may be dismissed, or if undocumented may face deportation, as a result of union activity; others change employment because of the seasonality of the work or return to their native country. But campaign efforts have won improved conditions in the industries involved and have had a positive effect on the image of the Dutch unions as a whole. One of the leading organizers for *Bondgenoten* told us that such organizing was not cost effective, but said it was necessary to stand up for the poorest and most exploited workers as a matter of principle. It remains unclear, however, how many unions are willing to expend resources over several years for workers who do not then remain members.

As in Austria, FNV has created a structure for self-employed workers (*FNV Zelfstandigen*), offering tailored 'packages' of services from which members can choose. In 2010 it had 13,000 members, with another 19,000 in sections for self-employed workers in other FNV unions; but the potential is estimated at 650,000.

As we have seen in the first two chapters, the 'southern' countries display some similarities in institutional context and trade union traditions, but there are also important differences. It has often been argued that most French unions see little need for dues-paying members: they require a limited cadre of activists and a larger body of workers who are not necessarily members but vote for their candidates in workplace elections and follow calls for strike action; financial resources derive in large measure from indirect state subsidies rather than membership subscriptions. Certainly union density, always low, has fallen further in recent decades. The main exception to the general pattern is the CFDT, which as part of the process of *recentrage* in the 1980s placed considerable emphasis on building up a base of paying members, and has proved more stable than most of its rivals (Andolfatto and Labbé 2006; Bévort 1994). Union density in France is the same (low) level for male and female workers, but there is a big disparity between permanent and temporary workers, and unionization of younger workers (who often have fixed-term contracts) is particularly low. While Italian unions are also ideologically divided and traditionally politicized, membership is far higher than in France; and though unions have lost members, the decline has been less severe than in many other countries (even disregarding the high membership among pensioners). Membership in northern Italy is higher than in the south. Women have only two-thirds the unionization rate of men, and fixed-term workers only half the density of permanent workers. Young workers, most of whom are unemployed or in precarious forms of work, have a low unionization rate, though the disparity is less than in France.

Young and precarious workers are therefore a major focus for recruitment and organizing in both countries. In France, the CGT has a dedicated youth organization, formed in 1968 and known since 2003 as *CGT Jeunes*. The CFDT has devoted resources to recruiting trainees and students, and also young workers in call centres and temporary work agencies, but has no specific young workers' organization. Both confederations developed close links with students' unions and other independent youth organizations in the course of nationwide protests in 2006 against the *contrat première embauche*, which we discuss further in Chapter 6. Both have dedicated resources to campaigns among agency workers and those with fixed-term and other precarious forms of employment, many of whom are not only young but also foreign-born or of minority ethnic origin. The CGT established a union for agency workers (*Union syndicale de l'intérim*) as early as the 1970s, and has undertaken a number of high-profile campaigns, for example in fast-food outlets (Bouffartigue 2008; Mabrouki 2004) and in shopping centres. It has also devoted considerable energy to work with undocumented migrants, achieving some gains in regularizing their status and some improvements in employment rights at the often small enterprises where they work. Such efforts usually depend on the commitment of local or regional structures—which are long-established in the CGT, but not the standard practice in the CFDT or FO—rather than the industrial federations. It is the latter rather than the local structures that have the main resources; and the sectoral federations 'applaud these initiatives but do little to support them' (Béroud 2009: 85). Normally these campaigns have propaganda value but result in no sustained gain in membership.

In Italy, all three major confederations have created separate unions for temporary workers: CGIL-NIdiL, founded in 1998, which appears to be the most active, CISL-FeLSA and UIL-Temp@ (Burroni and Carrieri 2011; Leonardi 2001). Together the three unions claim a membership of some 120,000—a small proportion of the total precarious workforce, but more impressive than parallel efforts in other countries. As well as a national agreement signed in 2007, the unions have negotiated a range of sectoral and company agreements regulating the use of temporary workers and their conditions of employment (Burroni and Carrieri 2011). In some ways, organizing atypical workers into entirely separate unions is structurally easier than accommodating them within existing union bodies. However, this may also be seen as marginalizing them, rather than mainstreaming their organization within the core sectoral union structures. It also raises acutely the problem of cross-subsidizing the recruitment and representation of precarious workers, which almost inevitably involve more resource costs per member than for 'typical' workers. The relative transparency of such cross-subsidies makes it more likely that sectoral unions will resist the shift in resource allocation required. A leading CGIL official told us that the sectoral unions, since they oppose the existence of precarious forms of work, would not organize such workers; it was a major organizational challenge to convince these unions to integrate the interests of precarious workers in their own activities. However, the view seemed widespread that a separate structure had not really worked: unionization rates remained very low among precarious workers. Another response to the problem of recruiting and retaining workers who often change jobs and sometimes occupations is to strengthen the territorial basis of organization. For example, CGIL in Milan has turned its *Camera del Lavoro* into a 'one-stop' trade union office for precarious young workers, so that they do not need to keep changing their industrial affiliation every time they change jobs and occupations. As in other countries with both a territorial and a sectoral confederal structure, the relative distribution of resources can be highly contentious; but the CGIL conference on organization in 2008 agreed to increase the funding for local structures.

Unions in Britain and Ireland have been particularly receptive to US conceptions of the 'organizing model', not only for obvious linguistic reasons but also because they lack most of the institutional supports common in continental Europe and have to recruit and negotiate company by company. The decline in membership density, severe in both countries, and the rise of new forms of atypical work which 'hollow out' the individual employing organization, thus pose distinctive problems to which American recipes can seem an attractive solution. Women have a slightly higher membership density than men in the UK, and slightly lower in Ireland, and fixed-term employees are very weakly unionized in the UK (although because 'permanent' workers have very limited job security, the numbers on temporary contracts are low). In both countries, workers aged under 25 are far less unionized than older groups. Both countries opened their labour markets to workers from CEE in 2004, and both experienced a substantial wave of immigration, primarily from Poland (Clark and Hardy 2011; Hughes 2011). Migrants are often agency workers with far inferior conditions to those of native-born workers, posing a threat to established standards; and in both countries, unionization rates are far lower. Hence unions in both countries have moved towards an 'organizing culture', particularly aimed at young, migrant, and precarious workers.

British trade unions stand out for their explicit embrace of the organizing concept. Following lengthy debates on responses to protracted membership decline, in 1998 the TUC opened its Organising Academy (OA), consciously imitating the US Organizing Institute although structured very differently. As a TUC official put it, 'for the first time the TUC had taken a proactive role in terms of union organizing and recruitment'. The OA takes on twenty to thirty trainees a year for a twelve-month programme, each sponsored by an affiliated union with the expectation that they will join its full-time staff. Just over half are women but efforts to attract ethnic minorities have not been very successful (Holgate and Simms 2008). The initiative both reflected and reinforced a 'turn to organizing' in most large unions—but there were very different understandings of what this meant in practice. Simms and Holgate (2010b: 158) have argued that 'the insistence of the TUC on allowing scope for different unions to develop different purposes for organizing means that the term is now so flexible that it can mean almost anything to anyone'. For the TGWU (now Unite) it meant establishing and resourcing an organizing department which now employs roughly a hundred staff (Graham 2007). The other main general union, the GMB, rejected this approach in favour of 'mainstreaming' organizing as part of the profile of all officials (Simms and Holgate 2010b). Other unions, such as Unison in public services and USDAW among shopworkers, have placed primary emphasis on training lay activists and devolving responsibility for organizing to workplace and branch representatives (Nowak 2010). The main problem with this approach is that such representatives, typically overworked, often give priority to servicing existing members (Waddington and Kerr 2009). Conversely, in unions which develop a specialist organizing function, most trained organizers become stuck in junior positions— sometimes on fixed-term contracts—without a specialist career structure (Holgate and Simms 2008; Simms and Holgate 2010a; Simms et al. 2013).

Union efforts face the familiar dilemma that groups of workers with the greatest need for collective representation and solidarity are often hardest to organize. In part this reflects the vicious circle, in countries where unions must win representative status workplace by workplace, that potential members will only join a union if it shows its effectiveness by gaining recognition and negotiating improvements; hence membership remains low and the employer can refuse bargaining rights (Gall 2005: 60). The most cost-effective measure is thus 'infill' recruitment, directed at non-members where unions are already recognized; hence part of the TGWU/Unite strategy has been a '100 per cent Campaign'. As one official explained sadly, '[if] I had half a million pounds to spend on organizing, would I be best trying to organize a hotel down the road that had no recognition agreement, high staff turnover, a lot of migrant and vulnerable workers, or do I go and organize where I've got a recognition agreement, I've got access, and it's more likely when I get members that they're still going to be in employment in two years' time?' Unite has also targeted sectors where it seemed possible to develop strategic power resources: meat processing, budget airlines, logistics.

Nevertheless, unions have also devoted considerable resources to much more 'difficult' workers. For example, in 2005 the TGWU launched its 'Justice for Cleaners' campaign in London's financial district, closely modelled on the 'Justice for Janitors' initiative in the USA, and directed at a largely female and minority ethnic workforce. This 'was a really important campaign symbolically, but you would never be able to justify it on a cost–benefit analysis because it would never pay for itself'. In this respect there are obvious parallels with the Dutch union campaign for cleaners. The TGWU/Unite has also worked with undocumented migrants in the food-processing sector, helping to achieve the 2006 Gangmasters Licensing Act which limited some of the worst abuses of such workers.

More efforts have been made to recruit and represent migrant workers in Britain than in any of our other countries. Here it is important to differentiate between minority ethnic workers, most of whom are UK-born or settled residents and have long had representative mechanisms in most unions, and migrant workers, some of whom are from ethnic minorities (and often undocumented) but many of whom are from other EU countries, particularly Poland, often sent by foreign agencies. For the latter, since 2006 the TUC has changed its policy 'from having a separate migrant worker strategy to including migrant workers under the umbrella of vulnerable workers' (Fitzgerald and Hardy 2010: 137). In 2007 it established a Commission on Vulnerable Employment which produced a detailed report, including recommendations for union organizing (TUC 2008). Some unions have used language training as a recruitment mechanism (Heyes 2009; Martínez Lucio and Perrett 2009a); several, such as Unite in food processing and UCATT in construction, have appointed officials fluent in the languages of migrant workers, although this can be very resource-intensive (Hardy et al. 2012).

Heery (2009) and other writers have identified a need to 'move away from the enterprise' in activity involving or on behalf of precarious and atypical workers. British unions have created networks for organizing in small firms, sometimes with the support of an official covering a large geographical area, although these efforts are not always specifically aimed at 'atypical' workers. Yet commonly, 'organising initiatives have become about training organizers, union officers and activists to deploy a depoliticised toolbox of practices to build collective support for workplace unionism...Unions have generally given little attention to the interests and solidarities that could unite workers beyond their workplaces' (Simms 2012: 106). Hence the turn to organizing has been framed by pre-existing conceptions of what trade unions are and what they are for. At the heart of these conceptions—in the majority of unions—are the individual workplace and the boundaries of interests that are socially constructed within it. Within this fragmented model, it is easy for minority interests to be marginalized or excluded altogether.

In their overview of the turn to organizing among British unions, Heery and Simms (2011: 42–3) conclude that 'the findings are mixed'. Unions have deployed 'new techniques...particularly those that seek to mobilize member support through an integrated and planned campaign'. In addition, 'most campaigns have built workplace organization—they are organizing not just recruitment campaigns—and there has been the development of a diversity agenda around organizing'. On the other hand, 'there is conservatism in the selection of campaign targets' and 'the level of resource invested has often been modest and resulting outcomes in many campaigns have been poor'. Hence 'the "organizing turn" in UK unions since the mid 1990s has at best stabilized union membership rather than generated renewal'.

'Ireland has been an outlier amongst the Anglo-Saxon economies in that organizing has only recently begun to emerge as a priority' (Donaghey and Teague 2007: 25). While union density has been declining since 1980, the pace accelerated in the 1990s, from 57 per cent in 1990 to 40 per cent in 2000 (even though, in a booming labour market, the actual number of union members increased). Unions faced a growing problem of anti-union employers, often US multinationals, and the government refused to introduce effective recognition legislation. The opening of the Irish labour market after EU enlargement brought a substantial influx of CEE migrants, and was followed in 2005 by two high-profile disputes over the exploitation of migrant workers, involving the large construction company GAMA, which paid its Turkish workers €2–3 an hour, and Irish Ferries, which attempted to replace its seafarers by low-paid agency workers from CEE.

While many unions have embraced an organizing model in recent years, two—SIPTU and Mandate—have done so most comprehensively. Both have been influenced by the American policy of 'like recruits like', employing women, young workers, and CEE migrants as organizers (Murphy 2011).

SIPTU, by far the largest Irish union, set up an Organising Unit in 2004 and began to hire dedicated staff for recruitment, an innovation in Ireland. It has since carried out many organizing campaigns, often aimed at mainly immigrant workers in low-paid service sector, construction, and food-processing jobs. Some of these closely resemble campaigns in the Netherlands and the UK. As with these cases, they have led to some general improvements in the conditions and legal protection for migrant workers, but not always to a sustained increased in membership. Other campaigns, however, do seem to have been more successful in this respect (Murphy 2011). SIPTU brought in Mike Crosby, well known in Australia and the USA as an exponent of the organizing model (Crosby 2005), to head a review of the union. His wide-ranging report in 2008 recommended a reduction in the proportion of resources devoted to handling individual worker grievances, and the commitment of at least a quarter of contribution income to organizing—the proportion was then well under 10 per cent. These changes were implemented in the following two years.

Mandate, the third largest union, which covers the retail sector and bar staff, has also devoted considerable resources to recruitment and organizing. Like SIPTU, it hired dedicated staff and commissioned a large-scale internal strategic review in 2006. Its general secretary told us that officials had become 'full-time service providers' and 'our solution was to empower all members to deal with a lot of their own issues, free up resources to start organizing and recruiting'. He insisted that the policy was to 'appoint organizers, not just recruiters'. In 2010 the union set up its own organizing and training centre, adopting the slogan 'organise, campaign, train, recruit': 'we want members to be active and to take an interest in Mandate rather than just seeing us as a glorified insurance scheme'. It is interesting that, like its British counterpart in the retail sector, USDAW, Mandate sees workplace activists as the key resource for organizing: thus its primary strategy is 'talent-spotting' of potential activists, providing training which will help them become effective organizers.

Though these initiatives have been undertaken by individual unions, the ICTU has also played a role, launching an 'outreach' recruitment drive in 2007 funded by SIPTU, Mandate, and three other large unions, and targeted particularly at younger workers in the 'new economy' and involving online and telephone access. As part of this initiative, the ICTU has created a UnionConnect website through which interested workers can be directed to the union covering their area of employment. The turn to organizing in Ireland does appear to have yielded positive results, with union density increasing in the mid 2000s; but these gains, not surprisingly, have been lost with the economic crisis.

Comparing the diverse range of national experience, we can see a number of successes in trade union responses to membership decline; and a number of similarities but also contrasts emerge. One example is the contrast between the greater success of the GPA in Austria in recruiting new, mainly young and female members in the private sector, compared to that of *ver.di* in similar industries and among similar groups of workers (Pernicka and Aust 2007). This does not mean that *ver.di* has been any less committed or imaginative: quite the contrary; but it has worked against the grain because the institutional context—with relatively low collective bargaining coverage and the virtual impossibility of extending sectoral agreements—is very unfavourable. Another, more striking, contrast is the unionization of women in Germany and the Netherlands. In the former, the gender gap has remained unchanged over the past two decades; over the same period, Dutch unions have almost halved the gender gap (women's density rose from 11 per cent in 1987 to 17 per cent in 2008; men's fell in the same period from 36 per cent to 25 per cent). Two decades ago, German women were twice as likely to be unionized as their Dutch counterparts; now their density is lower. This contrast may also in part reflect the declining coverage of collective bargaining in Germany as against high and stable coverage in the Dutch labour market.

The meaning, purpose, and function of trade unions differ between our countries, along with the meaning of membership and therefore of recruitment. The degree of integration of unions into industrial relations institutions, party systems, and state administration varies considerably, in line with different varieties of capitalism. Thus recruitment is traditionally less important, or not seen as important, in highly institutionalized industrial relations systems. This is obviously the case in countries with Ghent-type systems—Belgium, Denmark, and Sweden—but the 'curse of institutional security' (Hassel 2007) in Germany and Austria has similar effects. In the Netherlands, too, the turn to an 'organizing model' has been uneven and has occurred relatively late. The same is true in France and Italy, where institutional security of a distinctive kind has long reinforced union status.

There has been much discussion of the appropriateness (or otherwise) of many of the American organizing techniques in European contexts. These campaigns tend to be concentrated in low-wage sectors; union movements which are confident (or complacent) regarding their strength in traditional manufacturing industries or the public sector are unlikely to see the need to devote resources to such efforts. As our national accounts indicate, it is far from clear whether organizing campaigns among precarious workers in poorly unionized sectors yield enduring results in terms of membership. But they certainly help bolster the image of unions as defenders of the weak and vulnerable. Without such efforts, there is no possibility of advance: the trend towards a two-tier workforce will be irresistible. Whether the effort is systematically made is in large measure the outcome of trade union strategic choices. As a corollary, 'a successful implementation of the "organising model" might be thwarted by an inadequate or excessively limited shift in resources, a hesitant or less-supportive union leadership or union bureaucracy, insufficient involvement (or participation) of union representatives or union members, a lack of clarity in terms of the unions' self-identity [and] broader union politics and purposes'; while policies and strategies are 'obviously also influenced by vested interests, internal discussion and conflict' (Vandaele and Leschke 2010: 21).

Representation: Institutional Arrangements and the Bargaining Agenda

The full adoption of a comprehensive organizing model requires not only the successful recruitment of new members but also changes in internal union structures and an openness to new interests and new demands. In this section we focus primarily on attempts to make unions more attractive to under-represented groups—women, ethnic minorities, and younger workers, and in some countries pensioners, LGBT workers, those with disabilities, and the unemployed—by creating dedicated structures to pursue their interests. Our main focus is on the representation of women, since this has been the primary area of structural adaptation. We look more briefly at changes in the bargaining agenda, paying specific attention to efforts to close the gender wage gap.

The representation (or under-representation) of women's interests has long been a contentious issue for unions in most of the countries, and almost universally there now exist special structural arrangements. In nearly every confederation there is a women's committee, usually prescribed in the constitution and with input to the collective bargaining process. The exceptions are the Dutch unions and the Danish and Swedish white-collar and professional confederations. The official explanation, which has some plausibility, is that these unions already had effective equal opportunities policies in place before separate committees became the norm elsewhere. A particularly contentious question has been the introduction of women's quotas or reserved seats in decision-making bodies. Less prescriptively, there have also been moves to provide special training to encourage women's participation in representative positions. A more recent policy issue has been gender mainstreaming, which means monitoring and where necessary changing all union activity to ensure gender equality; this has been recommended by the European Trade Union Confederation (ETUC) since 1999. According to a survey undertaken by Sechi (2007: 22–5), 'almost all confederations reported that they do implement gender mainstreaming. However, some trade union policies are more targeted than others. Only one third of them incorporate systematically gender mainstreaming in all their policy, as this principle requires... Only three action plans appear to include all of these elements, targets, timetable, monitoring procedures and evaluation mechanisms.' We give some examples of these various initiatives below.

The manual worker confederations in the Nordic countries were among the first to create specific representative structures for women members and to target training and other initiatives at them. In Sweden, the *Kvinnor i facket* programme launched by women LO activists in 1986 aimed to increase the number of women in leadership positions (Mahon 1996). *Kommunal* had the first woman president in Sweden in 1988 and others followed, leading to the election of Wanja Lundby-Wedin as first woman LO president in 2000 (she has since been succeeded by a man). Some TCO unions have also introduced mentoring programmes for women, and the current president is female. The effective representation of women's interests can also be seen in the early adoption of family-friendly policies and the advocacy of a supplement to the wages of low-paid women to compensate for the gender pay gap (Tsarouhas 2011). TCO argues that there is no need for special policies to promote women within its ranks (Sechi 2007: 24).

In Denmark, Hansen (2004: 132–3) noted that while almost half of LO members were women, they formed only a fifth of the members of its executive. In part this reflects the fact that (as in Sweden) the LO executive consists primarily of the presidents of affiliates, the majority of which are small, male-dominated unions; women comprise half the members of the full-time secretariat. Hansen reports strong resistance to reserved seats for women or self-organized groups, but in 2000 LO agreed to adopt gender mainstreaming and to introduce the *Starlet* programme providing women-specific leadership training. In 3F, formed by amalgamation of the large general union SiD with the women-only KAD in 2004, there is a formal commitment to gender equality and an equal opportunities secretariat.

All German unions have women's committees, some long-established, and in many cases there are strict rules for proportionality in executive bodies (Blaschke 2011). Some committees have extended their power base, manage their own budgets, and have authority to make policy statements on behalf of their unions (Koch-Baumgarten 2002: 145). Perhaps the most comprehensive policy commitment to gender equality is in *ver.di* (with a 50 per cent female membership): it has strong women's committees, women-only training courses, and provisions for parity of representation in committees and conferences. Indeed the majority of the executive (*Bundesvorstand*) elected at the 2011 congress are women. However, as in almost all countries with effective proportionality on elected committees, this is not matched in full-time officer positions and the top leadership (Kirsch 2010)—though the position is better than in most other unions. The union also has special working groups for migrant, disabled, and LGBT members.

In Austria, the ÖGB federal executive adopted a gender mainstreaming plan in 2001 and set quotas for women in all representative bodies in 2006. Among its affiliates, only the GPA has adopted a strict proportionality rule for women in leadership positions; this has proved effective in representative bodies, and women are not far short of proportionality in full-time officer positions (Blaschke 2011). In other ÖGB affiliates there has been far less progress.

As noted above, Dutch unions do not have separate women's committees, treating gender equality as part of a broader equal opportunities agenda. FNV does possess a specific women's network, *FNV Vrouw*, with a mandate to pursue equality issues and address policy questions related to women's socio-economic position. There is a view that the key battles have been won; as Agnes Jongerius, FNV president until 2012, told us: 'we don't have this problem with women any more in the Netherlands'. Other forms of inequality seemed more important, notably the involvement of minority ethnic members: 'we are quite white in the leadership...you also should have some mixture in your leadership'.

The three Belgian confederations adopted a joint charter on gender mainstreaming in 2004, to enhance women's participation in decision-making processes (Dean 2006: 36–7). This included encouragement of positive action, training and awareness-raising processes, monitoring procedures, and annual progress reports. In the case of the ACV/CSC, mainstreaming has included an action plan adopted in 2002, setting a timetable to achieve at least a third of women in key executive bodies, a target also specified for sectoral unions (Sechi 2007: 25).

In France, Ardura and Silvera (2001: 7) write of 'undeniable advances in the integration of equality in the main unions...but also persistent obstacles to genuine parity in their executive bodies'. The CFDT, with some 45 per cent female membership, has been seen as a pioneer of women's representation (Guillaume 2007); it adopted a policy of positive discrimination and reserved seats on its *Bureau national* as early as 1982. Nicole Notat, its general secretary from 1992 to 2002, has been the only woman to head a major French confederation. The CGT, with a lower female membership, adapted its structures later but more radically: in 2003 it agreed to elect equal numbers of men and women to its *Commission executive* and *Bureau confédérale*. Within the sectoral federations, representation in leadership positions should be proportional to the membership. The CGT has also created a *Commission femmes-mixité* with its own budget and responsibility for assuring that gender issues are taken into account in all decisions. However, the attempt in 2012 by the outgoing general secretary to secure his succession by a woman, Nadine Prigent, provoked intense internal conflict and failed (though not primarily because of her gender). The FO has no formal rules on proportionality but has established a network of equality officers in its different structures to encourage women in positions of leadership. All three confederations have devoted considerable energy to representation within the union for women and also increasingly for young and ethnic minority members. Much of their attention has focused on improving the traditionally very limited number of women (and young or ethnic minority) members as activists and workplace representatives.

Of the Italian unions, CGIL stands out in terms of women's representation in leadership. In 1996 it adopted a rule that all official bodies should contain at least 40 per cent women, and two years later it established a forum to coordinate the activities of women leaders and representatives of self-organized groups and to develop equal opportunities initiatives (Dean 2006: 32). Today (as in the CGT) there are equal numbers of men and women on the executive, and the general secretary elected in 2010, Susanna Camusso, is the first woman to head any Italian confederation. The general secretary of one of the sectoral federations, herself the first woman to lead her union, told us that the formal rule on women's representation had been necessary in order to change the culture, but that it had now served its purpose. Attention has now moved to young and precarious workers: the 2008 *conferenza di organizzazione* agreed a target of 20 per cent of workers aged under 35 in decision-making bodies, but without a rulebook requirement. Less radically, CISL has agreed that at least one woman should be elected to each of its secretariats. Both CGIL and CISL devote resources to representing and providing services—such as legal and language training—to immigrant workers, most of whom are also in precarious forms of work, and CISL has a separate organization for migrant workers. According to Beccalli and Meardi (2002: 133), there is a contradiction between 'the distinctive egalitarian policy of the Italian unions and the unique alliance they formed with the feminist movement' and the fact that 'the unions as organizations have remained rooted in basically male social, cultural and organizational models and they find it increasingly difficult to cope with the emerging issues of diversity (an example being the enduring diffidence towards potentially women-friendly atypical and part-time jobs)'.

British unions have a relatively long history of equal opportunities initiatives. As a result of pressure from feminist activists, the TUC in 1979 adopted a Charter for Equality for Women within Trade Unions, recommending affiliates to establish women's committees and implement measures to increase the proportion of women in decision-making bodies. It has since become commonplace for unions to establish women's committees and conferences, appoint national equality or women's officers (sometimes both), reserve seats for women on executives, and provide women-only training courses. Also from the same period, many unions have put in place separate arrangements for ethnic minority members (Kirton and Greene 2002). The TUC itself has had special provisions for almost a century: when the General Council was created in 1921, two seats were reserved for women; a women's committee and annual conference were established soon afterwards. Later, representative structures were created for young and black workers, and more recently for disabled and LGBT workers. Currently there are reserved seats on the General Council for four women, three black members of whom one must be a woman, one LGBT, one disabled, and one youth representative; larger unions must also include at least one woman among their non-reserved nominees. In addition, the TUC publishes a biennial equality audit of its affiliates. In 2012 it elected Frances O'Grady as general secretary, the first woman to hold the post. All the main education unions are also headed by women.

Perhaps the most radical structural arrangements of any British union were adopted with the creation of Unison in 1993. These provided for 'fair representation' on elected bodies, covering gender, part-time/full-time and manual/non-manual status, age, race, sexual orientation, and disability. The rules also provide for self-organized groups at national and local levels, and for a learning agenda to encourage participation in union decision-making (McBride 2001).

Irish trade unions have adopted similar policies and structures, albeit rather later than their UK counterparts. For example, the ICTU has standing committees for the strategic implementation of its equality initiatives and also for women, disability, youth, retired workers, and racial and ethnic minorities. SIPTU declares its commitment to fighting discrimination on grounds of 'age, race, religion, disability, marital status, sexual orientation or membership of the traveller community, as well as gender or sex'. The reference to the 'traveller community', also part of the ICTU's own guidelines, is an indication that more generally applied European definitions of equality have been adapted to the specific Irish context.

In developing special arrangements for women, and also for 'minority' groups with distinctive interests, there has been an evident process of mutual learning. This has been significantly stimulated by the ETUC (which has its own women's and youth committees), which has issued a range of guidelines and disseminated 'best practice'. But some elements of this agenda can be contentious. The whole idea of special treatment, though designed to correct existing inequality of opportunity, may be seen as negating the principle of equality and non-discrimination. In France, Ardura and Silvera (2001: 7) note a widespread fear that special measures may create 'a risk of marginalizing or even "ghettoizing"' women and minorities. In part this may reflect the distinctive French conception of 'republican values': all citizens are equal and thus there should be no differentiation, for example through ethnic monitoring. But as we have seen, the fear that special arrangements may be divisive exists elsewhere, as in the Nordic countries.

The existence of special structures is no guarantee of their effectiveness in shaping policy or that they will be adequately resourced. Much of the literature on women's representation tends to argue that outcomes have been disappointing, though most writers agree that nevertheless there has been significant progress in recent years: is the glass half full or half empty? Vandaele (2012), in a survey of youth committees at confederal level, found that while most had a dedicated budget and some administrative support, almost all respondents felt that their resources were inadequate. Interestingly, representatives from countries where young workers had a reserved seat on the executive committee were least satisfied—though this might reflect higher expectations. And it is also likely that in most countries it is less the confederations than their affiliated unions which primarily shape interest representation.

The Bargaining Agenda

Dean (2006: 28) writes that 'it is not enough simply to implement gender equality policies. Objectives, targets and timetables need to be set and followed up in order to evaluate progress and verify that commitments are being translated into actions. Success depends on a commitment to follow through the polices.' For many observers, the acid test of equality policies in general is their impact on the collective bargaining agenda. Below we discuss briefly the evidence in respect of gender equality; some other gender-relevant bargaining issues are discussed in Chapter 5.

Writing over a decade ago—shortly after the Amsterdam Treaty enlarged EU competence in the equal opportunities field, and before the comprehensive Framework Directive of 2000—Bercusson and Weiler (1998: 40) produced a systematic analysis of collective agreements which 'range from challenging organizational cultures and work organizations, to the integration of equal opportunities policy within human resource management strategies, to equal opportunities policies and positive action plans'. They noted that most such agreements were negotiated within the public services.

In 2005 the ETUC and the European employers' organizations agreed a 'Framework of actions on gender equality' which committed affiliates to 'addressing gender equality through social partners' actions, at the appropriate levels, in accordance with national industrial relations practice, such as social dialogue, collective bargaining, joint statements, recommendations, etc.'. Their final evaluation report (European Social Partners 2009) included national reports from all countries covered by our study. These indicated general declarations of principle, many initiatives involving analysis and awareness raising, but very little evidence of active collective bargaining, except in some countries where all low-paid workers (who are disproportionately female) received higher percentage increases in national pay settlements. The most notable advance was in Belgium, where the 2007–8 intersectoral agreement included a commitment to improve equal opportunities, with a code of conduct and proposals for affirmative action in training. Subsequently, the gender pay gap was made a target for future collective bargaining.

Other sources also indicate an ambiguous record. In Denmark, there was a major public sector strike in 2008, primarily involving low-paid women members of FOA. This was generally regarded as unsuccessful, but it was followed by the formation of a Wage Commission to analyse pay relativities. The report (Lønkommissionen 2010) provided empirical evidence of the gender pay gap in the Danish public sector but made no substantive policy recommendations, and the issue was 'almost absent' from the next national bargaining round in 2012 (Borchorst and Jørgensen 2012: 9). However, FOA has secured a framework agreement on gender equality for local government, though its effectiveness is unclear. *Ver.di* in Germany has negotiated a number of sectoral agreements containing gender equality plans. In Austria, where the gender wage gap is far higher than the European average, the white-collar GPA proposed in 2011 a separate bargaining round to address gender inequalities, gaining the support of the ÖGB and some other affiliates, but the suggestion was strongly opposed by employers (Allinger 2011). However, the agreement for the primarily female retail sector, negotiated at the end of the year, brought significant improvements in the pay structure and also enhanced provision for child care. The French *loi Génisson* of 2001 required annual workplace negotiations on gender equality issues and sectoral negotiations every three years; this was reinforced by an intersectoral agreement in 2004. However, an official study a decade after the law took effect concluded that without effective sanctions or union bargaining strength in the workplace it had been generally disregarded.

The gender pay gap provides a hard test for the rhetorical commitment, at both EU and national levels, to the principle of equality. Almost universally the gap narrowed in the 1970s, and in most countries also in the 1980s, but then generally stabilized or even widened. For employers and governments, correcting the disparity—currently 16–17 per cent of gross hourly pay across the EU—would be immensely expensive, unless male workers accepted a corresponding pay cut. This is similarly an acid test for trade unions: those representing higher-paid (disproportionately male) workers are unlikely to accept sacrifices for their own members in order to reduce gender differentials. Where bargaining teams in sectoral negotiations, and workplace union representatives, are male dominated, the priority assigned to the issue is also likely to be reduced. A British study a quarter of a century ago (Heery and Kelly 1988) found that women negotiators gave higher priority than men to issues of particular concern to women—though this was less true of equal pay than of childcare and harassment. Since Heery and Kelly wrote, the importance of the substantive issues concerning women—and the other groups of workers we have discussed—have been increasingly recognized in most national trade unions; the bargaining agenda has broadened substantially over the past two decades and, as we have seen, there have been serious if uneven efforts to make union officials more representative of those they represent.

Mobilization

Mobilization is an essential element in translating association into organization: forming individual members, or potential members, into a collectivity who act together. We have already described several instances of such collective action in previous sections; the aim here is to relate these to more general arguments.

We start with the overview of mobilization theory presented by Kelly (1998) on the basis of the extensive US literature. Collective mobilization requires a conception of common interests; some form of collective organization; and a perception of opportunities for successful outcomes. Kelly places key emphasis on three factors: a sense of injustice which transforms individual dissatisfaction into collective grievance, an explanation which attributes responsibility for the injustice (for example, to the employer or the government), and a (formal or informal) leadership which helps frame workers' discontents as the outcome of injustice and helps shape collective demands and forms of action.

Certainly many of the initiatives we have described in previous sections can be understood in these terms. What types of collective response can newly unionized workers make to advance their interests, if and when they identify their discontents as a collective injustice? And what can unions do, first to encourage a sense of common identity and interests, second to facilitate collective action? Opportunity structures may be very restricted: we have already noted some of the obstacles to united action. As we discuss in Chapter 5, the balance of power in industrial relations generally has shifted radically with high unemployment and economic internationalization, and this is an important part of the explanation for the almost universal decline in strike activity. The power resources of precarious workers, who have been a key target of organizing drives, are particularly modest: they are often separated from others doing similar work by bargaining unit, by location, by task, or by formal employer; and typically they are easily replaceable. The difficulty of including atypical workers in traditional forms of industrial action has been commonly observed: in the German case, for example, even in engineering (Greer 2008).

One answer is to mobilize 'borrowed resources'. For example, in its campaign against a repressive anti-union management at the cut-price retailer Lidl, *ver.di* used many of the tactics of the US 'corporate campaign' model, in coalition with human rights NGOs (Gajewska and Niesyto 2009; Schreieder 2007). High-profile publicity was supported by 'flashmob' actions involving sympathizers: for example, *IG Metall* activists undertook disruptive protests within Lidl stores. Where traditional strike action is not on the agenda, demonstrations, occupations, and street theatre can play an important role: for instance, in the *Operation Übernahme* mentioned above, young *IG Metall* members themselves devised the campaign themes, materials, and actions (Dobbert 2010). It is also possible to give 'marginalized' workers a voice in framing union demands and for them to participate at least symbolically in the collective bargaining process (Brinkmann et al. 2008: 143–4). As a result of such campaigns, and of a more general militant stance, both *IG Metall* and *ver.di* claim gains in membership (Dribbusch 2011). There have been similar successes in several European countries through mobilization among service sector workers (Kocsis et al. 2013). We may also note the successes of two British unions well known for their readiness to support militant action. On the railways, the National Union of Rail, Maritime and Transport

Workers (RMT)—which claims to be Britain's fastest-growing union—has used strikes to win a series of improvements in wages and conditions, including for precarious workers in contracted-out services (Darlington 2009). In the civil and public services, the Public and Commercial Services Union (PCS) has also expanded its membership and has won a reputation for militancy, in part in defence of precarious workers in such services. As one of the union's leaders told us, strike activity was itself an effective organizing method. Conversely, he saw recruitment without activism as a recipe for failure: without an 'activist culture' that empowers members to fight for their interests, new recruits would feel they have been 'conned'.

Even precarious workers have on occasion undertaken successful collective action of a traditional kind. Probably the most notable was by Dutch contract cleaners on the Dutch railways and at Schiphol airport, as we outlined previously: the longest Dutch strike since the 1930s. This won improved pay and conditions for the workers, most of them from ethnic minorities, organized by *FNV Bondgenoten*. This struggle, and the similar campaign for a living wage for cleaners in London (Simms 2010), profited from coalitions between trade unions and community and religious groups (see Chapter 6). Similar successful strikes have been undertaken by mainly young, ethnic minority workers in Paris fast-food outlets, organized by the CGT (Mabrouki 2004). What is clear from these cases, however, is that success usually depends on long and careful preparation in order to build collective identity and collective confidence, and not all unions have the resources or commitment to make such an investment.

The whole issue of recruiting 'non-traditional' groups of workers raises important questions for trade union conceptions of solidarity. Unions were traditionally organized on the basis of particular constituencies: distinct occupations, specific employers, individual sectors of the economy. In uniting one group of workers, unions might divide them from others. To some extent, the ideal of solidarity was an effort to overcome such divisions. And typically, if different constituencies were able to unite it was not so much through common interests in the present as through a shared vision of the future: 'trade unionism often involved the articulation of an alternative social order comprising a wider class solidarity' (Richards 2001: 26). It is necessary to combine Kelly's presentation of mobilization theory with Touraine's theory of class (1966): collective consciousness involves a sense of common identity which is conditioned by perceptions of antagonism to an external threat (typically, the employer); but genuine solidarity requires an integrated understanding of the broader context, linked to a perception of a different form of economy and society and a belief that through unity this can be achieved. Some of the implications will be explored in Chapter 6.

Conclusions

In this chapter we have primarily discussed union organizing efforts in terms of recruitment, particularly of 'new' constituencies and 'atypical' employees. Yet organizing is not only a question of recruitment: it also involves (or should involve) representation and mobilization. Special arrangements for the representation of particular groups (through quotas and dedicated committees, for example), in particular for women, exist in the majority of our countries. However, these measures are generally distinct from recruitment and mobilization drives, and there is no clear causal link between improved representation as such and higher recruitment. Recruitment in turn is not always linked to mobilization, which in the traditional form of strike action is often extremely difficult for many of the target groups to undertake; but without some form of collective activity, recruitment gains may well prove short-lived. Many European unions are now grappling imaginatively with the underlying issues.

4

Restructuring Trade Unionism: Mergers and Organizational Redesign

As we saw in Chapter 2, one response to hard times has been to consolidate union forces by amalgamation. This is a major theme of the present chapter. However, we first survey the different structural patterns of trade unionism in our ten countries, including the relationship between confederations and their member unions. We also examine issues concerning union democracy, and more generally discuss internal organizational changes within individual unions.

Trade Union Structure

A century ago, Socialists who viewed trade unions as potential vehicles for revolution conceived the goal of creating 'One Big Union' (Peterson 1981). Most famously, the Industrial Workers of the World (IWW), originating in the USA, aspired to organize the working class globally in a single union. The objective was never achieved. Historically, the notion of a 'trade' union indicated that organization was structured according to membership of a specific skilled occupational group. The British *Trades* Union Congress was thus a confederation of unions in individual trades. For the Webbs (Webb and Webb 1897: 105), successful unions inevitably covered relatively narrow occupational constituencies; conflict would result from any attempt to combine disparate occupational groups within a single organization 'having a common policy, a common purse, a common executive, and a common staff of officials'.

History has proved wrong both the Webbs and the revolutionaries who formed the IWW—though both expressed partially valid arguments. When the Webbs wrote, there were around two thousand separate unions in Britain; today there are 170. Evidently some of the obstacles to common organization across occupational boundaries have been overcome. Today the very notion of a 'trade' sounds archaic; and indeed, even when the Webbs were writing there were major unions in industries such as coal, cotton, steel, or railways where 'trades' in the traditional sense barely existed. In reality, the extreme multiplicity of unions in Britain a century ago can be seen as a historical anomaly, which has been gradually transcended. In most countries where unions were created later than in the UK, it seemed self-evident that 'unity is strength' and that effective trade unionism required a broad membership base.

Yet the failure of the 'One Big Union' concept is also instructive: IWW membership was largely confined to low-skilled, marginalized, often immigrant workers. The risk which the Webbs identified of conflict between diverse occupational interests is real: unions with a heterogeneous membership do indeed face challenges in coordinating this diversity and sustaining a coherent common identity, as we shall see in particular when we discuss union mergers. There is a persistent tension between the ideal of workers' unity and the more parochial everyday concerns of most workers. In countries where an ideology of class solidarity is widely embraced, it may be easier to sustain broadly based organization; but nowhere are union movements genuinely unitary, though the degree to which they approximate this varies considerably cross-nationally.

Thus all trade union movements contain internal demarcations. In some cases (notably in southern Europe and also in the Benelux countries), as we saw in Chapter 1, the primary line of division is ideological, reflecting past conflicts between Socialist, Christian, Communist, and in some countries liberal conceptions of trade unionism. The sharpness of such divisions has weakened over time, and the degree to which they are translated into conflict varies, but in the main old organizational separations persist. Elsewhere there are clear divisions by occupational category (manual, white-collar, and professional), as in the Nordic countries (though the demarcation is sharper in Sweden than in Denmark). Historical origin is evidently an important explanation of cross-national variations in structural patterns. For example, in countries which industrialized early, employers were often small and there were more likely to exist self-confident craft groups which formed exclusive occupational unions; separate unions for lower-skilled workers developed later. In Britain, Ireland, and to some extent Denmark, a division between craft and 'general' unions has left its mark on current structure.

Conversely, the early presence of an influential Socialist movement encouraged industrial unionism among manual workers. Class-conscious unionists were often suspicious of white-collar workers because of their perceived proximity to the employer; and such suspicion has often been reciprocated. Hence notably, LO in Sweden refrained from recruiting white-collar workers, who unionized separately. In Germany, DGB unions competed for members with a separate white-collar confederation, until the latter merged into the broad services union *ver.di*; but a separate organization still represents most *Beamte*. In Austria, the principle of industrial unionism underlying the creation of the ÖGB was breached to allow the existence of a multi-industry white-collar union (GPA), which is now its largest affiliate. A similar organizational separation exists in most other national movements which otherwise follow an industrial structure; and where this is not the case, unionization levels are often much lower for white-collar than for manual workers, at least in the private sector.

Employers' organization and policies have also been important influences on union structure: strong sectoral employers' associations have encouraged integrated counterparts on the union side. Legal regulation of union recognition (certification) and rules on 'representativeness' have in some countries constituted obstacles to small occupational unions and provided incentives to the rise of more encompassing organizations. Finally, we should note that powerful, centralized union confederations may be able to regulate inter-union demarcations among their affiliates.

Turner (1962), in a study of the historical evolution of British trade unionism, presented a dynamic model in which some organizations based on narrow occupational groupings with a secure labour market status remained exclusive ('closed') whereas others became increasingly inclusive ('open'), creating a tendency towards 'general unionism'. Since he wrote, the latter tendency has been reinforced by structural changes in the economy and labour market: the number of protected occupational groups with robust structural power has dwindled, and unions in declining sectors of the economy have been impelled to merge with others to form 'conglomerate' unions, as we examine below.

Unions and Confederations

In all our countries, most (though usually not all) trade unions of any significance are affiliated to peak confederations. Only in Austria, Britain, and Ireland is there just one central body. Austria is exceptional in that—following post-war reconstruction and more recent mergers—there exist only seven trade unions, all affiliated to the ÖGB. In Ireland, very few unions, all small, are outside the ICTU. In Britain, the TUC contains only a minority of registered unions but almost 90 per cent of total membership; the only substantial unions outside its ranks are specialist bodies in the health service. A number of professional organizations have indeed shown significant growth in recent years (Wilson 2007). Though post-war German trade unionism was remodelled along similar lines to its Austrian counterpart, as noted above it has always faced rivals. Among *Beamte*, the DGB has only a third of the membership of the separate DBB. Some of its affiliates face a threat from the small *Christlicher Gewerkschaftsbund* (CGB), which has signed collective agreements undercutting its own demands, while non-affiliated unions among specialist groups such as doctors, airline pilots, and train drivers have posed significant challenges in recent years (Hoffmann and Schmidt 2009). The DGB today accounts for 80 per cent of total union membership in Germany.

Elsewhere there is greater diversity. In the Nordic countries, as we have seen, there are separate confederations for manual, routine white-collar, and professional employees. In Sweden, as noted in Chapter 1, membership of the two non-manual confederations now exceeds that of LO; whereas LO in Denmark, whose affiliates have been more willing to cross the (increasingly blurred) occupational boundaries, remains far more dominant. In both countries there are some non-affiliated unions, far more significant in Denmark where—as we saw in Chapter 2—there is also a growing Christian union offering cut-price membership.

In the remaining four countries, the primary basis of division is ideological. To qualify this point, competing confederations derive from *past* ideological identities which may have lost much of their force over time. This is most obvious in the Netherlands, where the Socialist and Catholic movements merged over three decades ago and where it seems possible that the small Protestant confederation may join a restructured FNV. Should this happen, the basic line of division will be occupational, as in the Nordic countries, with MHP competing with the main confederation for senior white-collar employees. In Belgium too, old ideological conflicts have become muted. We asked an official of the Socialist ABVV/FGTB what still differentiates his union from its Christian counterpart ACV/CSC; he replied that 'we prefer to focus on the 90 per cent that unites us rather than the 10 per cent that divides us'. In Italy the clear political differences which more than half a century ago split the CGIL into today's three main confederations have also become diluted, and a joint platform is often possible, though tensions frequently arise. There is also competition from numerous smaller organizations, some associated with right-wing political currents, others protagonists of militant sectionalism, particularly in the public sector. The most complex picture, however, is in France; the five confederations traditionally regarded as 'representative' face competition from a number of more recent rivals, including the radical leftist SUD. Unified action, whether in collective bargaining with employers or in political mobilization, is rarely achieved and is usually fragile. Whether the new rules on representativeness will simplify the picture of extreme fragmentation despite very low membership is as yet uncertain.

What do confederations do? Their relationships with their affiliates can vary along a wide continuum. At one extreme, individual unions are autonomous and merely delegate to the confederation certain functions which they feel cannot be undertaken separately, or at least only at greater cost, such as political lobbying and public campaigning. The British TUC is an obvious example: it was created by unions that were already well established but saw advantages in possessing a common voice. It is they who decide what resources to assign to the confederation and what authority to allow it. In Germany, though the DGB was in its early years more powerful, a similar relationship now exists. Here, debates about the future role and structure of the confederation have shown clear tensions between larger affiliates, which would prefer to provide the bulk of services 'in-house', and smaller unions which lack the resources to do so. In both countries, as Hartmann and Lau (1980) have shown, it requires astute manœuvring by the confederal leadership to assert their authority and to demonstrate to affiliates the value of their activities (as, for example, in the efforts of the TUC to coordinate the turn by British unions to the 'organizing model'). There are parallels in Ireland, where decades of centralized social pacts enhanced the authority of the ICTU.

At the other extreme, unions may be subsidiaries of the central confederation, to which they pay their subscriptions and which then distributes resources to its individual (usually sectoral) affiliates. While unions in some of our countries once approximated to this model, in general there has been a gradual loss of central authority. Today the closest example is the ÖGB in Austria. In theory, 'member unions are not independent associations, but sub-units of the ÖGB itself, which therefore exercises control over their finances, officials and negotiating function' (Blaschke 2005: 68). In practice, they possess far greater autonomy; but the confederation still has a significant say in collective bargaining strategies, as well as deriving considerable authority from its central role in 'social partnership'. LO in both Sweden and Denmark once had stronger control over affiliates than today, when collective bargaining is more decentralized.

The countries with ideologically divided movements have traditionally had strong confederal authority. This was particularly true of Communist trade unionism, where the ideal of class unity (as well as party control) allowed little space for internal diversity; today, however, it is possible to describe the internal politics of the CGT as 'more or less organized anarchy' (Piotet 2009), while its rival CFDT has much stronger central authority. It is interesting that in Italy, while the (formerly Communist) CGIL was a 'general confederation of labour' with industrial sections, its main rival CISL defined itself as a 'confederation of unions'—implying that its affiliates were more autonomous; here too, the old distinction has lost relevance. In both France and Italy, it is normal for all confederations to determine the subscription levels and the proportion of income to be allocated to the sectoral organizations, though in some cases the latter may choose to set additional fees to supplement their own funds. An important question, which links closely to the degree of autonomy in collective bargaining, is the payment of strike benefits. For example, in the Netherlands the FNV defines overall collective bargaining targets and provides the bulk of funding for strikes by its affiliates if their demands are within the specified limits; otherwise they have to use their own resources. In the Nordic countries, similar provisions apply.

In all countries, the shift in the weight of union membership towards the public sector has been a source of tensions. As we discuss further in the next chapter, concerns with competitiveness shape union bargaining policy in export-oriented industries, whereas the economic constraints in the public sector are very different. More than two decades ago, Swenson (1989) compared the different ways in which these potentially conflicting interests were (or were not) reconciled in Germany and Sweden. Today, when governments in all countries are imposing restrictions—often severe—on public expenditure, such conflicts assume new forms. Confederations face a challenging task in sustaining a common trade union front despite divisive pressures.

As well as comprising usually sectorally based affiliates or component unions, most confederations also have geographical substructures. These may be rudimentary, as in Britain: the TUC has eight regional councils, mainly responsible for campaigning and for organizing education and training for union representatives. In Germany the DGB—which receives 12 per cent of its affiliates' subscription income—has a far more elaborate structure of local and regional offices, though pressure by some unions for a substantial reduction in the number of officials resulted in agreement on economies in 2010. Confederations with greater central authority can in principle devote more resources to territorial organization. The constitution of the CGT in France is fairly typical: members pay subscriptions to the local union for their sector; this retains a third for it own activities and transmits the remainder to the confederation nationally, which distributes resources to the sectoral and territorial organizations in accordance with principles adopted by the national congress. As we indicated in Chapter 3, redistributing resources to strengthen the local cross-sectoral structures has often been proposed as a response to the less stable employment patterns of a growing proportion of the workforce. However, this usually encounters strong resistance from the sectoral federations, which would lose resources. For example, in Belgium (where the sectoral unions are known rather confusingly as 'centrals'), tensions around such issues have absorbed 'much energy and time' to little effect—except in the smaller liberal confederation, which lacks a sectoral structure (Faniel 2012: 23).

Union Democracy

Most trade unions insist, with reason, that they are democratic organizations. However, there is great diversity in the formal decision-making structures in unions, both within and between countries. The relative powers of national officers, executive committees, and conferences, the degree to which middle-range officials are elected from below or appointed from above, and the balance of authority between confederations and their affiliated unions all vary. Cross-national differences may reflect diverse understandings of the meaning of union democracy, but they may also derive from relatively contingent decisions made a century or more ago (for example, unions subject to state repression often adopted highly centralized, almost military methods) which have persisted despite changed circumstances. Unions in some countries (such as Germany) have a high ratio of paid officials to members, others depend heavily on 'lay' activists (as in Britain and France); such differences have evident implications for the internal distribution of power.

Real intra-union politics may differ significantly from rulebook decision-making structures. As we saw previously, Michels (1915: 32) argued (primarily on the basis of German experience) that trade unions and Socialist parties, though formally democratic, were subject to an irresistible 'tendency to oligarchy'. Subsequent scholarship (and debate among trade unionists themselves) has tended to focus on differences of power and interests within unions, but with two contrasting types of emphasis. One is hierarchical, giving primary attention to the roles and influence of leaders and other paid officials, as against rank-and-file activists and members more generally. This approach has often led to rather polemical arguments concerning the distorting effects of the 'trade union bureaucracy'. A second approach, particularly associated with feminist analyses, focuses on horizontal differences (occupation, sector, gender, age, ethnicity). From this perspective, trade unions not only redistribute power and resources between workers and capitalists but also *within* the working class. Since both paid officials and lay representatives typically derive disproportionately from relatively skilled, male, native-born sections of the workforce, their distinctive interests may shape the policies of the union as a whole. In recent years, unions in many countries have attempted to implement some form of 'proportionality' in order to address this problem, as we saw in the previous chapter.

A related debate concerns centralization as against decentralization in union policy-making. Are decentralized structures more democratic, in that they provide greater scope for membership involvement in decision-making? Such an argument is consistent with participative theories of democracy. But a counterargument is that (at least beyond a certain point) decentralization precludes overall strategic direction, a particular problem when key employer strategies are increasingly centralized (Streeck 1988). For some analysts, efficiency and democracy in trade unions are incompatible (Child et al. 1973). More constructive approaches investigate how the democratic vitality of decentralization and the strategic coherence of centralization might be reconciled; for example, Kjellberg (1983) has argued that Swedish unions combine both authoritative national decision-making *and* workplace-level autonomy over key issues, with close articulation between the two levels providing a source of strength *and* democracy. This is a theme to which we return in the final chapter.

Certainly there are great variations in the practical understanding of union democracy and the structures adopted to achieve it, across and often also within countries. In most unions, organizational structures exist at workplace level, but patterns of authority between such structures and the national, regional, or local union are complex and shifting; an added complexity in most of our countries is the relationship between workplace union representation and works councils. Where union decision-making has traditionally been centred on bodies outside the workplace, declining membership participation is a widespread problem. We discuss some responses to these issues below. First, however, we discuss the phenomenon of union mergers, which in many countries have radically transformed the organizational landscape in recent years.

Restructuring: Mergers

Almost universally, the number of trade unions has been reduced over the past decades through processes of amalgamation, takeover, or 'transfer of engagements'; in our discussion we refer to all these processes as mergers. In most cases this has involved the amalgamation of small unions or the absorption of a smaller by a larger partner, thus making little impact on the overall structural pattern; but some mergers have created conglomerate or 'megaunions' (Streeck and Visser 1997), with far more profound implications.

The process has been particularly notable in the UK, where the number of unions has fallen by three-quarters in the past half-century; but the pattern displays 'no apparent underlying rationale' (Waddington 2006: 636). Two organizations now account for 40 per cent of total union membership, and almost half the membership of the TUC. Unison was formed in 1993 through the merger of three relatively large unions covering local government, health services, and a range of other public (or former public) services. Unite was created in 2007 by the merger of Amicus and the Transport and General Workers' Union (TGWU). The TGWU was a general union which had itself absorbed a multiplicity of smaller organizations over the years; Amicus was a multi-sector, mainly white-collar union which was also the product of a succession of mergers. In Ireland too there has been a merger wave, less radical than in the UK (Donaghey and Teague 2007). The most notable amalgamation was in 1990 between two large general unions to form SIPTU, which now accounts for a third of total membership in the country.

Of our 'continental' countries, the trend to conglomerate unions has been most marked in Germany and the Netherlands. The DGB, which had seventeen affiliates in the 1970s, now has only eight. The most notable change was the formation of *ver.di* in 2001 by amalgamating five unions (including the non-DGB confederation which organized white-collar workers). The outcome was a union straddling a range of public and private services, together with transport. Its membership is roughly equal to that of *IG Metall*, which has itself absorbed the textile and woodworking unions. Together they account for 70 per cent of DGB membership. In the Netherlands a wide-ranging public services union, *AbvaKabo*, has existed since the creation of FNV three decades ago. A more protracted process of consolidation has occurred within the private sector, culminating in 1997 with the merger of the two multi-sector unions in manufacturing and private services, together with several others, to form *Bondgenoten*. With *AbvaKabo* it represents 60 per cent of FNV membership. In Austria there has also been considerable concentration: from sixteen ÖGB affiliates until the late 1970s to seven today. A series of amalgamations culminated in the creation of *Pro-Ge* in 2009, covering virtually the whole of manufacturing. In private services and transport, another conglomerate (*vida*) was formed in 2006 (Stern 2010). The three largest unions now contain 60 per cent of ÖGB membership. In Belgium, the number of unions in both main confederations has roughly halved over the past four decades; the process began earlier in the ABVV/FGTB, which now has just seven *centrales*; the main mergers in the ACV/CSC have been more recent, and there are now nine *centrales* in Flanders, seven in Wallonia.

Both Nordic countries have seen numerous mergers in their manual and white-collar confederations. However, for the most part these have involved rather small unions (Due and Madsen 2005; Kjellberg 2005). It is also notable that the professional confederations, SACO and AC, have been virtually untouched by the merger process. As a SACO official stressed to us, affiliated unions are strongly rooted in specialized professional identities; this has enabled them to recruit 90 per cent or more of their constituencies, which might be jeopardized by any merger.

In Sweden, the number of LO affiliates has fallen from forty-four in 1960 to fourteen today; those in TCO from thirty-five to fifteen. The most substantial merger was in 2008, between the white-collar manufacturing union SIF and the retail and commercial HTF to form *Unionen*, which now represents 40 per cent of TCO membership. In Denmark, LO had over sixty affiliates half a century ago, two-thirds of which had fewer than 5,000 members; today there are eighteen, and almost all the smallest unions have disappeared. The most significant merger was between the large general union SiD and the women's union KAD in 2004, to form 3F (Due et al. 2007); in 2010 it merged with TIB, which organized skilled building and wood workers. 3F is the largest LO affiliate and together with the retail and clerical union HK comprises almost 60 per cent of total membership. The white-collar confederation FTF has always possessed an unusually large number of affiliates, and today still has over eighty, though the number has roughly halved since 1970.

In the 'southern' countries there has been a gradual process of consolidation, though less radical than elsewhere. In France, the most notable change has been within the CFDT, which has reduced its number of federations by half to fifteen, sometimes against internal resistance (Thomas 2013): an indication of the high degree of central control within the confederation. Its two main rivals still have roughly double the number of sectoral organizations. Mergers have been more general in Italy: all three main confederations had around thirty sectoral federations in 1970 and have reduced the numbers by approximately half, with CGIL now having the fewest, only thirteen—though CISL is planning a more radical concentration.

Why merge? There is a broad consensus that 'the merger process in recent years has been essentially defensive and was primarily driven by adverse environmental circumstances' (Waddington 2005: 375): many unions have lost strategic, associational, organizational, and in some cases institutional power resources, a reflection of structural change in the economy, unemployment, and more hostile employer and government policies. In many cases, membership decline and the associated loss of income have resulted in budget deficits and put continued viability at risk. Traditional recruitment boundaries have been eroded. For example, technological change can break down the divide between manual and white-collar occupations in manufacturing; privatization undermines the separation between public and private services; the growth of new activities such as logistics bridges previously distinct sectors. The consequence may be sharp territorial conflicts between previously distinct unions, with merger a solution. Or unions which are still numerically and financially viable may merge in order to secure a long-term recruitment base. In addition, we may identify what could be called 'defensive-offensive' mergers: a union may take the initiative to amalgamate with another which is in the 'merger market' before a rival makes a successful bid.

How far have amalgamations improved the position of the unions involved? In the business world there are examples of successful mergers and acquisitions, but also many failures. Among trade unions the same seems to be true. In some cases—and here we return to the arguments of the Webbs—there is an unquestionable logic to integrating unions which compete for overlapping groups of workers and negotiate with the same employers; but most recent union mergers have involved far more heterogeneous constituencies. Over time, any union develops its own distinctive 'culture': shared beliefs, ways of working, relationships between different levels of the organization. Integrating different union cultures is a problem not always anticipated (Terry 2001); officials and activists may cling to their pre-merger identities and modes of action. 'We cannot expect other organizations to adapt overnight to our practices, ideology and orientation, which have evolved over many decades,' an official of the French CGT said to us with reference to mergers between sectoral federations; while in the CFDT, Barthélemy et al. (2009) report that the creation of a conglomerate *Fédération Communication, Conseil, Culture* means that postal workers complain they can no longer find an official who understands their sector.

Recent surveys of European experience have reached rather sombre conclusions. In general, membership decline has continued as before. Financially, mergers have offered in principle the scope for economies of scale; but agreement to amalgamate usually requires guarantees of job security to existing staff (who would otherwise be in a strong position to campaign against the merger). Hence initially there have often been high costs in providing generous early retirement or voluntary severance schemes. Aligning very different organizational structures is often difficult; so, for example, in the case of *ver.di* the 'matrix' structure of cross-cutting sectoral, geographical, and functional divisions was a compromise between conflicting organizational logics, and has proved costly and inefficient to operate (Kahmann 2009; Kirsch 2009). More generally, within merged unions organizational conservatism has in many respects predominated over innovation. It has remained easier to focus on the traditional (often dwindling) core membership than to pursue recruitment among expanding but more difficult groups of workers. Amalgamation can represent 'a low-cost alternative to the expensive, time-consuming and high-risk strategy of organising the unorganised' (Waddington et al. 2005: 239); thus 'the merger process has the potential to contribute to union revitalization, but very few examples have been unearthed where this potential has been realised' (Waddington 2005: 387).

An additional problem is that big is not necessarily beautiful. Rightly or wrongly, members may see the new 'super-unions' as remote, or may perceive their distinctive interests as no longer adequately represented. In the UK, Unison lost some of its manual membership (who now found themselves in the same union as their managers) to the general unions; conversely, *ver. di* in Germany has lost out to small, specialist associations. In this respect, it is significant that the mainly small professional unions in Sweden and Denmark, as noted above, have shown little appetite for amalgamation, believing that a distinct occupational identity is a powerful resource.

A final issue raised by large-scale union mergers is the impact on the role of confederations. As noted above, small unions often rely on their peak organization to provide services (advice to members, education and training, information on political and legislative developments, for example) which they cannot economically offer on their own resources. Large unions, conversely, may prefer to cover such activities on their own behalf and under their own control, and accordingly to reduce their contributions to the confederation. The rise of mega-unions shifts the balance in this respect. Streeck and Visser (1997: 327–8) note that in both Germany and the Netherlands, confederal affiliation fees are defined in the rulebook and can only be changed by a two-thirds majority vote. Today, *IG Metall* and *ver.di* acting in concert exceed this threshold. In Austria, in the aftermath of the 2006 BAWAG crisis, ÖGB affiliates—which had invested in the bank and suffered financially from its collapse—reduced their contributions by almost half. Though payments were slightly increased in 2011, the confederation will need to reduce its staffing and activities considerably.

Much more generally, the continuing trend to fewer unions, and with straitened financial resources, will intensify pressures to streamline confederal organizations and functions (Dufour 2009). 'The merger process has thus made a significant contribution to the opening of debates on the future of confederations [but] there is no convergence in the strategic options that are either being debated or implemented' (Waddington 2005: 387).

Restructuring: Internal Reorganization

If unions are to reverse their loss of membership and bargaining power, and recover their broader social and political influence, they must first change themselves. 'A prior internal renewal' may be a precondition of successful revitalization strategies (Heery 2005: 92). In this section we consider some of the ways in which unions in the ten countries have attempted to restructure their internal organization. In particular we focus on systematic programmatic reforms, often involving the use of external consultants; the adoption of practices more commonly associated with business management; and the use of new means of communication with members and the public more generally. We do not attempt to provide a systematic, comprehensive overview of each of the ten countries, but select specific examples for illustration.

Strategic Reviews and Consultancies

Trade unions normally change their internal arrangements very slowly, usually by minor adaptations rather than major restructuring. Periods of national reconstruction, as in some countries in the immediate post-war years, can permit more radical transformation of trade unionism. So on occasion can amalgamations, if what emerges is a new union rather than a mere integration of its former components. What is notable, however, is the extent to which unions and their confederations in recent years have engaged in a self-conscious review of their internal organization and have developed strategic plans for reconstruction. Yet implementing such plans has often proved more difficult.

It is true that unions in some countries have well established procedures for forward planning. For the past century, the executive of LO Sweden has regularly drawn up detailed organization plans, reviewing the structure of the movement and making proposals for reform. In 2007, TCO undertook a strategic review in response to membership decline and reorganized all its activities to focus on project work. A new department was established with a steering group comprising the leaders of all affiliates. In Denmark, HK has a research and analysis department responsible for strategic planning, and initiated a major review in 2006, developing a 'strategy map' setting out the union's mission and vision. In smaller Nordic unions, strategic planning is typically the responsibility of the president's office.

German unions (there are some parallels in Austria) tend to devote significant resources to strategic planning: the DGB and its affiliates have well staffed policy and planning departments. In 2005 the DGB launched its *Initiative Trendwende* (initiative to reverse the decline), and its congress the following year agreed to pursue a series of organizational reforms. However, disagreements among affiliates have entailed that actual changes have been modest.

The largest German union, *IG Metall*, produces a rolling five-year plan which encompasses organizational questions. In 1999 it launched a debate on its strategic aims and methods, involving a large-scale survey, a series of policy papers, and discussions in the branches and regions. This process culminated in the publication of a 'manifesto for the future' (*Zukunftsmanifest*) which was discussed at a special congress in 2002. The 2007 congress agreed to establish a project group to propose organizational reforms. This group issued a series of proposals for an organizing strategy (IG Metall Vorstand 2009); these were broadly accepted at the 2011 congress, held under the slogan *Kurswechsel: Gemeinsam für ein gutes Leben* (a change of course: united for a good life), a reflection of the union's increasing emphasis on the quality of work and life as a recruitment tactic. Likewise, *ver.di* adopted a strategy document *Chance*

2011 (Opportunity 2011) at its congress in that year, and has issued proposals entitled *Perspektive 2015* for its next congress.

There are some interesting parallels with the report of the CFDT (2009), *Oser le changement* (dare to change), which analysed the weakness of French trade unionism in the context of social and economic transformation and in particular advocated a stronger orientation to the workplace. This informed a resolution adopted at the union's congress the following year, which called for stronger organizational links between the confederation and the members and activists on the ground—without proposing detailed organizational reforms. A priority is to increase support services for local representatives (financed in part from the accumulated reserves of the union's strike fund).

The British TUC, with limited resources but attempting to coordinate trade union responses to the drastic loss of membership and influence under a hostile government in the 1980s and 1990s, launched its 'New Unionism' project in 1997. The aims were to support affiliates in increasing membership, particularly in less-unionized sectors of the economy and among women, young workers, black workers, and those on 'atypical' contracts; building effective workplace organization; and recruiting and training more workplace representatives. The main result was the establishment of the Organising Academy the following year, as we discussed in the previous chapter. This was followed by the report *Meeting the Millennial Challenge* (TUC 1999), which analysed the fall in union membership and the decline in workplace trade union coverage. It identified a range of areas in which change was essential: giving greater priority to organizing, improving workplace representation, reforming union structure, and enhancing the public profile of trade unionism. A further series of initiatives followed, including the appointment of a 'Promoting Trade Unionism Task Group' which we examine below.

In Ireland, the 2009 ICTU conference agreed to establish a Commission to review trade union organization; it comprised leaders of the main unions and was chaired by the general secretary of Union Network International (UNI) Global Union. Its report called for urgent action to strengthen the movement, including structural consolidation ('there are too many unions'), the adoption of 'strategic targets for organising campaigns', the redefinition of the trade union 'mission', and a more effective communications capacity. This was approved at the 2011 conference. A number of individual unions have also undertaken strategic reviews, often involving external consultants. As we saw in the previous chapter, SIPTU commissioned the Australian Mike Crosby to head a review of the union's future. This resulted in wide-ranging changes in policies and structure, including a strengthening of the sectoral structures (as in the union's main British counterpart) and a weakening of the influence of local branches in the union's governance. The retail union Mandate commissioned a strategic review in 2005 involving three consultancy firms. The union depended heavily on closed shop arrangements, but feared that these might face legal challenges; the entry of foreign-owned retail firms threatened to bring more hostile management policies; and retail employment was becoming increasingly unstable, with a growing proportion of migrant workers. Here, the key change proposed was a more systematic priority for developing local activists, and more generally to reform internal democracy to increase member and activist involvement. It is interesting that the union's Danish counterpart, HK, facing to some extent similar problems, also initiated a strategic review in 2006; this involved the executive committee working with external consultants. The outcome was a strategic plan developed over three years. One organizational change was a reduction in the number of branches from forty to seven, which meant that local officials now had to 'get out of the office' and spend more time visiting the members, we were told.

Why involve external consultants? The formal explanation is usually that these bring expertise in 'organizational development', in some (but not all) cases specifically in the trade union context. But a political explanation is often that recommendations by 'independent experts' carry legitimacy that proposals by a union's own leaders may lack; cynics may suggest that leaders select consultants whose recommendations are likely to suit their own wishes. A more general issue is whether management consultants, more familiar with business organizations, will always understand the democratic traditions of trade unions; this touches on questions that we discuss further below.

Managerial Unionism

Writing two decades ago—just before the idea of an 'organizing model' came into widespread currency—Heery and Kelly (1994) identified the rise in the UK of a form of unionism according to which 'union bureaucracy must become more managerial in its functioning, researching and monitoring employee needs, designing and promoting union services to match and planning the organization, training and deployment of its own human resources to support service delivery'. Their thesis—that in order to survive, modern unions would necessarily focus on actual and potential members as calculating individualistic consumers—now appears strangely one-sided: even unions which offer a comprehensive package of individual services also stress their role as representatives of *collective* interests.

Yet it is certainly true that unions in many countries have shown a growing interest in management techniques developed in the context of business enterprises, and which for that very reason would once have been regarded as incompatible with the democratic ethos of trade unionism. And indeed, the appropriateness in the trade union movement of practices obviously suited to organizations with hierarchical top-down authority is not always well scrutinized. Nevertheless, it seems evident that many management ideas, applied cautiously, can contribute to union renewal and effectiveness.

In Germany, where far more staff are employed by trade unions than in any of the other countries we survey, the notion of organizational development (*Organisationsentwicklung*) has long been common currency. The structuring and deployment of staff were a major issue with the creation of *ver.di*, with a total membership of 2.8 million. It took on some 5,000 staff (including about 2,000 secretarial and support staff) from its component unions, though numbers were subsequently reduced by over a third (by comparison, Heery and Kelly (1994: 34) estimated that in 1991 British unions, with over 9 million members, employed around 3,000 officers, excluding support staff). The new union established a staff development department (*Abteilung Personalentwicklung*), adopting a practice common in the German public sector where it had many members. The post-merger process involved a systematic analysis of skill requirements and training needs and the introduction of mentoring (in part involving external consultants) and team building (Serafin and van Kaldenkerken 2004); *ver.di* has also established seven training centres. One may note that ideas of 'coaching', mentoring, and team building have become widely integrated into training for union workplace representatives in both Germany and Austria.

In the UK, there has also been a trend towards more formalized processes of training for union officials. In the previous chapter we referred to the creation of the Organising Academy in 1998; the TUC has also initiated a leadership programme for senior union decision-makers, designed to develop strategic capacity, while TUC programmes train some 50,000 shop stewards a year. Writing two decades ago, Heery and Kelly (1994) described British union officials as exercising a high degree of autonomy; most considered themselves accountable to the membership and local lay representatives rather than to head office. Very few unions operated any formalized system of performance appraisal. However, this has changed significantly, partly as a result of widespread adoption of an 'organizing model' and partly also because of an increased emphasis on equality issues. Heery (2006: 454) notes that 'unions have strengthened their internal management...as a means of securing greater articulation of officer work and union policy...Most union officers now report regularly to a line manager, undergo formal appraisal, and set and review targets, at least for recruitment and organizing,' while formal training has become much more extensive.

Another innovation in many British unions—here too, imitating the practices of public sector employers—is the creation of senior management teams (SMTs). Like many other unions, the GMB general union made use of the Union Modernisation Fund (UMF), launched by the Labour government in 2005 and closed by its successor. A key element in the process was adoption of the 'SMART' management approach (specific, measurable, achievable, realistic and time-based goals) as a means of enhancing the effectiveness of the newly created fourteen-member national SMT and also for teams at regional level (Donaldson 2010). The retail union USDAW also used the UMF to introduce a 'balanced score-card' management approach (Stuart et al. 2009) and for a second project aimed at 'developing competent and confident managers' (USDAW 2010).

It has been traditional for unions to divide areas of policy-making among permanent committees, often specified in the rulebook. Another management practice has been to move increasingly towards ad hoc project groups, often appointed from above. For example, TCO in Sweden reorganized its work following its 2007 congress in order to establish separate projects concerned with improving organization among weakly unionized groups. The British TUC introduced radical changes as part of its 'relaunch' in 1994, closing many long-established standing committees and creating task groups for specific, time-limited projects (Heery 1998).

The case for many of these changes is undeniable. Trade unions are complex organizations; union leadership is not a task for amateurs. Unions with depleted resources have to deploy those that remain more effectively—developing strategic power resources. Representation at every level requires distinctive skills. The tradition of the 'all-round' union representative not only makes unions dependent on key individuals but also inhibits the collective integration of a range of expertise. Yet there are also dangers. Guillaume and Pochic (2009), in a study of the CFDT in France, diagnose the emergence of a trade union career trajectory in which formal qualifications increasingly exclude the great majority of members from entry to official positions. 'Whereas access to the position of union official was once seen as a culminating step in an activist's career, the managerial redefinition of the function implies a stronger valuation of formal education and an increasing differentiation between union officials and rank and file members' (Thomas 2013). Representatives schooled in managerial techniques may become closer to the employers with whom they negotiate and more distant from those they represent (Giraud 2007): privileging the logic of influence while marginalizing the logic of membership. It is ironical that the shift to 'organizing', presented as a means of empowering grassroots workers to *become* the union, can at the same time involve a consolidation of hierarchical authority at the centre; as Rehder (2008) notes, the American experience of the organizing model was primarily a top-down imposition of a new approach to union policy. Hence, for example, critics within *IG Metall* argue that the drive to adopt an organizing model, while presented as a means of empowering the membership, has been predicated on strengthening the central apparatus.

Reviving Union Democracy, Communications, and 'Outreach'

Though the mechanics of its implementation differ widely across (and to a lesser extent, within) countries, all trade union movements tend to embrace a two-way conception of democratic policy-making. In one direction, members at the grassroots level meet to discuss policy questions, not least in respect of collective bargaining, elect their own local officers and also choose representatives to participate in higher-level structures (district, regional, and ultimately national). As we have also seen, there may be vertical differentiation between union- or confederation-wide and sectoral or occupational structures. There is also a general principle that top officials are either directly elected or else are chosen by a representative conference or congress. In some countries, there is a strong tradition of election of lower-level paid officials as well. In the other direction, the democratic credentials of top leaders and executive committees give them the authority to prescribe a policy framework for the lower levels of the union.

We noted earlier the argument of Michels a century ago, that internal democracy simply did not function so that the members collectively could determine policy. Participating in meetings and debates requires an interest, and a commitment of time and energy, which only a minority of members display. Conversely, those in positions of leadership possess the organizational and rhetorical skills to ensure that their preferences normally prevail. Hence for Michels, there was a mutually reinforcing cycle of membership apathy and leadership oligarchy. This was particularly the case in unions with a heterogeneous membership; as Turner (1962) argued, with reference to British experience, these might well be called 'popular bossdoms'.

Even if many of Michels' arguments were one-sided and exaggerated, they contained an important core of truth. Even more today than when Michels wrote, unions struggle to attract a significant attendance at membership meetings. The trend towards 'mega-unions' increases internal heterogeneity. Workers have many more exciting ways of spending their leisure time than attending union meetings. Those who do participate tend to possess strong ideological commitments which may incline them to lines of policy which most members fail to endorse. Some of the educational initiatives which we discussed above can be seen as efforts to increase membership interest, enthusiasm, and involvement; but these rarely touch more than a small minority of trade unionists. Hence across our countries we see efforts to bridge the gap between leaders and rank and file through new channels.

We have already discussed one key approach in the previous chapter: the recognition of workforce diversity by creating special committees (notably for women, ethnic minorities, young workers, LGBT members), 'self-organized' groups and (as in the Austrian GPA) interest groups and 'thematic platforms'

(Stern 2010). This is a major area of structural change, but having addressed these developments already we do not discuss them further here.

A second major innovation is the use of membership surveys (sometimes extended to non-members as well) in order to establish their main concerns and opinions on union policy initiatives. In Sweden, LO has published very detailed surveys every few years since 1988, entitled *Röster om facket och jobbet* (views of the union and the job). As part of its *Zukunft* project, IG Metall in Germany undertook a wide-ranging survey in 2001 involving interviews, written and online questionnaires, and focus groups. More recently FIOM-CGIL, the main Italian metalworking union, organized a survey of 100,000 workers in the industry (Como 2008). The Danish public sector union FOA has commissioned membership surveys since 1998. HK, the Danish retail and commercial union, has also undertaken surveys since 2007; 'we ask them what we can do better, to see how we can transform satisfied members into loyal members'. The Dutch FNV has commissioned panel surveys of members and non-members, while the French CFDT, in its plans for organizational reform in 2010, also agreed to conduct occasional large-scale national surveys.

It is common for unions to ballot their members before calling strike action (in Britain, indeed, this has been legally required for the past three decades). In some countries, in addition, the practice has developed of holding membership ballots before approving collective agreements, particularly if the contents are contentious. Baccaro (2001) has described how bitter intra-union disputes over the 1992 agreement abolishing the *scala mobile* led the confederations to hold a binding referendum over the tripartite pact the following year, a mechanism which allowed union leaders to insist on the democratic legitimacy of the outcome. Similarly in the Netherlands, ballots have been held over peak-level agreements since 2003, and also before ratification of some sectoral agreements (van der Meer et al. 2009; Visser and van der Meer 2011).

The use of surveys and ballots can be seen as a complement to the institutionalized mechanisms of union democracy, involving decisions by elected executives and conferences; but it could also be viewed as a means of bypassing these. In FOA, we were told that some executive members ask: '[d]o we decide, or the surveys?' In the case of ballots on collective agreements, opponents often argue that the leadership monopolizes the presentation of the costs and benefits while the critics have no access to the official publicity mechanisms.

This links to our final theme in this chapter: the use of new mechanisms of communication to inform members and explain union aims and policies to the wider public. In Britain, one of the outcomes of the 'New Unionism' project, discussed earlier, was a set of proposals entitled *Reaching the Missing Millions* (TUC 2001). A key element was the launch of *workSMART*, a web-based service for workers in the 'new economy', providing advice and information on employment rights and some limited services as well as acting as a gateway to union membership. This was soon extended to provide special 'channels' covering health, pensions, and job searching.

Computerization and internet technologies have brought a virtual revolution in trade union communications, though the degree of impact varies cross-nationally. 'Communication power is at the heart of the structure and dynamics of society' (Castells 2009: 3), and today communication power is increasingly electronic. After a late start in many countries (Lee 1996), including the UK (Ward and Lusoli 2003), the use of such technologies has extended dramatically. Writing less than a decade ago, Greene et al. (2003: 284) argued that information technology offered scope for 'much more innovative, inclusive and potentially effective forms of organizing' than unions had as yet barely exploited. Likewise, Freeman (2005: 182) noted that 'unions may have adapted less rapidly than firms to the Internet, but even so unions are innovating and experimenting at unparalleled rates'. Today the scale of *qualitative* improvement is as striking as quantitative increase: union websites are now generally user friendly, even though differing in professionalism (which is indeed resource-intensive). For example, LO in Denmark publishes a weekly electronic magazine, *A4*, which is one of the most cited sources on labour market and welfare issues in the country.

Almost universally, workers can now join a union online; the one exception is Italy (in 2012, CGIL introduced online application, but actual affiliation is possible only by traditional means). Dedicated pages to which members and activists can log in are increasingly common. Many union websites now have Facebook and Twitter links, and some general secretaries provide their own blogs. Web TV is an increasingly common medium for spreading campaigning messages, used by all three Italian confederations, for example. FIOM-CGIL makes particularly effective use of social media. In some countries, unions are happy to collaborate with other online activists, as we explore in Chapter 6. The intranet has become a key resource for communication among officials and with workplace representatives, at least in northern Europe. Unison in Britain is an example of a union that has launched 'virtual branches' to link members without a fixed workplace. As Greene and Kirton have suggested (2003), electronic technologies allow members to adapt union activity to their own time constraints, and also provide 'safe spaces' for those, such as women, who find traditional union meetings an uncomfortable environment.

Much more generally, the Internet has become an important instrument for linking workers' representatives cross-nationally in the development of coordinated action. Perhaps the most notable example was the two-year dispute of Liverpool dock workers against mass dismissals, which commenced in 1995. Through the medium of *Labournet*, the strikers succeeded in achieving solidarity action from fellow dockers around the world (Carter et al. 2003). There are also examples of 'virtual strikes', often facilitated by international networks such as *LabourStart* or *Union Solidarity International*. One early success was the campaign in 2005 against the dismissal of a Dublin shopworker for wearing a trade union badge; another was a dispute at IBM in Italy in 2007 when sympathizers across Europe and beyond bombarded the company with messages.

In the main, union websites are under firm leadership control, at least in their public domains. 'One reason is that unions have shied away from developing interactive websites that might encourage members or others to be critical of union leadership and policies' (Freeman 2005: 165). Nevertheless, there has been some movement in this direction in most countries, particularly as local branches or workplace organizations open their own websites (now a topic of trade union education and training, for example in Austria). Many unions also use their websites for online surveys. In some countries, organized opposition groups have developed their own web presence. For instance, the platform of the left opposition in CGIL, *La Cgil che vogliamo* (the CGIL we want), has a highly visible web and Facebook presence.

Are new forms of electronic communication a threat to traditional mechanisms of union democracy, or can they enhance these? This is a vital issue which few unions have as yet systematically addressed.

Conclusions

In this chapter we have reviewed the ways in which unions as organizations are changing, outlining how the structural divisions in national movements differ cross-nationally, as well as the balance of authority between confederations and affiliates, and the contrasting ways in which union democracy is understood in different countries. We have examined in detail the process of mergers and amalgamations which are evident in most countries, and which in some have resulted in the emergence of 'mega-unions'. We have also considered some of the ways in which the internal arrangements of unions have been transformed, often drawing on management prescriptions developed in the context of private business. One theme which emerges clearly is the frequent conflict between measures adopted on grounds of enhanced efficiency and effectiveness, and traditional conceptions of union democracy. New information and communications technologies offer options for greater membership engagement in union policy, but in most countries they have been shaped by leadership priorities. Can efficiency and democracy be reconciled? We return to this question in our final chapter.

5

Bargaining in Adversity: Decentralization, Social Partnership, and the Crisis

All trade union movements—even if they hold strong political commitments—have a key role as collective bargainers. In some countries this has always been considered their primary function; in others, a serious orientation to bargaining with employers—and a willingness to agree to compromise settlements—has been more recent and has caused internal tensions. Much more generally, the dynamics of collective bargaining and unions' role within the process have shifted in recent decades as their traditional power resources have weakened.

The status of unions as collective bargainers is institutionally buttressed in countries where multi-employer agreements predominate, hence the patterns of bargaining coverage shown in Table 1.2; but almost everywhere there has been a decentralizing trend, confronting unions with significant challenges. This can mean—as has long been the case in Britain—that they must organize employer by employer in order to achieve collective agreements. This in turn creates a need for new power resources, hence the turn to 'organizing' discussed in Chapter 3.

Decentralization of bargaining towards the company level has coincided with, and indeed has been partly provoked by, growing competitive pressures in product markets and the increased salience of 'shareholder value'. A drive for reduced unit labour costs has been reflected in most countries in wage increases which lag behind productivity growth, and hence a falling wage share in national income (OECD 2012: ch. 3), as well as in the spread of more flexible forms of work organization, more intensive working-time arrangements, and the rise in 'atypical' employment even in core sectors of the economy (as discussed in Chapter 3). MNCs have been able to pressure unions into competitive concession bargaining by threats to divert investment and relocate production to sites with a more compliant workforce. Where national industrial relations regimes permit (and few preclude this absolutely), employers have often been able to make continued bargaining relations with specific unions conditional on compliance with corporate priorities. Making a virtue of necessity, some unions have enthusiastically embraced a role as partners in 'productivity coalitions' (Windolf 1989), making company competitiveness a priority in the interests of job protection. Such an orientation fits uneasily, at best, with traditional union identities as representatives of distinct employee interests which may conflict with employer priorities. Even in the absence of an explicit commitment to company-level 'partnership', we should note the almost universal decline in strike activity, conventionally if simplistically regarded as an index of union militancy.

Many European countries have traditions of 'social dialogue' or 'social partnership' at macro level, as we outlined in Chapter 1. In Austria, the Netherlands, and Belgium, formal institutions of peak-level tripartite concertation date back to the years of post-war reconstruction; in Sweden and Denmark, bipartite peak-level dialogue seemed firmly established (though in Sweden it broke down); while in Germany it was long accepted that changes in social and labour market policy should be based on consensus among the 'social partners'. Italy and Ireland have more adversarial traditions, but peak-level social pacts were agreed in more recent decades. The dynamics of such macro-bargaining have altered with changed economic conditions. In the early post-war decades, 'political exchange' (Pizzorno 1978) could be regarded as a positive-sum game: unions possessed the power resources to achieve inflationary wage increases, but (in those countries where they also possessed strong central authority) endorsed explicit or implicit wage restraint in return for enhanced social welfare and the promise of a share in future growth. Most notably, this was the principle underlying the Rehn–Meidner model adopted by Swedish LO in the 1950s.

The social pacts of the 1980s and 1990s, by contrast, were responses to twin crises, both linked to globalization: the erosion of national competitiveness, and the effort to reduce public deficits in line with the restrictive convergence criteria for EU economic and monetary union (EMU) (Avdagic et al. 2011; Crouch 2000b). In return for their assent, union signatories sought job creation strategies (or much more modestly, limitations on job loss); but this was not a trade-off which their counterparts in government and on the employers' side could readily deliver. Under harder economic conditions, and with trade union power resources diminished, 'political exchange' was increasingly a process of 'competitive corporatism' (Rhodes 2001), with unions seeking 'least-worst' outcomes rather than positive gains. Even on this defensive agenda, their bargaining power was limited unless governments themselves were contingently weak (Baccaro and Lim 2007). Even more than at company level, concession bargaining at the level of the state created tensions and dilemmas for trade unions.

Both conventional collective bargaining and peak-level dialogue have faced a particularly harsh climate after financial and economic crisis hit Europe in 2008. Economic and political difficulties can make bipartite agreements (union–employer) and tripartite deals (also involving government) more difficult though perhaps more necessary. As we see below, traditional mechanisms of peak-level dialogue in many of our countries moderated the labour market impact of the crisis. However, where governments have subsequently pursued severe austerity programmes, unions have usually seen little option but to resist.

Declining Strike Action: A Loss of Power Resources in Collective Bargaining?

Is strike activity an indicator of trade union strength? Some argue that strikes, particularly if effective, demonstrate cohesive collective organization and an ability to mobilize in support of union demands. Others insist that strong unions can normally calculate accurately the margin for concessions, whether with employers or with governments, and their counterparts take seriously their demands—so that it is rarely necessary to strike. Both arguments can be supported with evidence, which suggests that the issue is indeed complicated. Moreover, the relationship may well vary cross-nationally: in some countries, peaceful resolution of the bargaining process is the norm, and the mere threat of strike action is sufficient to force a reassessment of the positions adopted on each side; in others, at least token strikes are a routine indicator that a union is serious about its demands. These complexities affect any assessment of the general decline in strike activity over recent decades.

Discussion of strike statistics requires a health warning (Hyman 1989: 17–19). In most countries, the parties to a dispute are not officially required to report the details; data usually derive from labour inspectors or mediation officials who become aware of a strike, perhaps through the press. The thoroughness of reporting is likely to vary across countries (it is known, for example, that data for Belgium and Italy are incomplete) and may change over time (because of staffing cuts in relevant ministries, for instance). Criteria for inclusion differ: for example whether or not 'political strikes', or stoppages lasting less than a day, or workers indirectly affected are excluded. There are different measures of strikes: what is usually considered most reliable for comparative purposes is their 'volume' (workers involved × average duration), often termed 'working days lost', as a proportion of the workforce. Table 5.1 provides data for our ten countries for two periods in the 1970s and 2000s.

Writing in the 1990s, Edwards and Hyman (1994) undertook a comparative analysis covering all our countries except Belgium (because of inadequate

Table 5.1. Strike days per 1,000 workers, annual averages

	1971–7 [1]	2000–9 [2]
SE	54	20
DK	329	104
DE	43	5
AT	11	40
NL	39	8
BE	231	70
FR	229	78
IT	1497	80
UK	482	29
IE	520	44

[1] Own calculations, based on Aspalter (2001: 77).
[2] Figures kindly provided by Kurt Vandaele on the basis of Eurostat and other sources.

data). They showed that strong centralized unions and well established 'corporatist' institutions were associated with low strike levels, though in many cases there were occasional large-scale stoppages. They also found that in most, but not all, countries the extent of strike activity had fallen since the early 1970s. Table 5.1, updating the record, tells a similar story. What also emerges is that the previous distinction between countries with a very high strike volume (Italy, Ireland, the UK, and Denmark), medium (Belgium and France), and low (Sweden, Germany, the Netherlands, and Austria) is no longer so clear cut. It also shows a reduction, often very large, everywhere except Austria. Here, the figure for the 2000s would have been negligible but for an exceptional series of protest stoppages in 2003 against government changes in the pensions system, as well as a dispute over restructuring on the railways. It should also be noted that Denmark heads the rankings for the 2000s because of a single dispute, involving health-care and related workers in 2008. In addition, the Swedish figures would have been negligible but for a protracted strike by local government workers in 2003. (It is worth noting that the averages for both countries in the 1970s were dominated, though less overwhelmingly, by one single year.)

How can these figures be related to an analysis of power resources? One general answer is that strikes in most countries were historically concentrated in a small number of industries such as docks, railways, coal mining and metalworking. Workers in such industries often possessed considerable workplace bargaining power, in the sense that they could impose significant costs on the employer through disruptive action; sometimes they could inflict more extensive economic damage which would encourage governments to enforce a favourable settlement. Commonly these were trade union strongholds: in other words, workers possessed associational and organizational power resources. Employment in many of these traditional strongholds has declined substantially, and in most countries this can be seen as a major cause of falling strike activity. In addition, one consequence of globalization may be to weaken structural power in industries where production can be transferred to foreign locations (Scheuer 2006). (Conversely, though, the cross-national integration of global supply chains can create new points of vulnerability for MNCs.) Nevertheless, unions in many public services, such as urban transport, are hardly vulnerable to 'offshoring' and retain considerable power resources of a traditional kind. In many countries one can detect a widespread shift of strike activity towards such services, which commonly are, or until recently were, part of the public sector and have above-average levels of unionization. Attempts by public employers to impose cost-cutting and restructuring measures are another precipitating factor behind most recent large-scale conflicts.

For many unions, however, a loss of power resources has evidently spurred a search for alternatives to the traditional strike. Indeed, there has been long experience of selective or demonstrative action—including 'smart strikes' and 'virtual strikes'—which minimizes the costs for the unions and their members while raising the public profile of their grievances and in some cases exploiting employer vulnerabilities, for example by refusing to collect fares on public transport services. Public campaigns to mobilize external support may in some circumstances constitute an alternative, but in others a complement, to strike action, as with the Dutch cleaning workers' dispute described in Chapter 3. They are a means of mobilizing moral, collaborative, and in some cases strategic power resources.

A more fundamental strategic shift, at least for unions and union movements whose identities reflected a history of mobilization and struggle, is from adversarialism towards the pursuit of 'mutual gains' through what Walton and McKersie (1965), in a classic study, termed 'integrative bargaining'. This move from 'boxing' to 'dancing' (Huzzard et al. 2004) may reflect a pragmatic assessment that if unions have lost the power resources to compel employers (or governments) to accede to their demands, they must persuade them that at least some of their aspirations can be met in ways which serve the employers' interests as well. Bacon and Blyton (2004), in a study of union responses to workplace restructuring, have explored some of the ways in which traditional ideologies and identities interact with pragmatic policy choices. Unions whose ideological assumptions focus on the conflicting interests of workers and employers may be expected to resist workplace restructuring ('militant opposition'); those with an orientation towards social partnership to adopt an integrative, problem-solving approach ('cooperative engagement'). But circumstances may divorce practice from ideology. Unions whose identities are shaped by past conflict and struggle may nevertheless calculate that militant opposition will fail (as in Italy in the 1980s) and decide that a problem-solving approach, critically embraced, will yield better results ('militant engagement'). Another example at macro level is the decision by the leadership of *IG Metall* in 1995 to call for a *Bündnis für Arbeit* (Alliance for Jobs). Conversely, a union predisposed to cooperation may nevertheless decide that certain management initiatives are a frontal challenge to its status or its members' interests—as has been the case with many recent changes in the public sector—and that there is no alternative to resistance ('moderate opposition'). Here, the shift is from 'dancing' to 'boxing'. Both 'militant engagement' and 'moderate opposition' can prove internally contentious for trade unions and result in policy inconsistency. This stylized model of the interconnections between ideology and action is a useful way of framing the discussion of changes and tensions in collective bargaining that we develop in the remainder of this chapter.

Collective Bargaining: Diversity and Change

Despite diminished union power resources, collective bargaining in most countries remains institutionally robust (Dufour and Hege 2010, 2011). As we have seen, the coverage of collective agreements is very extensive except in the anglophone countries, where only a minority of the workforce is affected, and to a lesser extent in Germany; elsewhere, the rate is at least 80 per cent. Quantity is not, however, the same as quality; and one key dilemma for unions is whether to accept a dilution of the content of agreements, and perhaps also a reduction in their scope, as the price of sustaining a bargaining relationship. Another, as already indicated, is a shift in the key locus of bargaining from the national level, where unions benefit from economies of scale in the negotiating process, and where the outcomes are more transparent, to company level. Here it becomes necessary to possess competent negotiators in each bargaining unit, and it is far harder to ensure that minimum standards are maintained. Indeed, bargaining at company or workplace level has always been part of the industrial relations landscape; but normally this has supplemented the terms of multi-employer agreements. In many countries, a hierarchical relationship was formally prescribed: lower-level agreements could not undercut those at higher levels. But decentralization has involved a weakening of the regulatory compass of multi-employer agreements (for example, determining only minimum pay rates, not increases for those paid above the minimum); and there have been moves to allow company-level derogation from the terms of multi-employer agreements, at least in specific circumstances.

Writing in the 1990s, Traxler (1995) argued that the trend towards company bargaining, evident across Europe, did not necessarily mean the disintegration of multi-employer bargaining systems. Only in Britain had sectoral bargaining been displaced by company or workplace negotiations (or, far more commonly, no collective bargaining at all); here, multi-employer agreements have now almost disappeared in the private sector (Kersley et al. 2006). In most other countries, single- and multi-employer negotiations coexisted. Typically, what was occurring was a process of 'organized decentralization', with sectoral agreements devolving the application of specific agenda items to local negotiations.

Since then, the process of decentralization has continued, with negotiations at company or workplace level acquiring increased importance; in some countries it is now uncertain how far the shift in the locus of bargaining can still be considered 'organized'. As sectoral agreements have become more flexible, allowing growing scope for autonomous regulation at company level, a further and associated trend has been the individualization of conditions *within* companies through performance-related and 'merit' pay systems. This development has posed particular dilemmas for trade unions, given traditional assumptions that solidarity requires the standardization of conditions and rewards across the workforce as a whole.

In the Nordic countries, there has been a rapid shift towards a 'two-tier bargaining model' (Stokke 2008). In both Sweden and Denmark, most sectoral agreements no longer prescribe actual pay increases but set broad parameters for decentralized bargaining (Granqvist and Regnér 2008; Scheuer 1998). Such bargaining often encompasses individualized performance-related pay, so indeed these might be described as 'three-tier' systems. In contrast to most other countries we examine, individual and collective bargaining are closely intertwined, since unions negotiate the procedures for performance evaluation, advise individual members, and submit appeals against unfavourable outcomes. In general, the unions endorse such three-tier systems; in particular, professional unions see this as a means of achieving enhanced rewards for highly qualified employees (thus partially reversing the egalitarian outcomes formerly achieved by blue-collar unions). However, if unions are to retain effective oversight of the process, 'the organizational resources at local level are crucial' (Stokke 2008: 19). Our interviews with both LO and TCO in Sweden indicated growing unevenness in workplace organization, making it more difficult to control the wage determination process. Likewise, though opening clauses in Denmark require shop stewards to approve any deviations from sectorally agreed conditions (Ilsøe et al. 2007), Scheuer (2007) points to problems resulting from variations in union strength at company level.

Similar trends create more serious problems for unions with lower membership density and less integrated relationships between national and workplace structures. Germany is an obvious example (Bispinck et al. 2010). As the price of achieving a reduction in the working week in 1984, *IG Metall* agreed that the detailed application of the change should be determined at company level, setting in train a sustained process of devolution. After German unification in 1990, and the economic crisis in the east which soon followed, unions accepted the introduction of 'hardship' and 'opening' clauses in sectoral agreements, allowing firms in economic difficulties to undercut agreed conditions. A radical extension of such flexibility was adopted in the metal industry through the 2004 Pforzheim agreement, as 'a response to the political threat of even more drastic changes to the legal basis of German collective bargaining' (Bispinck and Schulten 2011a: 9). To some extent, this gave formal approval to the growing practice whereby works councils agreed concessions in return for undertakings to maintain production at their site. There has also been a trend towards pay individualization, notably in the banking industry through an agreement reached in 2002 whereby much of the prescribed pay increase would be performance-related. Haipeter (2011a, 2011b) has argued that decentralization provides opportunities for union renewal, in particular spurring *IG Metall* to involve rank-and-file members in the company-level bargaining process. Bahnmüller (2010: 105–6) has also suggested that decentralization is 'Janus-faced': it may be a means for employers to reduce standards, but also offers unions an opportunity to mobilize in support of their own demands. Where works councils are effective, they can be 'successful veto-players if employers press unacceptable demands' (Behrens 2009: 108).

However, such relatively optimistic assessments presuppose a capacity to sustain and extend organizational power resources at the workplace in a coordinated fashion. Many of the current debates within *IG Metall* concern whether, and how, the union can achieve this. A more pessimistic reading would be that reinforced mobilizing capacity in existing union strongholds is unlikely to suffice. The 'dismantling of the traditional architecture of German-style pattern bargaining' (Lehndorff 2012: 83) has been linked, externally, to the threat by MNCs to choose the exit option if unionized workforces *do* act as 'veto-players'; and internally, to a growing low-wage sector with a precarious workforce, weak unionization, and often an absence of either collective bargaining coverage or works councils. The challenge of competitive undercutting of standards may be impossible to resist on a company-by-company basis.

In Austria the architecture of centralized bargaining remains more robust than in Germany. An employer may negotiate a company agreement with the works council, but this may not undercut conditions agreed at sectoral level, and sectoral agreements very rarely contain opening clauses. However, as in other countries, there has been a reduction in the effective impact of higher-level agreements; in banking, for example, 'basic wage agreements provided for increases below inflation in several recent years, offset by growth in non-consolidated—and frequently non-negotiated—bonuses and other premiums' (Arrowsmith and Marginson 2008: 9). There has also been a trend towards allowing an uneven distribution at company level of sectorally agreed increases; in some cases this option was used to implement 'merit' pay, but in others it was applied to benefit lower-paid groups (Bispinck and Schulten 2011b: 5). With the company level increasingly important in determining real pay increases, unions face obvious difficulties in sustaining central coordination.

In both the Netherlands and Belgium, opening or hardship clauses have become common, though their impact seems to be less than in Germany. In the Dutch case, a two-year wage freeze contained in a tripartite agreement in 2003 also boosted company arrangements for performance-related pay; while in Belgium, a peak-level agreement in 2007 encouraged collective bonus schemes.

The rapid growth of enterprise collective bargaining has been one of the most notable features of French industrial relations. In 2010 there were over 33,000 company agreements (Ministère du Travail 2011), an increase from around 1,000 in 1980 (Goetschy 1998). As we noted in Chapter 2, for many observers this growth has been a reflection of union weakness and a façade for 'managerial unilateralism' (Goyer and Hancké 2004: 176). Until the recent changes to the rules on representativeness, the fact that a minority union could sign a valid collective agreement opened the possibility for 'sweetheart' deals that favoured the employer. There has also been a rapid spread of performance-related pay, though for manual workers this normally relates to collective rather than individual performance (DARES 2010).

Can French unions achieve a stronger influence in workplace negotiations? In principle, the new rules on representativeness place limits on employers' ability to divide and rule. It is also significant that the traditional reluctance of the CGT to accept compromise with the employer (long diluted in practice) has now been formally abandoned. In this respect, a common front at workplace level has become easier to achieve. It is also interesting that SUD, which to some extent has filled the vacuum of intransigence created by the CGT's *recentrage*, also finds it increasingly difficult to sustain an absolute rejection of compromise (Connolly 2010; Damesin and Denis 2005; Denis 2003; Sainsaulieu 2006). Yet union workplace representation possesses breadth rather than depth, with diminishing numbers of activists struggling to cope with the demands of increasingly decentralized industrial relations which require technical skills which most lack.

In Italy, by contrast, there is a long tradition of two-tier (or three-tier) bargaining (Cella and Treu 1989; Ferner and Hyman 1992; Regalia and Regini

1998). In the late 1960s there was an explosion of workplace bargaining, closely linked as both cause and effect to the 'hot autumn' of 1969; for several years, decentralized bargaining was often a vehicle for offensive workplace struggles. The balance of power shifted with economic adversity in the late 1970s, leading to some traumatic defeats—notably at Fiat in 1980—but because of the institutional power resources derived from the 1970 *Statuto*, a common outcome was negotiated change (Regini 1995). Decentralization created space for more participative involvement of rank-and-file members, but also made overall coordination of bargaining policy more difficult (Locke 1990: 372), sometimes entailing 'an employer-led process of disorganized decentralization' (Molina Romo 2005: 12).

Subsequently a dominant issue has been the articulation between interconfederal, sectoral, and company negotiations, with employers and governments arguing that the system was inflationary in its outcomes. A peak-level agreement in 1983 limited the scope for workplace renegotiation of issues already covered in sectoral bargaining, and was followed a decade later by a tripartite agreement which for the first time clearly defined the respective roles of the different bargaining levels and further circumscribed the agenda of company negotiations. The 1993 agreement also created scope for collective bargaining at regional level in areas where small firms without effective workplace organization predominated. Subsequent attempts to reconfigure the relationship between levels have been driven, as in other countries, by the managerial pursuit of flexibility—reinforced by the deregulation drive of the Berlusconi governments—and have proved more contentious. Sustained employer pressure to weaken sectoral agreements was blocked by resistance from the unions, in particular CGIL; but in 2009, CISL and UIL broke ranks to sign an agreement with *Confindustria*. Two years later CGIL, in the face of internal opposition, also signed a modified tripartite pact, which enabled company agreements to undercut sectoral standards if signed by unions representing the majority of the workforce. The new arrangements also imposed a peace obligation on signatories of company agreements.

As noted above, change in the UK was far more radical, with most multi-employer bargaining—at least in the private sector—ending two or three decades ago. As in other countries, there has been a rapid growth in individualized pay systems, extending to nearly half of all private sector workplaces by 2004 (Kersley et al. 2006: 190–1). Disorganized decentralization, together with the systematic removal of institutional supports for collective representation, has made the overriding priority for private sector unions the achievement and retention of bargaining relationships with individual employers. After a period of strategic disorientation, the dominant union response—spearheaded by the TUC in the 1990s—was to persuade employers that unions were willing to act as 'partners' in enhancing company performance.

The record of partnership has been intensely debated, with advocates insisting that a shift from adversarialism to constructive engagement was a means of winning the support not only of employers but also of employees, while critics argued that partnership involved an essentially subaltern role which obstructed the creation of independent, activist-based organization (Stuart and Martínez Lucio 2005; Terry 2004).

Formal partnership agreements actually proved relatively rare, with a few dozen signed in the course of a decade. Much more extensively, though, union recognition appeared to involve a tacit acceptance of a constrained trade union function (Brown et al. 2009; Kelly 2012; Marginson 2012). Workplace unions often focused more on individual representation than on collective bargaining; and unions' role on collective issues was commonly reduced from negotiation to consultation. There was also a growing focus on 'soft' bargaining issues, where employer opposition was less likely. Some unions, notably in public (or ex-public) services which are vulnerable to disruptive action, have pursued more combative strategies, at times linked to the type of organizing approach discussed in Chapter 3. Many others have oscillated between partnership and mobilization, or have attempted to vary their approach according to the nature of each workforce and its employer.

Ireland is a curious anomaly. For more than two decades, peak-level partnership agreements have set the framework of industrial relations, as we discuss in more detail below. However, while all other countries with cross-sectoral bargaining also have robust institutions at sectoral level, in Ireland (as in Britain) these largely disintegrated in the 1980s, partly because of the influx of foreign companies. Union attempts to achieve some peak-level support for their bargaining role at company level proved unsuccessful, resulting in a complete lack of articulation between centralized partnership and company industrial relations; here the Irish unions face the same difficulties as their British counterparts.

Innovative Collective Bargaining Strategies

Though the collective bargaining environment in all countries has placed unions on the defensive, there are also signs of innovative responses. In this section we do not attempt to survey the ten countries systematically, but provide some illustrative examples.

In a number of countries—notably Germany—trade unions have long played a role in initial vocational training, but influence on continuing career development has been less common. This has been a subject of contention for *IG Metall*, which achieved its first collective agreement on continuous vocational training in 2001. The EU vocational training centre Cedefop (2008) has surveyed a variety of initiatives in several of our countries, some primarily involving trade union advice to individual members but others including collective bargaining demands. In Belgium, biennial intersectoral agreements have since 1986 included provisions for funding vocational training, while in Denmark such frameworks are negotiated at sectoral level (Giaccone 2009). Elsewhere, any union bargaining role is usually more decentralized. One much-discussed example is the workplace learning agenda in the UK, which received financial and institutional support from the 1997 Labour government (Stuart et al. 2009) and was coordinated by the TUC. Enthusiasts argued that union learning representatives were able to develop both an advisory and a bargaining role, thereby strengthening workplace union organization; others (McIlroy 2008) are more sceptical, suggesting that there is little evidence that unions have succeeded in collectivizing the learning agenda.

'Humanization' of work was often a key trade union demand in the 1970s, resulting in significant improvements in the quality of work. But a shift in the balance of power from the 1980s, and a growing priority for job saving over job quality, resulted in a reversal of many of the gains, as is indicated by the European Quality of Work Surveys (Parent-Thirion et al. 2012). Work intensity has increased; a growing proportion of workers (almost half) perform monotonous work; exposure to most physical hazards has increased, as have feelings of insecurity—all factors which help explain the rise in work-related stress.

A decade ago, a comparative study (Llorens and Ortiz de Villacian 2001) found that stress had been addressed in collective bargaining in six of our countries. The most significant was Belgium, where an intersectoral agreement was negotiated in 1999. Stress obtained a more general profile when in 2004 the ETUC and the European employers' organizations signed an 'autonomous framework agreement on work-related stress'. Though the outcome has been uneven, unions in all countries have since given increased attention to the problem. Both of the largest British unions have issued guidance to workplace representatives (Unison 2002; Unite 2010) and have supported legal action against employers. In Denmark, FOA reached a comprehensive anti-stress agreement with the local government employers in 2005, resulting in a wide-ranging five-year campaign. In Germany, *IG Metall* has developed its own anti-stress campaign, including a support pack for workplace representatives and a draft legislative proposal (IG Metall 2012), in the context of the broader *Gute Arbeit* (good work) initiative which it launched in 2002. Since 2007 the DGB has organized a large-scale annual survey on the same theme, while *ver.di* has pressed for a collective agreement on stress in the health-care sector. More recently, TCO in Sweden has published a large-scale 'stress barometer' (Mörtvik and Fromm 2012). In France, where a peak-level agreement on stress was signed in 2008, the issue has assumed key importance for unions following a spate of work-related suicides, particularly at

France Télécom Orange. By raising the problem of stress and wider work quality issues on the bargaining agenda, unions in many countries have endeavoured to find new ways of mobilizing worker awareness that their personal job-related issues have broader collective relevance and that trade unionism can be part of the solution.

The concept of 'good work' also links closely to growing trade union attention to 'work–life balance' and 'family-friendly' work arrangements. In Sweden, work–life balance has been addressed in many collective agreements. In Belgium, this has been an element in intersectoral and sectoral agreements for the past decade. In Germany, *ver.di* launched a campaign in 2003 with the slogan *Nimm dir die Zeit* (take your time), in part as a reaction against company-level employer demands for increased working time, including at unsocial hours. Its interventions have included both sectoral bargaining demands and guidance to workplace negotiators (Bsirske et al. 2004). GPA in Austria has also made work–life balance a major bargaining issue, and has achieved some success in collective agreements (Demetriades et al. 2006). In both countries, unions have responded to employer demands for working time flexibility by insisting that this should provide workers with greater time sovereignty, and that there should be collective oversight of individual work schedules. In the UK, where working hours have traditionally been the longest in any of our countries, this has also been a major concern for trade unions. In the public sector, Unison has achieved many agreements on the issue (Gregory and Milner 2009), but in the private sector the ability to influence outcomes through collective bargaining has been very limited (O'Brien-Smith and Rigby 2010). Overall, Keune (2006: 16, 23–7) has found that 'there is no unified trade union point of view on working time flexibility'; and in terms of outcomes, 'there has been a steady increase in employer-oriented types of working time flexibility', while 'trade unions have difficulties achieving their objectives through collective bargaining under the present economic and political circumstances'.

When the Webbs first developed the concept of collective bargaining, they wrote of the 'device of the common rule' (Webb and Webb 1897: 715–39): a standard set of conditions which no individual contract of employment could vary, except upwards. With the advance of mass manufacturing industry ('Fordism') in the 20th century, the focus of trade union strategy in most countries was increasingly to achieve the greatest possible standardization of conditions, in order to minimize the risk of employers discriminating between workers. This neglected the extent to which workers' preferences might be differentiated, in part because of the diversity of their individual circumstances. One means of adapting to such diversity is the pursuit of more flexible forms of regulation, particularly in respect of the organization of working time.

A pioneer in this process has been the Netherlands, where in 1993 the STvdA approved a policy document, *Een nieuwe koers* (a new course), recommending more flexible agreements, particularly in respect of performance-related pay. This was followed by a 1999 agreement entitled *Naar arbeidsvorwaarden op maat* (towards customized working conditions). This encouraged the negotiation of 'à la carte' or 'cafeteria' collective agreements, allowing, for instance, a choice between increased pay or reduced working time (Delsen et al. 2006). For example, since 2002 collective agreements in the metal industry have offered a menu of higher pay, extra days off, career breaks, or early retirement (van Klaveren and Tijdens 2011). There have been similar developments in Denmark, with collective agreements providing 'free-choice accounts' which can be used for extra holidays, as pension savings, or taken as increased pay (Madsen 2003; Scheuer 2008).

Innovations in collective bargaining strategy are often designed to foster capacity building at workplace level. As we saw in the previous chapter, unions increasingly use surveys to identify workers' own priorities, and ballots to legitimize bargaining outcomes. Many recent initiatives can be understood in this light. An example is the campaign entitled *Besser statt billiger* (better rather than cheaper), launched by *IG Metall* in 2004, against the background of widespread employer demands for cost-cutting reductions on employment levels and adverse changes in work arrangements. In association with the campaign for 'good work' discussed above, the union aimed to move beyond a defensive and reactive response by developing alternative proposals for product innovation and new production methods, formulating arguments and analyses which could help mobilize members behind their workplace negotiators (Bromberg 2011; Korflür et al. 2010). Many of the new bargaining demands have been informed by surveys of workplace representatives or workers more generally. In the terms discussed earlier in this chapter, this could be seen as an approach of militant engagement; as one leading *IG Metall* official described it (Urban 2005), the union would act as a 'constructive veto player'.

In hard times, innovative bargaining approaches are increasingly necessary. Yet given the immensity of short-term challenges, they may often assume a low priority.

Political Exchange and Social Partnership

Writing half a century ago, Shonfield (1965: 66–7) sought to account for the superior economic performance of the 'modern capitalism' of many continental European countries compared to Britain or the USA. His explanation centred on 'the vastly increased influence of the public authorities on the management of the economic system'. A combination of long-range planning and publicly funded national welfare meant that 'the violence of the market has been tamed'. He also commented 'that full employment and the enhanced bargaining power of wage-earners have not resulted in the diversion of resources away from investment', and attributed this to 'the corporatist formula for managing the economy. The major interest groups are brought together and encouraged to conclude a series of bargains about their future behaviour' (1965: 5, 231). This idea of a 'corporatist formula' became a popular theme of industrial relations analysis in the following decade.

In many European countries, the 'post-war settlement' involved a Keynesian commitment to full (or near-full) employment, which in turn strengthened the labour market position of trade unions. Commonly the explicit or implicit corollary of expansionary macroeconomic policies was that unions should restrain their wage demands so as to avoid inflation and loss of competitiveness in export markets. As Katzenstein (1985) noted, this was particularly necessary in the small, export-oriented states that comprised much of western Europe. This was reflected in the formal tripartite institutions established in Austria and the Netherlands, and the more informal tripartism in Belgium, Denmark, and Sweden.

Institutionalized wage restraint was the expression of a distinctive strategic choice by trade unions: a calculation that their members would derive greater benefit from sustained employment security than from short-term maximization of pay increases. Such a strategic choice is obviously more attractive to unions that embrace an ideology of 'social partnership' than to those with more adversarial orientations. For Korpi and Shalev (1979), generalizing primarily on the basis of Swedish experience, the organizational strength of labour enabled unions to move from the (conflictual) defence of workers' interests in the industrial arena to the (non-conflictual) pursuit of shared interests in the political arena. This could facilitate high investment, hence economic growth, hence subsequent increases in both wages and social expenditure: a virtuous circle. A corollary of such schemes was that unions (and employers' associations) achieved a privileged position in macro-policy formulation, which enhanced their own organizational status and institutional power resources, and in turn made it easier for them to enforce moderation on their constituents. But to attain such a role, it was normally necessary that confederations already possessed sufficient authority; or, as a functional alternative, that large manufacturing unions in export-oriented sectors could anticipate the macroeconomic consequences of their own bargaining activity and should be able to set the pattern for wage bargaining across the economy, as in Germany (Olson 1982).

Analysis of such arrangements became a 'growth industry' in the 1970s (Panitch 1980). While some writers used the terms 'neo-corporatism' or 'concertation', others referred to 'political exchange' (Baglioni 1987; Pizzorno 1978; Regini 1984). Here, the argument was that governments with weak popular legitimacy—Italy was the paradigm case—were keen to make unions co-responsible for potentially unpopular economic policies. But by the 1980s, corporatist arrangements had come under increasing pressure and often unravelled. Corporatism had emerged as a mechanism for encouraging economic growth with positive-sum outcomes; now the economic situation was far less favourable, with inflation and unemployment both rising in many countries. In some, trade unions were weakened by recession and no longer needed to be 'bought off' by government; in others, their capacity to guarantee wage restraint had been undermined by rank-and-file revolts, or by challenges to the dominance of male manual workers in manufacturing unions by growing white-collar and public sector organizations with very different constituencies and interests. In the main, corporatism—both as practice and as theory—fell out of fashion.

Yet in the 1990s, peak-level concertation again became widely practised in western Europe, though in a form very different from that of previous decades (Berger and Compston 2002; Regini 1997). The previous agreements had been reached when unions appeared strong; employers were largely rooted in the national economy and national governments had considerable autonomy in determining fiscal and monetary policy. Now unions were far weaker, capital was more cosmopolitan and mobile, while financial liberalization constrained governments' economic policy discretion (formally so, within the eurozone)—issues which are considered further in the following section. The new 'social pacts' were primarily designed to reduce, or at least stabilize, unit labour costs and to reduce both corporate taxation and budget deficits (Fajertag and Pochet 2000; Rhodes 2001; Sisson et al. 1999). The agenda shifted from 'gain-sharing' to 'pain-sharing': unions were invited to maintain wage moderation but at the same time to accept cutbacks in the welfare state and often also some weakening of labour market regulation. The main goal was to achieve greater national economic competitiveness and more incentives for capital to invest in the country, thereby reducing unemployment. Governments, in many cases lacking the electoral base to push through unpopular policies unilaterally, were often keen to 'construct support coalitions' (Gourevitch 1986: 239) as a means of blame avoidance. Analysts increasingly employed such terms as 'lean corporatism' (Traxler 2004), 'competitive solidarity' (Streeck 1999), and 'competitive corporatism' (Rhodes 2001).

Post-Keynesian political exchange involved a new set of strategic choices for trade unions. In contrast to the positive-sum trade-offs of previous decades, the calculus often involved a search for 'least-worst' options, without specific compensation (except perhaps in bolstering unions' organizational status as 'social partners'). One key contextual change was the readiness of many governments to act unilaterally in the absence of union assent (Ebbinghaus and Hassel 2000); by showing willingness to endorse agreed policies, unions hoped at least 'to retain some influence over decision-making' (Fajertag and Pochet 2000: 19) and to avoid attacks on their institutional position, described by Ebbinghaus (2011: 329) as 'the ultimate "meta-reform"'. A strategy of 'militant opposition' might seem too high a risk.

Another important influence was the shift to 'non-accommodating monetary regimes' (Iversen 1999, 2005; Iversen et al. 2000) where governments and central banks no longer made full employment a policy priority, a regime which was externally reinforced under EMU (Crouch 2000b; Kauppinen 1998; Martin and Ross 2004). As Hancké and Rhodes (2005) suggest, while unions possessed significant bargaining power in the run-up to EMU (since they might have mobilized against the project), once EMU was adopted the scope to affect government policy largely disappeared. Nevertheless, unions in many countries have been able to ensure that 'deregulation' maintains a collective alternative to simple marketization. In Italy, for example, most relaxations of former statutory regulation have followed peak-level agreements, bolstering collective authority; in Belgium, 'derogation' from legislated rules is possible only by collective agreement; in the Netherlands, areas of public welfare have been delegated to sectoral collective bargaining (which in the Dutch case ensures comprehensive coverage) (Trampusch 2006).

National experience does not map easily against the four country groups which have framed most of our previous discussion. In Denmark, a peak-level tripartite agreement was signed in 1987; and though there was no formal successor, its basic principles continued to guide collective bargaining (Lind 2000). There has been no parallel in Sweden (though Finland has seen a series of formal pacts). In Germany, the *Bündnis für Arbeit* established in 1996 was a failure, and the attempt to negotiate a pact was not repeated; but peak-level concertation continued in Austria and Belgium, while in the Netherlands a series of pacts was negotiated. Peak-level consultations in France never seemed likely to result in formal agreement on major policy issues, whereas in Italy there has been a succession of pacts. In the UK, after the breakdown of the 'social contract' of the 1970s (a bilateral agreement between government and unions), governments have rejected the idea of peak-level bargaining; whereas Ireland saw a continuous series of three-year pacts from 1987.

Below we focus on the three countries which have seen the most extensive pattern of peak-level pacts since the 1980s, but first we refer briefly to some more general features of 'competitive corporatism'. The full title of the *Bündnis für Arbeit* was 'Alliance for Jobs, Training and Competitiveness', and despite the lack of formal outcome the unions endorsed the principle of 'employment-oriented' bargaining policy: a tacit acceptance of wage restraint (Bispinck and Schulten 2000). Despite more militant public assertions, German unions accepted modest pay settlements that contributed to the falling wage share in national income. Wage moderation in Germany had knock-on effects in the enlarged deutschmark zone and later the eurozone, as unions in each country accepted the need for parallel restraint in order to maintain national competitiveness. Erne (2008: 71–3) notes that following the Maastricht Treaty which initiated EMU, real wage increases no longer followed productivity growth, 'a clear indication of wage moderation'. In Sweden, while there was no return to interconfederal bargaining, in 1997 the unions (both manual and white collar) in the manufacturing sector signed the 'Industrial Agreement' (*Industriavtalet*), which set a framework for pay bargaining oriented to the 'Europe norm' (Elvander 2002). A decade earlier, the tripartite agreement in Denmark (where the krone, unlike the Swedish krona, was tightly linked to the deutschmark) accepted the principle that labour costs should reflect trends in competitor countries. As Lind comments (2000: 155), 'most trade unions and especially their main organizations, the LO, the FTF and the AC, have realised that moderation of pay claims (and increased labour market flexibility etc.) will result in more jobs because the economy will be more competitive'. A similar principle received legal backing in Belgium (without union opposition) in 1989, authorizing government intervention if average overall wage increases adversely affected competitiveness; a more specific law in 1996 required that labour costs should not exceed a 'wage norm' based on projected increases in Germany, France, and the Netherlands. Intersectoral agreements have embraced the same constraint—even if, in theory, 'trade unions refuse to follow the logic of wage competitiveness and argue that collective bargaining should concentrate on quality competitiveness' (Keune 2008: 13–14). We return to this theme in Chapter 7.

The Netherlands stands out among the Nordic and 'central' countries for its succession of formal tripartite agreements. In the Wassenaar agreement of 1982, the unions formally accepted the centralized imposition of wage moderation after more than a decade of 'free collective bargaining'. Visser and Hemerijck (1997: 81–2) point to three main motives. First, unemployment had risen sharply and in consequence union membership had fallen; a social pact which increased profits and restrained wages was the precondition for employment-creating measures. Second, the employers signalled that as part of a deal they would be willing to negotiate over shorter working time, which they had previously resisted. Third, it was clear that the government would impose a freeze (as it had done several times before) in the absence of 'voluntary' restraint. Following Wassenaar, a series of peak-level policy initiatives on such issues as training, minimum wages, and unemployment reduction was approved in the STvdA and the SER (Hemerijk et al. 2000: 263).

Concertation temporarily broke down in 1991 when the employers insisted on cuts in social expenditure, in particular on disability benefits, which often functioned as a form of redundancy compensation; the coalition government (in which Wim Kok, former head of the NVV/FNV, was deputy premier) imposed reductions unilaterally, followed by threats to curtail the extension of collective agreements. After tense negotiations, the unions agreed—as in Wassenaar—to wage moderation in return for working time reduction. This 1993 agreement also approved more flexible working arrangements and further decentralization of collective bargaining. This was followed by a four-year framework agreement in 1997. Another central agreement in 1999 opened up the possibility of à la carte agreements, discussed above. Further strains occurred in 2003–4, in a phase of economic recession. Under a right-wing government, following the electoral defeat of the PvdA, the FNV agreed to a pay freeze in return for assurances on welfare reforms; to head off rank-and-file opposition, the union organized a referendum which showed narrow support for the 'emergency pact' (Baccaro and Simoni 2010; van der Meer and Visser 2010). The government then insisted on removing tax incentives for early retirement, resulting in another union referendum which rejected the proposals, and a series of strikes and mass demonstrations. A compromise pact was agreed in 2004; 'having gained a number of concessions and fighting back from the brink, the unions claimed victory' (Visser and van der Meer 2011: 221).

Dutch experience shows that peak-level concertation can be a highly conflictual process. The FNV leaders often accepted 'least-worst' options reluctantly, in recognition of their own diminished power resources, in turn provoking internal opposition. Such tensions came to a head during the current economic crisis, as we discuss below.

Italy also has a long history of peak-level tripartite bargaining: the concept of political exchange (*scambio politico*) derived from experience in the 1970s, when weak governments sought the support, or at least acquiescence, of the unions for unpopular social and economic restructuring and when CGIL, as part of the 'historic compromise' adopted by the PCI, was willing to participate in negotiated reforms. Here too, the process engendered tensions. Political exchange in the 1970s was based on consensus among the three main confederations, and in 1983 resulted in a formal tripartite agreement on anti-inflationary measures; but unity collapsed in the following year when the Communist majority in CGIL rejected a new agreement which substantially weakened the *scala mobile*, one of the major achievements of the previous decade.

A new era of formal social pacts began in the 1990s, when the post-war political order had collapsed and Italy faced mounting economic difficulties (Molina and Rhodes 2007; Regini and Regalia 1997). In 1992, after several years of inconclusive negotiations, it was agreed to abolish the *scala mobile* and impose a temporary freeze on company pay bargaining. In the face of sharp internal criticism, the CGIL leader, Bruno Trentin, symbolically offered his resignation. A more extensive pact was agreed the following year, in the run-up to EMU, involving more counter-inflationary restraints, the reform of the collective bargaining and workplace representation machinery, and the introduction of active labour market measures. An agreement on pensions reform in 1995 was 'a relative success for the unions' (Regini and Colombo 2011: 130). But a further pact in 1998 on social and regional reforms was followed by breakdown, as the employers' organization *Confindustria* adopted a tougher negotiating stance (Negrelli and Pulignano 2010). With the right-wing Berlusconi government in office for much of the period since 2001, the potential for negotiated policy diminished. CGIL refused to sign the 2002 'Pact for Italy', though under the brief centre-left government of 2006–8 it accepted the 2007 pact on welfare reforms; but after Berlusconi's re-election it again rejected the tripartite agreements signed by CISL and UIL, as we outline below.

Italian experience shows the complexity of sustaining a united trade union front (the same could be said for the employers), with CGIL in particular less willing than its two rivals to compromise on issues with high symbolic value, insisting that a number of established worker rights were non-negotiable (Carrieri 2003: 175). Part of the reason is that the union is itself riven by very public internal conflicts. In the case of the most sensitive concession, the abolition of the *scala mobile*, Regini and Colombo (2011: 127) cite the atmosphere of crisis; according to a leading union negotiator, 'had the CGIL not signed, the economic crisis would have further deepened and CGIL would have been held responsible'. Hence one benefit was blame avoidance. Conversely, the rationale of the two smaller confederations could be understood in part as wrong-footing CGIL and forcing it to take the blame in case of breakdown. To head off internal resistance, CGIL submitted subsequent contentious pacts to a membership referendum before final signature (Baccaro 2001).

In Ireland, formal three-year 'partnership' agreements were in force continuously from 1987 to 2009. Most traded wage restraint and constraints on company pay bargaining against tax cuts, preservation of transfer payments, and formal government commitments on social and welfare policy. The initial agreement was a response to economic crisis: a weak government wanted to avoid confrontation over the introduction of austerity measures. Opinion on the union side was sharply divided, but unemployment was over 17 per cent and many unions were concerned that nominal wage increases were being eroded by taxation. The government persuaded employers to agree a reduction in the working week; and there was also a widespread concern to avoid the type of confrontation with government which resulted in union defeat in

Britain (Baccaro and Lim 2007; O'Donnell et al. 2011; Roche 2007). Initially, social partnership appeared to bring real wage gains as the 'Celtic tiger' boom took off; but from the late 1990s, economic slowdown and the impact of the Maastricht convergence criteria meant that the benefits for most wage earners declined, while inequality increased rapidly (Hardiman 2005; O'Donnell et al. 2011; O'Donnell and O'Reardon 2000). Nevertheless, some argue that Irish unions still fared better under social partnership than their counterparts in other anglophone countries (Donaghey and Teague 2007).

After the narrow acceptance of the first pact, the unions approved subsequent agreements by more comfortable majorities, though always with some opposition; and after 2000 their renegotiation became more difficult and more protracted. In some respects, Irish trade unionism became locked into the social partnership system; according to Donaghey and Teague (2007: 39), the unions had gained 'an institutional veto' over labour market policy, and partnership had become 'the only game in town'. The institutionalization of partnership also inspired a shared discourse of competitiveness as the priority for a small open economy (Regan 2010); and critics failed to 'articulate a viable alternative' (O'Donnell et al. 2011: 113). For opponents, not only did peak-level partnership carry no complementary support for union organization at company level, but the constraints on workplace pay bargaining eroded existing power resources. Even a union leader who strongly supported the agreements told us that they were 'a lazy route to influence'; while another, more critical, said 'we were happy to sit back and negotiate tripartite three-year agreements which gave pay increases and other benefits in terms of legislation and tax concessions, but we didn't actually build our own organization capacity'.

For Visser and Rhodes (2011: 61), the social pacts of the 1990s were 'highly contingent and fragile constructions'. Their analysis stresses the complex triangular dynamics of inter- and intra-organizational bargaining; but gives no systematic comparative interpretation of the strategic choices of trade unions within this process. It seems evident that there were very different constellations of interests, perspectives, and power resources in each of the three countries discussed above. The balance has shifted in different ways with the current economic crisis, as we explore below.

Responses to Economic Crisis and Austerity: The Limits of Radicalism

The global economic crisis began with the collapse of the US housing bubble at the end of 2006 and escalated in 2007 into a banking crisis within a largely deregulated financial system, which had developed ever more complex speculative instruments. By the end of 2008, financial instability hit the 'real' economy, with a fall in demand, plant closures, and job losses. Meanwhile banks that were 'too big to fail' received massive government bailouts, creating a 'sovereign debt' crisis. The neoliberal recipe was austerity, with cuts in public expenditure, meaning public sector job losses and attacks on social benefits and public services: a policy which depressed demand and thus merely aggravated the problem.

Though Europe was severely affected by these interrelated crises, the impact varied considerably across countries, as Table 5.2 indicates. Of those in our study, Ireland—with its own US-style housing bubble and deregulated financial sector—was the first victim; the cost of rescuing failed banks more than doubled government debt between 2008 and 2010. In consequence, the government itself obtained a bailout in 2010 from the 'Troika' of the EU, European Central Bank, and IMF, at the price of a drastic austerity package which has prolonged the recession and caused increasingly high levels of unemployment. More generally, countries in the 'southern' and anglophone groups have fared worst. Sweden and the countries of the 'central' group have recovered fastest. Interestingly Germany, whose government lectures others on the need to reduce government debt, had one of the highest debt ratios at the outset of the crisis. Drastic austerity programmes have been far from universal, occurring either in exchange for rescue packages or because of the ideological proclivities of national governments (as in the UK). Since austerity is self-defeating, cross-national differences between winners and losers are likely to intensify (Weeks 2013).

Unions with depleted resources were not well placed to respond to the crisis. An official of *IG Metall* insisted (Guggemos 2009): 'nobody today can

Table 5.2. Dimensions of the crisis

	GDP growth (%)						Unemployment (%)					Government debt/ GDP ratio (%)		
	2006	2007	2008	2009	2010	2011	2008	2009	2010	2011	2012	2008	2010	2012
SE	4.3	3.3	−0.6	−5.0	6.6	3.9	6.2	8.3	8.4	7.5	7.8	38.8	39.4	37.2
DK	3.4	1.6	−0.8	−5.8	1.3	0.8	3.3	6.0	7.4	7.6	8.0	33.4	42.9	45.1
DE	3.7	3.3	1.1	−5.1	4.2	3.0	7.5	7.8	7.1	5.9	5.5	66.7	83.0	81.6
AT	3.7	3.7	1.4	−3.8	2.1	2.7	3.8	4.8	4.4	4.2	4.5	63.8	71.9	73.5
NL	3.4	3.9	1.8	−3.7	1.6	1.0	3.1	3.7	4.5	4.4	5.3	58.5	62.9	66.8
BE	2.7	2.9	1.0	−2.8	2.4	1.8	7.0	7.9	8.3	7.2	7.4	89.3	96.0	101.8
FR	2.5	2.3	−0.1	−3.1	1.7	1.7	7.8	9.5	9.7	9.7	10.6	68.2	82.3	89.2
IT	2.2	1.7	−1.2	−5.5	1.8	0.4	6.7	7.8	8.4	8.4	10.7	105.7	118.6	123.3
UK	2.6	3.6	−1.0	−4.0	1.8	0.8	5.6	7.6	7.8	8.0	8.0	54.8	79.6	86.4
IE	5.4	5.4	−2.1	−5.5	−0.8	1.4	6.3	11.9	13.7	14.4	15.0	44.2	92.5	108.5

Source: Eurostat.

claim to know all the answers to all the challenges of the crisis. We are simply learning from day to day.' In similar vein, a leader of the CFDT commented (Grignard 2009): 'it is clear that we were not prepared for this...We face the first systemic world crisis, for which we had no experience. We see a chain reaction...' There is evidence of both radical and conflictual responses, and of a reinforcement of cooperation and partnership. Often the two types of response have been paradoxically interconnected. Radical actions, whether national general strikes or company-level conflicts, have tended to be defensive in objectives. Conversely, efforts to seek consensual solutions through social dialogue have confronted an intensified opposition of class interests (who will pay for the crisis?) and a diminished space for positive-sum outcomes. As Dufour and Hege comment (2011: 546), 'the brief resurgence of the spirit of pacts during the economic and financial crisis of 2008–9 was succeeded by austerity plans which the unions fought'.

The slogan *Noi la crisi non la paghiamo!* (*we* are not paying for the crisis!) first appeared in Italy in the autumn of 2008, began to figure prominently in translation at demonstrations across Europe in the spring of 2009, and was adopted by many trade unions. It expressed a high degree of public anger: the 'fat cats' whose greed and recklessness caused the crisis were still protected, being bailed out with huge sums of public money, while ordinary workers were suffering job losses, pay cuts, and loss of pension rights, and would be expected to pay the long-term bill to redress public finances.

'There can be no return to business as usual': this was the unanimous trade union response to the crisis. Yet was the aim to negotiate with those wielding political and economic power for a tighter regulatory architecture for financialized capitalism, or to lead an oppositional movement for an alternative socio-economic order? Two familiar and intersecting contradictions of union action were evident. One was the dilemma of short-term imperatives versus long-term objectives. 'The situation really is not simple for trade union organizations,' a leader of the Belgian ABVV/FGTB told us in 2009. 'The analysis of the crisis is not complicated: neoliberalism cannot deliver. The difficulty is that today, discourse is not enough. It is easy to say: we need to change the balance of forces. But that does not tell us how to proceed: there are contradictions.' Referring to the crisis in the Belgian banks—one of which, Fortis, was partially sold to the French BNP Paribas with the remainder nationalized—he added that 'we have 25,000 members whose jobs are at risk. Do we just say: let Fortis go bankrupt? Our members expect us to look after their immediate interests.' The leader of FIOM, the CGIL metalworkers' union, made a rather similar point. 'Right now it is difficult to discuss strategy, insofar as we are bound to react to situations of crisis...The absolute priority is to be a force for collective initiative, to counter tendencies to individualization and despair.' He added—demonstrating a more strategic reaction—that 'as the first priority we have demanded an end to dismissals, then the application of every means of income maintenance, after which we can develop general analyses of industrial reconversion'.

The second contradiction was between a global economic crisis and trade union action that is essentially national or indeed sub-national in character. The international trade union organizations produced powerful analyses and progressive demands, but their impact on day-to-day trade union practice was non-existent. Indeed, the dominant response was to defend and enhance competitiveness, meaning a struggle of country against country, workplace against workplace, intensifying the downwards pressure on wages and conditions.

The crisis provoked a variety of conflictual responses at workplace level, including a spate of sit-ins against job cuts and plant closures, reminiscent of the struggles of the 1970s. In France this was given distinctive character in the spring of 2009 with a number of episodes of 'boss-napping', when senior managers were held hostage by workers; in three cases, workers threatened to blow up their factories with gas cylinders. Undoubtedly the most publicized British dispute against job losses began in 2009 at the Lindsey oil refinery in Lincolnshire, owned by the French multinational Total. The company subcontracted a construction project to an Italian firm employing only foreign labour—displacing existing workers—on terms inferior to those specified in the British collective agreement for the sector. An unofficial strike quickly escalated, with sympathy action across the country. (We refer to this again in Chapter 7.) Yet radical forms of action did not imply similar radicalism of objectives. In most cases, such workplace struggles seemed gestures of defiance and despair, with little belief that they would prevent announced closures or job losses. Rather, the aim was commonly to limit the number of dismissals or to achieve improved redundancy packages. For this reason, such disputes were usually relatively easy to resolve. 'When you are preoccupied with survival, how you are going to eat tomorrow, that does not necessarily make you militant,' a CGT official told us in 2009, adding that many workers would rather take the redundancy pay than fight to retain their jobs.

In a survey of responses to the crisis, Glassner and Galgóczi (2009) found widespread agreements on 'partial unemployment' or short-time working—though they noted (2009b: 10) that in the banking sector 'many believe that the current crisis is often being used by employers as a pretext for laying off staff sooner than originally planned'. Such agreements were often buttressed by partial pay compensation from public funds as well as by company negotiations to enhance compensation above statutory levels. Some such schemes led to inter-union conflicts, notably in countries where white-collar workers enjoy stronger statutory protections than manual workers. In Germany too, though more systematic job-saving measures were pursued, in many companies (often with at least tacit union approval) the protection of the 'core' workforce was at the expense of temporary workers (Lehndorff 2012: 89; Urban 2012: 230); the same occurred in Austria (Hermann and Flecker 2012: 125). In Denmark, badly affected by the crisis, numerous company agreements provided for work sharing (Lallement 2011: 634). The Dutch government subsidized short-time working and temporary lay-offs for firms in difficulties; while in Belgium, a substantial recovery package included funding for 'technical unemployment' and special provisions for short-time working and temporary lay-offs. In France too, the government funded a programme of 'partial unemployment' (*chômage partiel*); nevertheless, temporary workers bore the brunt of the crisis (Jany-Catrice and Lallement 2012); a CFDT official told us it was a major challenge to persuade permanent workers of the need for solidarity. In Italy, a long-established system of lay-off pay (*cassa integrazione guadagni*) was widely used to cushion job losses (Simonazzi 2012). One possible counter-example is Sweden, where work sharing and temporary lay-offs have not traditionally been adopted; in consequence there was a sharp decline in employment, particularly of temporary and agency workers, and unemployment among young workers remains very high, as Table 2.1 indicated (Anxo 2012: 35); however, Rychly (2009: 19) refers to a national agreement in manufacturing permitting short-time working.

Another demand pursued successfully in some countries, primarily at company level, was for temporary periods of slack demand to be used for vocational (re)training rather than resorting to lay-offs. Again, this was facilitated in some countries by state subsidies: Rychly (2009: 20) cites examples from France and Italy.

One outcome of the crisis was a widespread reinforcement of wage moderation, with employers in some cases pressing for downwards renegotiation of existing pay agreements. This was particularly notable in France: in 2009, over 80 per cent of workers were subject to nominal pay freezes, and in some cases reductions (Vandekerckhove et al. 2012: 6); much more generally, pay increases were below the rate of inflation. Negotiations over restructuring and job reductions, with the aim of agreeing some form of 'social plan', were common across our countries. Haipeter and Lehndorff (2009: 27) amplify this analysis, with particular reference to Germany, and focus on 'deviant collective bargaining agreements' at company level which 'are increasingly becoming instruments allowing for unspecified or restricted undercutting of standards agreed at industry or national levels'. Typically these involved a local trade-off in which job losses were avoided or postponed in exchange for concessions on pay or work organization.

In some cases they note what they term 'forced voluntary redundancies' (2009a: 5)—for example eliminating transport services provided for long-distance commuters, and then offering supplementary payments to those who resigned their jobs. In her seven-country analysis of responses to the crisis in the banking sector, Glassner (2009) likewise identifies a diverse range of trade union action, often reflecting a combination of collective mobilization and negotiation and dialogue.

At national level, there has also been a complex mix of confrontation and accommodation. General strikes were threatened in protest against government responses (or lack of response) to the crisis in a number of countries. In some, as in Ireland, threats were a pressure tactic not ultimately activated. Actual general strikes mainly involved the 'usual suspects' with a history of such action, notably France and Italy (and, of course, Greece and Spain) (Hamann et al. 2013). Other protest action was essentially demonstrative. The ETUC convened European Action Days in May 2009, with four Euro-demonstrations in Madrid, Brussels, Berlin, and Prague. It should be noted that for European trade unions, reactions to the economic crisis coincided with growing anger at the implications of recent ECJ decisions that ruled that market freedoms have priority over the protection of decent work by national law or collective agreement, discussed in Chapter 7. Yet the tide of mass protests across Europe subsided rather rapidly.

Even in parallel with symbolic protest action, unions in most countries endeavoured to manage the crisis through peak-level social dialogue: what Urban (2012) has called 'crisis corporatism'. In some countries, however, there were no serious efforts to obtain tripartite agreement on responses to the crisis; in others, such efforts failed, or provoked serious divisions among the parties involved. Even in countries with a tradition of national pacts, the crisis thus made peak-level dialogue very difficult. Since government action underlay national responses to the crisis, macro-dialogue was inevitably tripartite rather than bipartite. The outcome typically involved ad hoc, narrowly focused agreements—if any.

A key initiative in many countries was the relaxation of rules governing short-time working, often linked to government funding for short-time work schemes as an alternative to redundancy so that loss of wages would be minimized. For example, in Austria a tripartite agreement in 2009 provided for a 90 per cent replacement rate for hours not worked (Allinger and Hermann 2011; Hermann and Flecker 2012). A notable German response in 2009 was a joint union–employer approach to the government which led to temporary subsidies for scrapping old motor vehicles (*Abwrackprämie*) when replaced by less-polluting models; this boosted demand and helped prevent redundancies (Dribbusch 2012).

However, on broader issues of pay policy and restructuring of pensions and other social benefits the process of peak-level bargaining became fraught, with a breakdown of negotiations in some countries and in others serious inter-union divisions. Initially, Belgium seemed a relative success story. The two-yearly national pay negotiations for 2009–10 were tense, with a 'day of action' (described by the ABVV/FGTB as a general strike) in October 2008; but government mediation resulted in an 'exceptional' agreement at the end of December, given legal backing in March 2009. The unions, which complained that purchasing power had fallen substantially, agreed to a limited pay rise weighted towards the lowest paid, and to 'soft' increases (such as luncheon vouchers and travel subsidies) which added little to employers' labour costs; benefits for the unemployed and pensions were increased, while employers' taxes were reduced. There was significant opposition to the terms in all three confederations. A further agreement provided for the payment of 'eco-cheques' which workers could spend on ecological products; while in April 2009 there was a tripartite agreement on crisis measures for white-collar workers.

The following round of peak-level negotiations was even more difficult. A draft agreement provided for real wage increases of only 0.3 per cent over two years, and for measures to harmonize the employment status of manual and white-collar workers that involved some losses for both. After internal consultations the draft was accepted by two to one in the ACV/CSC but rejected by three to one by the Socialist union and by a narrow majority by the liberals; the terms were then applied by legislation. Subsequently, after almost two years without a government, a new administration took office at the end of 2011 and initiated a major austerity programme, including cuts in social benefits and a two-year increase in the retirement age. All three confederations participated in a public sector strike in December 2011 and a general strike in January 2012. Further conflict was heralded by a National Bank report which criticized the Belgium indexation system for determining increases in wages and benefits. All three unions objected strongly.

In the Netherlands, despite fundamental differences there was agreement on a crisis package in May 2009; this involved wage moderation in exchange for some measures to tackle unemployment. Government proposals to increase the retirement age were strenuously opposed by the FNV, and unions and employers were given six months to negotiate an alternative pensions plan. Shortly before the deadline the employers broke off talks and FNV organized a series of mass protests and strike actions. Compromise proposals for a phased increase in the retirement age were endorsed by the CNV (the minister of labour, a Christian democrat, was a former member of its advisory board) and MHP but not FNV. Visser and van der Meer have commented (2011: 208–9) that 'there is one unwritten rule, *unanimity*... Neither employers nor governments have ever contemplated an agreement or pact without the FNV, even when that organization appears isolated.' It was evident that this rule would be breached, and in June 2011 the agreement was signed by the FNV president and subsequently endorsed by a majority of the executive.

As we have explained in previous chapters, the two largest affiliates, with the majority of the membership, were strongly opposed and the result was to tear the FNV apart.

In France, internal divisions among the unions weakened their capacity to influence government responses to the crisis. Since the onset they mobilized a series of national strikes and demonstrations to call for more effective job-saving initiatives and to oppose a range of austerity measures; in many cases all the main unions participated, but often with evident differences of perspective. Proposals to raise the retirement age and to end the statutory thirty-five-hour working week provoked several such actions in 2008; one of the largest national days of action for many years took place in early 2009, demanding measures to save jobs and increase minimum pay; there were national strikes against changes to pensions in autumn 2010; and another mass protest against austerity at the end of 2011.

However, unions such as the CFDT were more anxious to seek negotiated solutions. Freyssinet (2011) has documented an 'intense renewal of peak-level bargaining', with a series of agreements on social benefits and labour market policy since 2006, including eight in 2011 alone; but almost all were rejected by the CGT. The change of government in 2012 was followed by a *grande conférence sociale*; initial union reactions were positive, but it is unclear whether the changed political context will result in more consensual policy outcomes.

In Italy, likewise, the initiatives of the Berlusconi government split the unions. As we saw above, most previous pacts—typically negotiated under centre-left or 'technocratic' governments—provoked internal opposition within CGIL in particular. In May 2008, just after Berlusconi's return to office, all three confederations agreed a joint platform (though FIOM, which headed the internal opposition in CGIL, was against). But in January 2009, in a break with precedent, a pact was implemented which was signed by CISL and UIL but not CGIL; this revised the collective bargaining system, devolving more responsibilities to the company level, extended the duration of sectoral wage agreements to three years, and included a new (and more limited) inflation index as a guideline for pay negotiations. CGIL held a referendum (boycotted by CISL and UIL), and called a general strike soon afterwards, partly in opposition to the agreement and partly in protest at the inadequate government response to the economic crisis. CGIL also opposed an agreement for central government workers in the same month, and organized strikes and sit-ins against public sector job cuts. A year later, CGIL called another general strike.

In practice, however, the three confederations maintained a united front in most sectoral negotiations—though not, most notably, in metalworking; here, CISL and UIL alone signed an agreement, in line with the new bargaining rules. A more moderate position was signalled at the CGIL congress in May 2010, when FIOM was largely isolated; this was confirmed with the election of Susanna Camusso as general secretary, despite FIOM opposition. In October 2010, all three confederations agreed a list of common objectives in response to the economic crisis. Then in June 2011 they agreed new rules on bargaining and representativeness, amending the 2009 agreement along lines more palatable to CGIL. The three unions also presented a common front against the liberalization of labour law pushed by the new 'technocratic' Monti government in the spring of 2012, though this unity was strained at a number of points, and CGIL backed down from a threatened general strike.

In Ireland, there was record union support for the November 2008 'Transitional Agreement' which amplified the partnership pact of 2006, providing for a 6 per cent pay increase over twenty-one months. But the subsequent government crisis package resulted in a breakdown, particularly over its imposition of a 'pension levy' which involved in effect a cut in public sector pay, and allegations that it was allowing employers to renege on the pay increases. The problem of public finances was particularly serious in Ireland because of the low-tax regime which two decades of social partnership had reinforced; the government thus endeavoured to blame wage costs in the public sector, and the role of public sector unions, for the economic crisis (Regan 2012: 484). The ICTU attempted to maintain a united front, issuing in February 2009 a ten-point plan (entitled *A Better, Fairer Way*) designed to meet the interests of both public and private sector workers. This was followed by a 'day of protest'—the biggest mass demonstration in Ireland for thirty years; but the ITUC general secretary assured us that 'there isn't as such a crisis in the social partnership system, it's just that we can't agree'. A general strike was threatened but was called off pending further talks.

In late 2009 a new phase of confrontation began, and the partnership agreement was suspended (O'Donnell et al. 2011: 117). However, in June 2010 the conflict in the public sector was temporarily resolved though the Croke Park Agreement, in which the government agreed not to impose compulsory redundancies or further pay cuts, while the unions agreed to abandon strike action and to cooperate in public sector reforms. A further financial crisis at the end of the year forced the government to apply for a bailout from the EU. To meet the cost-saving conditions it announced a substantial cut in the minimum wage and an increase in VAT, and the ICTU responded with another mass protest demonstration in November 2010. In February 2011 a new government was elected, with Labour as a junior partner; it partially improved the industrial relations climate by restoring the minimum wage to its previous level. The government also suggested re-establishing a more modest version of partnership under the label 'social dialogue'.

In the absence of peak-level dialogue in Britain, responses to the crisis have been particularly tense. The right-wing government elected in May 2010 made debt reduction a political mantra. As Table 5.2 indicates, the debt ratio was actually lower than in Germany, whose government preached austerity for others but did not practise it at home. In consequence, UK debt actually increased after two years of austerity while that in Germany fell. The government programme involved some half million public sector job cuts, a pay freeze, and major reductions in public sector pensions, as well as massive inroads into welfare spending (Grimshaw and Rubery 2012). Identifying a general problem for unions facing public service cutbacks and restructuring, Schelkle (2011: 310) has written that 'public opinion has not, on the whole, been favourable to strike action since this can be portrayed as openly fighting for privileges. Hence, trade unions have had to tread carefully when seen as political actors, even in underpaid public sectors.' TUC leaders were well aware of the risks, particularly given experience in Ireland. On the basis of a large-scale opinion survey they launched an extended campaign of argument and protest, under the titles *All Together for Public Services* and *A Future that Works*. A massive national day of action was organized in March 2011, and another in October 2012. Some affiliates, such as the civil service union PCS and the general union Unite, favoured a far more militant response, and a number of one-day public sector strikes took place. The TUC congress in September 2012 adopted a tougher position, pledging support for coordinated strike action by public sector workers and calling for assessment of the 'practicalities of a general strike'—the first time this was officially contemplated since the 1920s. At the time of writing, the outcome is far from clear.

Conclusions

In this chapter we have surveyed the different trade union approaches to collective bargaining, including the (limited) development of innovative approaches, and have examined the trend towards 'competitive corporatism' at both company and national levels. We then considered the impact of the economic crisis, which has strengthened the pressures towards concession bargaining but has also provoked new forms of conflict at times; crisis has also created 'growing interest cleavages' (Brandl and Traxler 2011: 15). Finally, we have discussed the challenges resulting from government austerity measures. The results have been complex and contradictory, but all these developments have exposed the limits of trade unionism centred primarily on 'free collective bargaining'. As we explore in the final chapters, these limits have impelled many unions to seek broader social, political, and also international forms of intervention.

6

Unions and Politics: Parties, Alliances, and the Battle of Ideas

In this chapter we focus on trade unions' role in politics, and their relationships with governments and political parties. Unions are not merely economic (or 'industrial relations') actors: they are necessarily protagonists in the political arena. Regulating the labour market is a question of political resources. Historically, most unions in the countries we examine have had close (and sometimes formal) links with specific parties with a shared ideological heritage—Social democratic, Christian democratic, or Communist—but these political identities have almost universally weakened. The relationship has also become strained as allied parties, reluctantly or otherwise, have implemented market- and employer-friendly policies that challenge trade union aims and interests.

Politics concerns not only relations with governments and party-political affiliations. In Chapter 2 we argued that with the erosion of many of their conventional power resources, unions are obliged to seek new forms. One of these we termed 'collaborative': if unions' own capacities diminish, they need to pool their resources with allies. Forming alliances is itself a complex political process, as we explore below.

We also referred to 'moral' power resources. It is widely accepted that trade unions require a coherent social vision if they are to win members, inspire the activists on whom much of their work depends, and sustain their societal legitimacy. They need to be seen as a 'sword of justice' rather than a 'vested interest'. In many countries, unions have seemingly lost such a vision, with the exhaustion of all three main ideological traditions within which most were founded, and as neoliberal ideas have become almost hegemonic. However, there have been serious attempts by unions to reposition themselves as bearers of an alternative to the market liberalism which is widely seen as the cause of the current crisis. We discuss how unions have attempted to recreate a sense of purpose which they can convey to a wider public.

Why politics?

In most of Europe it is taken for granted that trade unions are political actors. This is not universally accepted, however: Perlman (1928) famously insisted that trade unions adopted political programmes only under the malign influence of (mainly Socialist) intellectuals. For many American writers on trade unionism in the 1950s and 1960s, strong political engagement was an index of 'immaturity' which would become marginalized with a shift to collective bargaining. And within European trade unions today, many members criticize their organizations' political attachments, and some workers cite these as a reason for non-membership.

What then is the rationale for engagement in the political arena? Taylor (1989: xiv) insists succinctly 'that unions are inevitably *political*, whether they or politicians like it; that within capitalist industrial states they are relatively *powerless*; and that unions are primarily *reactive* and *defensive* in their political behaviour'. As one of us has written (Hyman 2001: 13–15): 'regulating the labour market involves political issues...The state is not only the ultimate guarantor of contracts, including employment contracts; whether by active intervention or by default, it underwrites a particular (im)balance between different participants in market relations. At a very minimum, unions have to influence the ways in which the state shapes the rules of the game in the labour market, including their own right to exist, to bargain collectively and to mobilize collective action.' Following the Keynesian transformation of economic theory and economic policy, unions universally recognize that the parameters of supply and demand, and hence the whole terrain of collective bargaining, are subject to the influence of government intervention. Workers, moreover, are not simply concerned with their nominal wages or salaries: their interest extends to the real wage, taking account of price movements; the net wage after taxation; and the 'social wage' constituted by transfers and services provided by the welfare state. In countries with institutions and traditions of peak-level tripartite bargaining, all of these elements are part of a composite agenda involving complex trade-offs—'political exchange', as we discussed in the previous chapter—and even in the absence of these institutional arrangements, unions everywhere attempt to influence welfare and taxation policies. Finally, unions which represent public sector employees—who today, almost universally, comprise the majority of members—must inevitably address the policies of the state.

Unions Between the Industrial Relations and Political Arenas

In most European countries, 'political action is used in varying degrees and forms, partly as a substitute but more generally as a complement...to economic bargaining' (Cella and Treu 2001: 456). Unions that define their function primarily in terms of negotiation with employers are still 'compelled to seek ways of influencing public policy' (Sturmthal 1972: 45). Yet if unions are inescapably both economic and political actors, the relationship between the two roles is complex and contradictory, and the priority assigned to each varies across countries and over time. Four factors seem of particular importance in explaining these distinctive patterns: ideology, power resources, opportunity structures, and contextual challenges.

In many European countries, trade unionism was an offshoot of an emergent working-class movement in which political radicalism aiming at systemic transformation shaped unions' identity and action. Unions were 'schools of war', as Engels put it: their task was to challenge capitalism, not to seek modest reforms within it. Where more moderate, Social- or Christian-democratic trade unionism prevailed (or displaced earlier, more radical forms), the focus was still on societal change, alongside the more prosaic functions of collective bargaining. Ideologies inherited from the formative period of trade unions have proved persistent, shaping identities that do not easily change (Hyman 2001). This has been most evident in the reorientation of (former) Communist unions in southern Europe: the increased priority assigned to collective bargaining in the Italian CGIL from the 1970s, and much more recently in the CGT in France, has in each case provoked substantial resistance from 'traditionalists' (who have often accused the leadership of betraying the principles on which their unions were founded).

Power resources clearly shape trade union politics. In order to give priority to collective bargaining, at least if their membership is in the private sector, unions typically require relatively high membership density (associational and organizational power) and the financial resources to sustain prolonged disputes where necessary. If such resources are modest, mobilization on the streets may be easier to conduct than sustained strike action—which (as we discussed in the previous chapter) is a component of bargaining power, even if not its only source. As an extreme example, the fragmented French trade unions with minimal density in the private sector have virtually lost the capacity to organize strikes there; while public sector strikes have been facilitated by the tendency (now diminishing) of public employers to agree settlements whereby strikers do not lose pay for lost time. Clearly there can be a self-sustaining elective affinity between trade unions' ideological orientations and their organizational capacities.

The persistence of political self-definitions has a material basis. In part this reflects opportunity structures. In most countries, early trade unions were subject to systematic repression, and the state was inevitably a target for collective action. Only when the legal status of union activity was secured could 'free collective bargaining' become a priority. And where employers remained resolutely opposed to union recognition, unions in turn still saw pressure on the state as an effective option to resolve their grievances. This was the classic argument of Shorter and Tilly (1974) in explaining the highly politicized character of French industrial relations: a pattern which seems more generally applicable across southern Europe. Conversely, 'business unionism' can also be considered an outcome of distinctive opportunity structures. In countries (including most of those in western Europe) where the state was from the outset an overt protagonist in the shaping of a market economy (Crouch 1993), the political dimension of labour market intervention was self-evident. Conversely, in countries where the emergence of capitalism was less dependent on active state initiative, and where the political system made alternative forms of regulation difficult to achieve, unions might conclude that there was no practicable option but to play the market as it currently existed. This was certainly Perlman's argument regarding the USA (1928: 196–7): 'American governments are inherently inadequate as instruments of economic reform [and] it is to this situation, more than to anything else, that the stubborn "economism" of the American Federation of Labor must be traced.'

Historical contingency shapes the objective challenges confronting trade unions and the appropriateness of different strategies. For example, Daley (1992) described how American steelworkers, confronted by restructuring and the threat of plant closure, responded by attempting to mobilize their traditional industrial strength. But strike action is ineffectual in preventing closures, since the employer no longer requires the workers' labour power. By contrast French unions, because of their organizational weakness, pursued political pressure and struggle, achieving greater success in saving jobs. In the past two decades of drastic structural changes in employment, reduced industrial strength through membership losses, and the pressures of intensified product market competition, unions that traditionally relied substantially on economic strength have often sought alternative forms of action. One notable example, discussed further below, is the conversion of German trade unions to the goal of a statutory minimum wage. The opening up of the German labour market through EU enlargement, and the rapid growth of a sector covered neither by collective bargaining nor by works councils, demonstrated that unions' purely economic strength had eroded and required political-institutional reinforcement.

In Europe as a whole, the economic crisis of 2007–9 made the state a key interlocutor, as we saw in the previous chapter, even in countries in which trade unions traditionally drew a line between 'economic' and 'political' action. Financial assistance to struggling employers, special subsidies to sustain income in cases of short-time working, and extensions to active labour market policies—all widespread trade union demands—necessarily required engagement in the political arena. Conversely, government attempts to tackle unprecedented budget deficits through attacks on public sector jobs, pay, and pensions, and more general assaults on the welfare state, have involved even reluctant unions in sharp political conflicts.

Trade Unions and Political Parties

For Ebbinghaus (1995), trade unions and their allied parties are 'Siamese twins', mutually dependent organizations (which in the view of some observers should be separated for their mutual good). There have been many attempts to classify their interrelationship. For example, Hayward (1980: 5–6) identifies four types: first, a 'Leninist model' in which the party seeks to control the policies and actions of its associated union; second, more exceptionally, the British case in which the unions themselves created the Labour Party and saw their task initially as to dictate its policies; third, a more general Social-democratic pattern involving 'interdependence and symbiosis'; finally, a position in which unions, even if politically engaged, refuse any alliance with political parties. It should be added that while most writers have focused on union links with Social-democratic or Communist parties, in several countries the relationship between Christian-democratic unions and parties has been of great importance.

Ebbinghaus (1995) identifies all four models as outcomes of the fundamental cleavage between labour and capital, but stresses two other cleavages. Where there was historically a sharp confrontation between church and state, divisions between secular (commonly Socialist) and religious identities resulted in an ideological segmentation of unions and parties competing for working-class allegiance. These divisions were in turn often fertile ground for a third cleavage, between reformist and revolutionary unions and parties. Notably in southern Europe, the resulting fragmentation of the labour movement was a source of organizational weakness and reinforced the bias towards political protest rather than bargaining.

Though orientations and relationships can often be traced back to the sequencing of industrialization and the struggle for democracy, they are not immutable, and below we explore how recent changes in opportunity structures and objective challenges have affected party–union relationships. It is notable that almost universally, relationships of intimate mutual dependence have over time given way to looser attachments and sometimes to complete divorce. Historical examples include the rejection by German unions of SPD hegemony at the start of the 20th century; later, in several countries the growing autonomy of Christian trade unions from church or party control; finally, the detachment of Communist-oriented unions from their parent parties, spearheaded in the early 1970s in Italy when the CGIL (seeking unity with the two rival confederations) agreed the principle of *incompatibilità*—that its leaders could no longer participate simultaneously in the ruling bodies of the party. But formal differentiation may still permit close informal interlinkages.

Three key developments in the past few decades have affected all our countries, though to differing degrees. The first is cultural and ideological: unions have been subject to 'ideological blurring' (Pasture 1996: 380). Secularization has undermined the identities of formerly Christian-democratic unionism (Pasture 1994): the only significant exceptions in our ten countries are the Belgian ACV/CSC and the much smaller Dutch CNV. A parallel process of deconfessionalization has turned most Christian-democratic parties—even if their titles are unchanged—into conventional centre-right political actors, while others have dwindled into insignificance (again, the Benelux countries are obvious exceptions). In the extreme Italian case, the *Democristiani*, who dominated national politics for almost half a century, imploded in the 1990s. Hence Christian democracy as a nexus between unions and party has all but disappeared. An analogous process occurred in countries with mass Communist parties and satellite trade unions. In France, electoral support for the PCF fell below 2 per cent in the 2007 presidential election; in 2012 it campaigned under the umbrella of the *Front de gauche* rather than independently. In Italy, the PCI disbanded in 1991 and after several changes of identity is now the dominant component of the *Partito democratico* (PD), which no longer defines itself even as Socialist (though its representatives in the European Parliament sit with the Socialist group). The left minority of the PCI who formed *Rifondazione comunista* retained significant support until the disastrous elections of 2008. In effect, both ex-Christian and ex-Communist unions have embraced forms of Social democracy; but in a post-Keynesian world, it is no longer clear what Social democracy stands for. Hence there is a 'crisis of social-democratic trade unionism' (Upchurch et al. 2009), resulting in ideological disorientation which constitutes a major theme of our discussion below: the crisis of Social democracy is inseparable from the crisis of European trade unionism.

The second key development is structural. Traditionally, both trade unions and left-oriented parties found their core support among manual workers in cohesive industrial communities. The decline of old manufacturing and extractive industries, the growth in white-collar and professional occupations and, more generally, rising educational levels have posed challenges for both unions and parties. As we have seen, many union movements have had difficulties recruiting these expanding occupational groups (at least in the private sector); where they succeed, this dilutes the homogeneity of interests and identities within the membership. In the Nordic countries, where separate confederations cover white-collar occupations and graduate professions, these insist on political neutrality (even though their leaders are typically Social democrats). Many observers see structural and ideological shifts as mutually reinforcing, causing the erosion of membership support for any political project, let alone a specifically Socialist one. Social-democratic parties for their part have tended to take their dwindling working-class base for granted while targeting the 'median voter', resulting in a policy convergence with their opponents to the right.

The third key change is the advance of neoliberalism. The pursuit of international competitiveness, efforts to contain public finances, loss of faith in Keynesianism, and conversion to 'lean government' have become as much the hallmarks of centre-left as of right-wing governments (Moses 1994; Notermans 1993). Neoliberal restructuring places inevitable pressures on the party–union nexus: electoral expediency, or simply the limited room for manœuvre in the management of national economies within global economic disorder, places Social-democratic parties on a collision course with union movements whose own commitments include the defence of workers' incomes and the social achievements of past decades (Piazza 2001). Little is left of a Social-democratic 'project' to inspire either parties or unions and to bind them together.

If the historical ties between unions and parties have lost most of their material and ideological foundations, little but inertia can sustain them. It is unsurprising therefore that they have proved fragile. There is no uniform process of distancing or divorce but evident cross-national variation. We survey some of these below. First, though, it is useful to provide a simple map of the variable geometry of left parties' electoral success (or failure) in our ten countries. Table 6.1 shows the widespread decline in Social-democratic representation, and also rising support for alternative left and/or green parties in a number of countries. Notably, in France, Germany (almost), and the Netherlands the combined representation of these two groups in the 2009 European elections equalled or exceeded that of the Socialists or Social democrats (though given the low turnout and the opportunity for protest voting, these results are an imperfect indicator of popular opinion). Even more notably, in the German parliamentary elections of 2009, under a quarter of trade union members in the east voted for the SPD while a third supported *die Linke*; in Germany as a whole, the Left and the Greens combined scored virtually the same as the SPD. In many other countries, right-wing nationalist parties have attracted considerable backing from working-class voters.

In both Nordic countries there was for many years a particularly close institutional linkage between Social democracy and the dominant manual trade union confederations. In Sweden, the relationship with the SAP came under strain in the 1970s, as the party increasingly adopted economic policies that clashed with LO interests. In part, this distancing reflected party efforts to attract non-manual voters affiliated to the expanding minority union confederations. The proportion of LO members voting and supporting the SAP

Table 6.1. 'Left' seats in most recent national[1] and European[2] elections

Country	Year	Seats available		Social Democrats[3]		Other left[3]		Greens[3]	
SE	2010	349	(18)	112	(5)	19	(1)	25	(3)
DK	2011	179	(13)	44	(4)	28[4]	(1)	4	(1)
DE	2009	622	(99)	146	(23)	76	(8)	68	(14)
AT	2008	183	(17)	57	(4)			20	(2)
NL	2012	150	(25)	38	(3)	15	(2)	6	(3)
BE	2010	150	(22)	30	(5)			13	(4)
FR	2012	577	(72)	280	(14)	14	(4)	18	(14)
IT	2013[5]	617	(72)	292	(21)	48[6]		6	
UK	2010	650	(72)	258	(13)	6[7]	(1)[7]	1	(2)
IE	2011	166	(12)	37	(3)	5[8]	(1)		

[1] National elections: lower house only. Source: *Election Resources on the Internet*, http://electionresources.org/.
[2] 2009 European Parliament election (in parentheses). Source: *Results of the 2009 European Elections*, http://www.europarl.europa.eu/parliament/archive/elections2009/en/new_parliament_en.html.
[3] All these categories are inevitably somewhat arbitrary: for example, neither the Italian PD nor the British Labour Party labels itself as Social democratic; the boundaries of 'other left' parties are imprecise; the Green/EFA group in the European Parliament includes representatives of regionalist parties which are neither environmentalists nor left oriented, and other parties which we have categorized as 'left' in national elections.
[4] The Red–Green Alliance (*Enhedslisten*) won 12 seats, here listed as 'Other left'.
[5] February election: another election anticipated before the end of the year. Note the Italian election law providing an automatic addition to the seats of the largest party bloc; the left bloc actually gained 29.5% of the popular vote.
[6] Includes the Green–Left alliance (*Sinistra ecologia e libertà*).
[7] Including the Welsh nationalist *Plaid Cymru*. In addition, the Irish nationalist *Sinn Féin*—which is on the left in terms of labour policies—won 5 seats in the national elections and 1 European seat.
[8] In addition, *Sinn Féin* won 14 seats.

fell from 65–70 per cent in the 1980s to 50 per cent in the 1990s, while in 1998 some 20 per cent backed the *Vänsterparti* (Left Party) (Bengtsson 2008: 11). LO ended its collective membership of the SAP in 1987, though local union branches can still affiliate, and the confederation still nominates a member to the party's executive. Since the election of a strongly right-wing government in 2006, which has clashed with the unions over cuts in welfare provision, relations between LO and the party have somewhat improved.

In Denmark there was historically a similarly intimate relationship between LO and the *Socialdemokraterne*, with each organization represented on the other's executive committee; but surveys in the 1990s showed that these links were unpopular amongst the membership, and were cited as one reason why many had joined the 'yellow' *KriFa* (Bild et al. 1998: 203). A union leader told us that the formal link to the party had cost members: 'you can't keep your members if you try to make them Social democratic against their will'. As in Sweden, LO agreed to sever the ties, in 2003, although many individual unions remain affiliated. Given the high union density in Denmark, the right-wing government in office from 2001 to 2011 seemed keen to win trade union assent for its social and labour market policies—ironically, perhaps more so than the *Socialdemokraterne*. This created a certain dilemma for union leaders, evident in other countries also: in negotiating a policy consensus they can moderate attacks on members' conditions but thereby add legitimacy to a politically uncongenial government.

In the 'central' group of countries there is a long tradition of both Social- and Christian-democratic trade unionism; in three cases (though only exceptionally in Germany) coalition governments involving both Social- and Christian-democratic parties are the norm. In both Germany and Austria, the post-war reconstruction of the trade union movement transcended former ideological divisions. In the German case, this involved formal party-political neutrality. Most union leaders have always been Social democrats (though Frank Bsirske, president of *ver.di*, is a member of the Greens).

By convention a minority of seats on executive bodies has been reserved for Christian democrats, who have their own organized fraction, the *Christlich-Demokratische Arbeitnehmerschaft* (CDA). This was important in maintaining relatively labour-friendly policies in the conservative *Christlich Demokratische Union* (CDU); the minister of labour throughout the sixteen years of the Kohl government (1982–98), Norbert Blüm, was a leader of the CDA and a member of *IG Metall*. Its influence in both the party and the unions has, however, declined; indeed, it is not represented on the current *IG Metall* executive. Traditionally most SPD parliamentarians, and a significant minority of the CDU, have been trade union members; but the proportions have fallen over time, and today many politicians hold union membership primarily because it 'looks good on their CV' (Hönigsberger 2008: 172). The predominant union backing for the SPD—on occasion a source of sharp criticism from CDA members—has been subject to three related challenges in recent years. First, the traditional manual worker core constituency of both unions and SPD declined not only in numerical importance but also in party loyalty, particularly under the red–green government of 1998–2005 (Schroeder 2007: 5). Second, that government's *Agenda 2010* reforms provoked sharp conflict with the unions as well as internal disarray within the party. Third, rivals to the left have gained ground at the expense of the SPD; and a number of regional union officials support *die Linke* (Deppe 2012: 78–9; Seibring 2010).

In Austria, political pluralism within the ÖGB connects to a semi-official structure of fractions, represented in leadership positions in relation to membership support (as reflected by votes for their separate lists in works council elections). The SPÖ traditionally attracts about two-thirds of the votes in these elections, followed by the Christian-democratic ÖVP and a series of smaller lists. Even more clearly than in Germany, this ensures that there is a strong trade union presence within the governing party or parties. In a country with an exceptional tradition of institutionalized 'social partnership', top union leaders are commonly also members of parliament and hold seats on the executive committees of their parties—in almost all cases the

SPÖ, though the head of the public sector *Gewerkschaft Öffentlicher Dienst* is a key figure in the ÖVP. The then ÖGB president, Rudolf Hundstorfer, was appointed minister of labour in the new SPÖ-led government in 2008. However, many see the degree of union–party intimacy as excessive. In an era of austerity, governments increasingly pursue unpopular policies, and 'the ÖGB as active participant in the workings of the Austrian state has had to endorse and defend policies that not always directly benefit its membership and has found itself on occasion out of step with its membership and fellow citizens' (Suschnigg 1998: 348). Disenchantment with the establishment politics of social partnership and the SPÖ/ÖVP has contributed to the electoral rise of the far right—which in the 2008 elections gained almost 30 per cent of the popular vote, more than the ÖVP and almost the same as the SPÖ. In 2008 the executives of both SPÖ and ÖGB agreed that it should no longer be possible to hold leadership posts in both.

As we saw in Chapter 1, Dutch trade unionism in the first post-war decades was dominated by three ideologically oriented organizations. The largest, NVV, developed from a strong Socialist background towards a moderate Social-democratic position and maintained close but informal links with the PvdA. The Catholic NKV and the smaller Protestant CNV were both associated with different Christian-democratic parties (which have since merged). In the 1970s, as seen in Chapter 4, there was a move to unite the three unions; though CNV withdrew, the other two amalgamated in 1981 to establish the FNV. This required greater distance from the PvdA, though the party still received the support of the majority of FNV members and officials. The traditional Dutch 'polder model' entailed a commitment to consensual public policy, and all confederations were strongly involved in peak-level bipartite and tripartite bargaining. As we saw in the previous chapter, this consensus has been under repeated strain in the past two decades beacause of cutbacks in the welfare regime, imposed by governments in which the PvdA has often been a junior partner. In recent years, FNV appears to have moved towards a more assertive and independent political stance, perhaps aiming to connect with widespread popular disaffection with the political elite (which includes the PvdA)—and to respond to the growing willingness of union members to support other left-wing parties (notably the SP) and also the far-right *Partij voor de Vrijheid*.

Belgium is the one country outside the 'southern' group in which trade unionism remains firmly divided between ideological 'pillars', though political-party links are complex, partly because of the intersecting division between the French- and Dutch-speaking communities with separate party structures. The largest confederation, the ACV/CSC, is part of the Christian workers' movement *Algemeen Christelijk Werknemersverbond* (ACW)/*Mouvement ouvrier chrétien* (MOC), and through this is associated with political Christian democracy. Today this comprises the centre-right *Christen-Democratisch en Vlaams* (CD&V) and a more centrist French-language counterpart, now known as *Centre démocrate humaniste*. While MOC adopted in 1972 a policy of political pluralism, ACW retains a 'privileged relationship' with CD&V. The confederation has long observed the principle that officials should not be elected to parliament, and its leaders have developed some distance from the formerly allied parties: they clashed in the 1990s with the policies of prime minister Dehaene, and now criticize the neoliberalism of the CD&V (Cortebeeck 2008). The ABVV/FGTB has traditionally been linked to the Socialist Party, now regionally divided into the *Parti Socialiste* (PS) and the *Socialisten en progressieven anders*, with union leaders holding a consultative role on both party executives. The third, much smaller, confederation was traditionally linked to the Liberal Party; but in 1961 the latter adopted a neoliberal, anti-union programme. In 1962 the union asserted its autonomy from political parties (Faniel and Vandaele 2011: 35–6).

There is a two-way interconnection between the political and industrial relations realms in Belgium. On the one hand, peak-level collective agreements may require government subventions—as with the provisions for short-time working agreed at the end of 2008—or may provide guidelines for legislation. On the other, the government often intervenes forcefully in the collective bargaining process, for example threatening legislation in the absence of an agreement which it considers acceptable (Arcq 2008: 70). It can also facilitate peak-level bargaining by lowering employers' social security contributions. Despite the considerable potential for conflict, the unions appear broadly content with the system.

Industrial relations in France has always been highly politicized, since 'the French state is not reticent in enacting by law or regulation the norms (on pay, working time, health and safety) that elsewhere are left to other social actors' (Lallement 2007: 453). Despite the high formal coverage of collective bargaining—largely because of state extension of agreements—its real impact is far less than that of statutory determination, and the legislative route is typically the line of least resistance in regulating labour issues. The *Code du travail* defines a wide range of employment conditions; the national minimum wage (SMIC) is a point of reference for collective agreements; the unions derive the majority of their resources from subventions linked to their privileged role within a complex network of state institutions (Andolfatto and Labbé 2000: 61–4).

The party-political constellation is also exceptional: France, like Italy, was marked for the first post-war decades by the dominance on the left of a Communist party closely linked to the majority trade union and 'there has long been no large "catch-all" party of the left' (Amadieu 1999: 127). The *Parti socialiste* (PS) has never been a mass working-class Social-democratic party in the same way as its counterparts in other countries; the fragmented trade union movement—for much of the post-war era dominated by the CGT—never shared a Social-democratic identity, though both the CFDT and FO could be described as broadly Socialist. With the eclipse of the PCF, the CGT gave increasing emphasis to collective bargaining—'a compromise is not the same as a sell-out' (*compromis ne veut pas dire compromission*) declared its leader in 2009. In 2003 the union cut its links with the party, declaring that 'debate with democratic political parties precludes support for or joint elaboration of any kind of political project'. Ironically, this was a return to the principle of party-political neutrality adopted by the original CGT a century earlier, and sustained by FO from it formation in 1948. The CFDT was close to the left of the PS in the 1970s, but in 1978 reoriented its position away from political attachments. After backing Mitterrand for president in 1981, it has not endorsed any party in subsequent elections. Nevertheless, its position is somewhat ambiguous, recently described by its leader as *ni neutre, ni partisane* (Barthélemy et al. 2009). Conversely, SUD has informal links to the anti-capitalist parties which have performed strongly in recent elections. Yet the distancing of the main unions from political parties coexists with a role in which the state remains a major focus of action. In the context of continued government efforts to restructure the labour market and the welfare state, unions have been torn between sustaining their status as privileged interlocutors and militant defence of members' interests, with the CFDT most ready to favour the former and CGT and FO (and particularly SUD) more oriented to resistance on the streets—where 'protesters have largely won small victories while losing the war' (Howell 2009: 230).

The changing political environment of Italian trade unionism contrasts markedly in significant respects. In France, the Communist vote was far higher than the Socialist until the late 1960s, but then the positions were reversed and from the late 1970s the PCF went into rapid electoral decline. But in Italy, Communist support remained well above that for the (divided) Socialists, reaching a third of the popular vote in 1976. In the corruption scandals of the early 1990s, the *Partito socialista italiano* (PSI) was severely compromised, its electoral support collapsed, and it was dissolved in 1994. Though the PCI was dissolved after the fall of the Berlin Wall, its post-Communist inheritors constituted the only significant party of the left—apart from *Rifondazione* and its successors, linked to a powerful minority fraction within CGIL. By contrast CISL, founded in 1948, reflected the tradition of Catholic trade unionism, though it professed political neutrality. During the 1960s it accepted the principle of *incompatibilità*—officials could no longer hold political office. The third main union, UIL, was a mainly Social-democratic breakaway from CGIL. Despite the shift of all three confederations to formal autonomy from political parties—and a far more effective turn to collective bargaining than in France—informal links remained close and the political arena remained a common priority.

From the 1970s, as discussed in the previous chapter, political exchange became a key element of Italian industrial relations, in part because unstable governments saw union endorsement of their policies as a source of legitimacy (Baccaro and Lim 2007)—notably over the fraught issue of pensions reform in the 1990s. Yet the new bipolar character of Italian politics, with a weak and divided left facing an ascendant right under Berlusconi, imposed serious strains within and between the unions and between them and the government. As we saw in the previous chapter, CGIL took a harder line than the other two confederations under the Berlusconi governments in office for most of the decade 2001–11, and the same was true under the 'technocratic' government which succeeded him. Conversely, critics accused CGIL of undue acquiescence to the demands of the 2006–8 Prodi government, with which it was politically sympathetic. Intriguingly, the mainly ex-Communist PD, formed in 2007, includes the former left-Catholic *Margherita* party and embraces leading members of all three confederations; but the unions seem as far away as ever from a common strategy adapted to the new political conjuncture.

In Britain, where—exceptionally—most main unions (though not the TUC itself) retain a collective affiliation to the Labour Party, the strains in the 'contentious alliance' (Minkin 1991) intensified with the rebranding of the party as 'New' Labour in the 1990s. Party leaders viewed the formal links with the unions as an electoral handicap and attempted both to reduce their financial dependence (unsuccessfully, because of the collapse in individual party membership) and to demonstrate their readiness to adopt policies which provoked union opposition. The role of trade unions in party decision-making and in the selection of parliamentary candidates was substantially reduced; while the enthusiasm of the government elected in 1997 for privatization and public sector budgetary constraints provoked conflict with most trade unions and was one reason for the election of a new generation of more militant leaders popularly dubbed the 'awkward squad' (Charlwood 2004). The fraught relationship resulted in the Fire Brigades Union disaffiliating in 2004, while the RMT rail union was expelled after supporting rival left candidates in opposition to party nominees. Other unions have retained their links, but in many cases have reduced their financial support for the party and have used their funds for a wider range of political interventions (Hamann and Kelly 2004: 95–6).

In Ireland, politics remains shaped by the struggle for independence in the early 20th century: as we saw in Chapter 1, nationalism has overridden class politics. Labour is thus a minority party, though occasionally (as at present) it has been junior partner in coalition governments. Some unions, notably the largest—SIPTU—are affiliated to the party but with less influence than their British counterparts. In practice, most Irish unions seek to work with whatever government is in office, hence the two decades of social partnership agreements.

The Search for Alliances

The weakening of trade unions' influence over their traditional 'fraternal' parties can be interpreted as part of a more general decline of their own representativeness and mobilizing capacity. In terms of the power resources discussed in Chapter 2, unions have lost elements of their former structural, associational, and organizational power; while the diminished effectiveness of long-established political channels can be regarded as one index of the erosion of their institutional power. In this section we turn to one alternative form of power resources, coalitional power, and conclude the chapter by considering moral or discursive power.

Frege et al. (2004: 139–41), surveying trade union coalition building in five countries (including three of those covered in this book), suggest five main reasons why unions may seek alliances with other organizations or groups. The first, to gain financial and physical resources, is in our view rarely significant: most alliances are with bodies less well endowed in this respect than unions themselves. Second is access to new constituencies: this is particularly important for efforts to recruit previously unorganized (or weakly organized) groups of workers, as discussed in Chapter 3. Third is the ability to draw on specialist expertise, for example when unions formulate policies on sustainable development. Fourth, coalitions may be a source of added legitimacy for union campaigns: working with community or religious organizations may help unions recruit ethnic minority members, and a common campaign with relevant NGOs may strengthen union claims to represent a broad public interest. Finally, alliances can strengthen unions' mobilization capacity, particularly when working with NGOs that possess a vibrant activist base.

The same authors note that alliances with other organizations may involve one-off actions, intermittent joint activity or continuous collaboration; and that unions may in some cases (attempt to) set the agenda, while in others they collaborate as equal partners, and in yet others lend their support to NGOs which have already defined the aims and tactics. Frege et al. present a further distinction, drawing on McIlroy (2000: 3), between collaboration with institutionalized and respectable 'insider' NGOs to create 'coalitions of influence' within mainstream politics, and cooperation with more radical, 'outsider' groups to create 'coalitions of protest'.

Relations with external organizations and groups can involve serious tensions. Union officials often stress that their organizations possess a substantial paying membership and established procedures of internal democracy, unlike many other 'civil society organizations'. Conversely, some NGOs—and in particular 'outsider' groups—often regard unions as part of the establishment, reluctant to engage in radical action which might threaten their institutional status. Certainly there is some basis for the latter view. In particular, most unions are very hesitant in associating with groups engaged in extra-legal (even if non-violent) direct action, partly because their own material resources might be exposed to sanctions, but more fundamentally because their own ideology and identity are often centred around their role as 'social partners'. Frictions can also arise from jurisdictional conflicts: for example, do unions or women's groups have the primary right to represent the distinctive interests of women workers?

The issues involved in common action tend to shape the type of coalition partner and the nature of the relationship. Five broad themes may be identified. The first two link directly to what, in most countries, has traditionally been viewed as unions' 'core' function in defending workers' economic interests. One, which has already been explored in Chapter 3, is the effort to recruit and represent vulnerable groups of workers, and in some cases to support them in strike action. The campaigns among mainly female and minority ethnic cleaners in the Netherlands and the UK, for example, involved collaboration with a range of community and religious groups: both to gain access to the target workers and win their trust, gaining 'access to social capital' in minority ethnic communities (Martínez Lucio and Perrett 2009b: 704), and to convince broader public opinion of the justice of their case. While such alliances are often ad hoc and temporary, more enduring relationships may evolve—as, for example, with The East London Communities Organisation (TELCO), which has spread beyond its original geographical base and campaigns on such issues as wages, housing, safer streets, and immigration (Wills and Simms 2004). Readiness to form such coalitions is obviously closely associated with the adoption of an 'organizing model'.

A second theme, particularly important for public sector unions, is the effort to construct alliances between 'producers' and 'consumers' of goods and services. While there is a long history of unions seeking allies in organizing consumer boycotts of employers with which they are in dispute (the *ver. di* campaign against Lidl is an obvious recent example), such collaboration has become a vital element in the defence of public services in the face of privatization and budget cuts. Perhaps the most notable example is the initiative of the British TUC, together with a number of its public sector affiliates, which in 2010 funded the launch of False Economy: a web-based campaign bringing together trade unions and a range of national and local groups and social media campaigners to develop anti-cuts activities. Similarly in France, the CGT helped launch the *Convergence Nationale des Collectifs de Défense et de Développement des Services Publics*, which coordinates a range of local and service-specific campaigns.

A third focus, which to some extent overlaps with the first, concerns issues of equality and identity which (as we saw in Chapter 3) have become part of the union agenda in all countries. In general, unions have been relatively late to embrace the rights of women, migrants and ethnic minorities, workers with disabilities, and the LGBT community; in all these cases, advocacy groups and organizations pre-existed trade union engagement. Moreover, in many cases those campaigning *within* trade unions for the rights of such groups are also active as part of external collectivities, hence bridging the different components of emergent alliances. Particularly in the case of representation of the interests of minority ethnic workers, collaboration with other groups fighting discrimination may lead directly to broader anti-racist and anti-fascist campaigns. For example the British TUC, and many of its affiliates, have from the 1990s engaged with anti-racist and community groups to combat right-wing extremism and xenophobia, including the organization of an annual 'Respect' music festival since 1996.

The need to collaborate with established issue-specific NGOs is even more evident in the case of wider, more overtly political issues with which unions increasingly engage. One of these—our fourth theme—concerns the environment, and more specifically proposals for sustainable development in industries where unions organize. Germany, where *die Grünen* have been an important actor for several decades, is a pioneer in this respect. The DGB adopted its first environmental programme in the 1970s, and *IG Metall* established a working group on alternative production in 1981. At its first conference in 2001, *ver.di* included a section on sustainable development in its constitution, claiming that 'environmental protection creates jobs'. *IG Metall* has argued similarly, insisting that 'sustainable transportation' is the only means to ensure the future of employment in its core industries. Another interesting example is the issue of nuclear energy, divisions over which in the 1970s 'endangered...the very organizational existence' of the DGB, with some service sector unions opposing nuclear power but industrial unions, notably those organizing energy sector workers (the predecessors of the current IG BCE) supporting its continuation (Jahn 1988: 330). Today, even IG BCE accepts the phasing out of nuclear power. In the environmental field we can identify a dual reciprocity. On the one hand, environmental groupings and NGOs apply pressure both within trade unions and from without in order to shift their policies; on the other, once unions have embraced a commitment to sustainability, they often collaborate with specialist NGOs in order to formulate concrete strategies. For instance, British unions have worked with NGOs such as Friends of the Earth and Greenpeace in the development of 'green workplaces' projects. In Italy, FIOM-CGIL has cooperated with more radical social movements on environmental issues.

Finally, a theme which we address in greater detail in the next chapter is union engagement in issues of international solidarity (including ethical trading), resistance to neoliberal attacks at EU and global level, and anti-war struggles (Gallin 2000). Here, the tension between 'coalitions of influence' and 'coalitions of protest' is often particularly pronounced. This can be seen, for example, in the case of the European Social Fora (ESFs). In the first, held in Florence in 2002, the Italian unions, in particular CGIL, played an important organizing role, and unions from Belgium, France, Germany, and the UK also participated (Bieler and Morton 2004); trade unions from many countries (in particular their youth organizations) have maintained a presence in subsequent years. Connecting to our second theme, public sector unions have been particularly involved, given the threat from global and EU liberalization policies to established public services, most notably the Bolkestein directive on service liberalization in 2004–6 (Marcon and Zola 2007). Moissonnier (2009) writes of a 'cautious rapprochement' between unions and *altermondialistes*, with the ACV/CSC, CGIL, and CGT being most closely involved. But a cultural divide has typically existed between leaders of 'insider' unions delivering formal speeches, and younger, sometimes anarchistic participants more interested in direct action. There are parallels with relations in many countries between unions and ATTAC, founded in France in 1998; we give some examples below.

We now provide a brief overview of trade union–NGO relations in our various countries. In both Nordic countries, involvement is relatively limited and relates mainly to international issues. This can be attributed to the continuing strength of unions' own associational and organizational resources. It is interesting that when the retail workers' union *Handels* was fighting for recognition by the US multinational Toys R Us in 1995, it called for a consumer boycott but relied less on community organizations than on secondary action by other unions, notably in transport—action that is subject to far fewer legal constraints than in most countries (Vandenberg 2006). Peterson et al. (2011: 17, 23) note a 'general lack of interest among the Swedish trade unions' in joint action with NGOs, and to the extent that collaboration does occur it normally involves the more 'respectable' organizations. Hence the municipal workers' union *Kommunal*, in some respects one of the more radical LO affiliates, describes itself as 'an organization that uses socio-political cooperation and not confrontation...We seldom are seen on the streets...Reformism is the way we work.' The LO, and some TCO affiliates, helped organize the 2008 ESF in Malmö, but this seems to have been exceptional. In general, the strongest links are with officially recognized bodies working in the fields of overseas development and trade. The same is true in Denmark; the only NGO mentioned by LO in a recent annual report (2009) is the Ethical Trading Initiative.

Collaboration with outside organizations is rather more developed in Germany, largely because of the need for external allies in campaigns to organize weakly unionized sectors. For example, *ver.di* undertook joint action with ATTAC in its Lidl campaign. According to one commentator, 'ATTAC seems to have everything that *ver.di* lacks: rapid growth and a big, encompassing theme—globalization. ATTAC activists compensate for lack of money with imagination and commitment' (Rickens 2006: 128). Indeed both *ver.di* and the teachers' union GEW are affiliated to ATTAC, as are some local *IG Metall* branches. But as in the Nordic countries, German unions at official level seem most comfortable in dealing with NGOs in the field of international development: for example, in 2002 the DGB signed a declaration with ATTAC and VENRO (an umbrella body of development NGOs) on 'creating a fair globalization' (*Globalisierung gerecht gestalten*). More generally, as Kröck (2005: 43) notes, considerable suspicions exist on both sides, with many leading trade unionists still committed to working exclusively within traditional political channels.

Analogous suspicions occur in Austria. In an interview, an *Arbeiterkammer* official contrasted unions, with a 'transparent' system of internal democracy, and NGOs, which 'have no democratic basis'. Yet she added that 'NGOs can act spontaneously, they are not committed to being very correct and serious, they can have more imagination and vision'; the future of trade unionism required mutual cooperation. As examples, she mentioned that 'we work with ATTAC, which is a bit more moderate in Austria than in France, with Greenpeace over the environment and creating new workplaces, with Amnesty over ILO [International Labour Organization] labour standards and with churches and related NGOs over social inclusion and anti-poverty'. However, such collaboration was 'not undisputed': some unions wanted to protect their status as privileged social partners and resisted any involvement with 'outsider' bodies.

Similarly in the Netherlands where, as we have noted, *FNV Bondgenoten* developed cooperation with churches and community organizations in its attempts to unionize migrant workers, the commitment to social partnership institutions tends to limit unions' willingness to collaborate with other social organizations. The main areas of joint action are in the field of international development, as in the other countries we have mentioned. The same is true of Belgium, though it should be noted that the history of 'pillarization' means that, particularly in the case of the ACV/CSC, there exists a wide range of social organizations that form cooperative actors in the same 'family'. Beyond these 'privileged' partners, however, the ACV/

CSC 2010 confederal congress called for collaboration with groups representing women, young people, immigrants, undocumented workers, and persons with disabilities. All three confederations are affiliated to umbrella NGOs in the field of overseas development, and also participate in joint work with environmental organizations. One major difference is that the Socialist ABVV/FGTB has worked closely with LGBT organizations in its equality work, while the ACV/CSC, with its Catholic orientation, ignores issues of sexual orientation.

In France, as elsewhere, the most developed union–NGO cooperation concerns international development, with less extensive relationships on domestic issues. In the case of the CGT, there is a past tradition of cooperation with 'front' organizations, as for example in the peace movement. This has, however, now broadened considerably: an official mentioned that involvement in the ESF and World Social Fora 'has brought us close to the NGOs', including environmentalist organizations such as Greenpeace. Indeed, all main confederations participated with various NGOs in the *Grenelle de l'environnement*, a round table launched by the government in 2007, and have also collaborated on issues of 'corporate social responsibility' (CSR). In the words of a CGT representative (Geneste 2010), discussing initiatives for 'green' workplaces, 'it is obvious that the voluntary sector has genuine expertise on environmental issues, and their expertise is valuable for union officials. On our side, we have better negotiating skills; in essence, this makes a productive complementarity.' As in other countries, collaboration is predominantly with 'respectable' NGOs; the clear exception is *SUD-Solidaires*, which reports links with over 50 organizations, many of which are radical activist groups.

More than in any other of our countries, Italian unions tend to regard themselves as encompassing NGOs, concerned with the broad interests of workers as citizens and not only their employment status: hence, notably, their function as organizations of pensioners as much as of actual employees. Such an orientation is particularly evident in the case of CGIL (as with CGT in France) because of its ideological heritage. Like its French counterpart, the union has been notably active in campaigning for the rights of immigrants and asylum seekers, in alliance with a range of NGOs, in response to the racist policies of the Berlusconi government. NGOs are themselves employers, and because of limited and unpredictable funding can often provide poor employment conditions. An interesting development was the framework agreement negotiated in 2004 between the Association of Italian NGOs and the temporary workers' unions of all three main confederations, laying down minimum standards, following negotiations which according to the NGOs were 'thorough and not always easy'.

As we have seen, the turn to 'organizing' has involved a range of alliances between British unions and community groups. A decade ago, Heery and Abbott (2000: 165–6) pointed to community organizing, derived from US experience, as one element in the adoption of an 'organizing culture'; more recently, Wright has presented several case studies of 'community engagement' and concludes (2010: 16–17) that effective alliances usually require 'a long-term commitment of resources' as well as 'trust and reciprocation between unions and community groups'. Often, however, such alliance building has been primarily opportunistic (Parker (2008: 572), but there are also signs of more strategic engagement. The largest UK union, Unite, has appointed a network of regional community organizers and has also launched a 'community membership' scheme for those not in employment. Another interesting example is the former steelworkers' union, which in 2004, as part of a merger process and in response to the decline of its traditional industrial base, changed its name to 'Community' and now places significant emphasis on representing interests beyond the workplace.

At national level, unions have long collaborated with a range of NGOs, and this was made more systematic with the 'relaunch' of the TUC in the 1990s (Heery 1998), involving closer relations with the voluntary sector, campaigning organizations, and churches. Several of the main unions funded the 2004 ESF in London. A TUC official told us that in the past the typical trade union approach to NGOs could be caricatured as 'when you're in trouble, reach for the community and get them to do what you've got on your agenda. Well...that doesn't work, you have got to have mutual respect, mutual understanding for your different objectives, recognising that they won't always coincide.' Careful coordination has been particularly important in the anti-cuts campaign, including the False Economy initiative mentioned above. More generally, the TUC has attempted to collaborate with digital activists, in 2012 launching Netroots UK in order to draw on the expertise of grassroots campaigners. As the incoming TUC general secretary told the founding conference, 'none of us has all the answers, but our different strengths, our different skills, our different passions combined mean that we can complement each other, benefit each other, learn from each other'.

In Ireland, experience has been similar, with a wide range of joint initiatives with NGOs; and indeed, from 1997 the national 'social partnership' discussions included voluntary and community organizations. However, unions have made less resort to the 'community unionism' approach than their British counterparts. It is interesting, given Ireland's reputation as a conservative Catholic country, that in 2011 the ICTU in conjunction with the Gay and Lesbian Equality Network produced a Guide to support equal treatment for LGBT workers and to encourage them to 'come out' in their union.

The Battle of Ideas

'What are we here for?' one former British union leader used to ask. There is a paradox at the heart of trade union identity: at one and the same time, unions are social movements with the goal of social betterment, but also often conservative bureaucracies which opponents can depict as defending the vested interests of the relatively protected. Unions require stable organization if they are to be effective, and established procedures if they are to be democratic; and they cannot ignore the core membership who pay their contributions. But unions require power resources of a normative character: they are not mere insurance companies, and can survive only if they express a social ideal and a social mission. In times of crisis, managing this paradox demands great strategic imagination. In this final section of the chapter we do not attempt to provide a systematic survey of national experience, but offer some illustrative examples of attempts to transcend the paradox.

The development of moral or discursive power resources requires first a normative content or set of values in order to demonstrate 'what we are here for'. Any live and democratic movement will contain areas of debate and division over the precise answer to this question. The different ideological traditions discussed earlier in this chapter have embodied very different conceptions of a better socio-economic order and the means to attain this. The erosion of these traditional identities may make it easier to pursue an overarching common vision, but may also lead towards convergence on a form of 'business unionism' bereft of broader normative content. For example, in 2007 the Swedish LO published in ten languages its 'trade union vow' (*Det fackliga löftet*) designed to encapsulate the movement's purpose; but the sole focus was on collective defence of wages and conditions against employer attempts to reduce standards. Yet LO itself conceives solidarity in a much more encompassing manner; and its Danish counterpart adopted a far broader 'value statement' in 2003, as we outline below.

A normative vision becomes a power resource only when effectively communicated: 'collective strength comes from communication, or it withers away' is the title of an article by a former DGB official (Arlt 1994). Communication has both an internal and an external dimension. Arlt focuses primarily on the first: for a union to create a genuine collective identity, a lively internal exchange of information and opinion is essential, with critical debate over arguments and positions in order to develop an enlightened commonality. But traditional trade union culture, Arlt argues, involves a 'laager mentality': rather than reveal internal differences in the face of the 'enemy', the official reflex (even in unions which have long abandoned the notion of class struggle) is often to contain and suppress debate and to ritualize internal communication. Clearly this is incompatible with aspirations to constitute an agency of industrial democracy.

External communication is no less important, especially in an era when the mainstream media are anything but sympathetic to trade unionism. We have already touched on this issue, in particular in Chapter 4: in most countries, unions have in recent decades become far more professional in the public presentation of their policies and positions, with large unions in many countries appointing specialist communications officers or using public relations agencies. However, a recent British overview (Stanley et al. 2011) identifies problems which are evident in many other countries: officials and leaders who lack media training and are unaware that they need it; time-honoured jargon which 'serves to create a cadre of cognoscenti' but 'bewilders anyone new to a union, or contemplating joining one'; a preference for 'comfortable narratives—rich in class conflict—that appease our current base of fellow members' but fail to offer a positive image; the staging of conferences which are a public relations disaster, seemingly confirming hostile media stereotypes. This is one area where cross-national exchange of union practice and experience can be particularly valuable.

This links closely to a third issue: the 'framing' of the unions' case. In communication, the key issue is less what is *said* than what is *heard*. Everyone possesses a world view, however inchoate, a set of beliefs and assumptions which make sense of a complex social environment and act as selective filters for what is communicated. Today, such world views are predominantly shaped by the 'common sense' of neoliberalism: the notion that acquisitiveness is an unquestionable virtue, that money is the measure of all things, that 'free' markets are unquestionably efficient and virtuous. Crafting an alternative which penetrates the dominant perceptual filters is a challenge, and it is easy to surrender to the dominant frame: 'the increasing takeover of everyday life by market logic means the takeover of even those places in everyday life where we build our ability to resist. The trade union itself becomes colonized by the market, its relationships commodified into services and consumers' (Edwards 2007: 127). Hence the key issue is how to subvert the dominant frames by 'amplifying' and 'extending' those elements which can be aligned to the movement's own objectives, thus transforming and reshaping their master narratives (Snow et al. 1986). So, for example, the central purpose of trade union action can be presented as the pursuit of social justice; the struggle for economic and industrial democracy; the defence of humanity and autonomy against precariousness and stress at work; the search for opportunities for self-development in employment. All share a master narrative: trade unions are collective means for workers to defend their human rights against the dehumanizing imperatives of profit. Framed in these terms, union policies and actions can resonate with deeply held, if often subsidiary, elements in everyday understandings of economy and society.

We end with five examples of the battle for ideas: two of broad presentations of union values; two of defensive struggles; and one of a positive campaign for rights.

The first example is the statement of fundamental values (*Værdigrundlag*) adopted by Danish LO at a special congress in 2003, when it severed formal links with the *Socialdemokraterne*. With the overarching argument that 'solidarity creates opportunities', the statement developed five specific themes. First, while we can achieve some of our goals as individuals, together we can do more: an argument which challenges the simple dichotomy between individualism and collectivism. Collective agreements are a means to secure the rights of workers as individuals, enhancing their capacity to develop their personal abilities. Second, all humans are different but they all have equal value and must have equal rights and opportunities. The labour market must be open and inclusive; and the trade union movement itself must be an inclusive community with space for diversity, which must be reflected in its democratically elected bodies. Third, all workers have the right to a job where employee participation and skills development go hand in hand with decent wages and decent working conditions. The trade union movement must promote the creation of workplaces that treat employees as the most valuable resource and that make room for marginalized groups of workers. Fourth, unions work to achieve a welfare state that is inclusive and redistributive, providing equal access to fundamental social resources. Fifth, solidarity is global: LO contributes to developing workers' rights across the world, and accepts that rich countries should help those who live in poverty and destitution. As a whole, the document presents a positive statement of union objectives, both for members and for the broader public, in plain language and covering many of the key themes that trade unionists in any country would emphasize.

A second example provides an interesting parallel but from a very different ideological tradition, the analysis presented by the Belgian ACV/CSC for its congress in 2010 and disseminated almost a year in advance for discussion, under the title 'Let's build tomorrow together' (*Morgen mee maken* or *Construisons demain*). The aim was to provide a long-term understanding of the key challenges—but also opportunities—facing trade unions and to develop responses, with the argument that 'another future is possible'. Three 'mega-trends' were discussed: first, demographic ageing, youth unemployment, and growing labour force diversity; second, the rapid increase in economic and financial globalization without matching forms of social regulation; and third, the impact of climate change. The policy implications derived from this analysis were: a struggle to make the economy serve society, and finance serve the economy, and not the reverse as at present; the need to relate a vigorous response to the current crisis to a longer-term strategy; the pursuit of sustainable development; and the key task of developing innovative trade union ideas while also seeking to collaborate with others who share similar objectives. Produced as the economic crisis unfolded, this effort to define a union strategy for the longer term is particularly impressive as an attempt to propagate a positive trade union vision.

A notable instance of successful defensive struggle is the resistance in France in 2006 to the introduction of the *contrat première embauche* (CPE). Ostensibly a response to high levels of unemployment among young people, this relaxation of French equal opportunity legislation authorized a new form of contract for workers aged under 26, allowing dismissal without justification in the first two years of employment. According to the government, this would encourage employers to take on new recruits. The change to the law provoked massive student protests, and all significant trade unions—very unusually—mobilized together against what they perceived as a threat to job security. The unions framed the new contracts, first as a form of discrimination (hence contrary to republican principles), and second as paving the way to reduced job security for all workers (hence an issue of direct concern to all). Opinion polls showed that some two-thirds of the French population opposed the CPE, and a similar proportion blamed the government rather than the unions for the confrontations. Following mass demonstrations and both local and national strikes, the government withdrew the legislation. The lesson seems to be that, when speaking with one voice, unions with few members can nevertheless campaign persuasively against the damaging policies of an apparently strong government.

Another example of imaginative engagement in a battle of ideas is the resistance by British unions to austerity and public sector cuts, to which we have alluded previously. From the outset, most unions' objective has been to understand and engage with public attitudes, drawing on survey evidence and where necessary commissioning their own opinion polls. These were 'designed to test which of our many arguments against the austerity policies of the coalition government were most effective in shifting people into our camp, and which government arguments worked best for ministers. The polling exercises consisted of a series of focus groups used to narrow down and refine the messages under test—and a big quantitative poll. This was of sufficient sample size to allow it to be split in various ways allowing different language and ways of presenting our arguments to be tested' (TUC 2012: 12).

The TUC described its response as a 'battle of ideas' and a 'battle for a narrative'. Initially, a majority of the population had accepted government arguments that cuts were unavoidable because of the size of government debt; that they would be implemented fairly; that expenditure could be reduced by eliminating 'waste' without reducing core services; and that union resistance reflected an attempt to preserve the 'privileges' of public employees. In part the unions attempted to demonstrate that the austerity measures were economically counterproductive (a 'false economy'), would hit both private and public sector workers, were unfairly targeted at ordinary people while protecting the rich, and reflected an ideologically driven agenda to cut back the welfare state, including the popular National Health Service. But the aim was also to convey a positive message: to 'provide some alternative vision and hope', as a TUC official described it to us. According to the TUC general secretary in 2010, 'it is now clear that there is an economic alternative available. We can have a more sensible timetable for deficit reduction, a fair tax system and policies to stimulate green growth.' The campaign 'All Together for Public Services' involved a range of local and regional activities as well as national action. The mass demonstration held in October 2012 adopted the slogan 'A Future That Works'. The message was that there *is* a credible alternative to austerity.

As the government's measures began to take effect, this narrative began to achieve an impact. Public opinion increasingly regarded the cuts as too drastic and unfair in their application. The government's reputation for economic competence fell rapidly, and its overall profile in opinion polls collapsed. Of course the TUC and its affiliates were only one element in the counterargument to austerity; and at the time of writing the government has not altered its policies. But smart engagement in a battle of ideas has shifted the terrain of political debate and has enhanced the unions' own status.

We end by considering the campaign for a statutory minimum wage in Germany. Traditionally, German unions (like their Nordic counterparts) saw minimum wage legislation as incompatible with the principle of *Tarifautonomie*; the one exception was NGG in the food, hotel, and catering sectors, which called for statutory regulation from the late 1990s. Attitudes began to change with the growth of a low-wage sector only weakly covered by collective agreements, particularly following the introduction of a 'workfare' system by the Schröder government in 2003. This had serious implications for *ver.di*, which now endorsed the idea of a minimum wage; and *IG Metall*, also facing low-wage competition through subcontracting, joined the campaign. In 2006 the DGB endorsed the demand for a statutory minimum of €7.50 an hour (now €8.50). Only the chemical workers' union IG BCE opposed, and it has since altered its position.

In contrast to their British counterparts, who used mainly 'insider' pressure through the Labour Party to achieve the minimum wage in the 1990s, German unions launched a high-profile campaign with simple slogans, posters and display advertising, eye-catching public events, a dedicated website, and a broad-based online and SMS petition. Supporters were also encouraged to press their local parliamentary representatives to endorse the call. By framing the issue in terms of fairness and the need to end the growing scandal of poverty wages (which 'make Germany poor'), the unions have won extensive public support: surveys tend to show that 75 per cent or more strongly agree that a statutory minimum is desirable. While the SPD and other left parties endorsed the demand at an early stage, only in 2012 did the governing CDU agree to support the principle of a statutory minimum, though with loopholes that the unions consider completely unacceptable (a 'minimum wage light'). Though the unions seem to have won the public argument, the outcome will await the result of parliamentary elections in 2013.

Conclusions

Political influence is a function—as both cause and effect—of union vitality. Declining influence in most countries stems in part from the constrained policy options of national governments in an era of neoliberal globalization, but also reflects a general weakening of unions' organizational power resources. This in turn limits trade union strategic options, yet 'union leaders...retain some leeway in which forms of political action they choose to pursue' (Hamann and Kelly 2004: 108). Increased autonomy from their associated (and often 'parent') parties both requires, and enables, unions to rethink their social purpose. What *are* we here for? The whole idea of a labour *movement* implies a goal, a vision, which transcends the immediate task of representation in the workplace, however important this may be. As we have explored briefly in the latter part of this chapter, unions have increasingly attempted—albeit to varying degrees and with different evidence of effectiveness—to develop new political resources through cultivating alliances with other progressive organizations and groups, and by taking more seriously the need to define a social vision and craft an effective language to propagate it.

7

Beyond National Boundaries: Unions, Europe, and the World

Trade unions are primarily national organizations; and became consolidated in the 20th century as interlocutors of nationally based employers and national governments; but—as we explained at the outset of this book—they act within an economy which is increasingly integrated internationally, and in Europe within a polity—the EU—which increasingly affects national labour markets. Hence one theme in the 'revitalization' debate, as we saw in Chapter 3, has been the need to strengthen international trade union cooperation.

In this chapter we begin by addressing the global level, describing the evolution of international trade union organization, debates about the nature and rationale of international action, and approaches to internationalism in our different countries. We then turn in more detail to the European level, where most unions increasingly focus their attention. Here we discuss the institutional framework of the EU, the impact of its policies on national trade unions, and the role of the ETUC and the associated European Trade Union Federations (ETUFs). We also consider other initiatives, including the development of European Works Councils (EWCs) and the negotiation of transnational company agreements. We discuss the tensions which can occur (in a time of scarce resources) between national, European, and global activities, and the degree to which international commitments actually engage with the day-to-day work (and members) at home. We end by relating our account to the theme of power resources.

The International Level of Trade Union Action

International trade union organizations emerged at the end of the 19th century, at roughly the same time as the major national confederations themselves. The earliest internationals were industry based, becoming known as International Trade Secretariats and subsequently renamed Global Union Federations (GUFs). The first cross-sectoral body was founded in 1901, became the International Federation of Trade Unions in 1913, and was reconstituted in 1919, acting as the main representative of world labour within the newly created ILO. But the international labour movement soon split along ideological lines, with the foundation of the *Confédération internationale des syndicats chrétiens* (CISC) in 1920 and the Red International of Labour Unions (RILU) in 1921.

A new global organization, the World Federation of Trade Unions (WFTU), was founded in 1945, but never included the Christian unions. In 1949, most non-Communist affiliates broke away to form the International Confederation of Free Trade Unions (ICFTU). In 1968 CISC 'deconfessionalized' and became the World Confederation of Labour (WCL) (Pasture 1994). WFTU, now consisting mainly of national centres from Communist and/or developing countries, lost membership rapidly with the rise of 'Eurocommunism' followed by the fall of the Berlin Wall in 1989. From 1974, most European affiliates of both ICFTU and WCL had joined the newly created ETUC, which was formally autonomous of both international confederations. This was a precedent for creating, in 2006, a new unitary organization at global level, the International Trade Union Confederation (ITUC), bringing together ICFTU and WCL affiliates and a number of independent centres, some of which had formerly belonged to WFTU. A functional division of labour remains between the ITUC and GUFs, which concentrate on organizing work, bargaining strategy, and solidarity action within their sectors. The ETUC also remains formally autonomous.

European trade unions played a key role in constructing international trade union organizations; indeed, in the early years these were almost exclusively European in membership (Gumbrell-McCormick 2008). They were dominant within both the ICFTU and WCL, and were particularly influential in the formation of the ITUC. But how do national unions engage internationally? At international as at national level, unions operate within a regulatory system which structures their actions. This system is, however, distinctive in its structures and their internal decision-making processes, the timescale of their development, the type of governance, and the extent of their regulatory competence. Governments assign only limited powers to intergovernmental institutions, imposing decision-making rules which restrict the chances that they will be bound by policies to which they object. Similar constitutional limitations apply in the case of international organizations of trade unions.

Trade unions have varying motives for involvement at international level. They are clearly motivated by solidarity, but there are many forms of solidarity (Hyman 2001; Waterman 2001). Some writers stress economic considerations.

For Logue (1980), unions engage internationally to advance the short-term economic interests of their members. Haworth and Ramsay (1984) show how changing patterns of ownership and control of individual companies and industrial sectors structure workers' interests over time; while Anner et al. (2006) argue that contrasts in the form and extent of cross-national union solidarity in shipping, textiles, and car manufacturing can be explained by differences in production organization and product and labour market competition. The increased integration of the world economy, particularly within Europe, was indeed mentioned by many of the officials we interviewed as a prime motive for international action.

Other students of the labour movement have treated political considerations—either unions' own ideological convictions or those of their national governments—as the key to understanding international organization. Here we may note Hyman's argument (2005a) that a political logic seems best to explain the development of cross-sectoral international organization, while a more economic logic is reflected in the history of the GUFs. A third consideration is that institutional: unions (or their leaders) seek to enhance their institutional power resources; while within unions, international work can be seen as a form of reward or prestige.

Visser's discussion (1998b) of 'push' and 'pull' factors in transnational union organization is also pertinent: national unions may be 'pushed' towards supranational activity by economic factors (such as globalization) or political dynamics (European integration), but they may also be 'pulled' by the opportunities and resources (material assistance or status and legitimacy) available on the international stage. This may be one explanation for the increased focus on European as opposed to international work more generally, to which we return.

International trade union bodies rely on much more meagre resources than most national confederations and many sectoral unions. The ETUC is somewhat better resourced than the ITUC. The latter charges its wealthiest affiliates more (in 2010, €197 per thousand members as against €161 by the ETUC), but most ETUC affiliates are in the higher-fee category, whereas the opposite is the case with the ITUC. In addition, the ETUC benefits from substantial resources from the EU, as we indicate below. The differences are reflected in staffing. The ITUC, with its global remit, listed seventy-four headquarters staff in 2011. The ETUC listed fifty-two, but with an additional sixty-four in the European Trade Union Institute (ETUI) (Cotton and Gumbrell-McCormick 2012).

Membership decline at national level has caused a reduction in payments (as well as late payments) to the international bodies. Further, affiliation fees are weighted by the level of national income in each country; in 2009 the ITUC fee was €191.45 per thousand members for unions from the richest countries, only €3.1 for those from the poorest. The GUFs have similar arrangements, as has the ETUC. This weighting means that any fall in paying membership in the wealthiest countries has a disproportionate impact on the resources of the global unions. In addition to affiliation fees, the ITUC receives roughly €1 million a year in voluntary contributions to its Solidarity Fund, just over half coming from its German and Japanese affiliates. Far more substantial—about €7 million a year—are the project-oriented Development Aid Funds. Almost half this funding comes from the Dutch government and trade unions, with other substantial contributions from the Swedish unions. Given the political shifts in western Europe, these funds are increasingly dependent on ability to show concrete outputs and benefits for the donor countries.

The unions we examine operate within this configuration of international organizations, but do not act only through them. The degree of involvement in, and commitment to, the ETUC and ITUC, and the closely linked European and global sectoral federations, varies considerably. Further, most national confederations also engage in bilateral links with other unions in the industrialized countries; as mentioned above, some also maintain bilateral solidarity or assistance links with unions in developing countries or in CEE. The degree to which the membership is interested, and actively involved, in international work also varies, although it is fair to say that in most countries, international trade union action is the concern of a tiny minority.

Trade unions face particular difficulties at the international level. National union capacity is ultimately determined by members' willingness to act, the internal cohesion of the organization, and its responsiveness to members' concerns. This cannot apply in the same way to the international level, which involves *organizations of organizations*. While national action must depend ultimately on individual members, in practice at the international level the main question is the willingness to act of the national affiliates. National rivalries proved a major obstacle to international action in the Cold War period, particularly between WFTU affiliates and unions affiliated to the ICFTU and WCL, as well as between the latter two. These rivalries have not fully disappeared even within Europe, and in the ETUC there are often different positions between union confederations of northern and southern Europe. Nonetheless, the European affiliates continue to play a dominant role within the ITUC and the GUFs; while within Europe, certain national centres and a few individual national unions wield particular influence. This is often relatively covert. Traditionally, leadership positions in international union organizations have been held by officials from smaller countries (though as we will see, this has been changing); as a counterbalance, the larger affiliates often coordinate informally to shape policy (Cotton and Gumbrell-McCormick 2012).

National Approaches to Internationalism

Nordic trade unions have long punched above their weight at international level. Unions in both Sweden and Denmark are noted for their commitment to international work, through involvement in the ITUC and its predecessors, and especially through funding international solidarity work with unions in the developing countries and contributing to their education programmes (Peterson et al. 2012). Union leaders from both countries have served as top officials of the ICFTU/ITUC and the GUFs, and more recently of the ETUC and the ETUFs. Swedish LO president, Wanja Lundby-Wedin, was ETUC president from 2007 to 2011, the first woman and the first Swede in the post. Unions in both countries are also known for a relatively high membership involvement in international and European affairs. Attention to European affairs has increased in recent years and perhaps now overshadows global involvement. Another important area of international action is the Nordic region, through *Nordens Fackliga Samorganisation* (NFS), as well as the wider Baltic region, through the Baltic Sea Trade Union Network (BASTUN) (Larsson et al. 2012).

In both countries, the largest confederations determine international and European policy at their national congresses, and congress reports contain substantial sections on international affairs. These show a consistency of approach: for example LO Sweden places strong emphasis on trade union rights and support for international development work. Both LO confederations pay increased attention to newer issues such as CSR. LO Sweden's executive approved a model agreement for future International Framework Agreements (IFAs) in spring 2012, while LO Denmark made detailed proposals along the same lines in a 2006 English-language report, *Denmark in a Globalised World*, and has published a handbook for shop stewards on CSR and IFAs. The responsibility for international affairs differs somewhat between confederations and has varied over time. The president of LO Sweden is in charge of international and EU work and has always tended to play an important role within the international trade union organizations, as have many leaders of TCO. In LO Denmark, international affairs are currently the responsibility of a confederal secretary; but in the past, leaders such as Thomas Nielsen played a key role in the ICFTU. In 2011, LO Denmark reorganized its international department in order to give more weight to European affairs (*Danish Labour News*, September 2011).

In both countries, the strength and legitimacy of the large confederations contribute to an effective articulation of interests between levels—local, sectoral, national, and international; and international policy and action are coordinated between the confederal and sectoral levels. Sweden in particular has a strong tradition of informing and involving the membership in international affairs. Unions in both countries often work closely with NGOs such as the Fairtrade Foundation; LO Sweden and the official church jointly own the Fairtrade mark for Sweden. This interest in international affairs is not necessarily shared by all workers, however. In Denmark, a union-sponsored Gallup survey of over 2,000 employee representatives showed a lack of basic knowledge about European and international issues (*Danish Labour News*, September 2011), although, interestingly, manual workers tended to be better informed than white-collar workers. A recent Swedish study (Peterson et al. 2012) found a strong interest in international affairs among LO activists, and a motivation for international action based on both identification with workers in other countries and a desire to protect the conditions of workers in Sweden.

Unions in the 'central' countries also have long traditions of international involvement, though patterns differ considerably. German unions were largely responsible for the creation of the first international trade union organizations over a century ago, exerting a decisive influence. Understandably, history has created some sensitivities about their role in modern international trade unionism; one official told us that unions in other countries expect the Germans to take initiatives, but if the Germans do so, the same unions are likely to complain of German domineering. The DGB president is directly responsible for international policy, and the current occupant, Michael Sommer, is also president of the ITUC, where he has played a significant and often conservative role. This may be seen as a continuation of the DGB's cautious policies over many years within the ICFTU. The head of *IG Metall* is traditionally also president of the relevant GUF (now IndustriALL) (Rüb 2009). While most of its international work is focused on European issues, *IG Metall* has also played a significant role in key international issues, such as the struggle against apartheid, where it gave crucial support to black South African unions organizing at Volkswagen (Gumbrell-McCormick 2000: 408). It is important to note that *IG Metall* and *ver.di* are each far larger than most national confederations; hence they can develop independent international policies which do not always coincide with those of the DGB.

An important channel of German influence at global level is the *Friedrich-Ebert-Stiftung* (FES), a foundation linked to the SPD which, like all main political parties, receives public funding in proportion to its parliamentary representation. Many of its officials have close trade union links; activities include education programmes in Latin America, Africa, and Asia and its influence and global reach probably exceed those of any single European trade union. The FES is reported to have organized most of the seminars and conferences in Latin America around the creation of the ITUC, helping reconcile the differences between the ICFTU and WCL regional organizations (Collombat 2011).

The primary focus of the ÖGB is on Europe, with special attention to neighbouring CEE countries. It also carries out other international work, much of it multilaterally through the ITUC International Solidarity Fund (Prausmüller and Sauer 2007), as well as through its separate development association, *weltumspannend arbeiten*, which receives support from a number of affiliates and the AK as well as from the government. Much of the focus of this work is on child labour, and involves cooperation with unions in Africa and Asia. The 2007 congress called for a strengthening of ÖGB's international work and collaboration on international issues with NGOs. Some affiliates also carry out international work: GPA works closely with UNI Global and UNI-Europa, and carries out dedicated training on international issues.

Unions in the Netherlands and Belgium, like their Nordic counterparts, have traditionally played a disproportionate role in international activities. The FNV (and the CNV to a lesser degree) is a major sponsor of international development assistance in developing countries, often with the backing of government funds. The Belgian unions also have international solidarity projects, especially in Africa (in part reflecting the country's colonial past). Dutch and Belgian trade unionists have long held officer and executive positions at international level, providing four out of seven ICFTU general secretaries and similarly dominating the key positions in the WCL. Belgian unions, especially the ACV/CSC, played a key role in negotiations between the WCL and ICFTU and were instrumental in the formation of the ITUC. Unions in both countries are also deeply involved in the ETUC and ETUFs.

In the Netherlands, international and European affairs are the responsibility of the top leaders of both the FNV and CNV. In FNV, European affairs have received growing attention in recent years and are now handled separately, increasingly 'mainstreamed' through sectoral unions. Some of these carry out their own international work, in particular *Bondgenoten* and *AbvaKabo*. A separate body, *FNV Mondiaal*, was set up to channel government and other external funds to international projects, of which there are between 100 and 200 in any given year. Many of these have to do with child labour and the informal economy, both top priorities for the confederation, along with CSR. FNV works closely with a number of NGOs, and has a long association with the Clean Clothes Campaign. With its affiliates it has often sought to involve the membership in international issues, in recent years in campaigns by sectoral unions to negotiate IFAs, and over a longer historical period in international solidarity campaigns by the then largest sectoral union, *Industribond*, to put pressure on Dutch-based MNCs such as Unilever to improve conditions in developing countries. It remains to be seen, however, whether and to what extent international work will remain a priority for the *Nieuwe Vakbond*: discussion of its creation has paid little attention to international affairs beyond proposing that international work be carried out 'in-house' by the confederation rather than by the sectoral unions. A recent survey found a low interest in international affairs among the Dutch population as a whole, although this was higher among trade union members (van der Meer et al. 2009: 456). The CNV, for its part, has fewer resources and much less focus on European work. It continues to work closely with the Belgian ACV/CSC in international solidarity projects with former WCL affiliates in developing countries.

As the major funder of the WCL, the ACV/CSC played a vital role in the process leading to the creation of the ITUC, convincing other affiliates (including the CNV) to wind down their separate world body (Gumbrell-McCormick 2013). Since the foundation of the ITUC, it has played an important role in the leadership of the new organization, with its then president Luc Cortebeeck elected as deputy president. The confederation's strong focus on international affairs, based on its Christian-inspired conception of solidarity, can be seen in its attention to the plight of the poorest workers such as domestic workers, child labour, and the informal economy. It has relatively less involvement in forms of solidarity such as IFAs, although it is committed to CSR and has traditionally had very close links to NGOs (Moissonnier 2009), in particular through the other organizations within the Catholic Workers' Movement. The ABVV/FGTB has a much stronger focus on Europe, but has a department for international affairs headed by the president, Rudy De Leeuw, who is a member of the executives of the ITUC and ETUC. The federation has many international projects, often with additional government funding, especially in African countries such as Congo and Rwanda, as well as in Latin America; some are undertaken in cooperation with sectoral unions such as the construction workers. Increasingly, the confederation attempts to integrate international work with that of other departments, but there is little involvement of the wider membership on international, as opposed to European, issues. Like the ACV/CSC, the ABVV/FGTB works closely with various NGOs, including the Clean Clothes Campaign.

Trade unions in France and Italy, as we have seen, are strongly divided along ideological lines; and while the three main confederations in Italy tend to cooperate on European and international affairs, the same cannot be said of France. This has a rather paradoxical effect: the division and enmity between the French confederations weaken their presence and effectiveness in international work, but the competition between them has also encouraged all to become involved at international level. For decades, FO effectively vetoed the participation of the CGT and, for a time, the CFDT in the ICFTU and ETUC, but all three confederations were free to pursue European and international links outside the official bodies, through development projects and bilateral contacts with unions in other countries.

The end of the cold war led eventually to a thaw in the attitude of FO towards CGT membership of the ETUC, finally agreed in 1999, and the CGT was a founding member of the ITUC in 2006. Given its only recent participation in the mainstream European and international trade union bodies, or perhaps in response to its previous isolation, the CGT has developed particularly extensive programmes of education and training for its activists and officials on EU and international questions. It carries out consultations at sectoral and regional levels on major international and European issues, and the latter are integrated into national work. Nonetheless, the confederation is clearly 'top-down' in its decision-making on international policy: many activists were initially opposed to entry into the ETUC and ITUC, for example, but clearly the decision had already been taken by the leadership. The CGT has emerged as a leader of the 'left' unions within both the ETUC and the ITUC. It has a long tradition of cooperation with NGOs in its international work and takes part alongside a wide spectrum of civil society organizations in a national forum on CSR, along with the CFDT. The latter confederation has played an important role in European affairs for a much longer period, through the ETUC and the ETUFs, and has also developed a strong involvement in CSR and transnational company agreements. Both confederations carry out solidarity work in developing countries, in particular in former French colonies in Africa as well as in Asia and Latin America. International affairs are the responsibility of a member of the CFDT executive, not the general secretary. FO, which for many years was the only French affiliate to the ICFTU, has long been a major player on the international stage, particularly within the ILO.

CGIL, CISL, and UIL usually collaborate on international issues, for example by agreeing common positions and lists of candidates for office; and indeed the then CISL president, Bruno Storti, a former ICFTU president, was a strong advocate of the admission of CGIL to the ETUC in 1974 (a move opposed by FO) (Gumbrell-McCormick 2000: 356–7). But this does not mean that there is no difference between their positions. Like the CGT in France, the CGIL adopts a more radical position within the ETUC and ITUC, and has pushed for a stronger common stance on globalization within both bodies. The 2009 *conferenza di organizzazione* called for a major increase in the resources devoted to international and European work, including the expansion of training on international issues, and also proposed the creation of a permanent coordinating body of the three confederations to make their international work more coherent and less 'episodic'.

Of the two anglophone countries, British unions have long been key international actors and were a major player in the creation of WFTU as well as the ICFTU. In the immediate post-war years, and in the period of decolonization thereafter, the TUC continued to exert considerable influence at international level, particularly in the former colonies, and helped establish a Commonwealth Trade Union Council. It continues to work with unions in developing countries, especially in former British colonies and in Latin America, on education and other development projects, and in campaigns in support of human and trade union rights. It pursued many bilateral relationships with trade unions in other countries, sometimes in contradiction to ICFTU policies. For example, with several of its sectoral unions it developed good relations with the French CGT and other unions outside the ICFTU 'family' during the Cold War period, reflecting a commitment to unification of the entire trade union movement at European and world levels. It was one of the strongest advocates of broadening ETUC membership beyond its original ICFTU constituency. In recent years, EU issues have gained priority; as part of the 'relaunch' of the TUC, its international department was renamed the European Union and International Relations Department, an indication of the relative salience of the two arenas.

Widely regarded as an agent of British government foreign policy (Harrod 1972), the TUC for a time lost influence within international trade unionism. In more recent years, it has regained an important role in the ITUC and the GUFs, as well as the ETUC. Indeed despite the traditional implicit principle that trade unionists from the largest affiliates should not hold top posts in the international and European trade union bodies, British trade unionists have occupied key positions, notably John Monks as general secretary of the ETUC from 2003 to 2011 and Guy Ryder at the ICFTU/ITUC from 2002 to 2010. As the then TUC general secretary quipped at the ITUC founding congress, 'there is one area where Britain excels, and that is the export of trade unionists'.

Many of the larger TUC affiliates have their own international departments, including Unison and Unite, running international projects and maintaining bilateral relations with unions in other countries. Unite, indeed, has officially 'merged' with the US Steelworkers' Union in a 'global' organization, but this has had no discernible effect on its day-to-day operations. Many British unions have an international or European component to trade union education and training, and involve themselves in solidarity campaigns on major international issues.

Though Ireland is Europe's most open economy, its trade unions have traditionally been very little involved in European and international affairs, a point made in the report to the ICTU Biennial Delegate Conference in 2011. The conference recommended creating the post of international secretary to address this problem. In the meantime, the ICTU has received government funding to introduce trade union training and consciousness raising on international development issues. The sectoral unions nonetheless do engage in European affairs, in particular through EWCs.

Despite the many differences between the countries of our study with regard to the focus and extent of international work, we can draw some preliminary conclusions. First, we have said relatively little about what trade unions actually *do* internationally. Trade unions in Europe, despite their pronouncements on the need for international action, are still mainly focused on their own national issues, and what attention they do give to international questions has increasingly focused on Europe, which we discuss below. Second, international issues remain distant from the average member and even the average activist, with a few notable exceptions. Yet the need for greater knowledge about international affairs and greater coordination, at least among European national centres, was mentioned by many of our interviewees: '[w]e don't know enough about what other countries are doing well,' said one French official. Clearly, trade unions have to do much more in terms of communication and information, an elementary form of international action. Third, much international work is bilateral, devoted to various types of 'charity' rather than more egalitarian forms of solidarity, and in many countries much of this work is at least partially funded by national governments. Finally, there are important differences between the way unions handle global and European issues. While it is possible (indeed necessary) for EU-related issues to be functionally integrated into national work, and while national (and sometimes local or regional) officials are often able to handle European questions, strictly international issues such as dealing with the ITUC or ILO generally require specialist competence.

The European Dimension

As we have noted, for most of its history, trade union internationalism has been primarily European in composition and focus: all formal organizations of global unionism have been based in Europe, headed by Europeans (though the ITUC now has an Australian general secretary) and largely funded by European affiliates. If one source of tension in international trade unionism has been a belief that the movement was dominated by 'a powerful European club' (Gumbrell-McCormick 2000: 336), the opposite concern—that European unions would do less at global level—has existed ever since the creation of the (then) European Economic Community (EEC) in 1957. What was initially a common market between six western European countries has now become the European Union (EU) of twenty-seven member states, encompassing virtually the whole of western Europe and the majority of CEE countries. Three additional countries (Iceland, Liechtenstein, and Norway) form part of the European Economic Area (EEA) and are bound by the rules of the internal market. Unlike other free trade areas, the EU possesses an elaborate regulatory architecture, including the capacity to legislate on a wide range of employment issues. Increasingly, European economic integration has set the parameters of trade union action, encouraging 'an extension to the European level of the role unions had sought for themselves in national planning' (Cox 1971: 562). As one union official responsible for international affairs told us, what is discussed today in Brussels may shape national legislation in three years' time, so it is essential to be involved. Hence for unions in Europe today, 'international' is often understood primarily to mean 'European'.

The formation of the ETUC in 1973, as a body autonomous of existing global union structures, was widely viewed as a signal of a shift of interests and resources. At the outset there were two main contentious issues among European affiliates of the ICFTU. First, should there be a single organization encompassing both EEC member states and those outside; second, should the new body be open to non-members of the ICFTU? After intense debate, it was agreed to create a broad European structure, followed by a decision to open membership to all bona fide unions except affiliates of WFTU. In 1974, the ETUC admitted all main European affiliates of the WCL. Later the same year, CGIL—which ended its full membership of WFTU—was also admitted, to be followed significantly later by all major (ex-)Communist unions in western Europe (Moreno 2001). With the fall of the Iron Curtain in 1989, membership was extended eastwards, though again with considerable debate whether the former 'official' unions should be admitted.

The ETUC was founded with seventeen affiliates in fifteen countries; this has increased to eighty-five organizations in thirty-six countries. Creating a coherent common programme despite growing diversity of interests, experiences, and traditions is a daunting task. At the same time, the challenges facing trade unions have magnified radically; yet in a period of straitened union finances, income from affiliates has not kept pace in real terms with membership, particularly since unions from CEE pay pro rata only a quarter of the fees of those in the west. For much of its work, the ETUC depends on subsidies from the European Commission. Most notably, its research arm, the ETUI, is largely funded by the Commission—more than €10 million was paid for its 2009–10 work programme, substantially above the annual affiliation fee income—while major sums are also received for other projects. In addition, considerable support for workshops and conferences—meeting facilities, interpreters, travel costs—comes from the same source. The ETUFs, previously known as European Industry Federations, almost all of which are (more or less autonomous) regional organizations of the GUFs, likewise receive significant Commission subsidies.

Gläser (2009) has suggested that the ETUC faces two dilemmas that are a source of inescapable weakness. The first is between representativeness and capacity to act—a tension between the logics of membership and of influence, or between broad coverage and homogeneity (Braud 2000). The second is between political independence and financial dependence on the European institutions; or in the words of Martin and Ross (2001), 'the dilemma of borrowed resources'. The resulting contradictions have provoked intense debates among unions at national level, sometimes overt but often implicit.

The European Union: A Complex and Contested Political Space

The EU is something of an enigma for social scientists. As noted above, it is not just a regional trading bloc; it possesses a significant administrative infrastructure with authority of a political nature. But nor is it, as sometimes asserted, a 'super-state': the competence of EU institutions is limited to the agenda specified in the governing Treaties, and the principle of 'subsidiarity' insists that the European level should regulate only when this cannot be accomplished effectively at national level (though it is less clear who is to judge whether this is the case). It is also a complex political system with many veto points.

A key question for trade unions is the character of European integration. Initially, most assumed that as the importance of the European level increased, this would entail a growing body of European rules regulating employment and the labour market. But subsequently a more sceptical position argued that integration occurred primarily through weakening or eliminating national rules which constrained cross-national economic activity—'negative integration' (Scharpf 1999)—without necessarily establishing supranational rules in their place. A common market can be understood primarily in terms of freedom *from* regulations inhibiting cross-national exchange, whereas the creation of a social community depends on *rights* entrenched in new regulatory institutions. For example, the single European market is founded on the 'four freedoms' of movement (for goods, services, capital, and labour). Freedom of movement means eliminating national barriers; but for neoliberals and advocates of flexibility, it is neither necessary nor desirable to create positive regulation at European level.

This question overlaps with the relationship between economic and social integration. The 1957 Treaty of Rome established a European *Economic* Community (or Common Market), and market integration was in the eyes of many observers (both supporters and opponents) the be-all and end-all. However, there were fears that countries with inferior employment conditions would gain an unfair advantage in the common market (what would later be described as 'social dumping'). For this reason, the original Treaty of Rome included a clause enabling the Commission to propose measures aimed at the harmonization of working conditions, and another prescribing equal pay for women.

In the 1970s (when centre-left governments were in power in many member states) there were more ambitious efforts to adopt directives (the main form of EU legislation) which would ensure upwards harmonization of employment standards. This was halted with a shift to the right in European politics (notably Thatcher's election in Britain in 1979) and enthusiasm for labour market deregulation. A new phase began when Jacques Delors became Commission president in 1985: he helped drive the 'single market' project, but insisted that greater integration must possess a 'social dimension'. The 'social chapter' agreed at Maastricht in December 1991 enlarged EU competence in the employment field and extended the range of issues on which directives could be adopted by qualified majority voting (QMV).

A key element in the Delors initiative was the 'social dialogue' between unions and employers at European level. By cultivating authoritative interlocutors from the two sides of industry, the Commission might strengthen its own authority and acquire greater room for manœuvre within the complex politics of EU decision-making. The Maastricht Treaty gave the 'social partners' at European level the right to negotiate agreements that could be implemented as directives by a 'Council decision'. Maastricht was followed by significant new employment legislation, but from the late 1990s the pace slowed again: right-wing governments now dominated western Europe, while eastwards enlargement has created a bloc without the traditions of 'social Europe' and with a competitive interest in weak employment regulation.

There is a familiar imbalance within the institutions of the EU itself: the Parliament, the most 'popular' (directly elected) element in the decision-making architecture, and the most reliable supporter of an effective social dimension to European integration, is also the most limited in its powers. The Commission, while dependent for its own status on the extent of EU regulatory capacity, has in recent years been dominated by neoliberal fanatics. This has involved a sustained drive to enforce market 'freedoms', pressure to weaken national welfare and labour market protections and the imposition of binding instruments of fiscal rigour and budgetary austerity. The Council, comprising representatives of each national government, reflects the dominant political coloration of Europe; and given the limited scope for QMV on industrial relations issues, contains multiple veto points against an extended social dimension. Finally, the ECJ, with judges from all member states, has since enlargement in 2004 given market 'freedoms' primacy over social protection, as we discuss below.

To these biases is added the imbalance of influence between labour and capital. This is not simply a matter of organizational resources. In many respects, the ETUC is more robust than the employers' organization BusinessEurope, though we should not forget the ranks of lobbyists and representatives retained in Brussels by individual companies and national associations, vastly outnumbering the European officials of national trade unions. Even greater power is exercised by the European Round Table of Industrialists comprising heads of leading MNCs: the single market project of the 1980s and the more general commitment to liberalization of European societies were largely outcomes of its strategic initiative (Balanyá et al. 2003; van Apeldoorn 2000). But the issue is also structural: employers and industrialists work with the grain of entrenched EU policy, while trade unions (if they are serious about 'social Europe') seek a major change of course. In such a context, veto power is typically more effective as well as more discreet. The normal economic rationality of company decision-makers has a political significance which may not even be intended.

Trade Unions and European Integration

European economic integration provoked conflicting reactions among trade unions. To some extent, these reflected familiar political divisions. Unions affiliated to, or sympathetic with, WFTU denounced the original EEC as the institutional expression of the interests of monopoly capital. Conversely, affiliates of the ICFTU and WCL tended to a more positive view: European integration was inherently progressive, not least as heralding the end of military conflicts among (west) European nations. But national circumstances were also important. Marks and Wilson (2000), in a study of party-political attitudes to European integration, suggest that Social-democratic parties with limited strength and effectiveness at national level tend to regard European integration positively, while those with a greater power to shape national policy resist the idea of subordinating national decision-making capacity to an (almost certainly more conservative) European regime. A similar distinction applies to trade unions: where Labour or Social-democratic governments have been relatively common (as in Britain and the Nordic countries), unions have been more sceptical of European integration. Confronted with the tension between a process of European integration that seems in principle desirable, and the potential threats from economic integration to national industrial relations practices, unions have responded in four different ways. The most negative could be termed 'no, because': for example, the French CGT long opposed actually existing Europeanization as a conspiracy driven by multinational capital to undermine workers' rights. A more nuanced position could be termed 'no, unless': the position of opposition groups within many trade union movements, particularly in the Nordic countries. This shades into what might be termed the 'yes, if' stance: for example, the Austrian ÖGB in 1988 endorsed accession to the EU but with nine important conditions. More positively, many trade unions have embraced a 'yes, and' posture: their support for integration is virtually unconditional, but they articulate a 'wish list' of desired accompaniments to Europeanization. This has been the traditional position of the ETUC.

Dølvik (1997: 29) has argued that 'the incentives for trade unions to engage in Europeanization...are influenced by interplay between the particular structure of opportunities related to the social dimension and the structural bias of the broader trajectory of European integration'. As this interplay has developed, both ideological and nation-specific sources of resistance weakened over time: it is possible to discern a 'conversion experience' (Martin and Ross 1999: 355) through which initially sceptical organizations changed position. This conversion owed much to the exhaustion of the old ideologies (Communist, Christian, or Social democratic) which once provided a vision and utopia for trade union movements: 'Europe' seemed a new moral inspiration. For this reason, the shift in EU policy towards uncompromising neo-liberalism has caused considerable trade union disorientation, particularly as anti-EU sentiments have increasingly marked popular opinion in the countries in our study. One indicator of changing union policies and of national differences is provided by the results of popular referendums on European issues (Hyman 2010), and we refer to these in the following discussion—even though this means neglecting Germany, where no referendums have been held, and Italy, where there was one, almost wholly uncontentious, referendum in 1989.

The Nordic countries have been described as 'reluctant Europeans', suspicious of the risks of EU membership in terms both of national economic interests and the viability of their distinctive social models (Miljan 1977). In general the official trade union organizations have assessed the economic benefits of integration as outweighing the risks, but have not necessarily convinced their memberships.

In Sweden, until the 1990s EU membership was generally considered inconsistent both with Swedish neutrality and with Sweden's highly developed welfare state. But the end of the Cold War and escalating economic problems changed the calculus (Archer 2000; Misgeld 1997). EU accession was initiated by a Social-democratic government, but with considerable internal opposition. Leaders of both LO and TCO in general supported EU membership; but there were major internal divisions, and officially LO took a neutral position. In the accession referendum in 1994, 'grass-roots union members, especially in the blue-collared sector, provided one of the main sources of opposition' (Archer 2000: 104). Similar divisions occurred over EMU membership in 2003 (Bieler 2006). LO was split: the manufacturing unions *Metall* and *Industrifacket* were strongly in favour of the euro, *Handels* and *Transport* were equally strongly opposed, with most other unions lukewarm; hence LO decided not to take a formal line on the referendum. Nevertheless, its president, Wanja Lundby-Wedin, signalled her personal support. In the event, euro entry was decisively rejected. LO members voted almost two to one against, and TCO members were evenly divided.

Denmark joined the EU in 1973, and has held six referendums on EU-related issues. In the view of Franklin (2002: 752), the Danes 'have by far the best developed views on European integration of any voters in the European Union'. As one union official told us, his area's delegate conferences are usually quiet until the EU is mentioned, when twenty members will be on their feet wanting to speak. In the original accession referendum, the LO leadership stressed the economic advantages of membership and campaigned strongly in favour. However, two major unions (SiD and *Metal*) were opposed, and a special LO congress endorsed accession by a relatively narrow majority. Left-wing criticism persisted after accession, and the unions were again divided over the Single European Act (SEA) referendum in 1996; thus LO adopted no formal position (Haahr 1993: 207–10). The SEA was eventually endorsed by a 56 per cent vote, based mainly on solid support from right-wing parties.

Denmark was one of three countries to hold a referendum on the Maastricht Treaty and the only one to vote against (by a very narrow majority). The Treaty was endorsed by the leaders of the *Socialdemokraterne* and the LO, the latter citing in particular the 'social chapter' as a reason for support. The opposition was led by the left-wing *Socialistisk Folkeparti* (SF), which highlighted the negative implications of EMU, together with two smaller right-wing parties. In the event, almost two-thirds of *Socialdemokraterne* supporters voted against, hence the majority of trade union members. In the political turmoil that followed, a 'national compromise' was reached setting the terms on which SF would end its opposition, and these in turn were accepted by other EU member states. In the second referendum the Treaty was approved, but the great majority of SF supporters, and almost half the Social-democrat voters, still voted 'no', with manual workers and public sector employees most strongly opposed (Svensson 1994, 2002; Worre 1995). At the next referendum, on the Amsterdam Treaty in 1998, LO mounted a well resourced campaign in favour, on the theme of *Fagligt Europa* (a trade union Europe) (Petersen 1997). This time the 'yes' majority was comfortable. The governing *Socialdemokraterne* initiated a referendum on euro membership in 2000, with the backing of most political parties, even though popular support for the single currency was extremely limited. The top leadership of LO also gave strong support (Marcussen and Zølner 2001: 387). Yet the unions were in practice divided; 'the members don't trust us on European issues', a senior LO official told us after the referendum, adding: 'and they shouldn't'. The outcome was a narrow 'no' majority. Danish unions remain 'passive supporters' of European integration, and at times resist ETUC demands for more EU labour market regulation as a threat to their own bargaining-based model (Knudsen and Lind 2012: 393).

Of our 'central' group of countries, Germany, Belgium, and the Netherlands were all members of the original EEC, and membership has traditionally received strong public support, including from the trade unions—although, as we will see, this has changed in recent years. Only one referendum has been held in these countries, the Dutch vote on the Constitutional Treaty (TCE) in June 2005. This took place three days after the French rejection, discussed below, and was even more decisive, with a 62 per cent 'no' vote on a relatively high turnout. This was the more remarkable because organized opposition was minimal and was led by parties outside the political mainstream. The FNV urged its members to vote 'yes': 'the European Constitution is a step forward'; but it did not engage actively in the campaign. The arguments of the 'no' camp—criticisms of EU neoliberalism, together with fears that the Netherlands, a small country, was losing its autonomy and cultural identity, that it was paying too much to Brussels, and that the euro had hit consumers' pockets (Lubbers 2008)—resonated with many union members.

Austria, partly because of its post-war neutral status, joined the EU only in 1995. The SPÖ had long opposed membership as incompatible with Austrian neutrality; but attitudes changed in the mid 1980s, and in 1989 the party leadership endorsed accession with minimal internal opposition (Kaiser 1995: 412). Within the ÖGB, reservations were at first stronger. A special conference in July 1988 set nine conditions for accession, but these were rapidly sidelined—in part, perhaps, because of the leading role of its leader, Fritz Verzetnitsch, within the ETUC (he was to become its president in 1993). In March 1989 the ÖGB signed a joint statement with the employers supporting accession, on condition that Austrian neutrality was preserved. By the time of the referendum, the publicity material issued by the ÖGB was almost exclusively in favour of a 'yes' vote. As a senior official told us, there was a systematic process of propaganda: all the structures of the ÖGB were expected to be opinion leaders, and hundreds of events were organized across the country. The outcome was a two-thirds majority for accession. However, scepticism remains widespread, particularly regarding free movement of labour post 2004, as we discuss below.

Both France and Italy were among the six founding members of the EEC. The largest (Communist-dominated) unions in each country were hostile to the original EEC; but attitudes changed, much earlier in Italy (with the turn to 'Eurocommunism') than in France. Conversely, the other main unions in each country were strong supporters of economic integration. Only in France have referendums been held on European issues. The first, in 1972, endorsed the first wave of EEC enlargement. Twenty years later, when President Mitterrand called a referendum over Maastricht, a bare majority of voters approved the Treaty. The campaign saw most mainstream politicians in the 'yes' camp; both the PCF and the far right campaigned against. Among the unions, the Treaty was actively supported by the CFDT and opposed by the CGT. Both the government and its critics on the left presented monetary discipline, institutional reform, and curbs on public spending as necessary responses to the single market and the future single currency (Milner 2000; Ross 1998). Such considerations primarily contributed to the size of the 'no' vote, which 'was working-class, with industrial and inner-city areas voting heavily against, notably areas of high unemployment' (Criddle 1993: 235). As Moss argued (1998: 70), 'this was not a nationalist vote but a class vote of protest by those who associated sound money and the single currency with unemployment'.

Such protests came to the fore in 2005 with the referendum on the TCE, which was derailed by French rejection. The ETUC strongly supported the Treaty, despite explicit qualifications. It had campaigned vigorously for the Charter of Fundamental Rights, adopted on a non-binding basis in 2000, to be given legal status within the new Treaty; when this was achieved, it was endorsed by overwhelming majorities in the steering and executive committees. Though arguing that 'the Constitution must represent a base from which to promote the construction of more Social Europe', the ETUC concluded that 'support is the only pragmatic and realistic approach for trade unions'. In the event, only the French FO voted against, while twelve affiliates including the TUC, CGT, and TCO abstained.

In the French referendum, the PS was deeply divided, as were the Greens. Smaller left-wing parties were actively opposed, while a leading role was taken by ATTAC. As in 1992, the unions were split. The CFDT was again a strong supporter, listing 'ten good reasons to say yes', and was joined by two smaller confederations. As noted above, the FO was the one ETUC affiliate to vote against the TCE at the executive meeting, and insisted that it did not consider itself committed by the decision in favour. Its main objection was that the TCE entrenched a neoliberal policy regime destructive of employment rights and welfare provision. FO did not actually call on its members to vote 'no', since it was 'confident of their astuteness and power of reasoning'—but the message was clear. As noted above, the CGT abstained in the ETUC vote, perhaps restrained by its recent (1999) acceptance into the ETUC and the election of its international secretary, Joël Decaillon, to the ETUC secretariat in 2003. Its initial assessment of the Treaty in May 2004 was rather neutral, echoing both the positive and negative comments of the ETUC. But at the national committee in February 2005 there was in effect a rank-and-file revolt, committing the CGT to campaign for rejection of the Treaty by a vote of over 80 per cent. The most unambiguous trade union opposition came from the smaller left-wing SUD, which called for a vote against neoliberalism but for a different Europe.

The popular verdict was a 55 per cent 'no' vote on a high turnout. As in 1992 (and in other countries), the 'no' vote was firmly rooted in the working class, indicating 'a clear-cut class cleavage opposing the haves and the have-nots in contemporary French society' (Ivaldi 2006: 57). The connection was again made between deflation and deregulation at home and the policies being driven by the European Commission and symbolized by the draft Bolkestein directive for liberalization of services—against which the ETUC had organized a European demonstration in March 2005. This was 'a vote against a particular Europe, an economically liberal Europe' (Brouard and Tiberj 2006: 266).

The two anglophone countries present interesting contrasts. Both joined the EEC in 1973, in the British case under a Conservative government. After Labour was elected the following year, a referendum was held—the first and only such measure in the UK—in 1975; the result was a two-to-one vote to remain in the EEC. The TUC campaigned for a 'no' vote and its majority position remained hostile until the 1980s, when the 'social dimension' of the EU became far preferable to the market liberalism of the Thatcher government.

The TUC response to the SEA was to 'maximize the benefits, minimize the costs'; and its general council overwhelmingly backed Maastricht and opposed calls for a referendum. Despite qualifications and internal divisions, it also supported EMU entry. Rank-and-file opinion has been far more negative: one 1999 survey found 61 per cent of union members opposed to joining the euro, only 23 per cent in favour (Mullen and Burkitt 2003: 333). A leftward switch in the leadership of two of the largest unions—Amicus in 2002, TGWU in 2003, now amalgamated in Unite—resulted in a more EU-critical position. In addition, the strongly pro-EU stance of the TUC general secretary from 1993, John Monks—who left in 2003 to head the ETUC—gave way to a rather more cautious approach by his successor. Congress rejected the TCE in 2005, seeing it as entrenching economic liberalization, and in 2007 voted in favour of a referendum on the Lisbon Treaty, largely as a protest against the UK opt-out from the Charter of Fundamental Rights—although a motion to campaign for a 'no' vote was defeated.

As in several other member states, unions in Ireland have shifted from a primarily anti-EU stance to support for further integration—though ironically, this change has coincided with declining support for the EU in popular referendums. Ireland joined the EU in 1973 together with Britain and Denmark, and is the only one of the trio to have entered the eurozone. Constitutionally, Ireland is required to conduct referendums on any treaties affecting national sovereignty, and eight have been held on EU issues. In 1972 the unions campaigned against accession, but the electorate endorsed membership by a massive majority; unlike their British counterparts, the Irish unions then engaged fully in the EU institutions. The ICTU took no formal stance on the SEA;

while on Maastricht, it 'evaluated EC membership and the prospects of further commitments positively in the 1992 campaign' (van Wijnbergen 1994: 186). The outcome was a decisive 'yes' vote.

In the 1998 vote on the Amsterdam Treaty, all mainstream political parties supported the Treaty. The main arguments against centred on a perceived threat to Irish neutrality, the EU's democratic deficit, and the subordination of social to economic policy. The ICTU backed the Treaty as embodying employment and social inclusion as EU priorities. After a low-key campaign the Treaty was comfortably approved. For the 2001 vote on the Nice Treaty the political line-up was largely the same, and the campaign centred around familiar themes, though EU enlargement added issues regarding Ireland's increased contributions to the EU budget, the dilution of its influence on decision-making, and the opening of the labour market to CEE workers. Though the ICTU was strongly in favour (only one member of the executive voted against) it did not campaign actively. There is evidence of complacency among supporters of the Treaty, but the result was a narrow 'no' majority on a very low turnout. For the second referendum sixteen months later the 'yes' camp mounted a far more active campaign (Gilland 2003), and the ICTU and its affiliates engaged far more vigorously, spelling out what were seen as the benefits for workers, countering the core arguments of opponents, and denouncing 'scare-mongering about floods of immigrants from Eastern Europe taking Irish jobs after enlargement' (ICTU press release, 16 October 2002). The outcome was a much higher turnout and a clear 'yes' majority.

Ireland was again the only country to hold a popular vote on the Lisbon Treaty. While the campaign was in many respects similar to those on previous occasions, there were two important changes. First, Irish opposition was informed by the ideas and arguments of the 2005 French campaign, to some extent cross-fertilized by involvement in the ESF. Second, the industrial relations climate had been inflamed by the bitter confrontation at the end of 2005 between SIPTU and Irish Ferries, discussed in Chapter 3. One consequence was that the unions were more divided. Perhaps most importantly, SIPTU demanded a government commitment to legislate for stronger controls over agency workers and to protect trade union rights; when this was refused it made no recommendation to its members, widely seen as a tacit call to reject the Treaty. The referendum result, a narrow no majority, was widely predicted. 'Voting was heavily class-correlated' (Storey 2008: 77), with three-quarters of manual workers in the 'no' camp (Chari 2008). In its own reaction, the ICTU insisted that in supporting enlargement at the time of the Nice referendums, it was not aware that the Irish labour market would be immediately opened to the new member states, and was not consulted on this; a particular problem because Ireland had a small and 'virtually unregulated labour market' (ICTU Briefing, July 2008).

As with the Nice Treaty, a second referendum reversed the popular verdict. The government obtained a set of 'legal guarantees' aimed at addressing issues raised by the 'no' campaign. Perhaps more important was the impact of the global economic crisis, which seemed to underline the vulnerability of an Ireland committed to 'going it alone'. The ICTU executive again backed a 'yes' vote, though agreeing that affiliates could adopt their own position in the campaign. SIPTU now gave its backing, although expressing a series of reservations and also emphasizing that concerns over the ECJ judgments had not been adequately addressed. In the event, the result was a two-to-one majority in favour of Lisbon, with the highest turnout on a European referendum in Ireland since accession in 1972.

This overview reveals considerable cross-national diversity but also some common themes. Over recent decades, there have been two conflicting trajectories. The first is a shift in union attitudes towards European integration from suspicion or even antagonism towards acceptance and even enthusiasm. In an important sense, union leaders became professional Europeans, insiders in a process of integration but with their own agenda of moderating the neoliberal priorities that have come to dominate the EU. At the same time, popular acquiescence in the elite project of Europeanization has been extensively shaken. Though the dynamics of each referendum campaign have been unique, the British situation in which the 'eurosceptic' agenda is shaped primarily from the political right is not typical of western Europe: in most campaigns the prominent arguments have favoured a more social and more democratic Europe. Surveys have shown virtually without exception that manual (and to a lesser extent, routine white-collar) workers—the core constituency of trade union membership—have been disproportionally represented in the 'no' camp. In this sense, the policies of most unions are clearly out of step with the attitudes of their memberships.

Unions and 'Free Movement'

The EU Treaties provide for the 'free movement' of goods, persons, services, and capital, and also for the 'freedom of establishment' of economic activities. These principles were contained in the original Treaty of Rome, but it was assumed for almost half a century that governments could impose specific regulations on the exercise of these freedoms as long as these did not discriminate against citizens of other member states. Hence, for example, collectively bargained employment rules could be applied to workers exercising the right to freedom of movement from another member state. Such assumptions have been challenged in two key respects. The first concerns the labour market implications of eastwards EU enlargement in 2004. There have always been cross-national disparities in wage levels in the member states, in particular after the accession of Greece, Portugal, and Spain in the 1980s, but the west–east differences vastly exceeded those between north and south, and this was even more the case when Bulgaria and Romania joined in 2007. In order to cushion the effect on western labour markets, it was agreed that free movement of workers could be restricted for up to seven years, and we discuss national trade union policies below. The second challenge, to which we have already alluded, stems from the forceful assertion of the primacy of market freedoms by the ECJ, itself transformed in character by the addition of judges from the new member states. We explore a number of aspects of the new legal regime and trade union responses.

Writing on the eve of enlargement, Meardi (2002) documented reservations among west European trade unions, not least because many post-Communist countries had embraced policies of market liberalism which conflicted with the presuppositions of the 'European social model'. He noted that German unions, in an attempt to cultivate good relations with their Polish counterparts, agreed not to demand transitional periods in respect of free movement of labour, but did not object when the German government imposed limitations. The most restrictive position was adopted by the ÖGB, which argued that free entry should be permitted only when wage levels in the country of origin had reached 80 per cent of those in Austria. A leading ÖGB official told us that it caused some embarrassment when the far-right FPÖ declared that it endorsed the union's policy. Both Germany and Austria are on the borders of the old Iron Curtain, and fears of the effects of a sudden opening of their labour markets are not surprising. We should note that in both countries, attempts have been made to cooperate with unions in the east; and as we saw in Chapter 3, in Germany in particular there have been efforts to develop unionization among CEE migrant workers.

In Ireland, Sweden, and the UK, no restrictions were imposed in 2004. Austria and Germany were the only countries to apply a seven-year transitional period; all others enforced restrictions of up to five years. The impact of the immediate opening of the labour market in Ireland—which has the smallest population of any of our ten countries—was particularly marked. Union officials complained that they had not been consulted by the government, and that the low levels of labour market regulation made social dumping a serious threat. In Britain there was also a substantial inflow, particularly from Poland. The TUC, and most of its affiliates, strongly supported immediate free movement, fearing that workers from the accession countries would otherwise be forced to take on irregular work (Clark and Hardy 2011: 4). LO in Sweden adopted a similar position, though a senior official told us that it was difficult to convince some affiliates that the entry of east European workers would be easier to regulate if they were allowed to work legally. Indeed, in a statement in 2005 the ETUC reported claims by affiliates in some countries that had imposed restrictions that these had caused adverse effects, such as an increase in undeclared work and false self-employment, and exploitation and discriminatory treatment; while Meardi (2012a: 93) notes 'a pathologically high rate of self-employment' among migrant workers in Germany. Both Britain and Ireland imposed restrictions on the entry of workers from Bulgaria and Romania after 2007. This was condemned by the British TUC, which pressed for a relaxation of the rules. By contrast, the ICTU gave qualified support to the limitations, arguing in particular that it would be dangerous to allow unrestricted access to the Irish labour market if the UK acted differently (Krings 2009).

In the countries which adopted some transitional restrictions but not for the full seven years, patterns varied. The typical Nordic approach, adopted in Denmark, was to allow permits for any worker who obtained a job in accordance with collectively agreed conditions. This might also have been the Swedish position, but details were not agreed before the deadline. In the Netherlands, unions were divided: the FNV opposed transitional restrictions, arguing that these would encourage illegal working; but the CNV supported such measures to cushion the impact of labour migration. The latter view was endorsed by most right-wing parties, and also by the SP on the left, and limitations were imposed. In Belgium, by contrast, there was broad consensus on the need for restrictions, and these remained in place for five years. An official of the ABVV/FGTB told us that they accepted free movement in principle, but insisted on conditions, including strengthening the labour inspectorate to prevent abuses, and they supported the maintenance of restrictions in sectors where migrants were used to undercut standards. In both France and Italy, restraints were imposed by right-wing governments, to some extent pandering to xenophobic pressure. In France, all the main unions called in 2006 for the lifting of restrictions; a CGT official declared that 'we cannot have first- and second-grade workers and citizens'. The rules were eventually abolished in mid 2008. In Italy, the unions had not called for controls, and when the centre-left Prodi government was elected in 2006 it did not extend the restrictions, as the defeated Berlusconi government intended to do.

The ECJ: Liberalization versus Employment Regulation

'Expanded judicial review in the European Union simultaneously has empowered judges, shifted agenda-setting powers away from the member states toward the European Commission, altered the character of discourse over policy reform, transformed the kinds of policy instruments that decision makers prefer to use, and dramatically changed the value of political resources traditionally employed by interest groups' (Pierson 2004: 109). Though in the past the ECJ used its discretionary competence to enhance employment protections (notably in the field of equal opportunities), it has increasingly interpreted the Treaty commitment to market freedoms as overriding national employment protection rules (Höpner and Schäfer 2010). Its landmark decisions in the Viking and Laval cases in 2007 insisted that, although there was a 'fundamental' right to strike, this was less fundamental than the right of businesses to supply cross-border services. Irrespective of national law, industrial action which interfered with market freedoms was legitimate only if it satisfied strict tests: it must be justified by overriding reasons of public interest, must be undertaken as a last resort and must be 'proportionate' to the union objectives. Such an assessment was ultimately for the courts to make, under direction from the ECJ (Bücker and Warneck 2010).

The Rüffert and Luxembourg cases in 2008 raised somewhat different issues, both severely limiting the capacity of public authorities to prescribe employment standards if these interfered with the freedom to provide services. In Rüffert, the ECJ ruled that a German local authority was not entitled to require a contractor to force subcontractors to observe collectively agreed conditions of employment, since these conditions were not universally binding. The Luxembourg case was brought by the Commission against the national government, arguing that its implementation of the 1996 Posted Workers directive (PWD) breached market freedoms. The directive was intended to prevent a service provider—particularly in the construction industry—from 'posting' workers from a lower- to a higher-wage country and paying only their home-country wage rates, by defining 'a hard core of minimum prescriptions' where the law or collective agreements of the host country should prevail (Cremers 2010: 298). The ECJ (as in the preceding Laval judgment) treated the terms of the PWD as the maximum permissible employment protection compatible with market freedoms, rather than a minimum as originally intended. This was particularly serious because, in general, there was no provision for transitional restrictions regarding posted workers, and the use of posting expanded rapidly in countries which imposed limitations on free entry of workers (as the ETUC had warned).

In their discussion of some of the implications, Dølvik and Visser point to a 'trilemma' in EU policies, that rest on three 'fundamental principles'—market freedoms, equal treatment, and collective employee rights—which 'cannot be realised in equal measure' (2009: 493). But the severity of the contradictions varies cross-nationally. The priority assigned to market freedoms is most evidently a challenge to 'voluntarist' industrial relations systems, as in the Nordic countries where both the Viking and Laval cases arose (Finland and Sweden respectively) and where unions rely on the threat of industrial action to sustain high bargaining coverage. Germany, with no statutory minimum wage and with collective agreements rarely made generally binding, faces similar problems. By contrast, countries with a tradition of statutory regulation (or the legal extension of collective agreements) can argue that labour market rules are applied in a universal and hence non-discriminatory fashion. Moreover, while unions in western Europe focus on the risk of social dumping, some counterparts in the east welcome unrestricted access to western labour markets.

The ETUC called in 2008, in the aftermath of the ECJ judgments, for a 'social progress protocol' to be incorporated in the EU Treaties, specifying that 'neither economic freedoms nor competition rules shall have priority over fundamental social rights and social progress'. This hardly seems attainable within the current EU political conjuncture, but is strongly supported by affiliates in many countries, including LO Sweden and the DGB. At national level, union pronouncements in most of our countries are today marked by much sharper criticisms of the nature of European integration, with calls for a fundamental reorientation of union policies (Urban 2009).

The combination of ECJ attacks on trade union rights and EU-driven austerity has certainly helped shift the ETUC from an 'insider' role within institutionalized social dialogue procedures to a more 'outsider' stance in an effort to mobilize popular opinion, with frequent protests and mass demonstrations. Some such mobilizations have targeted specific Commission initiatives. One example was the Bolkestein directive, already mentioned. The initial draft in 2004 would have enabled a service provider to follow the regulatory standards of the 'country of origin' rather than the country of operation, providing a green light for social dumping. The ETUC and national unions organized large-scale protests, and the directive was significantly amended (though many of the original intentions have been restored by the ECJ judgments). Another significant campaign was the mobilization by the European Transport Workers' Federation and national unions against Commission efforts to liberalize port services. Following an imaginative publicity and lobbying campaign, the European Parliament rejected the initial proposals in in 2003; and joint action with those employers who would be adversely affected blocked a second Commission attempt in 2006 (Turnbull 2010).

A very different form of mobilizing response is industrial action to combat social dumping, regardless of court decisions. The most notable example was mentioned in Chapter 5: the unofficial strike by British construction workers at the Lindsey oil refinery in 2009, against the use by an Italian contractor of workers on inferior wages and conditions. Though widely depicted as a xenophobic incident, the strike is better regarded as a (largely successful) effort to defend collectively agreed conditions against attempts by a foreign service provider to undercut these (Barnard 2009; Meardi 2012b).

A third type of response is to strengthen cooperation with unions in the new member states. In the Laval case, the contractor colluded with a Latvian union to agree wage levels far below those collectively agreed in Sweden; but critics suggested that the Swedish union *Byggnads* should have done more to seek a common position with its Latvian counterpart (Gajewska 2009: 68–70). Subsequent attempts have been made to repair the damage, both bilaterally and through BASTUN. Similarly, there has been an increase in bilateral cooperation between German and Polish unions; much more generally, the ETUC's Interregional Trade Union Councils, ten of which bridge unions in east and west, serve to regulate cross-border movements of workers and the conditions under which they work.

Transnational Organization and Action at Company and Sectoral Levels

The increasing openness of the European economy, and the global economy more generally, created the potential for competitive undercutting of employment standards (social dumping). This is most commonly discussed in terms of the shift of production by MNCs from low-wage to high-wage countries, or the movement of workers in the reverse direction. However, competitive pressures between countries with high employment standards can also have serious effects: most notably, wage restraint in Germany has constrained pay bargaining in neighbouring countries. In this section we briefly discuss attempts to coordinate pay bargaining cross-nationally, before turning to a more detailed discussion of EWCs and framework agreements.

Bargaining Coordination

As we discussed in Chapter 5, 'competitive corporatism' has involved sustained wage moderation, which in turn has been one of the causes of the declining wage share in national income. This has stimulated a range of union attempts to limit downwards competitive pressures.

At its 1999 congress, the ETUC adopted the principle of a 'European solidaristic pay policy' which would 'guarantee workers a fair share of income; counter the danger of social dumping; counter the growing income inequality in some countries; contribute to a reduction in disparities in living conditions; and contribute to an effective implementation of the principle of equal treatment of the sexes'. This was followed in 2000 by a 'European guideline' for national bargaining: 'nominal wage increases should at least exceed inflation, whilst maximizing the proportion of productivity allocated to the rise in gross wages in order to secure a better balance between profits and wages; any remaining part of productivity increases should be used for other elements in the collective bargaining agenda, such as qualitative aspects of work where these are quantifiable and calculable in terms of cost'. Affiliates were asked to report annually on the application of this guideline (Schulten 2004). However, reporting was only partial (Mermet 2002), and all the evidence shows that affiliates failed to achieve the targets—which themselves were an attempt to stabilize the existing wage share rather than recover the losses of previous decades (Erne 2008). This lack of success was perhaps unsurprising, given that many of the parameters of the guideline could hardly be measured exactly, that decentralization of collective bargaining reduces the authority of national unions, and that bargaining outcomes depend more on employers and governments than on the unions themselves.

In any event, the ETUC delegated the main responsibility for coordination to its affiliates. Indeed, the policy of bargaining coordination stemmed from the 1997 initiative of the 'Doorn group' of confederations from Germany and the Benelux countries. The European Metalworkers' Federation (EMF, now IndustriALL) adopted a 'European coordination rule' in 1998, prescribing a pay target of inflation plus productivity growth, and established an information network, Eucob@n. This initiative was one outcome of the 1996 Belgian law (noted in Chapter 5) which prevented pay increases above the average in neighbouring countries (Erne 2008; Marginson and Sisson 2004).

For Schulten (2004: 307) the key problem with all such initiatives is their voluntaristic nature: ETUFs possess few sanctions over their affiliates, and enthusiasm for coordination differs considerably across countries. Busemeyer et al. (2008: 443) note that 'trade union leaders in the Scandinavian countries fear that collective wage bargaining on the EU level undermines their ability and power in national level wage bargaining'. On the other hand, 'union leaders in Southern countries supported stronger coordination of wage agreements. Some unions who have sceptical views on coordination were at least in favour of stronger consultation and exchange of information.' Erne (2008: 88) reports that his interviewees in Germany, Italy, France, and Belgium all 'accepted that national wage bargaining is losing much of its autonomy in the eurozone', though support for cross-national coordination differed between countries.

Yet in the absence of hierarchy, networks can achieve some effects. For Erne (2008: 103) it is important 'that national union leaders feel a moral obligation to explain their policies within a European framework'. The introduction of the euro reinforced such pressures; Traxler et al. (2008) find evidence of de facto 'cross-border pattern bargaining' in the metal industries in Germany and Austria. In addition, Traxler and Brandl (2009: 186) argue that even Nordic unions (and despite non-membership of the eurozone) participate in coordination: 'the northern network, bringing together *IGM[etall]* district *Küste*, the Danish *CO-Industri* and Sweden's *Svenska Metall*, holds regular meetings to exchange information and discuss strategies for the coming bargaining rounds...Longer-established cooperation exists among the Nordic metal unions... Compared with other macro regions, this cooperation by the Nordic unions is the most advanced in Europe, together with the most developed *IGM* networks.'

European Works Councils

From its inception, the ETUC pressed for European legislation prescribing transnational works councils or similar bodies in MNCs, arguing that nationally based rights of employee participation were being outflanked. The long campaign culminated in the 1994 EWC directive, which provided for information and consultation mechanisms in larger companies with employment in at least two EEA countries. The limited powers of EWCs were somewhat enhanced by the 'recast' directive adopted in 2009. Where employees demand such a mechanism, the 'default option' is an EWC of up to 30 members drawn from existing employee representatives, to discuss transnational issues in an annual information and consultation meeting with top management. The operating costs are met by the enterprise. The complexity of the procedure for establishing an EWC (and the scope for hostile managements to obstruct the process) means that only just over a third of the companies that meet the size threshold actually possess an EWC—though coverage of larger multinationals is far greater. Just under 1,000 exist, the majority in the metal and chemicals sectors, particularly in companies with headquarters in Germany, the USA, the UK, France, and Sweden.

What do EWCs mean in practice? Streeck (1997) argued that they were 'neither European nor works councils' but mere token mechanisms, lacking the powers of national representative institutions and typically ancillary to national procedures in the companies' home countries. Subsequent research has revealed a more nuanced picture. Lecher et al. (1999) distinguish four types: many are purely symbolic; others provide a servicing function, primarily through information exchange; some develop their own autonomous initiatives; a few exert a significant influence on company policy. It seems that problems of language and of different national industrial relations backgrounds inhibit cross-national unity among employee representatives, and in times of restructuring and redundancy they are often preoccupied with protecting their own 'national interests'. Nevertheless, in a minority of cases EWCs have developed into genuine transnational actors with a quasi-bargaining role (Fitzgerald and Stirling 2004; Hertwig et al. 2011; Whittall et al. 2007). In a few cases they have also extended their focus and composition beyond the EEA, developing into a form of World Company Council.

There are important organizational issues for unions: for example, do they assign responsibility to a European or international department, or to officials responsible for negotiating with the company at national level?

This can be a major source of intra-union friction. In *IG Metall* this led in 1995 to the creation of a special cross-departmental EWC Team (Rüb 2009: 253). Given the extensive literature that now exists on EWCs, we will not discuss their operation in detail, but rather focus on trade union policies. First, it must be stressed that EWCs—indeed, like most national works councils—are not formally trade union bodies, and in many cases at least some of their elected members are non-unionists. Hence an EWC may be a 'central ally' for trade unions but also a potential rival (Müller et al. 2011: 221). Most were established in the 1990s, and the ETUFs took an active role in identifying target MNCs and coordinating negotiations for creating the new structures. For example, in 1996 the EMF created a special Task Force that prescribed a privileged role for unions in the process. EMCEF (now also part of IndustriALL) adopted a similar approach in the chemicals sector. There are significant differences between (and also within) countries in the extent to which unions are involved in EWC activities, and indeed the degree to which these are regarded as a key issue for union policy. But most ETUFs were 'initially overwhelmed by the scale of EWC activities' (Waddington 2011: 52).

Telljohann concludes (2005: 34–42) that there is a positive and fairly close relationship with trade unions in most cases. Some unions delegate support to the international department, others to sectoral specialists. In some EWCs, full-time officials are members, in others they act as external experts. There is a tendency for unions to focus on home-country companies—where, Telljohann comments, the value added is least; and indeed, the EMF policy from 2000 was to assign each EWC a national representative, usually from the home country (Rüb 2009). In general, an EWC seemed 'a structure disconnected from the shop-floor and reserved to an elite of pioneers'. How it functions then depends on the existence of 'political entrepreneurs' at company level, and the strategic choices which they make (Greer and Hauptmeier 2008).

Whittall and Kotthoff (2012) find that full-time officials in most countries are too overloaded to give detailed attention to individual EWCs, once these have been established. In Germany, the headquarters of the largest single number of EWCs, trade unions are relatively well resourced but so are national works councils. Typically the (full-time) president of the national (group) works council also chairs the EWC, and often seeks autonomy from the external union (Müller et al. 2011). By contrast, in Britain, with no national tradition of works councils, unions are often suspicious of EWCs because of the participation of non-unionists, and seek to maintain a 'strong and clearly defined role' in almost all cases (Fulton 2005: 61). In France, Rehfeldt (2009: 178) reports 'a degree of EWC-monitoring fatigue', and this is almost certainly true of other countries with limited union resources.

Transnational Company Agreements

More complex issues of conflicting competences arise in the case of transnational company agreements, in which EWCs often play a key role despite their lack of formal collective bargaining capacity. 'By early 2012, 224 such agreements were known in 144 companies employing over 10 million people' (European Commission 2012: 4). These are typically 'framework' agreements, less binding or detailed than international collective bargaining agreements but more formal than any agreements that preceded them. The first was between the International Union of Food and Allied Workers' Associations and the French multinational BSN-Danone in 1988 (Hammer 2005: 515), but most have been agreed since 2000.

It is common to distinguish between international and European framework agreements (IFAs and EFAs): the former with global scope, the latter covering only Europe (Telljohann et al. 2009). On this basis, it is estimated that roughly equal numbers of each type exist. However, the distinction is far from clear cut. Almost all companies signing IFAs have European headquarters, primarily in France or Germany, and the extent to which their scope is global rather than European is a matter of degree. Perhaps the most important difference concerns the content of agreements. IFAs 'typically focus on fundamental rights or address the different aspects of corporate social responsibility' and are primarily designed to regulate employment in non-European subsidiaries. EFAs 'tend to have as their core aim the establishment of partnerships to deal with restructuring' and also 'address specific subjects such as health and safety at work, equality in employment, training and mobility, planning of employment and skills needs'; they mainly regulate conditions for the 'core' European workforce (European Commission 2012: 4).

Early IFAs stemmed from efforts by the ICFTU and the GUFs to regulate the overseas practices of MNCs based in industrialized countries, with the aim of establishing more mandatory norms than purely voluntary exercises in CSR. They almost always included references to ILO core labour standards, and often provided for independent monitoring by NGOs or by the unions themselves. Hence in their origins, IFAs were top-down initiatives. But 'second-generation' IFAs, and almost all EFAs, have been bottom-up initiatives by well established EWCs. Both processes can result in tensions. Top-down agreements can cause 'resentment among...workers' representatives at lower levels about...perceived interference with national systems of industrial relations and norms, resulting from the absence of mandating procedures and mechanisms to link the levels' (European Commission 2012: 6). Conversely, the GUFs (and some ETUFs) became increasingly alarmed that EWCs—not formally trade union bodies—were encroaching on their own sphere of competence without any representative mandate. As a result, clearer rules have been developed prescribing closer consultation between EWCs, ETUFs, and GUFs, and often requiring that one of the latter should be at least co-signatory of any agreement (Schömann et al. 2012: 198–201).

Internationalism and Trade Union Power Resources

We end by linking unions' international activities to our previous discussion of power resources. Trade unions as national institutions clearly face a loss of structural power: this is the main motive for international collaboration. Yet it would be wrong to regard unions as victims of overwhelming external forces. For example, MNCs with elaborate global supply chains may often be able to outflank national unions, but can be vulnerable to action which targets weak points in the chain.

International union organization clearly represents a form of associational power, though national unions' willingness to pay is circumscribed. We have seen that at European level, organization has access to 'borrowed resources'; but as some critics insist, this may be a Faustian bargain. In any event, associational power is rarely translated into organizational power; if internationalism is primarily an issue for full-time specialists, it cannot engage the members; what is required is sustained membership involvement. There have indeed been moves in this direction; but as Tu (2008) shows in a study of the main French unions, education and training are typically technical in nature and oriented to immediate bargaining issues. Membership engagement may be easier, though still precarious, at transnational company level, as the experience of some EWCs indicates (Bernaciak 2010; Whittall et al. 2007). With the growing use of web-based communication, however, there is scope for more systematic membership involvement, as some unions have recognized.

In general, institutional power resources are far more limited at international than at national level. Given the relative weakness of the ILO, this is obvious at global level. At European level the position is somewhat different, though with the rise of neoliberalism, unions' status as social partners has been seriously weakened. Despite the limited formal powers of EWCs, some have been able to accumulate significant institutional power resources, as the development of transnational agreements demonstrates.

This leaves a substantial need for alternative power resources. Unions have certainly attempted to cultivate moral power resources in the international field: notions of solidarity remain resonant, though their meanings differ according to national and ideological traditions. The search for moral legitimacy is one reason why unions have embraced the ILO's somewhat anaemic notion of 'decent work', and place such emphasis on the idea of 'social Europe'—or as Swedish LO puts it in an educational textbook, 'a just Europe'

(*Ett rättvist Europa*). These are at first sight powerful slogans: there are few explicit advocates of indecent work or an unjust Europe. By the same token, they must be translated into a concrete and plausible vision of an alternative globalization and an alternative Europe: re-envisioning an international identity, democracy, and economy (Schmidt 2009). This is a task in which unions in many countries have now become actively engaged. This process also requires coalitional power resources; and as we showed above and in the previous chapter, international work is one important area in which unions have formed alliances with other progressive movements. Perhaps the most challenging task is to develop strategic or logistical power: international union action remains an arena of diverse forms of organization and multiple levels of initiative; their integration and coordination remain severely underdeveloped.

Conclusions

National trade unions have long recognized the need to act beyond national boundaries, and most appreciate the growing urgency of effective international organization. In this chapter we have given an overview of different levels of engagement: global, European, sectoral, company. We have also explored similarities and differences in the approaches to international work in our ten countries. As we have seen, European unions have increasingly embraced 'Europe' as a new progressive ideal, but this has caused disorientation as actually existing European integration has assumed an ever more neoliberal character—at the same time as ordinary members, for good reasons as well as bad, have become increasingly 'eurosceptic'. There is a fundamental tension in international policy: is this a specialist issue which should be left to 'international experts', or a mainstream concern for all members and activists? While some unions have made serious efforts to 'mainstream' internationalism, others have tended to avoid internal discussion and debate on international issues for fear of provoking dissension. This dilemma forms part of a broader tension between the needs for effective strategy and vigorous democracy. In the concluding chapter we examine how the two may be reconciled.

8

Hard Choices: Reconciling Strategy and Democracy

A study such as this does not permit a conventional conclusion. The previous chapters have examined diverse patterns of change, and the one certainty is that often unpredictable changes will continue. Many of the trade union initiatives that we have discussed have been path dependent; but path dependency is a challenge, not a fate. Our focus in this chapter is on two key themes which have figured persistently in our earlier discussion: strategy and democracy. We consider in particular how they can be rendered compatible and indeed complementary.

Trade unions are democratic organizations—or at least, to use contemporary management-speak, they are 'striving to be democratic'. In order to function effectively, unions depend on the legitimacy of their mandate, and also on their members' willingness to act. Yet democracy is a contested concept, not least in the context of trade unionism, and its meanings differ considerably across countries. Thus we return to some of the issues already addressed briefly in Chapter 4.

Unions are also 'intermediary organizations', as we noted in Chapter 1: their main task as collective actors is to mobilize workers' own resources in engaging with those who exert power over them. Since these external actors differ in structure and objectives between one country and another, this is in itself a source of cross-national variation in trade unionism. Unions' intermediary character also means that they are typically reactive organizations, responding to an agenda which is externally defined. But in hard times there is also a need for proactive intervention: diminished traditional power resources require the development of strategic or logistical power, as we argued in Chapter 2, in order to leverage most smartly and effectively those other resources which remain to hand. In this final chapter we discuss how this can be achieved.

Hard times may result in strategic paralysis, but can also stimulate the framing of new objectives, new levels of intervention, and new forms of action. Underlying such choices is the question noted in Chapter 6: 'What are we here for?' Unions face both ideational and practical challenges which require credible answers to this question. Hence another underlying theme is whether, and how, unions in different countries respond strategically in defining their priorities. Is there coherent articulation between industrial and political action, for example? Do unions act with a long-term perspective, or do they primarily react to immediate events? We give a differentiated answer: strategic capacity seems to vary substantially across (but also within) countries, and the prospects of unions regaining the initiative differ likewise.

What is Strategic Capacity?

The notion of strategy is often used loosely. Originally a military metaphor, deriving from the Greek for a general, 'strategy' denotes the planning of a whole campaign or war in contrast to the tactics deployed in a single battle. This clearly requires long-term planning and also effective overall coordination. This is particularly important, since a union (or any other organization) does not itself 'act': its members, activists, and officials are the ones who act in its name and with its resources. These social and political processes are obscured by attributing the essentially human process of action to 'the union', though this is a shorthand we ourselves have used in this book. The democratic character of unions can make effective coordination of these myriad actors particularly difficult to achieve.

As its literal origins suggest, strategy is closely related to leadership. This concept often causes unease to those committed to union democracy. 'Who says organization, says oligarchy,' Michels concluded. Union democracy clearly requires adequate scope for all categories of members to shape the priorities and programmes of their organizations. It also requires appropriate *structures* for participation, involvement, and self-activity at rank-and-file level. Yet grassroots self-determination alone, as Streeck (1988: 312) has argued, seems a recipe for a 'multitude of small, narrowly based collective action units competing with each other for organizational resources and political influence' and lacking 'a capacity to deliberate and control the macro-level outcomes of their actions'.

The potential anarchy of purely decentralized democracy can be transcended only when articulated—a point developed further below—by overarching coordination. Union effectiveness requires 'the capacity to interpret, decipher, sustain, and redefine the demands of the represented, so as to evoke the broadest possible consensus and approval' (Regalia 1988: 351). This is one of the functions of leadership, which is therefore a prerequisite for participative democracy to deliver beneficial results. As Barker et al. insist (2001: 15–17), it is crucial to differentiate between *authoritarian* and *authoritative* leadership, and between leadership as *hierarchy* and as *process* or *function*: 'leadership is exercised at all manner of levels and locations...and not only by those obviously designated as "leaders"'. Gramsci's notion of the 'organic intellectual' is relevant here: grassroots activists may develop a breadth of information and analytical capacity that distinguish without distancing them from their colleagues. Hence there can, and must, be a complex dialectic between leadership and democracy.

One subtle attempt to explore trade union strategic capacity in terms of this dialectic is the study by Ganz of unionization among California farm workers in the 1960s. The United Farm Workers possessed only limited resources, but compensated for this through what Ganz terms 'resourcefulness'. This derived from the interaction between the personal qualities of the leadership team and the union's internal organizational structures. 'Strategic thinking is reflexive and imaginative, based on how leaders have learned to reflect on the past, pay attention to the present, and anticipate the future' (2000: 1009). Such creative thinking, argues Ganz, is essentially collective; it is most likely when there is a leadership team from diverse backgrounds and with a range of organizational experiences, and is least likely when there is a homogeneous leadership group deeply embedded in bureaucratic routines. The organizational characteristics which Ganz emphasizes are 'deliberative arrangements, resource flows, and accountability structures' (2000: 1007). Where there are effective channels of both horizontal and vertical dialogue over aims and methods, with democratic involvement of activists and the general membership and a recognition that union effectiveness depends ultimately on the members' willingness both to pay and to act, the scope for successful strategic initiative is enhanced. This point has been reiterated by Heery (2005) in Britain and by Milkman (2006: 152–3) in the USA: successful organizing requires an interconnection between 'top-down' and 'bottom-up' approaches.

Strategic capacity can be understood as the ability to assess opportunities for intervention; to anticipate, rather than merely react to, changing circumstances; to frame coherent policies; and to implement these effectively. It seems obvious that some European trade union movements possess this quality to a far greater degree than others. We may define key elements as *structure*, *intelligence*, and *efficacy* (Hyman 1997). Structure indicates the degree to which national trade unionism is unified or fragmented between rival organizations, and hence possesses the competence to aggregate diverse perspectives into a common set of priorities: themes we have considered in Chapter 4. Intelligence is in part an organizational matter: the extent to which unions and confederations possess specialist expertise in research, education, and information-gathering (or have the support of union-related 'think tanks'), and the means to disseminate knowledge throughout the organization (which is also in part a question of resources). Moreover (and perhaps more importantly) it is a matter of the degree to which, at all levels within union movements, knowledge is seen as an essential component of union power. Effective strategy depends on organizational procedures and traditions that link knowledge to action through analysis of circumstances, evaluation of alternative options, and planning of objectives and forms of intervention. Finally, efficacy partly reflects the attainability of union policies within the objective context, and the overall coherence (notably, between and within unions) of aims—which is more easily achieved where a reasonable degree of centralized authority exists. It also involves the degree to which union members (and other workers) 'own' the strategic priorities and are willing to take action in their pursuit—which calls for scope for decentralized initiative, as we discuss further below.

There are many obstacles to strategic reorientation in trade unions. Inherited identities and ideologies often create a strong path dependence. For example, unions whose traditional raison d'être rests primarily on control of the labour market through pay bargaining with employers (as in the UK) will be more sensitive to an erosion of economic bargaining power by membership decline than those (as in France) oriented more to mobilizing workers, whether or not union members, to press government for improvements in minimum wages and social benefits. Similarly, those embedded in 'social partnership' arrangements may feel institutionally secure even if membership density falls, as we saw in Chapter 2. Inherited identities also shape the likely trajectory of union renewal if a need for change is recognized. Trade unions rarely overturn all their past definitions of character and purpose; rather, they adapt selectively, and seek to persuade members and activists that any changes remain consistent with the fundamental values and objectives of previous generations.

Internal organizational politics are likewise of key importance. Any political system—and trade unions, like any other organizations, are systems of internal politics—contains built-in checks and balances which give opponents of change a degree of veto power. Such obstacles to strategic change are greatest, first, when a union (or union movement) comprises a diverse range of occupational and sectoral interests, which must be maintained in some form of equilibrium to maintain organizational integrity; second, when there is sharp rivalry among different ideologically based factions, none of which can dominate internal politics. In Figure 8.1 we present a stylized model of such internal political processes. Where there is a high degree both of diversity of internal interests and of ideological conflict, the outcome may well be

Figure 8.1. Strategic unionism: A stylized framework for comparison

'bounded anarchy': any coherent strategy, and in particular any effective process of strategic innovation, faces enormous obstacles. One reason why union mergers are often problematic is the multiplication of interest-based and factional conflicts. Where differentiation is high but there is relative ideological consensus, the diversity of interests may be accommodated by internal negotiation processes. Conversely, where there is relative internal homogeneity of interests together with marked ideological differences, factional conflict may inhibit strategic coherence. The capacity for collective strategic leadership is likely to be greatest where there is relative homogeneity both of ideology and of membership interests.

We term this a stylized model because reality is far more complex than any four-part typology. First, what we identify are tendencies and pressures, not deterministic 'laws'. Second, in any national trade union movement there are important differences between unions, and also between levels of decision-making. Third, any such model must be dynamic, not static: organizational politics changes according to external circumstances and the ways in which these are perceived. Fourth, and perhaps most importantly, the essence of effective trade union leadership is to manage these tensions. Interests are not objectively given: they can be framed and interpreted as conflicting or complementary, and one task of leadership is to emphasize solidaristic understandings. Likewise, to pursue the argument addressed in Chapter 6, competing political orientations may be skilfully reconceptualized to fit a common 'master narrative'. How far this is achieved, or even attempted, may depend on how union democracy itself is understood: a 'federal' or 'consociational' model of democracy presupposes a search for reconciliation between different interests and perpsectives, in contrast to a 'winner-take-all' model where achieving a majority is the key objective (Roland Erne, personal communication).

Organizational Learning

The notion of organizational learning has received growing attention within management literature. While it is misleading to suggest that organizations as such can 'learn'—any more than they can 'act'—they are clearly contexts within which learning can occur, and organizational effectiveness may well depend on the capacity of those within them collectively to learn appropriate responses to new challenges. One application of the organizational learning literature in the trade union context is the study by Huzzard and Östergren (2002) of the Swedish union SIF (now part of *Unionen*). They point out that theories of organizational learning were developed within a unitarist, managerialist framework, tending to neglect internal diversity and conflict over organizational identity and purpose (Huzzard 2001). This is particularly a problem in the context of trade unions, which—unlike business organizations—have an explicit democratic rationale, and in which competing ideological tendencies possess at least a degree of legitimacy. Huzzard and Östergren found a major disjuncture between the 'modernizing' conceptions of the SIF leadership—pursuing a more individual-oriented service to workers and greater partnership with employers—and the continued commitment of most local leaders to the values of collectivism, solidarity, and (if necessary) militancy. The authors describe this as a 'barrier to organizational learning'. An alternative reading, however, is that local activists fully understood the problems which the national leaders identified and the responses they proposed, but rejected these as the *wrong* lessons. This indeed is the message of their conclusion (2002: S58): trade unions 'have difficulties in developing shared meanings, visions, ideologies and identities'; but 'if learning is a *dialectical* process, then ideological differences may even promote reflection and learning rather than hinder them'.

Two further considerations on organizational learning are important. Huber (1991: 100) argues that 'organizations often do not know what they know'. Of course, organizations as such do not 'know', either; knowledge is a human capacity, though the knowledge of many individuals is synthesized, disseminated, retained, and remembered within organizations. However, experience acquired at specific levels or in particular locales within a union (or any other organization) may not be generalized. To return to the analysis which Ganz develops, effective intra-union communication channels—what Culpepper (2002), in a different context, calls 'dialogic capacity'—are of key importance; and to the extent that the most serious challenges today concern labour movements as a whole, effective *inter*-union (and indeed international) channels are essential. In many of our countries, inter-union conflict is a major contributor to union weakness and strategic disarray.

The second point is that before we can learn we may have to *unlearn* established routines and responses that are no longer appropriate. Hall (1993: 279), in discussing 'social learning' at the level of the state, has argued that 'policymakers customarily work within a framework of ideas and standards that specifies not only the goals of policy and the kind of instruments that can be used to attain them, but also the very nature of the problems they are meant to be addressing'. And it is certainly true that trade union policy-makers 'tend to rely on familiar repertoires or behavioral scripts when faced with new conditions' for which old tactics may be inappropriate (Johnston 1994: 37). Milkman (2006) has shown how the organizational approaches which served effectively a few decades ago for American industrial unions in large-scale manufacturing industries were totally unsuited to the growing numbers of low-paid, insecure service employees often working for small subcontracting employers; local unions without a traditional industrial background were more successful in organizing such groups. This argument clearly resonates with themes we addressed in Chapter 3. In the management literature, the notion of 'competency traps' (Levitt and March 1988) is familiar: skill in applying methods which worked well in the past is an obstacle to innovation in changed circumstances. Within trade unions, particularly those long established, respect for precedent and protocol means that the traditions of all the dead generations inhibit learning; unions 'tend to move in directions which will not threaten shared ideas, values, and habits and their organizational learning will be skewed towards what is already known' (Ross and Martin 1999: 4). To overcome such conservative bias, strategic innovation may require a process of creative destruction.

Reconciling Strategy and Democracy

In Chapter 4 we noted briefly the 'efficiency versus democracy' thesis. According to this analysis, in order to apply the 'logic of influence'—or, from a more militant perspective, to act as effective fighting organizations—unions must match the hierarchical and elitist decision-making of their opponents or interlocutors. At best, it is argued, unions should practise *representative* democracy, with those in leadership positions free to take informed policy decisions with only intermittent accountability to the membership. Yet a diametrically opposite argument is possible. If effectiveness requires members' willingness to act and not merely to pay, they must identify with their union's goals and methods; and this is far more likely if they have an opportunity to help shape these. Thus union democracy needs to be *participative*: democracy is both an end in itself and also a means to other valued ends.

A complementary perspective on this debate can be drawn from the literature on the 'democratic deficit' in EU policy-making. Scharpf (1999: 6) distinguishes between 'output-oriented legitimacy' ('government *for* the people'), whereby leaders are judged primarily by the results they deliver; and 'input-oriented legitimacy' ('government *by* the people'), where the key criterion is the opportunity for involvement in policy-making. These two conceptions map closely with the competing understandings of union democracy, and also with the contrast between 'servicing' and 'organizing' models of trade unionism, discussed in Chapter 3. In an attempt to reconcile these two approaches, Schmidt proposes a third conception, 'throughput legitimacy', or 'government *with* the people'. This requires 'more accountable, transparent and accessible processes' and also 'more productive deliberative interrelationships among actors' (2010: 24). To highlight themes which we examine further below, for effective 'input' it is necessary to sustain a sense of collective identity among the membership—maintaining a 'demos' within the union constituency—and to foster the 'social capital' of members to facilitate their effective participation. Coherent 'throughput', in turn, requires a sophisticated structure of internal union institutions, procedures, and networks that facilitates a multidirectional, interactive relationship among leaders, local officials, activists, and ordinary members.

In Figure 8.2 we present a model developed by researchers in Germany (Schoefer 2000; von Alemann and Schmid 1993). From their studies of the main predecessor of *ver.di*, they identify a virtuous circle (or 'magic triangle'): a transparent process of strategic leadership enables and encourages rank-and-file participation in debates and decisions; more informed and engaged

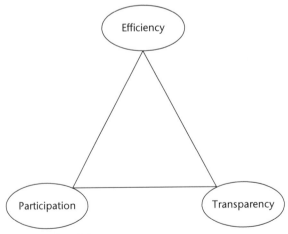

Figure 8.2. The 'magic triangle'
Source: adapted from Schoefer 2000; von Alemann and Schmid 1993.

members display greater willingness to act, enhancing union effectiveness; this in turn provides the organizational capacities and leadership confidence that facilitate transparency and participation. In the final sections we develop these themes further.

Membership Activism, Participation, and Social Capital

The argument above is that strategic capacity in trade unions is, in part, a product of *both* leadership *and* internal democracy. In his classic comparative study, Kjellberg (1983) argued that the most effective union movements combined, in an articulated manner, strong central organization (coordinated leadership) with vibrant local activity (high membership participation). This combination was in his view one of the explanations of the exceptional unionization rate in Sweden. As we saw in Chapter 2, a similar thesis has been presented by Lévesque and Murray (2003), who explore the means of refashioning trade union power in the face of economic internationalization. They propose a triangulation (which is similar, but certainly not identical, to the 'magic triangle' described above) between the strategic capacity of workplace union organization (its ability to develop a proactive agenda rather than simply reacting to management's initiatives); the internal democratic life of the union, which enables members to identify with the policies pursued on their behalf; and 'external solidarity', the degree to which broader national (and international) organizational resources and commonalities of interest shape local priorities. Their conclusion is that unions need to build a virtuous circle of proactive capacity, active democracy, and higher-level strategic support as the basis for an effective strategy for labour: 'it seems more and more obvious that these three levers of power are mutually reinforcing' (2003: 22). These are powerful arguments, though we must recognize that in an era when employment is increasingly precarious and thus fewer workers possess a fixed workplace, traditional models of workplace union organization have declining purchase. As we saw in Chapter 3, the foundations of collective organization must increasingly be found, at least in part, outside the workplace.

In a subsequent study, Lévesque et al. (2005: 402) suggest that workers' identification with trade unionism has been undermined by a 'radicalization of difference. Divergent social identities challenge traditional notions of collectivity and lead to an erosion of the relevance of traditional frames of reference.' Their survey of union members in Québec found that those who felt that they were consulted over union policy and had an opportunity to shape its direction were also most likely to see trade unionism as relevant to their own circumstances. 'Democracy is a building block in the construction of union identity' (2005: 409).

Richards argues (2001: 35–6) that 'labour solidarity has always been a constructed and contingent phenomenon built on local foundations. It is now more so than ever in an era of generally decentralized industrial relations, increasingly localized threats, fragmented work forces and growing corporate power.' Yet a fragmentation of solidarity, in a context where localized workers are increasingly compelled to compete with those in other localities, is no effective solidarity at all. This means, to return to our earlier argument, that local activism is necessary but not sufficient for effective union strategy. How can fragmentation be overcome?

In the past, unions have often striven to overcome differentiation by imposing uniformity—what Webb and Webb (1897) termed a 'common rule', a kind of 'mechanical' solidarity enforced from above (Hyman 2004). But the 'radicalization of difference' means that diversity cannot be suppressed; it must be accepted, even welcomed. The issue is how actual and potential trade union members can be encouraged to perceive common interests despite difference, and to negotiate the tensions that often exist between their own multiple social identities in a way which is compatible with collectivism. This raises difficult questions of human subjectivity and intersubjectivity. As Zoll has insisted (1991: 392), increased differentiation of circumstances and interests, and the growing uncertainty of social norms and values, make effective unity of action possible only if trade unions become 'discourse organizations'. This, he argues, is far more difficult in large than in small organizations, but may be facilitated by modern communications technologies (which have, of course, advanced exponentially in the two decades since he wrote).

Zoll focuses primarily on the need for appropriate structures to facilitate interaction and communication within unions, but also on the need for a culture of dialogue and mutual learning, rather than a simple confrontation of opposing arguments whereby conflicts are resolved by majority vote without a serious search for a synthesis. These are important points, but what is also necessary if unions are to develop discursive power resources is that members themselves possess the will and capacity to participate effectively. Here, the notion of social capital may be relevant.

Social capital is a notoriously problematic concept, popularized by Putnam (1993, 1995) in a manner which is 'potentially politically reactionary' (DeFilippis 2002: 791). Putnam's argument is that individuals benefit from social capital when they participate in a variety of social networks and voluntary organizations, and that a dense associational life contributes to the strength of the broader community and polity. In some respects this overlaps with much recent usage of the equally ambiguous notion of civil society. Critics have shown that Putnam's treatment neglects the role of power, inequality, and class in shaping individuals' social and economic opportunities; encourages a 'blame-the-victim' approach to disadvantage and social exclusion; and fails to recognize that dense social networks can exclude, oppress, and victimize 'outsiders'.

Nevertheless, the concept has a longer lineage, and in the case of writers like Bourdieu a very different meaning. The same is true of the cognate idea of civil society, which historically has had a variety of conflicting interpretations. What is the relevance to trade unions? Crucially, it seems to us, the idea of social capital can indicate that union organization derives its vitality from the networks of social relationships among the individuals who constitute the (actual or potential) membership, and that the quality of their interpersonal or 'sociable' relationships gives the union its human face and ultimately enhances its capacity to act. Understood primarily in collective rather than individual terms, social capital can define a potential resource for the relatively powerless and disadvantaged to challenge those who are economically and politically dominant, a basis for resistance and effective negotiation. This is certainly not what Putnam and his followers envisage. However, it has some affinities with the classic analysis of the Webbs, who saw the internal democracy of trade unions as a force for broader societal democratization, allowing workers 'to regain collectively what has become individually impossible' (Webb and Webb 1897: 850).

This collective dimension of social capital emerges clearly, for example, from the four-country research by Dufour and Hege (2002): 'representative capacity' derives in part from formal institutional provisions but depends no less on the quality of the interrelationships between representatives and their constituents, on the responsiveness of representatives to the often individualized everyday concerns of workers, indeed their readiness to act as a kind of social worker in dealing with issues arising outside work itself. Since networks of sociability pre-exist formal collective organization, they can provide the springboard for unionization (or conversely, for unwillingness to unionize) and the resource for effective intra-union dialogue (Ebbinghaus et al. 2011). This was demonstrated in the study by Batstone et al. (1978) of a British engineering factory: the workplace union leadership was able to shape the constituents' willingness to act by orchestrating debate and discussion through the network of first-line shop stewards down to informal groups of workers who ate lunch together, played cards during rest breaks, or debated the previous Saturday's football match. In the USA, Fantasia (1988) has described a similar articulation between informal social groupings and union solidarity.

In an analysis based on US experience, Jarley (2005) has argued for the development of what he calls 'social-capital unionism': trade unions should become facilitators of mutuality among workers, as a basis for recovering their membership and influence. He suggests that the 'servicing model' of unionism, by making members dependent on the full-time officials, actually weakens networks of collective mutual support among workers and thus reduces their social capital. The 'organizing model' in some respects devolves collectivism back to the workplace, but tends to replace dependence on officials with dependence on a core of committed activists who are themselves liable to victimization or to 'burn-out'. His alternative model creates a more diversified social network, with no clear demarcation between mutual support on issues which are 'union-relevant' as traditionally understood and those which are less obviously so; linkages built up over one type of issue can subsequently facilitate collective action over others. A study of two local branches of the United Food and Commercial Workers' Union (Johnson and Jarley 2005), again in the USA, suggests that such a model proved effective in recruiting and involving young workers in the union, as well as in broader political activism.

There are two particular advantages of 'social-capital unionism', Jarley suggests: it enables a union to 'borrow and extend the social capital of its most well-connected members' (2005: 12); and social networks, because not confined to purely workplace issues, can be sustained among workers who are mobile across employers, making union membership more readily 'portable across firms' (2005: 19). Interestingly, though Jarley does not develop this point, there are analogies both with the principle of 'mutual insurance' which the Webbs saw as the core of solidarity within early craft unions, and the efforts of early Socialist (and also Catholic) trade unions to organize a wide array of social activities to increase the cohesion and loyalty of their members. Whether or not Jarley's conception is considered practical as a model for European trade unions, the idea of reinventing broad networks of mutuality, potentially as a basis for 'insurgent social capital' (Law and Mooney 2006) to resist the relentless drive of neoliberalism, certainly deserves serious consideration. This is perhaps particularly important for the growing proportion of workers without a stable workplace.

Vocabularies of Motive, Ideologies, and Utopias

A theme of much of the preceding analysis has been that trade union strategic capacity can be—and needs to be—enhanced through internal dialogue, discussion, and debate. Uniform policy cannot be mechanically imposed when the 'average' member no longer exists (and probably never did); increasingly, unions need to be 'discursive' or 'dialogical' organizations, allowing the explicit negotiation of increasingly overt internal differences with the aim of achieving consensual policy outcomes. This prescription is not, of course, unproblematic: within any union, some individuals and groups are more motivated or able to voice their opinions and interests than others. Traditionally, as we saw in Chapter 3, the formal democracy of many unions has been a framework within which certain sections (male, full-time, native-born, relatively skilled) have dominated policy-making. Today, electronic communications permit far broader participation in strategic dialogue, but as anyone involved in union message boards appreciates, the most active participants tend to be self-selected advocates of a distinctive agenda. How to achieve 'bottom-up' dialogue which is truly representative of the diversity of rank-and-file opinion is a major challenge.

One answer is that 'social-capital unionism' would enhance the vocal capacity of the less articulate members and constituents. Another, which links back to Offe and Wiesenthal (1985), is that one of the leadership tasks in agenda setting is to transform particularistic and competitive demands and aspirations into more encompassing policy goals by redefining 'spontaneous' self-definitions of interest. And here, it is necessary to move beyond the *process* of discourse and dialogue (the foundation of 'throughput legitimacy') to the *content*. The fragmentation of employee identities and self-definitions of interest is not a 'natural' development but the outcome of politically driven efforts to erode national post-war industrial relations settlements and hence weaken or remove workers' social protections and set them in competition and conflict one with another. What is at issue is a radical shift in the balance of forces between labour and capital.

To defend employees at workplace level and no less within the national (and international) political economy requires a confrontation with the dominant policy logic of our age. This implies that unions must turn (or return) to a self-conception as organizations campaigning for rights and engaging in 'contentious politics' (Tarrow 1998), reasserting their identity as 'sword of justice': contesting oppression, inequality, and discrimination. As we saw in Chapter 6, it can also imply cooperation, often uneasy, with other social movements that in most countries have never acquired the respectability gained by trade unions. Potentially it redefines unions as outsiders in a terrain where until recently the role of insiders was comforting and rewarding.

The key issues here involve ideas, language, and mobilization. The decline of union organization is in part ideological in causation: European unions were able to thrive when the prevailing policy discourse made collective regulation, employment protection, and state welfare provision the common sense of the times. The ideological counter-revolution of the past three decades—which has proceeded further and faster in some countries than in others—has placed trade unions very much on the defensive. They are often seen as representing a vested interest: those who are already relatively secure in the labour market, and have relatively good wages and working conditions; those who are in most cases winners or at least not major losers in the process of economic restructuring. But unions have to convince themselves and others that they are the voice of the majority, that they represent the losers as well as the winners, and that they want to convert the losers *into* winners.

The battle of ideas is also a battle of words. Human actors 'discern situations with particular vocabularies, and it is in terms of the same delimited vocabulary that they anticipate consequences of conduct. Stable vocabularies of motive link anticipated consequences and specific actions' (Mills 1940: 906). Yet the vocabularies of motive which legitimated traditional trade union action have an archaic ring today. As Kelly (1997) has insisted, trade unions require effective linguistic means of 'framing' workers' perceptions of the circumstances that afflict them, of attributing blame for their problems, and of proposing credible remedies. If, for example, workers accept that deteriorating conditions of work, or threats of workplace closure, are the inevitable outcome of uncontrollable economic forces, collective resistance is futile. If they blame employers or governments for their predicament but have no conception of alternative policies, they may protest but are unlikely to prevail. If they conceive an alternative that they cannot *communicate*, it will be ineffectual.

Tilly has made an analogous point, that socio-political movements draw on 'repertoires of contention': forms of action that have been developed in the past and provide 'scripts' for the future, but which nevertheless are subject to constant innovation. Such repertoires, he suggests (2006: 184–5), contain three key elements: 'identity', the assertion that those involved are a group with distinctive interests and the capacity to pursue these vigorously; 'standing', the insistence that their claims and interests deserve to be taken as seriously as those of other more powerful socio-economic groups; and 'programme', an integrated set of demands. All three in his view are mutually supporting. Indeed, this is a useful prism through which to regard European trade unions: in their period of greatest strength they could credibly claim to represent a constituency with a strong collective identity, to possess the standing of a recognized actor in societal policy-making, and to articulate a programme which reflected the general interest. In more recent times, in most countries, all three claims have been weakened, and this weakening has been mutually reinforcing. New vocabularies which give meaning to the identity, standing, and programme of trade unionism are part of the key to union survival and renewal.

Union revitalization requires a new, imaginative—indeed utopian—counteroffensive: a persuasive vision of a different and better society and economy, a convincing alternative to the mantra of greed, commodification, and competitiveness...and austerity, a set of values which connects with everyday experience at the workplace (Huber 2010: 88). Whether this is described as 'good capitalism', post-capitalism, or Socialism is of secondary importance. The urgent need is to regain an inspiring vision of unions as a 'sword of justice', which many trade union movements seem to have lost. In other words, unions have to articulate a more humane, more solidaristic, and more plausible alternative if they are to vanquish neoliberalism, finding new ways to express their traditional core principles and values and to appeal to a modern generation for whom old slogans have little meaning. And since defending the weak is inescapably a question of power, unions have to help construct a new type of *politics*—in particular, as we insisted in Chapter 6, by engaging with campaigning and protest movements that attract the Facebook and Twitter generation in ways which most trade unions have failed to do (even if many have recently begun to make serious efforts in this direction). Do unions dare to abandon old rules and routines in order to create new strategies, or are they content to manage their own decline? We have shown that many have indeed embraced alternatives to their time-honoured traditions.

Conclusions?

As we insisted at the outset of this chapter, it would be futile to offer simple conclusions to a book that has ranged widely over time, place, and issues, charting complex and contradictory dynamics which will continue to develop in unexpected ways. What we have tried to do here is, first, to focus on how unions may attempt to regain the initiative by enhancing their strategic capacities; second, to insist that only as participative democracies can they enlarge their collective capacities to act; third, to propose that a broad orientation to the multiple identities and aspirations of their members can expand workers' social capital and hence facilitate their engagement with their unions; and finally, to argue that pursuing all these objectives requires a redefinition and reassertion of trade union purpose, presenting a persuasive vision in new language. Indeed, in our research we have found many examples of unions embracing all these objectives. However, unions still require a more systematic and generalized effort to develop innovative responses to hard times, nationally and internationally; as well as the internal democratic processes to ensure that effective learning is embedded within their organizations. If European unions are to survive as effective 'continuous associations', they must continuously reinvent themselves.

Afterword to the Paperback Edition

In the five years since we wrote this book there have been significant changes in European trade unionism and, even more, in the environment in which unions operate. But much has stayed the same. We have decided not to attempt to rewrite our text (which would require substantial new research), but instead to provide this Afterword which updates some of the tables and comments both on key developments in the countries we studied and on important new contributions to the literature. We organize our discussion according to the same structure as the chapters of the book.

Redrawing the Map?

Some critics have questioned what one reviewer (Erne 2013) termed the 'methodological nationalism' of our study. We focus on ten countries, and we decided, in presenting our analysis, to adopt a country-by-country approach (though within broader regional groupings). Such a mode of organization is of course open to criticism. But national identity was not at the heart of our research design, and certainly we nowhere suggest that national systems are self-contained and homogeneous. Indeed, our discussion of economic internationalization and European integration argues the opposite. Nevertheless, individual countries (or groups of countries) possess distinctive configurations of institutions which establish the terrain of trade union organization and action; labour law in many countries precisely defines the legitimate actors in industrial relations, the status of collective agreements, the legality of strikes, the mechanisms for remedying disputes; some 'state traditions', but not others, assign unions an accepted role in the formulation of public policy; and the institutional shape of trade unionism itself reflects processes of historical evolution which are often path-dependent and resistant to change; so, for example, ideological divisions which have lost much of their former resonance may still leave a powerful institutional heritage in conflicts between rival confederations which to the outsider possess little practical logic. One of our objectives was to explore how far such national distinctiveness persists, or how far 'converging divergences' have occurred, increasing within-country differentiation and across-country similarities.

Here we should also clarify our use of country groupings. As we explain at the outset, we locate our national cases within four familiar categories: Nordic, 'central', 'southern', and anglophone; and indeed our case selection was in part guided by the attempt to ensure that each group was represented. Of course, these are rough-and-ready categories, as our contrast between the 'telescope' and the 'microscope' makes clear. Italian writers in particular tend to object to any attempt to group their country with France as part of a broader 'southern' model, and, as we indicate, the differences between the two countries have increased significantly in recent decades. But as we also make clear, there is always a trade-off between parsimony and accuracy; country groupings are a heuristic device which makes a mass of detail more comprehensible to the reader.

We should also stress that the country groupings used as an organizing device were not intended to present 'typologies of trade unions', as some reviewers have inferred. In some cases, notably the Nordic countries, national models of trade unionism do indeed display important similarities, but we do not suggest that this is true of all our groups. In fact, much of our discussion involves an attempt to demonstrate how, and why, the nature and evolution of trade unions within each cluster have differed.

Since we wrote, such differences have increased. 'The cleavages between unions *within* the groups of countries are deepening . . . The country clusters frequently used in comparative trade union analyses make less sense today' (Lehndorff et al. 2017: 9, 24). This need not mean that the familiar groupings of European industrial relations systems have lost heuristic utility: the question, as we argued at the outset, is whether analysis requires fine detail or broad generalization. However, any attempt to systematize the patterns of industrial relations across Europe has become increasingly complicated because of the uneven impact of the crisis and subsequent EU initiatives to discipline national governments. Again, we must stress that such groupings should be treated as a framework for organizing our material on national developments, not as an assertion of common trends: though as Lehndorff (2015) demonstrates, the 'divisive integration' resulting from the constraints of eurozone membership and the deflationary force of the EU's 'new economic governance' have tended to reinforce the position of Nordic and 'central' economies as relative winners, and of most 'southern' countries as losers.

Power Resources: Old and New Challenges, Still Crafting Responses

In Chapter 2 we introduced the literature on power resources and trade unions. Analysis of trade unions through the lens of power resources has become increasingly common, particularly perhaps in German-language studies (McGuire 2014;

Schmalz and Dörre 2014). Some have suggested that our typology is over-elaborate, and we agree that parsimony is a virtue. Like many writers, Lehndorff et al. (2017: 10–11) offer a four-part model: structural, organizational, institutional, and societal. For our part, we were anxious to distinguish between associational power—the sheer weight of numbers—and organizational power, which requires welding members into a collectivity capable of framing goals and undertaking action in common; and indeed, Lehndorff et al. recognize that numbers alone are not enough. Further, they subdivide societal power into 'coalitional or collaborative power' on the one hand, and 'discursive or communicative power' on the other. In our view, it is not of primary importance whether one identifies six types of power resource, as we do, or four with subdivisions. The main substantive difference is that we also write of strategic or logistical power; again, it is in principle possible to treat this either as a separate resource, or as the capacity to make effective use of the other available power resources.

In Chapter 2 we also defined the key common external challenges faced by European trade unions as globalization and neoliberalism. For most of their history, unions were first and foremost actors in nationally bounded industrial relations systems; now they increasingly face employers that are no longer rooted in any single economy, and governments with less room for manœuvre in shaping economic and social policies and which often claim that 'there is no alternative' to a neoliberal regime. As we noted earlier, these policies have been intensified by the dominant politics of the EU. Despite formal commitments in 2017 to a 'European Pillar of Social Rights', market 'freedoms' are still assigned priority over social and employment protections; while the 'new economic governance' has entailed pressure on those member states, particularly in the south, which seek to avoid the neoliberal trend. In consequence, while in important respects the situation of different European countries has become more diverse, there is also an overarching trend for the erosion of worker and trade union rights. Baccaro and Howell (2011) wrote of a 'common neoliberal trajectory' across western Europe; and though they later (2017) qualified this argument, since the paths to labour market liberalization and the extent to which it has been accomplished have differed significantly according to national context, they argue that the direction of travel is almost universally the same.

We referred (pp. 35–6) to the pressures which stem from the growing financialization of European capitalism, itself facilitated by the deregulation of transnational financial movements and the liberalization of corporate governance and of rules on corporate takeovers. Despite the devastation wrought by the financial crisis which erupted in 2007–8, the unpredictability associated with neoliberal globalization has if anything intensified. This reinforces longer-term trends in employment from manufacturing to services, and from the public to the private sector, making unionization even more of an uphill struggle. Employing organizations have become increasingly opaque and transitory, while the hollowing out of companies through outsourcing and subcontracting of previously 'core' activities accentuates labour force fragmentation and insecurity. To these developments must be added another, virtually unknown when this book was originally published: the rise of the platform (or 'gig') economy, in which workers are in theory rendered self-employed entrepreneurs, often competing for brief, one-off tasks (as in the case of Uber taxi drivers), but in practice are often subordinated to the platform owner (Drahokoupil and Fabo 2016). Some writers see the development of artificial intelligence and the 'fourth industrial revolution' as an even greater threat to employment; as we discuss below, some unions have attempted to assess its implications, but this is in the future, and current challenges are demanding enough.

As we noted earlier, these common trends interact with the more differentiated impact of 'divisive integration' in Europe. Creating a common currency without the compensatory transfer mechanisms between regions with very different levels of economic performance has tended to reinforce, rather than alleviate, disparities. Hence, relatively successful economies have prospered while the less successful have been confirmed in their failings, kept afloat by unsustainable loans from the more fortunate member states. Though the 'new economic governance' has had damaging consequences for labour standards in all countries, it is those in the most unfavourable circumstances that have been most severely affected. This is particularly the case for the 'southern' countries. While the worst hit—Greece, Portugal, Spain—are not among those on which we focus, both France and Italy have been adversely affected.

The diverse trajectories in the last few years are to some extent demonstrated in Tables A1 and A2. Comparing 2010 (for most of Europe, the peak of the crisis) and 2016, unemployment continued to rise in France and Italy; but, with the exceptions of Austria and the Netherlands, it fell in all other countries (including Ireland, one of the first victims of the crisis). The same pattern is evident with youth unemployment, everywhere higher than for the labour force as a whole. This continued to increase in France and (particularly) Italy; and also in Austria and the Netherlands, though the disparity with the average rate is much less. What is also striking is that the proportion of temporary contracts, particularly among those aged 15–24, is in most countries in all regional groups very high, and in the majority of our countries has increased since 2010. Thus, new labour market entrants have been paying the price for any stabilization of the position of their seniors.

The impact on union density and bargaining coverage can be seen from Table A2 (here, the most recent available figures are for 2015). In this brief period, density has actually increased in Belgium and Italy, and continued to decline (often very slightly) in most other countries. In France, the ICTWSS and OECD databases show density stable at 8 per cent; note,

Table A.1. Labour market insecurity, 2010 and 2016 (%)

	Unemployment				Temporary contracts[a]			
	15–64		15–24		15–64		15–24	
	2010	2016	2010	2016	2010	2016	2010	2016
SE	8.6	6.9	24.8	18.9	12.6	13.2	56.7	53.2
DK	7.5	6.2	14.0	12.0	7.0	7.9	21.1	33.6
DE	7.0	4.1	9.9	7.0	11.0	10.2	57.2	53.2
AT	4.8	6.0	8.8	11.2	5.0	5.5	37.0	33.9
NL	5.0	6.0	8.7	10.8	13.0	14.3	48.3	55.6
BE	8.3	7.8	22.4	20.1	6.5	7.4	21.1	33.6
FR	9.3	10.1	22.8	24.6	12.2	13.2	55.1	58.6
IT	8.4	11.7	27.8	37.8	9.3	10.7	46.8	54.7
UK	7.8	4.8	19.6	13.0	4.7	4.5	13.8	15.2
IE	13.9	7.9	13.9	17.2	7.3	6.2	30.1	29.3

Source: Eurostat.
[a] Since apprenticeship contracts are fixed-term, countries with high proportions of apprentices are likely to show a high rate of temporary employees, especially for young workers. This is particularly the case for Germany; national statistics excluding apprentices reduce the percentage by more than half. Note, however, that whereas German apprenticeships were once a secure route to permanent employment, this is no longer the case.

Table A.2. Trade union density and collective bargaining coverage, 2010 and 2015

	Union density		Bargaining coverage	
	2010	2015	2010	2015
SE	69	67	91	90
DK	68	65	80	84
DE	19	18	62	57
AT	28	27	99	98
NL	19	18	82	79
BE	52	54	96	96
FR	8	8[a]	93	98[a]
IT	33	36	80	80
UK	27	25[a]	33	28
IE	37	33[a]	44	36

Source: ICTWSS database, derived from national sources (Visser 2015) and OECD.
[a] 2014.

Table A.3. Trade union density by age group, 2015

Age	15–24	25–54	55–64	Total
SE	30.6	70.6	80.7	67.0
DK	28.3	71.3	77.6	66.8
DE	11.0	17.4	25.9	18.1
AT	18.3	27.8	34.2	27.4
NL	7.3	17.7	27.8	17.6
BE	44.7	56.9	52.3	55.1
FR	2.8	11.5	15.7	11.3
IT	7.9	40.0	34.4	38.9
UK	9.2	26.4	32.9	24.7
IE	19.8	29.3	41.1	29.5

Source: OECD.

however, that official statistics since 2013 have used a different basis for calculation and now suggest a figure of 11 percent (DARES 2016). In Sweden, after a sharp decline following the changes in the 'Ghent' system, the situation has stabilized (Arvidsson 2014), and the same is true in Denmark; hence, the Nordic countries maintain their exceptional position. As we noted in Chapter 1, union membership does not correlate closely with bargaining coverage, because the latter reflects a variety of nation-specific institutional supports. Given the weakness of such supports in the anglophone countries, coverage has indeed declined in parallel with density; elsewhere there is no clear pattern, though Germany—already an outlier among the 'central' countries—has diverged further. Overall, as Table A3 indicates, unionization remains far lower among younger workers than for older groups.

Membership and Mobilization: How Much Light at the End of the Tunnel?

In the past five years, the literature on trade union 'renewal' and approaches to organizing has expanded considerably, in line with increasing efforts by European trade unions to respond to membership decline. In particular, there has been much attention to union efforts to recruit and represent 'vulnerable' workers such as young people, those on precarious contracts, and migrant or ethnic minority groups.

Research has tended to focus on three main themes. First, it has explored similarities but also differences in the 'turn to organizing' across countries (but also within them). Second, it has analysed the different interpretations and applications of the 'organizing model'. Third, it has attempted to explain differences in outcomes between different initiatives.

In a comprehensive overview, Ibsen and Tapia (2017: 180–1) identify three main conclusions in the recent literature. First, there has been a convergence on 'organizing' because unions in previously 'institutionally secure' countries have experienced government and employer attacks on traditional institutional supports. 'Thus, even in countries like Germany and the Nordic countries, unions are employing certain revitalisation strategies—most notably the "organising model" assumed to be more naturally suited for liberal market economies—while at the same time trying to defend their traditional strongholds of collective bargaining and corporatist policy-making' (2017: 180–1). Second, there has been growing scepticism about perceptions of 'organizing' as a simple panacea, a toolkit rather than a broader strategic or political vision for union change. 'As a result, the actual outcomes of union organising in terms of membership gains, collective bargaining power or internal union democracy have been less than was expected . . . especially in the countries where the institutional framework for union support is already weak.' Third, research has shown how unions can reinvent their 'repertoires of contention'; 'thus, tapping into a widespread sense of injustice since the 2008 recession, mobilisation power of trade unions has increased vis-à-vis governments in diverse countries like Finland, Belgium, Italy, Greece, Spain, France and even the US' (Ibsen and Tapia, 2017: 180–1). More specifically, Rego et al. (2016) argue that unions in a number of countries have successfully used social media to increase mobilization in protest actions. This has been especially important for efforts to redress the membership gap among young workers. For example, in the Netherlands the FNV youth section was relaunched in 2015 with the English title *Young & United*, and initiated a range of campaigns which made imaginative use of social media (https://www.youngandunited.nl/). An early success was to persuade the government in 2015 to abolish the rule whereby adult wages were payable only after the age of twenty-three. While media-based campaigns are typically intended to mobilize protest, this is not universally the case. For example, the Swedish white-collar confederation TCO launched a rap video in 2015 entitled *Business Like a Swede* (https://www.youtube.com/watch?v=OcVoKPTS7AU): the message was that the Swedish model meant that strong union organization brings gains for workers but also benefits for employers. What is also noteworthy, and perhaps novel, is the extensive 'use of social media by workers amongst themselves to organise industrial action, company-level protests, etc. This is indeed widespread amongst union members in German unions. There is widespread use of videos now by German unions not only to campaign but to document their activity' (Heiner Dribbusch, personal communication).

As we show in Chapter 3, and as Ibsen and Tapia (2017) comment, German unions have turned to 'organizing' as a solution to membership decline and the weakening of bargaining power; and their experience has been intensively analysed. Thomas, comparing their approach to that of their French counterparts, argues (2016: 326) that 'stronger centralization and the presence of more qualified staff predispose unions in Germany to be more receptive to new organizational techniques, whether related to the "organizing model" or to managerial forms of organization'. At the same time, central coordination has been stronger in *IG Metall* than in *ver.di*, where key initiatives have reflected commitment at the local level. Nicklich and Helfen (2017) suggest that there are 'tensions and contradictions' between top-down and bottom-up conceptions of organizing within *IG Metall*, linked to disagreements over competences and resources. On the other hand, Schmalz and Thiel argue that organizing in *IG Metall* involves a multi-level process, albeit with national leadership as the key actor. They insist (2017: 476) that

> the renewal of IGM cannot be attributed solely to national initiatives and to the union taking advantage of opportunity structures . . . The basis for revitalisation was a learning process that began at IGM's individual administrative offices and, with support from national funds, successfully united different levels of the organisation . . . This means that IGM members have not only regained visibility, reliability and the ability to act, but also that they more frequently have an impact on regional policy through networks aligned with unions.

Hence, recent initiatives also reflect a 'bottom-up dynamic of growing assertiveness of workers', demonstrated in particular in the increased recruitment of younger workers. In a cold climate, it is certainly an index of success that the union's membership was slightly higher in 2017 than in 2010. Somewhat similarly, unions in Austria have attempted to regain ground via workplace recruitment drives, coordinated by the works councils, and have registered some increases in membership (Guillas-Cavan 2017). In Sweden, LO has also responded to its substantial loss of membership by encouraging 'bottom-up' recruitment initiatives (Jolivet 2017: 153).

More generally across Europe, there has been considerable new research on trade union efforts to organize migrant workers. The edited collection by Marino et al. (2017) includes studies of eight of our ten countries (the exceptions are Belgium and Denmark). In Sweden, the dominant trade union approach is described as 'subordinated inclusion': unions have made efforts to recruit migrants, but have not developed special representation mechanisms. German unions have made some rather limited efforts to integrate migrant members and have also campaigned to regularize the status of undocumented migrants, launching a series of 'fair mobility' (*Faire Mobilität*) service centres. The policies of Austrian unions are still shaped by their basic assumption that immigrants threaten jobs, and their arguments identify 'exploitation' but not discrimination as the key issue. In the main, their efforts to recruit migrants focus mainly on the provision of individual services related to their integration into the labour market, rather than on collective resistance to disadvantageous conditions at work (Griesser and Sauer 2017). Conversely, Dutch unions have been active in pressing for equal rights for migrant workers. In 2013 they reached an agreement with employers to combat unfair competition, leading to legislation (the *Wet Aanpak Schijnconstructies*) making companies responsible for underpayment by subcontractors. The unions have continued a series of campaigns to represent vulnerable migrant workers. In the Southern countries, the commitment of French unions to 'universalism' has inhibited special arrangements for migrant workers; Italian unions, meanwhile, preoccupied with a range of other problems, seem to have placed less emphasis on integrating migrant workers into their structures. Finally, unions in both Britain and Ireland continue to devote considerable efforts to organizing migrants.

In an attempt to explain cross-national differences in approaches to migrant workers, Connolly et al. (2014) stress the importance of different conceptions of union identity and purpose. They argue (2014: 6) that 'union responses are stretched between different logics of action and meaning': for some, class unity is dominant; for others, a concern with community engagement encourages sensitivity to issues of race and ethnicity; for a third group, the priority is institutional regulation to underpin general social rights. The same authors (Martínez Lucio et al., 2017) also note structural problems within many unions, with a failure to integrate the activities of different functions such as organizing departments and migrant worker units. In a study of British unions, Alberti et al. (2013: 4144) identify a 'universalistic' logic whereby migrants are treated as workers rather than specifically as migrant workers: 'the question of the complex social identities of migrants as workers and as migrants and the irreducibility of their "difference" as compared to traditional forms of class and economic discrimination constitute a challenge to the occupational and industrial approaches to organising that are still dominant in the majority of trade unions in the UK'. Such an argument probably applies more strongly in a number of other countries.

Other studies of trade unions and vulnerable workers include the comparison of union policies towards agency workers in Belgium and Germany by Pulignano et al. (2015). German unions initially opposed agency work and hence were slow to attempt to organize such workers, and some unionized works councils negotiated protections for 'core' employees while regarding agency workers as a buffer labour force. Belgian unions, by contrast, have long sought to regulate agency work, achieving low thresholds for the proportion of agency workers in any company and negotiating better conditions than in Germany. Belatedly, however, German unions, and in particular *IG Metall*, have mobilized effectively on behalf of agency workers (Benassi 2015; Benassi and Dorigatti 2015; Kahmann 2017). In a comparison of seven countries (including five of those covered in our book), Keune (2013) shows that Dutch and Danish unions follow a similar approach, attempting to set maxima for the use of temporary contracts and to achieve equal pay for equal work. In Italy, as we showed in Chapter 2, there have been attempts to organize temporary workers in separate sections and also to negotiate social benefits for temporary workers; while in Britain, there have been serious efforts to organize precarious workers, but these face many difficulties.

As we have shown (p.34), new labour market entrants are particularly likely to be in precarious employment relationships. Representing young workers is thus necessary both in order for unions to secure their own future and to impose some regulation in the most exploitative elements of the labour market. Vandaele presents a comparison of union approaches to young workers in Sweden, Ireland, and the Netherlands, arguing in particular (2013: 392) that the youth section of the Dutch FNV has proved effective in creating 'discursive power and coalition-building capacity'. Subsequently (2015) he emphasizes the importance of 'deliberative vitality'—the integration of young people into union decision-making mechanisms—if organizing efforts are to be successful. In the main text (p.55) we identify a tension between union leaders' desire to harness the activism and enthusiasm of young people, and fear that self-activity may conflict with established policies and patterns of action. This tension is still very evident. Hodder and Kretsos (2015) offer a global overview of union approaches to young workers, though they identify rather few 'success stories'.

However, there are many examples of innovative initiatives, often developed by young trade unionists themselves. In Italy, CGIL launched a campaign against the exploitation of precarious contracts, with the title *Giovani NON +* ('young people will not take all that any more') (Nizzoli 2017). In Britain, as part of its biennial Equality Audit, the TUC (2014) found a significant increase among affiliated unions in the provision of special structures for young workers. The largest British union, Unite, undertook a cross-national study (2014) of trade union approaches to young workers and offered a series of strategic recommendations. In the same year it launched its 'Unite in Schools' programme, trained more than one hundred schools speakers, and developed a pack of films and interactive materials, with the aim of building familiarity with trade unionism before young people enter the labour market. Outreach to students is indeed a process well established in other countries, primarily in Northern Europe.

In Belgium, the Francophone CSC—acting separately from its Flemish counterpart ACV—has supported collective action by platform workers involved in fast food deliveries (Vandaele 2017), and launched a series of campaigns at the end of 2017, with the slogan *ça n'va nin !* (meaning 'that doesn't work' or 'we don't want that'). One of its first themes was to attack the extension of 'flexi-jobs', using a number of online videos (https://www.youtube.com/watch?v=uq1UfAKZgog). Likewise, a major focus of FNV Young & United is a social media campaign, using the tag *WTFLEX!*, highlighting that half of all young Dutch workers have a precarious contract.

New Structural Dilemmas

The merger process which we discuss in Chapter 4 seems to have reached saturation: there have been no new large-scale amalgamations in most of our countries. The main exception is the planned merger of Danish LO with the white-collar confederation FTF; if approved by special congresses of the two bodies, the new organization will be launched in January 2019. But, more generally, there have been reactions to the rise of 'mega-unions'. In the Netherlands, as we noted earlier (pp.18, 41–2), the dispute over pension reforms in 2011 threw the FNV into crisis, with its two largest affiliates outvoted. After lengthy and acrimonious debates (Wierink 2017), a 'new' FNV was established at the end of 2014. Both *AbvaKabo* and *Bondgenoten* were effectively dissolved into FNV to create 'a new hybrid structure' (de Beer and Keune 2017: 237): twelve smaller unions continue as separate affiliates, in parallel with fourteen sectoral or occupational groupings. Both constituencies are represented in a new members' parliament (*ledenparlement*), its 108 members directly elected by the membership. However, this initiative to enhance direct democracy does not appear to attract more than a low level of membership participation in elections for the new body.

A different form of reaction to giant unions can be seen in Germany. Here, the large DGB affiliates, and in particular *ver.di*, have faced growing competition from separate organizations representing skilled or professional occupations. These have been able to appeal to groups which often possess considerable structural power and which feel that their interests are submerged within the solidaristic bargaining policies of the conglomerate unions. The growing assertiveness of specialist unions has involved demands for separate bargaining rights, often backed by strike action (Müller-Jentsch 2017). Some of these organizations have a long history: notably, the engine drivers' union *Gewerkschaft Deutscher Lokomotivführer* (GDL) was founded a century and a half ago. The *Marburger Bund,* which represents doctors, dates from 1947. Others are newer. The *Unabhängige Flugbegleiter Organisation* (UFO), which represents aircraft cabin crew, broke away in 1992 from one of the predecessors of *ver.di;* the pilots' union *Vereinigung Cockpit* has existed for half a century but until 2000 it worked in conjunction with the white-collar confederation DAG which was about to merge into *ver.di;* while in the same sector, the air traffic controllers' union *Gewerkschaft der Flugsicherung* (GdF) was formed in 2004. Some such organizations have been growing, while *ver.di* lost 5 percent of its membership between 2010 and 2017.

Collective Bargaining: Increasing Adversity

As we discuss in Chapter 5, the context in which unions bargain with employers has become increasingly difficult in recent decades, and in some countries the problems have intensified since we wrote (Marginson 2016). The balance of power between unions and employers has become more adverse, while government support for 'organized' industrial relations has in many cases diminished; and the main institutions of the EU, while still paying lip service to the notion of a 'European social model', have increasingly seen trade union effectiveness as a threat. The relative importance of internal and external drivers of change in the structure and coverage of collective bargaining, and the degree to which these threaten the regulatory capacity of traditional institutional arrangements, entail major cross-national variations in the experiences of the past decade.

In a large-scale international analysis, Visser (2016: 30) remarks that

> the Great Recession has sharpened the divide between a smaller group of countries with more cohesive and coordinated industrial relations and wage bargaining institutions, and lower inequality levels, and a larger group of countries where "markets make policies", wage bargaining institutions are divisive and uncoordinated, and income inequality levels are higher.

He identifies an overall decline in bargaining coverage, though not primarily in western Europe (as is clear from Table A3, with Britain and Ireland, and to a lesser extent Germany, the main exceptions among the countries we analyse).

The impact of these trends in Europe has been mediated by specific interventions by the EU institutions. These have been most coercive in the case of countries forced to seek debt relief from the 'Troika', as shown in a study of collective bargaining in manufacturing by Koukiadaki et al., who focus (2016: 11) on seven countries which 'were among the European countries most affected by the economic crisis [and] have borne the brunt of the austerity measures'. These include Ireland and Italy from our national cases. Much more extensive, however, has been the effect of the 'new economic governance', described by Stierle and Haar (2012) as a 'Troika for everyone'. Since 2011, this has involved the publication of 'country-specific recommendations' which, while not formally mandatory, nevertheless exert coercive effects on individual countries (Bongelli 2018). As Van Gyes and

Schulten put it (2015: 9), 'the political emphasis is on "structural reforms" in order to increase the "downward flexibility" of wage development'. This has reinforced pre-existing pressures towards wage restraint. While trade unions at national and political levels have contested this policy logic and have insisted that wage increases are essential to boost domestic demand and hence to escape from recession, actual bargaining outcomes at sectoral and company level still tend to reflect the logic of 'competitive corporatism'.

Decentralization of bargaining, as we note in Chapter 5, has been a common European trend, though to varying degrees; this uneven process has continued under the impact of external pressures (Pedersini and Leonardi 2018). In southern European countries there has been a 'frontal assault' on multi-employer bargaining; while in northern countries there has been an 'incremental corrosion', with key issues increasingly devolved to company level (Marginson 2015). The study coordinated by Leonardi and Pedersini (2018) focuses primarily on five countries, four of which are covered in our book: Belgium, France, Germany and Italy. All have a long tradition of encompassing sectoral collective agreements; and in all cases their functioning has been changing in complex and uneven ways, making strategic trade union responses particularly difficult. Among these countries, Belgium stands out for the persistence of biennial peak-level bargaining and for the institutionalized linkage of wages to the cost of living. Sectoral bargaining is however the key form of regulation, though there has been some devolution to company level. An important shift has been a growing regionalization of bargaining, given the pressures for Flemish autonomy. Overall, the most important development under the impact of the crisis has been a growing tendency for governments to override collective bargaining by imposing restraint (Van Gyes et al. 2018).

In France, there is a formally impressive structure of collective bargaining but with limited depth, while the state maintains a key regulatory role. Governments have encouraged decentralization for more than three decades, partly to facilitate company-level 'modernization' and partly to 'empower' local actors; the number of company agreements has increased substantially, particularly since the turn of the century. This process has been accelerated by the El Khomri legislation of 2016 and the Macron ordinances of 2017, which have broadened the scope for derogation from sectoral agreements. In the context of weak (at least in numerical terms) and divided trade unions, this represented a political defeat for the unions and enhanced the powers of employers; however, the practical outcomes are as yet unclear (Rehfeldt and Vincent 2018: 107–32).

Italy also has a tradition of multi-level bargaining, but the process of reconfiguration described in our main text has continued. The economy was badly affected by the economic crisis and experienced no real recovery, with the highest levels of unemployment—in particular, among young workers—in any of our ten countries, as Table A1 shows. This has encouraged pressure by employers and governments for changes to the industrial relations system. The dominant private sector employer, FIAT, withdrew from the employers' confederation *Federmeccanica* in 2010 and insisted on a major worsening of employment conditions. FIOM-CGIL, the largest union, refused and was effectively excluded from the FIAT plants (Nuti 2011). Many observers saw this as heralding a general employers' offensive and a breakdown of coordinated bargaining, but this has not occurred. A series of cross-sectoral agreements between 2011 and 2014 recalibrated the structure of collective bargaining but sustained the priority of multi-employer agreements. In many respects, the most important recent change to the system (as in Belgium) has been far greater government intervention, despite trade union disapproval (Leonardi et al. 2018).

As explained in the main text, Germany has no tradition of cross-sectoral bargaining, but sectoral multi-employer bargaining has long been the norm. However, for some three decades there has been a process of decentralization of key decisions within the framework of sectoral agreements, together with a declining coverage of these agreements. This process has continued, with the result that 'the trend towards decentralisation has fundamentally changed the German system of collective bargaining' and has caused 'a significant loss of regulatory power on the part of both employers' associations and trade unions' (Schulten and Bispinck 2018: 103). This has placed increased demands on the capacities of workplace representation structures, which only a minority have been able to meet effectively. Nevertheless, sectoral bargaining can still achieve important results: for example, in February 2018, after a series of 24-hour strikes, *IG Metall* negotiated a 4.3 per cent increase over two years plus several additional one-off payments, and also the right to reduce weekly hours temporarily to twenty-eight and to take part of the pay supplement in the form of additional leave.

In our other countries, there has been less recent evidence of radical change. 'Organized decentralization' remains the pattern in Sweden, Denmark, Austria, and the Netherlands; both British and Irish bargaining remain highly decentralized (though with the collapse of peak-level 'partnership agreements' in the latter, as described in our main text (p.130)).

Decentralization has also affected the capacity—or the willingness—of unions to mobilize strike action. As Vandaele (2016: 285) shows, there has been 'an almost general downward tendency in strike frequency' (or at least, in strike volume), with bargaining decentralization encouraging a fragmentation of conflicts and with other social movements at times filling a vacuum of trade union militancy (Hyman and Gumbrell-McCormick 2017). Table A4 provides updated data on strike trends.

Table A.4. Strike days per 1000 workers, annual averages

	1971–1977[1]	2008–2015[2]
SE	54	6
DK	329	144
DE	43	18
AT	11	2
NL	39	9
BE	231	81
FR	229	132
IT	1497	n.a.
UK	482	23
IE	520	35

[1] Own calculations, based on Aspalter (2001: 77).
[2] Figures kindly provided by Kurt Vandaele on the basis of Eurostat and other sources.

To systematize the diversity of recent experience, we identify three main patterns, though the boundaries between these are relatively imprecise. At one extreme are countries subject to externally imposed austerity and more specific requirements to weaken employment protection legislation, liberalize precarious contracts, decentralize collective bargaining, remove the priority of higher-level over lower-level agreements, weaken or abolish extension mechanisms, and reduce minimum wages. The most radical cases are Mediterranean countries outside the focus of our book (notably Greece and Portugal), subject to the severe constraints of 'Memoranda of Understanding' with the Troika as conditions for debt relief. Measures included the weakening or elimination of extension mechanisms and the abolition of 'after-life' provisions which entailed that an expiring collective agreement remained in force until a replacement was agreed. Ireland was also subject to analogous constraints from the Troika, though its already weakly institutionalized industrial relations mechanisms were less radically transformed.

This category merges into a second, where less coercive external pressures have reinforced already strong domestic moves to liberalization. Here, Britain is the exemplary case: the financial crisis, and the subsequent government bail-out of failed banks, substantially increased public debt; but the radical austerity measures imposed after the 2010 election were largely the reflection of a domestic political agenda. Moreover, the new legislative attacks on trade unions' bargaining capacity were purely an exercise in political vindictiveness. The cases of Italy and France present some similarities. In the former, the 'secret letter' sent by the European Central Bank in 2011, when a default on government debt seemed possible, demanded radical changes in labour law and collective bargaining practices.

Nevertheless, liberalization of employment protection and collective bargaining was strongly embraced by both the Monti and Renzi governments, and the latter presented his 'Jobs Act' (choosing an English title) as a form of modernization necessary to remedy the labour market failings deemed responsible for high youth unemployment. Likewise, in France the El Khomri law of 2016 partly reflects the risk of EU sanctions for 'excessive debt' and the pressures from the Commission to cut labour costs and facilitate company-level derogations from sectoral collective agreements. Yet at the same time, this agenda was enthusiastically embraced by 'modernizers' within the Hollande government, and became central to the electoral programme of Macron in 2017.

As a third category, the Nordic and 'central' countries include the main winners from the eurozone and the 'competition Union' (Lehndorff 2015). Here, there were relatively few external demands to transform industrial relations during the crisis, and the pressures for weakening of employment protection and decentralization of collective bargaining have been primarily domestic. In these countries, it is a matter of debate how far recent changes have undermined the post-war industrial relations architecture. In the case of this group, many writers discern stability and continuity. But this must be read comparatively: as measured against the coercive destruction of regulatory institutions elsewhere in Europe, erosion is indeed limited. Whether even limited institutional erosion may escalate remains a serious question.

The Political Challenge: A Difficult Balance Sheet

We discuss in Chapter 6 the growing distancing between trade unions and the political parties with which many were traditionally associated—though Allern and Bale (2017) have recently argued that a general trend is difficult to establish empirically, primarily because these authors focus mainly on interpersonal rather than institutionalized links. We also note the secular decline in electoral support for social-democratic and other centre-left parties. Yet when we first wrote, such parties were in office in all but two of our countries, and headed the government in five of these. With the vagaries of the electoral cycle, the situation is now reversed: the centre-left heads just one government, in Sweden, but may not retain power after elections in September 2018; while in Germany the SPD remains the junior coalition partner. The centre-left is now in opposition in the other eight countries—unless the PD in Italy enters a coalition with the *Movimento 5 Stelle* (M5S), which at the time of writing seems improbable but not impossible. A comparison of Table 6.1 in our main text (p.139) with Table A5 below shows the extent of the losses.

The now-familiar alternation of office between left and right in the Nordic countries has seen the *Socialdemokraterne* defeated in the 2015 Danish

Table A.5. 'Left' seats in most recent national[1] and European[2] elections

Country	Year	Seats available		Social democrats[3]		Other left[3]		Greens[3]	
SE	2014	349	(18)	113	(6)	21	(1)	25	(4)
DK	2015	179	(13)	44	(3)	21[4]	(1)	4	(1)
DE	2017	622	(99)	153	(27)	69	(8)	67	(13)
AT	2017	183	(17)	52	(5)				(3)
NL	2017	150	(25)	9	(3)	14	(3)	19	(2)
BE	2014	150	(22)	36	(4)	2		12	(2)
FR	2012	577	(72)	30	(13)	27	(4)	1	(6)
IT	2018	630	(72)	113	(31)	14	(3)		
UK	2017	650	(72)	262	(20)	4[5]	(1)[5]	1	(3)
IE	2016	158	(12)	7	(1)	3[6]	(1)[6]	2	

[1] National elections: lower house only. Source: *Election Resources on the Internet*, http://electionresources.org/
[2] 2014 European Parliament election (in parentheses). Source: *Results of the 2014 European Elections*, http://www.europarl.europa.eu/elections2014-results
[3] All these categories are inevitably somewhat arbitrary: for example, neither the Italian PD nor the British Labour Party labels itself as Social-democratic; the boundaries of 'other left' parties are imprecise; the Green/EFA group in the European Parliament includes representatives of regionalist parties which are neither environmentalists nor left-oriented, and other parties which we have categorized as 'Other left'.
[4] The Red–Green Alliance (*Enhedslisten*) won 12 seats, here listed as 'Other left'.
[5] Including the Welsh nationalist *Plaid Cymru*, though it sits with the Green group in the European Parliament. In addition, the Irish nationalist *Sinn Féin*—which is on the left in terms of labour policies—won seven Northern Ireland seats in the national elections (which it refuses to occupy) and one European seat. We have not attempted to classify the Scottish National Party.
[6] In addition, *Sinn Féin* won twenty-three seats in the national elections and three European seats.

elections (though their vote increased slightly). The opposite occurred in Sweden in 2014, with the election of a 'red–green' minority government which has struggled to survive. In Germany, the SPD suffered its worst postwar result in the elections of September 2017, and initially decided to end its junior partnership in the 'grand coalition' in order to renew itself in opposition. But after Angela Merkel failed to construct an alternative coalition, the party leadership agreed in February 2018 to rejoin the government, provoking major internal divisions. A membership ballot gave two-thirds backing, a result widely attributed to fear that the alternative would be new elections in which the party would fare even worse. In Austria, the SPÖ sustained its vote in the 2017 elections but was ousted from the governing coalition following a collapse in support for the Greens. In Belgium, the Socialists had headed the government coalition from 2010 until 2014 but—although their share of the vote remained stable—they were displaced by a new centre-right coalition. According to the president of the ACV/CSC (which, as we indicated, was once close to the dominant Christian-democratic CD&V), the union now faced 'a right-wing government, poisoned by a dangerous cocktail of right-wing radicalismism and neoliberalism' (*De Morgen*, 23 April 2015). In the Netherlands, the PvdA fared disastrously in the 2017 elections, losing three-quarters of its seats and winning only nine (compared to fourteen each for the leftist SP and the *GroenLinks*).

Even worse was the performance of the SP in France in 2017 after five years of the lacklustre Hollande government. Internally divided over its choice of presidential candidate after Hollande agreed not to stand for re-election, it came fourth, behind Macron's newly formed party *En Marche!*, the far-right *Front National* (FN) and the left-wing *France Insoumise*. In the parliamentary elections that followed, *En Marche!* won an absolute majority while the PS was reduced to a rump of thirty seats. Italy stood out over the period with the government of the centre-left PD. But the party was an unstable coalition: Matteo Renzi ousted the incumbent premier in 2014, but in turn resigned after staking his position on an unsuccessful constitutional referendum in 2016, while remaining party leader. He eroded the already weak relationship between the PD and the unions, particularly by pushing through his 'Jobs Act', which involved 'a substantial liberalization of the labour market' (Fana et al. 2015: 2). Support for the coalition led by the PD fell from 30 per cent in 2013 to 19 per cent in 2018.

In Ireland, where the Labour Party had been an ineffectual junior partner in the coalition led by *Fine Gael*, it was punished by the voters, losing all but seven of its seats. At its following conference, the party voted to end collective trade union affiliations. The UK may be seen as a possible exception to the overall gloomy picture. After the disappointing electoral results of the 2015 election, the left-wing Jeremy Corbyn was unexpectedly elected leader of the Labour Party. He was opposed by most members of the party in parliament and was widely viewed as unelectable. His critics were confounded by the party's surprisingly strong performance in the 2017 general election, called by new prime minister Theresa May in a misguided attempt to strengthen her authority. Labour has been successful in boosting membership substantially, in particular among younger voters, and has established strong ties with key trade unions (Crouch 2018). Perhaps the only other evident case of centre-left revival, outside the countries on which we focus, is that of Portugal, where gains in the 2015 elections enabled the *Partido Socialista* to form a coalition with other left parties and to roll back some of the austerity measures imposed by the Troika.

In a few countries, the decline of support for centre-left parties has been linked to gains for parties further to the left: this is true of France and the Netherlands, and also—if *Sinn Féin* is so classified—of Ireland. But more generally, it is the far right which has captured the protest vote. In Sweden, the *Sverigedemokraterna* (SD), a party with Nazi origins, won 13 per cent of the vote in 2014 and became the third largest party. In Germany, the *Alternative für Deutschland* (AfD) entered parliament for the first time in 2017, with 13 per cent of the popular vote, likewise becoming the third largest party. In

Austria, the FPÖ almost won the 2016 presidential election, and gained 26 per cent of the vote in the 2017 legislative elections, obtaining key ministries in the new coalition led by the ÖVP, which had itself moved to the right in an effort to retain the xenophobic vote. In the Netherlands, the far-right *Partij voor de Vrijheid* (PVV) became the second largest party in 2017, with 13 per cent of the vote. In Belgium, the Flemish nationalist *Nieuw-Vlaamse Alliantie* (N-VA) became the largest party in 2014, with 20 per cent of the national vote (33 per cent in Flanders). The French FN came second in the 2017 presidential election, gaining 21 per cent of the vote in the first round and 34 per cent in the second (though it did less well in the legislative elections). The *Lega* in Italy, with xenophobic policies, dominates politics in the north and has now established a national presence; while the neo-fascist *Fratelli d'Italia* also attracts significant support. In Britain, the anti-EU United Kingdom Independence Party (UKIP), which has moved increasingly to the right on social and economic policy, won 13 per cent of the vote in 2015 but (partly because the Conservatives had taken over much of its programme) less than 2 per cent in 2017. However, its demand for UK withdrawal from the EU ('Brexit'), backed by many on the right of the Conservative party, was narrowly approved in the June 2016 referendum, despite opposition by almost all British trade unions. Significantly different in some respects is the case of Italy, where the anti-establishment M5S won a third of the popular vote in 2018 but is impossible to locate on a conventional left-right spectrum.

In most cases, far-right parties draw a significant part of their support from a working-class constituency which has traditionally provided much of the basis for trade union membership. For example, the AfD in Germany, founded only in 2013, has a primarily working-class base, with above-average support among blue-collar workers and trade union members; while in Austria, the FPÖ has 'eclipsed the SPÖ as the most popular party among blue-collar voters' (Luther 2017: 72). This poses serious challenges for unions, which in most cases wish to pursue progressive, anti-racist policies but are also reluctant to alienate members and activists with very different opinions. It also provides unions with a diminishing capacity to influence key political actors.

The International Dimension: Still Seeking Solidarity

'Realistically, the main focus for organized labor's struggle in Europe remains the national (or even subnational) level, not Brussels' (Schulze-Cleven 2017: 20). In Chapter 7 we discuss the obstacles faced by national trade unions in working together at the European and global levels: despite their long institutionalized transnational structures, particularly at the European level, the tension between the national and international levels of trade union identity, interests, and action remains strong; internationalism is not yet embedded in everyday trade union action and is still to a large extent the domain of 'experts'.

At the global level, European trade unions have retained their leading role in the ITUC, the GUFs, and other international bodies such as the ILO. While the ITUC has increasingly sought to strengthen its global representativeness, its core membership and its major political and financial resources still come from the western European confederations (with Nordic and Benelux unions playing an important role), along with the American AFL-CIO and a few other large national confederations. In opposition to what a French international officer has called the 'social democratic hegemony', the French CGT, Italian CGIL and a few other European confederations, along with the South African COSATU and some Latin American national centres, continue to enact an internal opposition to many of the decisions and policies of the leadership. As a partial legacy of its background in the WCL, the Belgian ACV/CSC continues to play a significant role, sometimes critical of the leadership. The Benelux countries also retain disproportionate influence within the ILO, with the election of Luc Cortebeeck (ACV/CSC) as president of the governing body in 2017, and of Catelene Passchier (FNV) as president of the Workers' Group in the same year.

There has been little change in the relationship between national confederations and the ETUC: the same tension between closer union and continued national autonomy remains. As the contributors to Ciampani and Tilly (2017) show, the priorities and forms of involvement of its affiliates have always been diverse. Issues such as a European minimum wage and wage coordination more generally remain contentious, with unions from the Nordic countries resisting any harmonization that might threaten their own standards, while those from CEE and some southern European countries are strongly in favour. However, Pernicka and Glassner (2014) conclude that there is indeed an emerging institutional field of European wage policy, offering scope for greater convergence should union actors so will. To some degree, solidaristic policies may thus counteract the pressures of 'competitive corporatism'.

At times, more general tensions are evident between unions from the older (western) EU member states and those from CEE that joined in the enlargements of 2004 and 2007. This has posed distinctive issues for cross-national solidarity. Workers and their unions in the west have often perceived labour migration from CEE as a threat of 'social dumping', while many MNCs have used lower labour costs in CEE locations as an argument for concessions in western plants. Conversely, workers and their unions in CEE have at times regarded their own 'inferior' conditions as a source of competitive advantage. According to one Polish union official (Adamczyk 2018), 'after

20 shared years in the ETUC, the two "union worlds" are still very far apart'. Nevertheless, it is important to note the increasingly targeted efforts of the ETUFs and GUFs, largely with special funding from western European affiliates, to spread organizing efforts to the CEE countries. The BASTUN network (mentioned on p.162) launched a Baltic Organising Academy in 2012, targeting specific companies for unionization drives (Häkkinen 2013). Perhaps most notably, in 2016 industriAll Europe initiated a project on 'Building Trade Union Power' as a key priority for its work. This has involved identifying target MNCs for transnational organizing campaigns, with unions from headquarter countries of MNCs supporting organizing efforts in subsidiaries where unionization is weak or non-existent. Another important initiative is that by UNI in the services sector to establish a Central European Organising Centre (*Centrum Organizowania Związków Zawodowych*, COZZ) which arranges workshops and training events in the Visegrád countries as a strategy to reverse the decline in union membership. A different type of action is the launch of Union Solidarity International (USI) in 2012 by the main British union, Unite, in an attempt 'to encourage and support transnational labour solidarity by harnessing the dynamism of the Internet and social media' (Geelan and Hodder 2017: 346).

Since the onset of the global economic crisis, there have been many mobilizations by trade unions; but in the view of Dufresne and Pernot (2013: 21), these have mainly 'been organised at national level without taking account of the timetable proposed by the ETUC . . . and most often lack a transnational dimension'. Hence, resistance to austerity has tended to involve a 'patchwork of often uncoordinated action' with 'no thought-through strategic plan for getting mass support to bring down the plans of the Commission', in the words of the former secretary of the EMF, now deputy general secretary of the ETUC (Scherrer 2011: 36).There has been an evident contradiction between a global economic crisis on the one hand, and trade union action that is essentially national or indeed sub-national in character. Lemb and Urban (2014: 50–1) conclude that while unions attempt 'in especially crisis-torn countries to brace themselves against the economically, politically, and socially disastrous crisis policy . . . there is little sign of a broad Europe-wide trade union resistance'. In Germany, they argue, 'the European crisis and the far-reaching economic, social, and political dislocations that neoliberal austerity policy has unleashed appears from those employed here as problems occurring far away [and] a solidary management of the crisis in Europe is less important or unimportant'. As Dribbusch concludes (2015: 182), '[t]he prospects of transnational trade union action are closely linked to the debate within unions on their future strategy on Europe, a debate that is located between the contending poles of supporting their own countries' attractions as locations of economic activity and trans-European cooperation.'

On p.188 we discuss the initiatives of European trade unions to negotiate transnational company agreements. The establishment of new IFAs and EFAs has slowed over the past few years, and there is still little take-up in companies based outside Europe. For this reason, the European national centres and the ETUFs continue to exert a strong influence in their operation.

By far the most significant recent development at the European level has been the June 2016 referendum in the UK, with a narrow majority voting to abandon membership of the EU. 'Brexit' was a major concern for trade unionists in most other EU countries, for there are important ramifications for unions across Europe as well as in the countries most directly affected: the UK itself and Ireland. The ETUC was quick to express its solidarity with the British TUC and with British workers. The ETUC held an 'extraordinary enlarged meeting' of its steering committee in London in July 2016, agreeing to 'reaffirm that there shall be no full access to the single market without applying the four freedoms linked to it, and particularly the free movement of people and workers'. Subsequently, the main resolution adopted at the TUC Congress in September 2016 declared: 'Congress resolves to stand in solidarity with all migrant workers, who contribute enormous value to society and support the right of all EU nationals living here to remain'. This was echoed in the address by ETUC general secretary Luca Visentini: 'we warmly welcome the TUC's campaign to maintain the rights of continental European workers here in the UK and to be sure, similarly, that the ETUC will call on EU governments to give British citizens and workers abroad the right to remain where they are.' Following this, in December 2017 the ETUC Executive called for a future partnership between the UK and the EU which would protect workers' rights.

The wider ramifications of Brexit involve the potential effects on labour rights in the rest of the EU, the impetus it has given to right-wing populism and the threat it poses to the solidarity and legitimacy of the EU, and, above all, its impact on EWCs. On labour rights, there could even be a positive impact, with the UK no longer able to block progressive employment regulation at the EU level. More realistically, though, countries (not least Germany) which have previously been happy to allow Britain to take the blame for blocking new labour rights would simply take over this role. In the UK itself, the potential impact could be disastrous, particularly if the right within the current government emerges victorious from the conflict over Brexit (Gumbrell-McCormick and Hyman 2017).

One of the main fears for trade unionists in the rest of the EU is that Brexit has boosted support for 'the poison of populism': the rise of far-right and xenophobic parties and movements which, as we noted earlier, have been the main beneficiaries of the decline of social democracy. Moreover, European trade unionists are concerned that the Brexit vote might weaken the unity of the remaining EU-27, in the extreme case leading to the breakup of the EU. Most other European governments would not contemplate a similar referendum, fearing the possible result. For many trade unionists, populist attacks on the EU are understandable outcomes of the policy orientation of European integration. 'As the triumph of two radical right-wing tendencies—a thoroughgoing version of economic liberalism and a form of xenophobic nationalism—Brexit strengthens disintegrative forces throughout the EU . . . The failure of EU leaders to address the social distress which, in a distorted way, finds expression in these forces, increases the danger' (EuroMemo Group 2017: 6). This argument was echoed by a leading official of the largest Belgian confederation, who insisted that unions must push within the ETUC and with their own governments for 'rights, rights and rights':

> we have failed altogether to involve ordinary people in the European project. Why? Because we did not manage to make the benefits of the European project visible for them . . . We turned a blind eye to the 'elephant in the room', to the growing distrust in a European project that only seemed to generate fear and indignation. (Serroyen 2016: 2)

Perhaps the most immediate practical impact of a 'hard' Brexit will be on EWCs, which we discuss on pp.186–7. Unless special arrangements are agreed with the EU, employment in the UK will not count towards the threshold for establishing an EWC. British-based firms which still meet the threshold would have to nominate a 'representative agent' within the EEA, as would non-European MNCs with European headquarters in Britain: a return to the pre-1999 situation. The numerical effect would be relatively small, since the smaller multinationals most likely to fall below the threshold after Brexit tend not to possess EWCs. As before 1999, but in a harsher economic and industrial relations environment, the question of British employee representatives could be contentious. One analysis (EWC Academy 2016) predicts that 'in practice, there will not be a massive loss of British mandates. The situation is different for EWC agreements based on British law. Here it remains entirely uncertain whether they will remain valid or will have to be completely renegotiated.'

Studies suggest that while managers in most firms with EWCs view the institution positively, roughly one in five do not (Waddington et al. 2016); hence, there could be resistance to retaining existing representation rights. There will probably be a multiplicity of time-consuming company-by-company negotiations, and it may be necessary to renegotiate the rules governing the selection, status, training, and protection of UK members of EWCs. For example, French union representatives have noted that in some companies, representatives of Swiss employees (who have no formal right to EWC membership) have only consultative status, and wonder if the same will happen to British members.

Strategic Choices: Where Are European Trade Unions Going?

Those responsible for policy-making in European trade unions have come to appreciate, sooner in some countries than in others, that there are no longer grounds for complacency and that institutional power resources alone are no guarantee for their future survival. Murray (2017: 9) refers to a 'long process of democratic experimentalism in union purpose and practice'. In the body of this book we chart aspects of this process; experimentation has continued, and in many countries has accelerated.

Since we wrote, there have been a number of attempts to explore issues addressed in our final chapter. For example, Gall and Fiorito (2016: 201–3) conclude their discussion of union effectiveness with the proposition that 'there is an overall dominant causal flow from environment to goals to strategy to structure to process to outcomes'. Similarly, Hodder and Edwards (2014: 849) suggest that while the external context shapes each union's 'purposes and overall objectives . . . unions engage in internal (democratic) processes of debate as well as external bargaining with employers and interactions with the state. Both these elements lead to the production of strategies for action. Finally, strategies generate outcomes.' Lévesque and Murray (2013 793–4) stress the importance of 'narrative resources' for rebuilding union power, adding that 'narrative resources and framing have to fit into a broader pattern or configuration of union capabilities'. Their argument complements our own emphasis on the importance of strategic capacity.

In many countries, the rapidly changing world of work and the potential advent of a 'digital economy' and a 'fourth industrial revolution' have stimulated strategic thinking. In Germany, the DGB at its 2014 congress called for a wide-ranging and intensive analysis of the implications. This resulted in a major study of 'the work of the future', coordinated by the union-related Hans-Böckler-Stiftung (Jürgens et al. 2017) and subsequently published in English (Jürgens et al. 2018). It will be debated at the 2018 congress. Whether this will result in a significant strategic advance remains to be seen; the outcome of previous German debates on the future of trade unionism has not been altogether encouraging.

After the Italian parliament published a report on 'Industry 4.0' in 2016, the CGIL established its own *Progetto Lavoro 4.0* (Project on Work 4.0), initiating a series of regional conferences in 2017 and publishing a preliminary report for further debate and discussion (CGIL 2018). Digitalization, financialization, and globalization, CGIL argues, imply radical changes in the shape of work and industrial relations in the future. The challenge for the union is to map likely scenarios and develop effective strategic responses. These require a strengthened model of participative governance and an adaptation of the structures of collective bargaining. The union itself must radically reform its structures in order to meet these challenges. The detailed CGIL strategy is still a work in process.

In Sweden, the future of employment was the key theme of the 2016 LO congress. Almost a year in advance, the union issued a report of over 400 pages on pathways to full employment and fair wages (Järliden Bergström et al. 2015); this was subsequently published in summary in English (LO 2017). It proposed a response to the growing problems of unemployment and inequality in Sweden, involving a return to expansionary macroeconomic policy, a strengthening of active labour market measures, improved continuing education and training, and a better system for the integration of migrants. LO emphasized (2016) that its traditional approach was to accept—indeed, to welcome—structural change, but that changes should be socially governed and the consequences should be equitably managed.

Not all programmatic initiatives unfold according to plan. We refer in the main text (p.85) to a description of the French CGT as 'more or less organized anarchy'. Since we wrote, internal disarray has increased. Bernard Thibault, the retiring secretary general, attempted to establish as his successor Nadine Prigent, who would have been the first woman to lead the union; but the choice was rejected by the key committee. Instead, Thierry Lepaon took over in 2013, but faced considerable internal opposition, and was forced to resign in January 2015 after revelations that some €160,000 had been spent on refurbishing his office and apartment. His succession was likewise strongly contested, and the whole affair damaged the union. In an effort to rehabilitate the CGT, the new secretary general presented a radical programmatic statement to its congress in April 2016. The policy document called for organizational restructuring designed to reinforce internal democracy, strengthen links with members, and give a greater role to regional committees in engaging with an increasingly fragmented workforce. More generally, the union should place greater emphasis on addressing young and precarious workers and on organizing smaller workplaces. The document was approved by the delegates, but received less than two-thirds of the votes—an unprecedented snub for the leadership (Noblecourt 2016). Only 58 per cent voted for the section on relations with other unions, political parties, and NGOs.

Less serious, but still embarrassing, was the outcome of the Belgian ACV/CSC congress in 2015. Its theme was participation, with the slogans *Zeg nu zelf* ('Have your say!') and *De vive voix* ('Speak up!'). The guidelines for action (*krachtlijnen* or *lignes de force*) were developed after consultation with activists and then debated within the union. Their central focus was the need to defend, extend, deepen, and update existing rights of participation in the face of structural changes in the economy and in employment. Within the union itself, there should be stronger provision for the representation of women, young people, precarious workers, the unemployed, and migrants. To connect with a broader constituency, the union should also develop greater creativity in its actions and improve its communications. In the main these guidelines were uncontentious, but very different was the proposal that the union should draw on broader European experiences of employee representation on company boards of directors and should press for legislative changes in Belgium to permit this. The idea of German-style board-level codetermination had long been opposed by the Belgian socialist union, but many ACV/CSC delegates expressed similar objections: sitting on company boards would subordinate representatives to the interests of 'their' enterprise, would prevent them from defending workers' interests, and would make them 'boot-lickers of the bosses'. The proposal was rejected. Evidently, one of the dilemmas of union democracy is that members and activists may not always embrace the strategic visions of the leadership.

In Conclusion

We have written this Afterword, like the book before it, not as a purely academic exercise. While it provides a large amount of information (perhaps too much), it was written as the outcome of dialogue with trade unionists in many countries and over many years. We have taken part in trade union training courses, attended congresses, and spoken to members and officials alike, not only in the context of formal research, but also in many different settings and situations. We ourselves are trade union members and activists, so we appreciate the challenges that recent years have presented to the trade union movement in our own country and throughout Europe. It is not for us to set up a ranking list of European trade unions, but rather to share a selection of examples of how they have begun to think strategically and to translate this into action. We have explored the constraints under which unions now operate and the ways in which they have responded, which often display both imagination and determination. Most importantly, we have sketched the different forms of union power and outlined why it is important for unions to respond strategically and as 'learning organizations' in an increasingly hostile climate. In the spirit of a call to further thought and action, this Afterword is intended to help those who read it to make their own history.

References

Adamczyk, S. (2018) 'Inside the trade union family: The "two worlds" within the European Trade Union Confederation', *European Journal of Industrial Relations*. doi.org/10.1177/0959680118760630.

Alberti, G., Holgate, J., and Tapia, M. (2013) 'Organising migrants as workers or as migrant workers? Intersectionality, trade unions and precarious work', *International Journal of Human Resource Management* 24(22): 4132-48.

Allen, K. (2009) 'Social Partnership and Union Revitalisation: The Irish Case' in G. Gall (ed.) *The Future of Union Organising*. Basingstoke: Palgrave Macmillan, 45-61.

Allern, E. H. and Bale. T. (eds) (2017) *Left-of-Centre Parties and Trade Unions in the Twenty-First Century*. Oxford: Oxford University Press.

Allinger, B. (2011) Union suggests wage bargaining for women. http://www.eurofound.europa.eu/eiro/2011/09/articles/at1109011i.htm

Allinger, B. and Hermann, C. (2011) Social Partners' Key Role in Austria's Labour Market Adjustment in the Face of the Crisis. Paper to IREC conference, Barcelona.

Amable, B. (2003) *The Diversity of Modern Capitalism*. Oxford: Oxford UP.

Amadieu, J.F. (1999) *Les syndicats en miettes*. Paris: Seuil.

Andolfatto, D. and Labbé, D. (2000) *Sociologie des syndicats*. Paris: La Découverte.

Andolfatto, D. and Labbé, D. (2006) 'Les transformations des syndicats français', *Revue française de science politique* 56 (2): 281-97.

Anner, M., Greer, I., Hauptmeier, M., Lillie, N., and Winchester, N. (2006) 'The Industrial Determinants of International Solidarity', *European Journal of Industrial Relations* 12 (1): 1-22.

Annesley, C. (2006) 'Ver.di and Trade Union Revitalisation in Germany', *Industrial Relations Journal* 37 (2): 164-79.

Anxo, D. (2012) 'From one crisis to another: The Swedish model in turbulent times revisited' in S. Lehndorff (ed.) *A triumph of failed ideas*. Brussels: ETUI, 27-40.

Anxo, D. and Niklasson, H. (2006) 'The Swedish Model in Turbulent Times', *International Labour Review* 145 (4): 339-71.

Archer, C. (2000) 'Euroscepticism in the Nordic Region', *European Integration* 22 (1): 87-114. Arcq, E. (2008) *La concertation sociale*. Brussels: CRISP.

Arcq, E. and Aussems, M. (2002) 'Implantation syndicale et taux de syndicalisation (1992-2000)', *Courrier hebdomadaire du CRISP* 1781: 5-36.

Ardura, A. and Silvera, R. (2001) 'L'égalité hommes/femmes: Quelles strategies syndicales?', *Revue de l'IRES* 37: 1-25.

References

Arlt, H.-J. (1994) 'Kampfkraft kommt aus Kommunikation, oder verkümmert', *Gewerkschaftliche Monatshefte* 5/1994: 281–9 6.

Arrowsmith, J. and Marginson, P. (2008) *Wage Flexibility*. http://www.eurofound.europa.eu/eiro/studies/tn0803019s/tn0803019s.htm.

Arvidsson, M. (2014) *Changes to the 'Swedish Model': Trade Unions under Pressure*. Berlin: Friedrich-Ebert-Stiftung.

Aspalter, C. (2001) *Importance of Christian and Social Democratic Movements in Welfare Politics*. Huntington: Nova Science.

Avdagic, S., Rhodes, M., and Visser, J. (eds) (2011) *Social Pacts in Europe*. Oxford: OUP.

Baccaro, L. (2001) 'Union Democracy Revisited: Decision-Making Procedures in the Italian Labour Movement', *Economic and Industrial Democracy* 22 (2): 183–210.

Baccaro, L. and Howell, C. (2011) 'A Common Neoliberal Trajectory: The Transformation of Industrial Relations in Advanced Capitalism', *Politics & Society* 39(4) 521–63.

Baccaro, L. and Howell, C. (2017) *Trajectories of Neoliberal Transformation: European Industrial Relations since the 1970s*. Cambridge: Cambridge University Press.

Baccaro, L. and Lim, S.-H. (2007) 'Social Pacts as Coalitions of the Weak and Moderate', *European Journal of Industrial Relations* 13 (1): 27–46.

Baccaro, L. and Simoni, M. (2010) 'Organizational determinants of wage moderation', *World Politics* 62 (4): 594–635.

Bacon, N. and Blyton, P. (2004) 'Trade Union Responses to Workplace Restructuring', *Work, Employment and Society* 18 (4): 749–73.

Baglioni, G. (1987) 'Constants and Variants in Political Exchange', *Labour* 1 (3): 57–94.

Bahnmüller, R. (2010) 'Dezentralisierung der Tarifpolitik' in R. Bispinck and T. Schulten (eds) *Zukunft der Tarifautonomie*. Hamburg: VSA-Verlag, 81–113.

Balanyá, B., Doherty, A., Hoedeman, O., Ma'anit, A., and Wesselius, E. (2003) *Europe Inc.* (2nd edn). London: Pluto.

Barker, C., Johnson, A., and Lavalette, M. (2001) 'Leadership Matters: An Introduction' in C. Barker, A. Johnson, and M. Lavalette (eds) *Leadership and Social Movements*. Manchester: Manchester University Press, 1–23.

Barnard, C. (2009) '"British Jobs for British Workers"', *Industrial Law Journal* 38 (3): 245–77.

Barthélemy, M., Dargent, C., Hilal, N., and Rey, H. (2009) *Les militants de la CFDT aujourd'hui*. Paris: CEVIPOF.

Batstone E., Boraston, I., and Frenkel, S. (1978) *The Social Organization of Strikes*. Oxford: Blackwell.

Beccalli, B. and Meardi, G. (2002) 'From Unintended to Undecided Feminism? Italian Labour's Changing and Singular Ambiguities' in F. Colgan and S. Ledwith (eds) *Gender, Diversity and Trade Unions*. London: Routledge, 113–31.

Behrens, M. (2009) 'Formen der Dezentralisierung', *WSI Mitteilungen* 2/2009: 102–9.

Behrens, M., Hamann, K., and Hurd, R. (2004) 'Conceptualizing Labour Union Revitalization' in C.M. Frege and J. Kelly (eds) *Varieties of Unionism*. Oxford: OUP, 11–29.

Benassi, C. (2015) 'From concession bargaining to broad workplace solidarity: The IG Metall response to agency work' in J. Drahokoupil (ed.), *The outsourcing challenge: Organizing workers across fragmented production networks*. Brussels: ETUI, 237–54.

References

Benassi, C. and Dorigatti, L. (2015) 'Straight to the Core: Explaining Union Responses to the Casualization of Work', *British Journal of Industrial Relations* 53(3): 533–55.

Bengtsson, H.A. (2008) *Nordische Erfahrungen: Das Verhältnis zwischen Gewerkschaften und Politik in Schweden*. Bonn: Friedrich-Ebert-Stiftung. http://library.fes.de/pdf-files/id/ipa/05862.pdf.

Bercusson, B. and Weiler, A. (1998) *Equal Opportunities and Collective Bargaining in Europe 3*. Luxembourg: Office for Official Publications. Berger, S. and Compston, H. (eds) (2002) *Policy Concertation and Social Partnership in Europe*. New York: Berghahn.

Bernaciak, M. (2010) 'Cross-border Competition and Trade Union Responses in the Enlarged EU', *European Journal of Industrial Relations* 16 (2): 119–35.

Béroud, S. (2009) 'Organiser les inorganisés', *Politix* 85: 127–46.

Béroud, S., Denis, J-M., Desage, G., Giraud, B., and Pélisse, J. (2007) 'Le changement de visage de la conflictualité en entreprise', *Les Mondes du travail* 3–4: 37–49.

Béroud, S., Denis, J-M., Desage, G., Giraud, B., and Pélisse, J. (2008) *La lutte continue? Les conflits du travail dans la France contemporaine*. Broissieux: Croquant.

Bévort, A. (1994) 'Le syndicalisme français et la logique du recrutement selectif:', *Le Mouvement social* 169: 109–35.

Bieler, A. (2006) *The Struggle for a Social Europe*. Manchester: Manchester UP.

Bieler, A. and Morton, A. D. (2004) '"Another Europe is Possible"?', *Globalizations* 1 (2): 303–25.

Bild, T., Jørgensen, H., Lassen, M., and Madsen, M. (1998) 'Do Trade Unions Have a Future? The Case of Denmark', *Acta Sociologica* 41 (2–3): 195–207.

Bispinck, R., Dribbusch, H., and Schulten, T. (2010) *German Collective Bargaining in a European Perspective*. Düsseldorf: WSI-Diskussionspapier 171.

Bispinck, R. and Schulten, T. (2000) 'Alliance for Jobs: Is Germany Following the Path of "Competitive Corporatism"?' in G. Fajertag and P. Pochet (eds) *Social Pacts in Europe: New Dynamics*. Brussels: ETUI/OSE, 187–217.

Bispinck, R. and Schulten, T. (2011a) *Sector-level bargaining and possibilities for deviations at company level: Germany*. Dublin: European Foundation.

Bispinck, R. and Schulten, T. (2011b) *Sector-level bargaining and possibilities for deviations at company level: Austria*. Dublin: European Foundation.

Blaschke, S. (2005) 'Austria: A Case of Limited Restructuring' in J. Waddington (ed.) *Restructuring Representation*. Brussels: P.I.E.-Peter Lang, 67–86.

Blaschke, S. (2011) 'Determinants of Female Representation in the Decision-Making Structures of Trade Unions', *Economic and Industrial Democracy* 32 (3): 421–38.

Bongelli, K. (2018) 'The impact of the European Semester on collective bargaining and wages in recent years', 189–207 in S Leonardi and R Pedersini (eds) *Multi-employer bargaining under pressure: Decentralization trends in five European Countries*. Brussels: ETUI.

Borchorst, A. and Jørgensen, H. (2012) The Equal Pay Issue and The Danish Labour Market Model. Paper to the Nordic Working Life Conference, Elsinore, April.

Bouffartigue, P. (2008) 'Précarités professionnelles et action collective', *Travail et Emploi* 116: 33–44.

Brandl, B. and Traxler, F. (2011) 'Labour Relations, Economic Governance and the Crisis', *Labor History* 52 (1): 1–22.

References

Braud, M. (2000) 'Représentation et représentativité syndicales au niveau européen', *Chronique Internationale de l'IRES* 66: 105–12.

Brinkmann, U., Choi, H.-L., Detje, R., Dörre, K., Holst, H., Karakayali, S., and Schmalstieg, C. (eds) (2008) *Strategic Unionism: Aus der Krise zur Erneuerung?* Wiesbaden: VS Verlag.

Briskin, L. (1999) 'Unions and Women's Organizing in Canada and Sweden' in L. Briskin and M. Eliasson (eds) *Women's Organizing and Public Policy in Canada and Sweden*. Montreal: McGill-Queen's University Press, 147–83.

Bromberg, T. (2011) *Rückenwind für Betriebsräte: Eine Analyse der 'besser statt billiger' Kampagne der IG Metall NRW*. Duisburg: IAQ-Report 2011-05.

Brouard, S. and Tiberj, V. (2006) 'The French Referendum', *PSOnline* April: 261–8.

Brown, W. A., Bryson, A., Forth, J., and Whitfield, K. (eds) (2009) *The Evolution of the Modern Workplace*. Cambridge: Cambridge UP.

Bsirske, F., Mönig-Raane, M., Sterkel, G., and Wiedemuth, J. (eds) (2004) Es ist Zeit: Das *Logbuch für die ver.di-Arbeitszeitinitiative*. Hamburg: VSA.

Bücker, A. and Warneck, W. (eds) (2010) *Viking, Laval, Rüffert*. Brussels: ETUI Report 111.

Bunel, J. and Thuderoz, C. (1999) 'Le syndicalisme entre participation et institutionnalisation', in H. Pinaud, M. Le Tron, and A. Chouraqui (eds) *Syndicalisme et démocratie dans l'entreprise*. Paris: L'Harmattan, 117–46.

Burroni, L. and Carrieri, M. (2011) Bargaining for social rights (BARSORI) country report Italy. http://www.uva-aias.net/uploaded_fi les/regular/BarsoriReport-Italy.pdf.

Busemeyer, M., Kellermann, C., Petring, A., and Stuchlik, A. (2008) 'Overstretching Solidarity?', *Transfer* 14 (3): 435–52.

Carrieri, M. (2003) *Sindacato in bilico*. Rome: Donzelli.

Carrieri, M. (2008) 'La necessaria immersione nel fost-Fordismo dei sindacalismi contemporaneii', *Economia & Lavoro* 42 (1): 71–83.

Carrieri, M., Ambra, M. C., and Ciarini, A. (2018) 'The "resistible" rise of decentralised bargaining : A cross-country and inter-sectoral comparison', 27–46 in S Leonardi and R Pedersini (eds) *Multi-employer bargaining under pressure: Decentralization trends in five European Countries*. Brussels: ETUI.

Carter, C., Clegg, S. R., Hogan, J., and Kornberger, M. (2003) 'The polyphonic spree: The case of the Liverpool dockers', *Industrial Relations Journal* 34 (4): 290–304.

Castells, M. (2009) *Communication Power*. Oxford: Oxford University Press.

Cedefop (2008) *Career development at work*. Luxembourg: Office for Official Publications.

Cella, G. and Treu, T. (1989) *Relazioni industriali*. Bologna: Mulino.

Cella, G. and Treu, T. (2001) 'National Trade Union Movements' in R. Blanpain and C. Engels (eds) *Comparative Labour Law and Industrial Relations in Industrialized Market Economies,* 7th edn. Deventer: Kluwer, 445–82.

Chaison, G.N. (1996) *Union Mergers in Hard Times*. Ithaca: ILR Press.

Chari, R. (2008) Why Did the Irish Reject Lisbon? Real Instituto Elcano Paper, http://www.realinstitutoelcano.org/wps/portal/rielcano_eng/Content?WCM_GLOBAL_CONTEXT=/Elcano_in/Zonas_in/Europe/ARI69-2008.

Charlwood, A. (2004) 'The New Generation of Union Leaders and Prospects for Union Revitalization', *British Journal of Industrial Relations* 42 (2): 379–97.

References

Charlwood, A. and Forth, J. (2009) 'Employee representation' in W. Brown, A. Bryson, J. Forth, and K. Whitfield (eds) *The Evolution of the Modern Workplace*. Cambridge: Cambridge University Press, 74–96.

Checchi, D. and Visser, J. (2005) 'Pattern Persistence in European Trade Union Density', *European Sociological Review* 21 (1): 1–21.

Child, J., Loveridge, R. and Warner, M. (1973) 'Towards an Organizational Study of Trade Unions', *Sociology* 7 (1): 71–91.

Ciampani, A. and Tilly, P. (eds) (2017) *National trade unions and the ETUC: A history of unity and diversity.* Brussels: ETUI.

Clark, N. and Hardy, J. (2011) *Free Movement in the EU: The Case of Great Britain*. Berlin: Friedrich-Ebert-Stiftung.

Clegg, H. A. (1976) *Trade Unionism under Collective Bargaining*. Oxford: Blackwell.

Como E. (2008) La Voce di 100.000 Lavoratrici e Lavoratori. http://www.fi om.cgil.it/inchiesta/libro_sintesi.pdf.

CFDT (2009) *Le syndicalisme à un tournant . . . oser le changement!* Paris: CFDT. CGT (2008) *Presence, Audience de la CGT.* Etude de la Commission ad hoc. Montreuil: CGT.

CGIL (2018) *Progetto lavoro 4.0: Primo report di attivitá* Rome: CGIL

CGT (2009) *Réflexions et pistes de travail sur les structures de la CGT.* Rapport de la Commission ad hoc. Montreuil: CGT.

Collombat, T. (2011) Several Souths: The Dynamics of the International Labour Movement in the Americas. PhD thesis, Carleton University.

Connolly, H. (2010) *Renewal in the French Trade Union Movement*. Oxford: Peter Lang.

Connolly, H., Marino, S., and Martínez Lucio, M. (2014) 'Trade union renewal and the challenges of representation: Strategies towards migrant and ethnic minority workers in the Netherlands, Spain and the United Kingdom', *European Journal of Industrial Relations* 20(1): 5–20.

Cortebeeck, L. (2008) *De solidaire samenleving*. Leuven: Davidsfonds.

Cotton, E. and Gumbrell-McCormick, R. (2012) 'Global Unions as Imperfect Multilateral Organizations', *Economic and Industrial Democracy* 33 (4): 707–28.

Cox, R.W. (1971). 'Labor and Transnational Relations', *International Organization* 25 (3): 554–84.

Crosby, M. (2005) *Power at work: Rebuilding the Australian union movement*. Sydney: Federation Press.

Cremers, J. (2010) 'Rules on working conditions in Europe', *European Journal of Industrial Relations* 16 (3): 293–306.

Criddle, B. (1993) 'The French Referendum on the Maastricht Treaty September 1992', *Parliamentary Affairs* 46 (2): 228–38.

Crouch, C. (1993) *Industrial Relations and European State Traditions*. Oxford: Clarendon Press.

Crouch, C. (2000a) 'The snakes and ladders of 21st-century trade unionism', *Oxford Review of Economic Policy* 16 (1): 70–83.

Crouch, C. (2000b) 'National Wage Determination and European Monetary Union' in C. Crouch (ed.) *After the Euro,* Oxford: OUP, 203–26.

References

Crouch, C. (2005) *Capitalist Diversity and Change*. Oxford: Oxford University Press.

Crouch, C. (2018) 'UK Labour: Credibly Redefining Left of Centre' in Social Europe and Friedrich-Ebert-Stiftung, *Social Democracy: A SWOT Analysis*. London: Social Europe, 44–74.

Culpepper, P. D. (2002) 'Powering, Puzzling, and "Pacting"', *Journal of European Public Policy* 9 (5): 774–90.

Daley, A. (1992) 'The Steel Crisis and Labor Politics in France and the United States' in M. Golden and J. Pontusson (eds) *Bargaining for Change*. Ithaca: Cornell UP, 146–80.

Damesin, R. and Denis, J.-M. (2005) 'SUD trade unions', *Capital & Class* 86: 17–37.

DARES (2010) *Les pratiques de rémunération des entreprises en 2007*. Premières syntheses informations 008.

DARES (2016) *La syndicalisation en France*. Paris: DARES analyses 025.

Darlington, R. (2009) 'Leadership and Union Militancy: The Case of the RMT', *Capital & Class* 98: 3–32.

D'Art, D. and Turner, T. (2008) 'Workers and the Demand for Trade Unions in Europe' *Economic and Industrial Democracy* 29 (2): 165–91.

D'Art, D. and Turner, T. (2011) 'Irish Trade Unions under Social Partnership', *Industrial Relations Journal* 42 (2): 157–73.

de Beer, P. and Keune, M. (2017) 'Dutch unions in a time of crisis' in S. Lehndorff, H. Dribbusch, and T. Schulten (eds) *Rough waters: European trade unions in a time of crises*. Brussels: ETUI, 221–44.

Dean, H. (2006) *Women in Trade Unions*. Brussels: ETUI.

DeFilippis, J. (2002) 'Symposium on Social Capital: An Introduction', *Antipode* 34 (4): 790–5.

Delsen, L., Benders, J., and Smits, J. (2006) 'Choices within Collective Labour Agreements "à la Carte" in the Netherlands', *British Journal of Industrial Relations* 44 (1): 51–72.

Demetriades, S., Meixner, M., and Barry, A. (2006) *Reconciliation of work and family life and collective bargaining in the European Union*. Dublin: European Foundation.

Denis, J.-M. (2003) 'Les syndicalistes de SUD-PTT', *Sociologie du Travail* 45: 307–25.

Deppe, F. (2012) *Gewerkschaften in der Großen Transformation*. Cologne: PappyRossa.

de Turberville, S.R. (2004) 'Does the "organizing model" represent a credible union renewal strategy?' *Work, Employment & Society* 18 (4): 565–76.

Dobbert, B. (2010) Organizing and mobilizing. Presentation to EMF Youth Conference, Šibenik, September.

Dølvik, J.-E. (1997) *Redrawing Boundaries of Solidarity?* Oslo: Arena/FAFO.

Dølvik, J. E. (2008) *The Negotiated Nordic Labor Markets*. Harvard: CES Working Paper 162.

Dølvik, J. E., Goul Andersen, J., and Vartiainen, J. (2011) The Nordic social models. Paper to the Council for European Studies 18th International Conference June.

Donaghey, J. and Teague, P. (2007) 'The Mixed Fortunes of Irish Unions', *Journal of Labor Research* 28 (1): 19–41.

Donaldson, H. (2010) *GMB: Developing our management structures*. London: BIS.

Dörre, K., Holst, H., and Nachtwey, O. (2009) 'Organizing: A Strategic Option for Trade Union Renewal?', *International Journal of Action Research* 5 (1): 33–67.

References

Drahokoupil, J. (ed.) (2015) *The outsourcing challenge: Organizing workers across fragmented production networks*. Brussels: ETUI.

Drahokoupil, J. and Fabo, B. (2016) *The platform economy and the disruption of the employment relationship*. Brussels: ETUI Policy Brief 5/2016.

Dribbusch, H. (2003) *Gewerkschaftliche Mitgliedergewinnung im Dienstleistungssektor*. Berlin: edition sigma.

Dribbusch, H. (2011) 'Organisieren am Konflikt' in T. Haipeter and K. Dörre (eds) *Gewerkschaftliche Modernisierung*. Wiesbaden: VS Verlag, 231–61.

Dribbusch, H. (2012) 'Sozialpartnerschaft und Konflikt', *Zeitschrift für Politik* 59 (2): 123–43.

Dribbusch, H. (2015) 'Where is the European general strike? Understanding the challenges of trans-European trade union action against austerity' *Transfer* 21(2): 171–85.

Due, J. and Madsen, J. S. (2005) 'Denmark: The Survival of Small Unions in the Context of Centralised Bargaining' in J. Waddington (ed.) *Restructuring Representation*. Brussels: P.I.E.-Peter Lang, 87–112.

Due, J., Madsen, J. S., Jensen, C. S., and Petersen, L. K. (1994) *The Survival of the Danish Model*. Copenhagen: DJØF.

Due, J., Madsen, J. S., Johansen, M. M., and Søndergård, K. (2007) *Den nødvendige fusion*. Copenhagen: Fagligt Fælles Forbund.

Dufour, C. (2009) 'Autriche', *Chronique internationale de l'IRES* 119: 3–12.

Dufour, C. and Hege, A. (2002) *L'europe syndicale au quotidien*. Brussels: PIE-Peter Lang.

Dufour, C. and Hege, A. (2010) *Evolutions et perspectives des systèmes de négociation collective et de leurs acteurs*. Noisy le Grand: IRES.

Dufour, C. and Hege, A. (2011) 'L'évolution de la négociation collective et de ses acteurs dans six pays européens', *Relations industrielles/Industrial Relations* 66 (4): 535–61.

Dufresne, A. and Pernot, J.-M. (2013) 'Les syndicats européens à l'épreuve de la nouvelle gouvernance économique', *Chronique Internationale de l'IRES* 143(4): 3–29.

Ebbinghaus, B. (1995) 'The Siamese Twins: Citizenship Rights, Cleavage Formation, and Party–Union Relations in Western Europe', *International Review of Social History* 40 (supplement 3): 51–89.

Ebbinghaus B. (2002) 'Trade unions' changing role', *Industrial Relations Journal* 33 (5): 465–83.

Ebbinghaus B. (2011) 'The role of trade unions in European pension reforms', *European Journal of Industrial Relations* 17 (4): 315–31.

Ebbinghaus, B., Göbel, C., and Koos, S. (2008) *Mitgliedschaft in Gewerkschaften*. MZES Working Paper 111.

Ebbinghaus, B., Göbel, C., and Koos, S. (2011) 'Social capital, "Ghent" and workplace contexts matter', *European Journal of Industrial Relations* 17 (2): 107–24.

Ebbinghaus, B. and Hassel, A. (2000) 'Striking Deals: Concertation in the Reform of Continental European Welfare States', *Journal of European Public Policy* 7 (1): 44–62.

Ebbinghaus, B. and Visser, J. (1999) 'When institutions matter: union growth and decline in Western Europe', *European Sociological Revue*, 15 (2): 135–58.

References

Edwards, G. (2007) 'Habermas, Activism, and Acquiescence', *Social Movement Studies* 6 (2): 111–30.

Edwards, P. K. and Hyman, R. (1994) 'Strikes and Industrial Conflict: Peace in Europe?' in R. Hyman and A. Ferner (eds) *New Frontiers in European Industrial Relations*. Oxford: Blackwell, 250–80.

Elvander, N. (2002) 'The New Swedish Regime for Collective Bargaining and Conflict Resolution', *European Journal of Industrial Relations* 8 (2): 197–216.

Erne, R. (2008) *European Unions*. Ithaca: Cornell UP.

Erne, R. (2013) 'National Unionism and Union Democracy in Crisis', *Labor History* 54(4): 471–6.

Esping-Andersen, G. (1990) *The Three Worlds of Welfare Capitalism*. Cambridge: Polity Press.

EuroMemo Group (2017) *The European Union: The Threat of Disintegration*. http://www.euromemo.eu/

European Commission (2012) *Transnational company agreements*. Brussels: SWD (2012) 264 final.

European Social Partners (2009) *Framework of Actions on Gender Equality*. Brussels: European Social Partners.

EWC Academy (2016) *Brexit: Welche Folgen entstehen für Europäische Betriebsräte?* http://www.ewc-academy.eu/de/consulting/brexit.html

Ewing, K. D. (2005) 'The Function of Trade Unions', *Industrial Law Journal* 34 (1): 1–22.

Fairbrother, P. and Yates, C. A. B. (eds) (2003) *Trade Unions in Renewal*. London: Routledge.

Fajertag, G. and Pochet, P. (eds) (1997) *Social Pacts in Europe*. Brussels: ETUI/OSE.

Fana, M., Guarascio, D. and Cirillo, V. (2015) *Labour market reforms in Italy: Evaluating the effects of the Jobs Act*. http://www.isigrowth.eu/wp-content/uploads/2015/12/working_paper_2015_5.pdf

Faniel, J. (2012) 'Crisis behind the Figures? Belgian Trade Unions between Strength, Paralysis and Revitalisation', *management revue* 23 (1): 14–31.

Faniel, J., Devos, C., Lannoo, S., and Mus, M. (2011) 'Les membres de la CGSLB et leur syndicat', *Courrier hebdomadaire du CRISP* 1781: 5–36.

Faniel, J. and Vandaele, K. (2011) 'Histoire de la Centrale Générale des Syndicats Libéraux de Belgique (CGSLB)', *Courrier hebdomadaire du CRISP* 2123–4: 1–53.

Fantasia, R. (1988) *Cultures of Solidarity*. Berkeley: University of California Press.

Fazekas, Z. (2011) 'Institutional effects on the presence of trade unions at the workplace', *European Journal of Industrial Relations* 17 (2): 153–69.

Feltrin, P. (2009) 'La rappresentatività dei sindacati ieri e oggi', *Formazione & Lavoro* 1/2009: 159–74.

Ferner, A. and Hyman, R. 1992. 'Italy: Between Political Exchange and Micro-Corporatism' in A. Ferner and R. Hyman (eds) *Industrial Relations in the New Europe*. Oxford: Blackwell, pp. 524–600.

Fitzgerald, I. and Hardy, J. (2010) '"Thinking Outside the Box"?', *British Journal of Industrial Relations* 48 (1): 131–50.

Fitzgerald, I. and Stirling, J. (eds) (2004) *European Works Councils*. London: Routledge.

Flanders, A. (1970) *Management and Unions*. London: Faber.

References

Franklin, M. N. (2002) 'Learning from the Danish case', *European Journal of Political Research* 41 (6): 751–7.

Freeman, R. B. (2005) 'From the Webbs to the Web' in S. Fernie and D. Metcalf (eds) *Trade Unions*. London: Routledge, 162–84.

Freeman, R. B. and Medoff, J. L. (1984) *What Do Unions Do?* New York: Basic Books.

Frege, C., Heery, E., and Turner, L. (2004) 'The New Solidarity?' in C. M. Frege and J. Kelly (eds) *Varieties of Unionism*. Oxford: OUP, 137–58.

Frege, C. M. and Kelly, J. (2003) 'Union Revitalization Strategies in Comparative Perspective', *European Journal of Industrial Relations* 9 (1): 7–24.

Frege, C. M. and Kelly, J. (2004) 'Union Strategies in Comparative Context' in C. M. Frege and J. Kelly (eds) *Varieties of Unionism*. Oxford: OUP, 31–44.

Freyssinet, J. (2011) *Un intense renouveau de la négociation interprofessionnelle en France*. Paris-Saint-Etienne: Lasaire.

Fulton, L. (2005) 'European Works Councils: The British Experience' in V. Telljohann (ed.) *Quality Inventories on the Operation and Results of European Works Councils*. Bologna: IpL, 51–66.

Gajewska, K. (2009) *Transnational Labour Solidarity*. London: Routledge.

Gajewska, K. and Niesyto, J. (2009) 'Organising Campaigns as a "Revitaliser" for Trade Unions?', *Industrial Relations Journal* 40 (2): 156–71.

Galbraith, J. K. (1952) *American Capitalism*. Boston: Houghton Mifflin.

Gall, G. (2005) 'Organizing Non-Union Workers as Trade Unionists in the "New Economy" in Britain', *Economic and Industrial Democracy* 26 (1): 41–63.

Gall, G. and Fiorito, J. (2016) 'Union effectiveness: In search of the Holy Grail', *Economic and Industrial Democracy* 37(1): 189–211.

Gallin, D. (2000) *Trade Unions and NGOs*. Geneva: UNRISD.

Ganz, M. (2000) 'Resources and Resourcefulness', *American Journal of Sociology* 105 (4): 1003–62.

Geelan, T. and Hodder, A. (2017) 'Enhancing Transnational Labour Solidarity: The Unfulfilled Promise of the Internet and Social Media', *Industrial Relations Journal* 48(4): 345–64.

Geneste, D. (2010) La CGT a travaillé avec les ONG bien avant le Grenelle de l'Environnement. http://ong-entreprise.blogspot.co.uk/2010/06/la-cgt-travaille-avec-les-ong-bien.html.

Giaccone, M. (2009) *Contribution of collective bargaining to continuing vocational training*. Dublin: European Foundation.

Gilland, K. (2003) 'Ireland's Second Referendum on the Treaty of Nice', OERN Referendum Briefing 1, http://www.sussex.ac.uk/sei/documents/irelandno1.pdf.

Giraud, B. (2006) 'Au-delà du déclin' *Revue française de science politique* 56 (6): 943–67.

Giraud, B. (2007) 'Le syndicalisme saisi par le management', *Politix* 79: 125–48.

Gläser, C. (2009) 'Europäische Einheitsgewerkschaft zwischen lähmender Überdehnung und umfassender Repräsentativität', *Mitteilungsblatt des Instituts für soziale Bewegungen* 42: 215–34.

Glassner, V. (2009) *Government and Trade Union Responses to the Economic Crisis in the Financial Sector*. Working Paper 2009/09. Brussels: ETUI.

References

Glassner, V. and Galgóczi, B. (2009) *Plant-level Responses to the Crisis*. ETUI Policy Brief 1/2009. Brussels: ETUI.

Goetschy, J. (1998) 'France: The Limits of Reform' in A. Ferner and R. Hyman (eds) *Changing Industrial Relations in Europe*. Oxford: Blackwell, 357–94.

Golden, M. and Pontusson, J. (eds) (1992) *Bargaining for Change*. Ithaca: Cornell UP.

Gorodzeisky, A. and Richards, A. (2013) 'Trade unions and migrant workers in Western Europe', *European Journal of Industrial Relations* 19 (3).

Gourevitch, P. (1986) *Politics in Hard Times*. Ithaca: Cornell UP.

Goyer, M. and Hancké, B. (2004) 'Labour in French Corporate Governance', in H. Gospel and A. Pendleton (eds) *Corporate Governance and Labour Management*. Oxford: OUP, 173–96.

GPA-djp (2012) *Migration und Integration im Blickfeld*. Vienna: GPA-djp.

Graham, S. (2007) 'Organizing als Kampf gegen den Niedergang' in P. Bremme, U. Fürniß, and U. Meinecke (eds) *Never Work Alone*. Hamburg: VSA, 135–52.

Granqvist, L. and Regnér, H. (2008) 'Decentralized Wage Formation in Sweden', *British Journal of Industrial Relations* 46 (3): 500–20.

Greene, A. M., Hogan, J., and Grieco, M. (2003) 'E-collectivism and Distributed Discourse', *Industrial Relations Journal* 34 (4): 282–9.

Greene, A. M. and Kirton, G. (2003) 'Possibilities for remote participation in trade unions: Mobilising women activists', *Industrial Relations Journal* 34 (4): 319–33.

Greer, I. (2008) 'Organised Industrial Relations in the Information Economy: The German Automotive Sector as a Test Case', *New Technology, Work and Employment* 23 (3): 181–96.

Greer, I., Ciupijus, Z., and Lillie, N. (2013) 'The European Migrant Workers Union and the Barriers to Transnational Industrial Citizenship', *European Journal of Industrial Relations* 19 (1): 5–20.

Greer, I. and Hauptmeier, M. (2008) 'Political Entrepreneurs and Co-Managers', *British Journal of Industrial Relations* 46 (1): 76–97.

Gregory, A. and Milner, S. (2009) 'Trade unions and work-life balance', *British Journal of Industrial Relations* 47 (1): 122–46.

Griesser, M., and Sauer, B. (2017) 'Von der sozialen Neuzusammensetzung zur gewerkschaftlichen Erneuerung? MigrantInnen als Zielgruppe der österreichischen Gewerkschaftsbewegung', *Österreichische Zeitschrift für Soziologie* 42(2): 147–66.

Grignard, M. (2009) 'Dire aux militants comment se préparer pour la rentrée', *Le républicain Lorrain*, 10 June.

Grimshaw, D. and Rubery, J. (2012) 'Reinforcing neoliberalism: crisis and austerity in the UK', in S. Lehndorff (ed.) *A Triumph of Failed Ideas*. Brussels: ETUI, 41–57.

Guggemos, M. (2009) 'Die Leute wollen kein Rädchen im Getriebe sein', *Die Mitbestimmung* 6/2009: 18–21.

Guillas-Cavan, K. (2017) 'Autriche: Le conseil d'entreprise au cœur des stratégies de resyndicalisation', *Chronique internationale de l'IRES* 160: 70–84.

Guillaume, C. (2007) 'Le syndicalisme à l'épreuve de la féminisation', *Politix* 78: 39–63.

Guillaume, C. (2011) 'La formation des responsables à la CFTC-CFDT', *Le Mouvement Social* 235: 105–19.

Guillaume C. and Pochic, S. (2009) 'La professionnalisation de l'activité syndicale', *Politix* 85: 31–56.

References

Gumbrell-McCormick, R. (2000) 'Facing New Challenges: The International Confederation of Free Trade Unions (1972–1990s)' in A. Carew, M. Dreyfus, G. Van Goethem, R. Gumbrell-McCormick, and M. van der Linden, *The International Confederation of Free Trade Unions*. Bern: Peter Lang, 341–540.

Gumbrell-McCormick, R. (2008) 'International Actors and International Regulation' in P. Blyton, N. Bacon, J. Fiorito, and E. Heery (eds) *Handbook of Industrial Relations*. London: Sage, 325–45.

Gumbrell-McCormick, R. (2011) 'European Trade Unions and Atypical Workers', *Industrial Relations Journal* 42: 3: 293–310.

Gumbrell-McCormick, R. (2013) 'The International Trade Union Confederation: From Two (or More?) Identities to One', *British Journal of Industrial Relations* 51 (2).

Gumbrell-McCormick, R. and Hyman, R. (2006) 'Embedded Collectivism? Workplace Representation in France and Germany', *Industrial Relations Journal* 37 (5): 473–91.

Gumbrell-McCormick, R. and Hyman, R. (2010) 'Works Councils: The European Model of Industrial Democracy?' in A. Wilkinson, P. Gollan, M. Marchington, and D. Lewin (eds) *Oxford Handbook of Participation in Organizations*. Oxford: OUP, 286–314.

Gumbrell-McCormick, R. and Hyman, R. (2017) 'What about the Workers? The Implications of Brexit for British and European Labour', *Competition & Change* 21(3): 169–84.

Haahr, J. H. (1993) *Looking to Europe: The EC Policies of the British Labour Party and the Danish Social Democrats*. Aarhus: Aarhus University Press.

Haipeter, T. (2011a) 'Works councils as actors in collective bargaining', *Economic and Industrial Democracy* 32 (4): 679–95.

Haipeter, T. (2011b) '"Unbound" Employers' Associations and Derogations', *Industrial Relations Journal* 42 (2): 174–94.

Haipeter, T. and Lehndorff, S. (2009) *Collective Bargaining on Employment*. Industrial and Employment Relations Working Paper 3. Geneva: ILO. Hall, P. A. (1993) 'Policy Paradigms, Social Learning and the State', *Comparative Politics* 25 (3): 275–96.

Häkkinen, M. (2013) *The Baltic Organising Academy: How to Build a Multinational and Multisectoral Organising Program*. Warsaw: Friedrich-Ebert-Stiftung.

Hall, P. A. and Soskice, D. (2001) 'An Introduction to Varieties of Capitalism', in P. A. Hall and D. Soskice (eds) *Varieties of Capitalism,* Oxford: Oxford UP: 1–68.

Hamann, K., Johnston, A., and Kelly, J. (2013) 'Unions against governments', *Comparative Political Studies* 46 (9).

Hamann, K. and Kelly, J. (2004) 'Unions as Political Actors' in C. M. Frege and J. Kelly (eds) *Varieties of Unionism*. Oxford: OUP, 93–116.

Hammer, N. (2005) 'International framework agreements', *Transfer* 11 (4): 511–30.

Hammer, N. (2010) 'Cross-border Cooperation under Asymmetry', *European Journal of Industrial Relations* 16 (4): 351–67.

Hancké, R. (1993) 'Trade Union Membership in Europe 1960–90', *British Journal of Industrial Relations* 31 (4): 593–613.

Hancké, R. (2002) *Large Firms and Institutional Change:* Oxford: Oxford University Press.

Hancké, R. and Rhodes, M. (2005) 'EMU and Labor Market Institutions in Europe', *Work and Occupations* 32 (2): 196–228.

References

Hancké, R., Rhodes, M. and Thatcher, M. (eds) (2007): *Beyond Varieties of Capitalism*. Oxford: Oxford University Press.

Hancké, B. and Wijgaerts, D. (1989) 'Belgian Unionism and Self-Management' in G. Széll, P. Blyton, and C. Cornforth (eds) *The State, Trade Unions and Self-Management*. Berlin: de Gruyter, 187–210.

Hansen, L.L. (2004) 'Does the Future of Unions Depend on the Integration of Diversity?', *Industrielle Beziehungen* 11 (1–2): 129–42.

Hardiman, N. (2005) 'Politics and Markets in the Irish "Celtic Tiger"', *Political Quarterly* 76: 37–47.

Hardy, J., Eldring, L., and Schulten, T. (2012) 'Trade Union Responses to Migrant Workers from the "New Europe"', *European Journal of Industrial Relations* 18 (4): 347–63.

Harrod, J. (1972) *Trade Union Foreign Policy*. London: Macmillan.

Hartmann, H. and Lau, C (1980) 'Trade Union Confederations', *International Studies Quarterly* 24 (3): 365–91.

Hassel, A. (1999) 'The Erosion of the German System of Industrial Relations', *British Journal of Industrial Relations* 37 (3): 483–505.

Hassel, A. (2007) 'The Curse of Institutional Security', *Industrielle Beziehungen* 14 (2): 176–91.

Haworth, N. and Ramsay, H. (1984) 'Grasping the Nettle: Problems with the Theory of International Trade Union Solidarity' in P. Waterman (ed.) *For a New Labour Internationalism*. The Hague: ILERI, 59–85.

Hayward, J. (1980) 'Trade Union Movements and their Politico-Economic Environments' in J. Hayward (ed.) *Trade Unions and Politics in Western Europe*. London: Cass, 1–9.

Heery, E. (1998) 'The relaunch of the Trades Union Congress', *British Journal of Industrial Relations* 36 (3): 339–60.

Heery, E. (2005) 'Sources of Change in Trade Unions', *Work, Employment & Society* 19 (1): 91–106.

Heery, E. (2006) 'Union Workers, Union Work', *British Journal of Industrial Relations* 44: 3: 445–71.

Heery, E. (2009) 'Trade Unions and Contingent Labour', *Cambridge Journal of Regions, Economy and Society* 2 (3): 429–42.

Heery E. (2010) 'Worker representation in a multiform system', *Journal of Industrial Relations* 52 (5): 543–59.

Heery, E. and Abbott, B. (2000) 'Trade unions and the insecure workforce', in E. Heery and J. Salmon (eds) *The Insecure Workforce*. London, Routledge, 155–80.

Heery, E. and Adler, A. (2004) 'Organizing the Unorganized' in C. M. Frege and J. Kelly (eds) *Varieties of Unionism*. Oxford: OUP, 45–69.

Heery, E. and Conley, H. (2007) 'Frame Extension in a Mature Social Movement', *Journal of Industrial Relations* 49 (1): 5–29.

Heery, E., Conley, H., and Delbridge, R. (2004) 'Beyond the Enterprise: Trade Union Representation of Freelances in the United Kingdom', *Human Resource Management Journal* 14 (2): 20–35.

Heery, E. and Kelly, J. (1988) 'Do Female Representatives make a Difference?', *Work, Employment & Society* 2 (4): 487–505.

References

Heery, E. and Kelly, J. (1994) 'Professional, Participative and Managerial Unionism', *Work, Employment & Society* 8 (1): 1–22.

Heery, E. and Simms, M. (2011) 'Seizing an Opportunity?', *Labor History* 52 (1): 23–47.

Hemerijk, A., Van der Meer, M., and Visser, J. (2000) 'Innovation through Co-Ordination: Two Decades of Social Pacts in the Netherlands' in G. Fajertag and P. Pochet (eds) *Social Pacts in Europe: New Dynamics*. Brussels: ETUI/OSE, 257–78.

Hermann, C. and Flecker, J. (2012) 'The Austrian model and the financial and economic crisis' in S. Lehndorff (ed.) *A triumph of failed ideas*. Brussels: ETUI, 121–36.

Hertwig, M., Pries, L., and Rampeltshammer, L. (2011) 'Stabilizing Effects of European Works Councils', *European Journal of Industrial Relations* 17 (3): 209–26.

Heyes, J. (2009) 'Recruiting and Organising Migrant Workers through Education and Training', *Industrial Relations Journal* 40 (3): 182–97.

Hodder, A. and Edwards, P. K. (2015) 'The essence of trade unions: Understanding identity, ideology and purpose', *Work, Employment and Society* 29(5): 843–54.

Hodder, A. and Kretsos, L. (eds) (2015) *Young Workers and Trade Unions: A Global View*. Basingstoke: Palgrave Macmillan.

Hoffmann, J. and Hoffmann, R. (2009) 'Prospects for European industrial relations and trade unions in the midst of modernisation, Europeanisation and globalisation', *Transfer* 15 (3–4): 389–417.

Hoffmann, J. and Schmidt, R. (2009) 'The Train Drivers' Strike in Germany 2007–2008', *Industrial Relations Journal* 40 (6): 524–33.

Holgate, J. and Simms, M. (2008) *The impact of the Organising Academy on the union movement*. London: TUC.

Holtgrewe, U. and Doellgast, V. (2012) 'A service union's innovation dilemma', *Work, Employment & Society* 26 (2): 314–30.

Hönigsberger, H. (2008) *Der parlamentarische Arm*. Berlin: Edition Sigma.

Höpner, M. and Schä fer, A. (2010) 'A New Phase of European Integration', *West European Politics* 33 (2): 344–68.

Howell, C. (2005) *Trade Unions and the State*. Princeton: Princeton UP.

Howell, C. (2009) 'The Transformation of French Industrial Relations', *Politics and Society* 37 (2): 229–56.

Huber, B. (2010) *Kurswechsel für Deutschland*. Frankfurt: Campus.

Huber, G. P. (1991) 'Organizational Learning', *Organization Science* 2 (1): 88–115.

Hughes, G. (2011) *Free Movement in the EU: The Case of Ireland*. Berlin: Friedrich-Ebert-Stiftung.

Huzzard, T. (2001) 'Discourse for Normalizing What?', *Economic and Industrial Democracy* 22 (3): 407–31.

Huzzard, T., Gregory, D., and Scott, R. (eds) (2004) *Strategic Unionism and Partnership*. Basingstoke: Palgrave Macmillan.

Huzzard, T. and Östergren, K. (2002) 'When Norms Collide', *British Journal of Management* 13: S47–S59.

Hyman, R. (1989) *Strikes* (2nd edn). Basingstoke: Macmillan.

Hyman, R. (1997) 'Trade Unions and Interest Representation in the Context of Globalisation', *Transfer* 3 (3): 515–33.

References

Hyman, R. (2001) *Understanding European Trade Unionism*. London: Sage.

Hyman, R. (2004) 'Solidarity for Ever?' in J. Lind, H. Knudsen, and H. Jørgensen (eds) *Labour and Employment Regulation in Europe*. Brussels: PIE-Peter Lang, 35–45.

Hyman, R. (2005a) 'Shifting Dynamics in International Trade Unionism', *Labor History* 46 (2): 137–54.

Hyman, R. (2005b) 'Trade Unions and the Politics of European Integration', *Economic and Industrial Democracy* 26 (1): 9–40.

Hyman, R. (2010) 'Trade Unions and "Europe"', *Relations industrielles/Industrial Relations* 65 (1): 3–29.

Hyman, R. and Gumbrell-McCormick, R. (2017) 'Resisting Labour Market Insecurity: Old and New Actors, Rivals or Allies?', *Journal of Industrial Relations* 59(4): 538–61.

Ibsen, C. L. and Tapia, M. (2017) 'Trade union revitalisation: Where are we now? Where to next?', *Journal of Industrial Relations* 59(2): 170–91.

Ibsen, F., Høgedahl, L., and Scheuer, S. (2012) *Kollektiv handling: Faglig organisering og skift af fagforening*. Frederiksberg: Samfundsvidenskaberne.

IG Metall (2009) *Sich ändern, um erfolgreich zu sein*. Frankfurt: IG Metall.

IG Metall (2012) *Anti-Stress-Verordnung: Eine Initiative der IG Metall*. Frankfurt: IG Metall.

Ilsøe, A., Madsen, J. S., and Due, S. (2007) 'Impacts of Decentralisation', *Industrielle Beziehungen* 14 (3): 201–22.

Ivaldi, G. (2006) 'Beyond France's 2005 Referendum on the European Constitutional Treaty', *West European Politics* 29 (1): 47–69.

Iversen, T. (1999) *Contested Economic Institutions*. Cambridge: CUP.

Iversen, T. (2005) *Capitalism, Democracy and Welfare*. Cambridge: CUP.

Iversen, T., Pontusson, J., and Soskice, D. (eds) (2000) *Unions, Employers and Central Banks*. Cambridge: CUP.

Jacobi, O., Keller, B., and Müller-Jentsch, W. (1998) 'Germany: Facing New Challenges' in A. Ferner and R. Hyman (eds) *Changing Industrial Relations in Europe*. Oxford: Blackwell, 190–238.

Jahn, D. (1988) '"Two Logics of Collective Action" and Trade Union Democracy', *Economic and Industrial Democracy* 9 (3): 319–43.

Järliden Bergström, Å.-P., Jonsson, C.-M., and de Toro, S. (2015) *Vägen till full sysselsättning och rättvisare löner*. Stockholm: LO.

Jany-Catrice, F. and Lallement, M. (2012) 'France confronts the crisis' in S. Lehndorff (ed.) *A triumph of failed ideas*. Brussels: ETUI, 103–19.

Jarley, P. (2005) 'Unions as Social Capital', *Labor Studies Journal* 29 (4): 1–26.

Jenkins, A. (2000) *Employment Relations in France*. New York: Kluwer. Johnson, N. B. and Jarley, P. (2005) 'Unions as Social Capital', *Transfer* 11 (4): 605–16.

Johnston, P. (1994) *Success while Others Fail*. Ithaca: ILR Press. Kahmann, M. (2009) 'La fusion comme processus et moyen de réforme syndicale', *La revue de l'IRES* 61: 39–73.

Jolivet, A. (2017) 'Entre attractivité et organizing: les stratégies des syndicats suédois pour (re)conquérir des adhérents', *Chronique internationale de l'IRES* 160: 143–57.

Jürgens, K., Hoffmann, R., and Schildmann, C. (2017) *Arbeit Transformieren! Denkanstösse der Kommission 'Arbeit der Zukunft'*. Bielefeld: transcript Verlag.

References

Jürgens, K., Hoffmann, R., and Schildmann, C. (2018) *Let's Transform Work! Recommendations and Proposals from the Commission on the Work of the Future.* Düsseldorf: Hans-Böckler-Stiftung.

Kahmann, M. (2017) 'Allemagne. Stratégies de renouveau syndical envers les travailleurs précaires: le cas des intérimaires dans la métallurgie', *Chronique internationale de l'IRES* 160: 52–69.

Kaiser, W. (1995) 'Austria in the European Union', *Journal of Common Market Studies* 33 (3): 411–25.

Katz, H. and Darbishire, O. (2000) *Converging Divergences.* Ithaca: ILR Press.

Katzenstein, P. J. (1985) *Small States in World Markets.* Ithaca: Cornell UP.

Kauppinen, T. (ed.) (1998) *The Impact of EMU on Industrial Relations in the European Union.* Helsinki: Finnish Labour Relations Association.

Kelly, J. (1997) 'The Future of Trade Unionism', *Employee Relations* 19 (5): 400–14.

Kelly, J. (1998) *Rethinking Industrial Relations.* London: Routledge.

Kelly, J. (2004) 'Social partnership agreements in Britain', *Industrial Relations* 43 (1): 267–92.

Kelly, J. (2012) 'The Decline of British Trade Unionism', *Industrial Relations Journal* 43 (4): 348–58.

Kersley, B., Alpin, C., Forth, J., Bryson, A., Bewley, H., Dix, G., and Oxenbridge, S. (2006) *Inside the Workplace.* London: Routledge.

Keune, M. (2006) 'Collective Bargaining and Working Time in Europe' in M. Keune and B. Galgóczi (eds) *Collective bargaining on working time.* Brussels: ETUI, 9–29.

Keune, M. (2008) 'Introduction: Wage Moderation, Decentralisation of Collective Bargaining and Low Pay' in M. Keune and B. Galgóczi (eds) *Wages and Wage Bargaining in Europe.* Brussels: ETUI, 7–27.

Keune, M. (2013) 'Trade union responses to precarious work in seven European countries' *International Journal of Labour Research* 5(1): 59–78.

Kirsch, A. (2009) Structural integration in merged unions. Paper to the IIRA Congress, Sydney, August.

Kirsch, A. (2010) Revitalization through Gender Equality. Paper to the IIRA European Congress, Copenhagen, June.

Kirton, G. and Greene, A.-M. (2002) 'The Dynamics of Positive Action in UK Trade Unions' *Industrial Relations Journal* 33 (2): 157–72.

Kjellberg, A. (1983) *Facklig organisering i tolv länder.* Lund: Arkiv.

Kjellberg, A. (1998) 'Sweden: Restoring the Model?' in A. Ferner and R. Hyman (eds) *Changing Industrial Relations in Europe.* Oxford: Blackwell, 74–117.

Kjellberg, A. (2005) 'Sweden: Mergers in a Class-Segmented Trade Union System' in J. Waddington (ed.) *Restructuring Representation.* Brussels: P.I.E.-Peter Lang, 87–112.

Kjellberg, A. (2009) 'The Swedish Ghent System and Trade Unions Under Pressure', *Transfer:* 15 (3–4): 481–504.

Kjellberg, A. (2011a) 'The Decline in Swedish Union Density since 2007', *Nordic Journal of Working Life Studies* 1 (1): 67–93.

Kjellberg, A. (2011b) *Växande avgiftsskillnader i a-kassan.* Research Report: Sociologiska Institutionen, Lunds Universitet.

References

Kloosterboer, D. (2008) 'Trade Union Strategies to Organise Young, Ethnic Minority and Atypical Workers', *Economia e lavoro* 42 (3): 119–30.

Knudsen, H. and Lind, J. (2012) 'Is the Danish Model still a Sacred Cow?', *Transfer* 18 (4): 381–95.

Koch-Baumgarten, S. (2002) 'Changing Gender Relations in German Trade Unions' in F. Colgan and S. Ledwith (eds) *Gender, Diversity and Trade Unions*. London: Routledge, 132–53.

Kocsis, A., Sterkel, G., and Wiedemuth, J. (eds) (2013) *Organisieren am Konflikt*. Wiesbaden: VS Verlag.

Korflür, I., Nettelstroth, W., and Schilling, G. (2010) '"Besser statt billiger" im Betrieb', *WSI Mitteilungen* 2/2010: 109–12.

Korpi, W. and Shalev, M. (1979) 'Strikes, Industrial Relations and Class Conflict in Industrial Societies', *British Journal of Sociology* 30 (2): 164–87.

Koukiadaki, V. A., Távora, I., and Martínez Lucio, M. (eds) (2016) *Joint regulation and labour market policy in Europe during the crisis*. Brussels: ETUI.

Krings, T. (2009) 'A race to the bottom?', *European Journal of Industrial Relations* 15 (1): 49–69.

Kröck, H. (2005) Investigation of the Interrelationships between Trade Unions and Social Movements in the Context of Globalisation with Particular Reference to Germany. MA thesis, Berlin School of Economics.

Lallement, M. (2007) *Le travail*. Paris: Gallimard. Lallement, M. (2011) 'Europe and the economic crisis', *Work Employment & Society* 25 (4): 627–41.

Larsson, B., Bengtsson, M., and Lovén Seldén, K. (2012) 'Transnational Trade Union Cooperation in the Nordic Countries', *management revue* 23 (1): 32–48.

Larsson, M. (2009) *Facklig anslutning år 2009*. Stockholm: LO. Law, A. and Mooney, G. (2006) 'Social Capital and Neo-Liberal Voluntarism', *Variant* 26: 18–20.

Lecher, W., Platzer, H.-W., Rub, S., and Weiner, K.-P. (1999) *Europäische Betriebsräte*. Baden-Baden: Nomos.

Lee, E. (1996) *The Labour Movement and the Internet*. London: Pluto.

Lehndorff, S. (ed.) (2015) *Divisive integration: The triumph of failed ideas in Europe—revisited*. Brussels: ETUI.

Lehndorff, S., Dribbusch, H., and Schulten, T. (eds) (2017) *Rough waters: European trade unions in a time of crises*. Brussels: ETUI.

Lemb, W. and Urban, H.-J. (2014) 'Can Democracy in Europe Still Be Salvaged?' in A. Buntenbach, F. Bsirske, A. Keller, W. Lemb, D. Schäfers, and H.-J. Urban (eds), *Can Europe Still Be Saved?* Hamburg: Redaktion Sozialismus, 44–55.

Leonardi, S. (2001) 'Sindacato, lavoro e classi sociali', *Rivista giuridica del lavoro e della previdenza sociale* 52 (2): 151–81.

Leonardi, S., Ambra, M. C., and Ciarini, A. (2018) 'Italian collective bargaining at a turning point', 133–61 in S Leonardi and R Pedersini (eds) *Multi-employer bargaining under pressure: Decentralization trends in five European Countries*. Brussels: ETUI.

Lehndorff, S. (2012) 'German capitalism and the European crisis' in S. Lehndorff (ed.) *A triumph of failed ideas*. Brussels: ETUI, 79–102.

Lévesque, C. and Murray, G. (2013) 'Renewing union narrative resources: How union capabilities make a difference', *British Journal of Industrial Relations* 51(4): 777–96.

References

Lévesque, C. and Murray, G. (2003) 'Le pouvoir syndical dans l'économie mondiale', *Revue de l'IRES* 41: 1–28.

Lévesque, C., Murray, G., and Le Queux, S. (2005) 'Union Disaffection and Social Identity', *Work and Occupations* 32 (4): 400–22.

Levitt, B. and March, J.G. (1988) 'Organizational Learning', *Annual Review of Sociology*, 14: 319–40.

Lind, J. (2000) 'Recent Issues on the Social Pact in Denmark' in G. Fajertag and P. Pochet (eds) *Social Pacts in Europe*. Brussels: ETUI/OSE, 135–59.

Lind, J. (2007) 'A Nordic Saga? The Ghent System and Trade Unions', *International Journal of Employment Studies* 15 (1): 49–67.

Lind, J. (2009) 'The End of the Ghent System as Trade Union Recruitment Machinery?', *Industrial Relations Journal* 40 (6): 510–23.

Llorens, C. and Ortiz de Villacian, D. (2001) *Work-Related Stress and Industrial Relations*. http://www.eurofound.europa.eu/eiro/2001/11/study/tn0111109s.htm.

Locke, R. M. (1990) 'The Resurgence of the Local Union', *Politics and Society* 18 (3): 347–79.

Locke, R. and Thelen, K. (1995) 'Apples and Oranges Revisited', *Politics and Society* 23: 337–67.

Logue, J. (1980) *Toward a Theory of Trade Union Internationalism*. Gothenburg: University of Gothenburg.

LO (2009) *LO's faglige-politiske Beretning 2008*. Copenhagen: LO.

LO (2016) *We like change! A progressive agenda for future jobs*. Stockholm: LO.

LO (2017) *Full employment and a wage policy of solidarity: Report adopted at the 2016 LO Congress*. Stockholm: LO.

Lønkommissionen (2010) *Løn, Køn, Uddannelse og Fleksibilitet*. Copenhagen: Lønkommissionen.

Lubbers, M. (2008) 'Regarding the Dutch Nee to the European Constitution', *European Union Politics* 9 (1): 59–86.

Luther, KR (2017) 'A Dying Embrace? Interlocked Party-union Directorates in Austria's Cartel Democracy' in E. H. Allern and T. Bale (eds), *Left-of-Centre Parties and Trade Unions in the Twenty-First Century*. Oxford: Oxford University Press, 70–92.

Mabrouki, A. (2004) *Génération précaire*. Paris: Cherche midi.

McBride, A. (2001) *Gender Democracy in Trade Unions*. Aldershot: Ashgate.

McBride, J. and Martínez Lucio, M. (2011) 'Dimensions of collectivism', *Work Employment & Society* 25 (4) 794–805.

McGuire, D. (2014) 'Analysing Union Power, Opportunity and Strategic Capability: Global and Local Union Struggles Against the General Agreement on Trade in Services (GATS), *Global Labour Journal* 5(1): 45–67.

McIlroy, J. (2000) 'The new politics of pressure', *Industrial Relations Journal* 31 (1): 2–16.

McIlroy, J. (2008) 'Ten years of New Labour', *British Journal of Industrial Relations* 46 (2): 283–313.

Madsen, P. K. (2003) '"Flexicurity" through labour market policies and institutions in Denmark' in P. Auer and S. Cazes (eds) *Employment stability in an age of flexibility*. Geneva: ILO, 59–105.

Mahon, R. (1996) 'Women Wage Earners and the Future of Swedish Unions', *Economic and Industrial Democracy* 17 (4): 545–86.

References

Marcon, G. and Zola, D. (2007) 'Le campagne europee per i servizi pubblici', *Quale Stato* 12 (3–4) 224–37.

Marcussen, M. and Zølner, M. (2001) 'The Danish EMU Referendum 2000', *Government and Opposition* 36 (3): 379–402.

Marginson, P. (2012) '(Re)assessing the shifting contours of Britain's collective industrial relations', *Industrial Relations Journal* 43 (4): 332–47.

Marginson, P. (2015) 'Coordinated Bargaining in Europe: From incremental corrosion to frontal assault?', *European Journal of Industrial Relations* 21(2): 97–114.

Marginson, P. (2016) 'Governing Work and Employment Relations in an Internationalized Economy: The Institutional Challenge', *ILR Review* 69(5): 1033–55.

Marginson, P. and Sisson, K. (2004) *European Integration and Industrial Relations*. Basingstoke: Palgrave Macmillan.

Marino, S., Roosblad, J., and Penninx, R., eds (2017) *Trade Unions and Migrant Workers: New Contexts and Challenges in Europe*. Cheltenham: Edward Elgar and Geneva: ILO.

Marks, G. and Wilson, C. J. (2000) 'The Past in the Present', *British Journal of Political Science* 30 (3): 433–59.

Martin, A. and Ross, G. (1999) 'In the Line of Fire' in A. Martin and G. Ross et al., *The Brave New World of European Labor*. New York: Berghahn, 312–67.

Martin, A. and Ross, G. (2001) 'Trade Union Organizing at the European Level' in D. Imig and S. Tarrow (eds) *Contentious Europeans*. Lanham: Rowman & Littlefield, 53–76.

Martin, A. and Ross, G. (eds) (2004) *Euros and Europeans*. Cambridge: Cambridge University Press.

Martínez Lucio, M. and Perrett, R. (2009a) 'The Diversity and Politics of Trade Unions' Responses to Minority Ethnic and Migrant Workers', *Economic and Industrial Democracy* 30 (3): 324–47.

Martínez Lucio, M., Marino, S., and Connolly, H. (2017) 'Organising as a strategy to reach precarious and marginalised workers: A review of debates on the role of the political dimension and the dilemmas of representation and solidarity', *Transfer* 23(1): 31–46.

Martínez Lucio, M. and Perrett, R. (2009b) 'Meanings and dilemmas in community unionism', *Work Employment & Society* 23 (4) 693–710.

Meardi, G. (2002) 'The Trojan Horse for the Americanization of Europe?', *European Journal of Industrial Relations* 8 (1): 77–99.

Meardi, G. (2011) 'Understanding Trade Union Cultures', *Industrielle Beziehungen* 18 (4): 336–45.

Meardi, G. (2012a) *Social Failures of EU Enlargement*. London: Routledge.

Meardi, G. (2012b) 'Union Immobility? Trade Unions and the Freedoms of Movement in the Enlarged EU', *British Journal of Industrial Relations* 50 (1): 99–120.

Meardi, G. (2012c) Peripheral convergence in the crisis? Paper to SASE Annual Meeting, Boston, June.

Mermet, E. (2002) 'The Coordination of Collective Bargaining at the ETUC' in J. Hoffmann (ed.) *The Solidarity Dilemma*. Brussels: ETUI, 145–93.

Michels, R. (1915) *Political Parties*. New York: Hearst's. Miljan, T. (1977) *The Reluctant Europeans*. London: Hurst.

Milkman, R. (2006) *L.A. Story*. New York: Russell Sage Foundation.

Mills, C. W. (1940) 'Situated Actions and Vocabularies of Motive', *American Sociological Review* 5 (6): 904–13.
Milner, S. (2000) 'Euroscepticism in France and Changing State-Society Relations', *European Integration* 22 (1): 35–57.
Ministère du Travail (2011) *La négociation collective en 2010*. Paris: Ministère du Travail.
Minkin, L. (1991) *The Contentious Alliance*. Edinburgh: Edinburgh UP.
Misgeld, K. (1997) *Den fackliga europavägen*. Stockholm: Atlas.
Moissonnier, L. (2009) 'La participation des syndicats européens aux mobilisations altermondialistes', *Politique européenne* 27: 153–76.
Mok, A.L. (1985) 'Arbeidsverhoudingen' in België', *Tijdschrift voor Arbeidsvraagstukken* 1 (1): 4–18.
Molina Romo, Ó. (2005) 'Political Exchange and Bargaining Reform in Italy and Spain', *European Journal of Industrial Relations* 11 (1): 7–26.
Molina, O. and Rhodes, M. (2007) 'Industrial Relations and Welfare State in Italy', *West European Politics* 30 (4): 803–29.
Moreno, J. (2001) *Trade Unions without Frontiers*. Brussels: ETUI.
Mörtvik, R. and Fromm, J. (2012) *Stressbarometer 2012*. Stockholm: TCO.
Moses, J. W. (1994) 'Abdication from National Policy Autonomy', *Politics and Society* 22 (2): 125–48.
Moss, B. H. (1998) 'France: EMU and the Social Divide' in B.H.
Moss and J. Michie (eds) *The Single European Currency in National Perspective*. Basingstoke: Macmillan, 58–86.
Mullen, A. and Burkitt, B. (2003) 'European Integration and the Battle for British Hearts and Minds', *Political Quarterly* 74 (3): 322–36.
Müller, T., Platzer, H.-W., and Rüb, S. (2011) 'European collective agreements at company level and the relationship between EWCs and trade unions', *Transfer* 17 (2): 217–28.
Müller-Jentsch, W. (1985) 'Trade Unions as Intermediary Organizations', *Economic and Industrial Democracy* 6 (1): 3–33.
Müller-Jentsch, W. (1988) 'Industrial Relations Theory and Trade Union Strategy', *International Journal of Comparative Labour Law and Industrial Relations* 4 (3): 177–90.
Müller-Jentsch, W. (2011) *Gewerkschaften und soziale Marktwirtschaft seit 1945*. Stuttgart: Reclam.
Müller-Jentsch, W. (2017) *Berufs- und Spartengewerkschaften: Neue Akteure und Perspektiven der Tarifpolitik*. Munich: Rainer Hampp.
Munck, R. (2000) 'Labour and Globalisation', *Work, Employment & Society* 14 (2): 385–93.
Murphy, C. (2011) Determining the Meaning of Union Organising Success in Ireland. Paper to IREC conference, Barcelona, September.
Murray, G. (2017) 'Union Renewal: What Can We Learn from Three Decades of Research?', *Transfer* 23(1): 9–29.
Negrelli, S. and Pulignano, V. (2008) 'Change in contemporary Italy's social concertation', *Industrial Relations Journal* 39 (1): 63–77.
Negrelli, S. and Pulignano, V. (2010) 'The evolution of social pacts in Italy' in P. Pochet, M. Keune, and D. Natali (eds) *After the euro and enlargement*. Brussels: ETUI/OSE, 137–60.

References

Nicklich, M. and Helfen, M. (2017) 'Trade union renewal and "organizing from below" in Germany: Institutional constraints, strategic dilemmas and organizational tensions', *European Journal of Industrial Relations* doi:1177/0959680117752000

Nizzoli, C. (2017) 'Italie: Du renouveau syndical sans stratégie?', *Chronique internationale de l'IRES* 160: 130–42.

Noblecourt, M. (2016) 'Congrès de la CGT: Camouflet pour la direction', *Le Monde* 19 April.

Notermans, T. (1993) 'The Abdication from National Policy Autonomy', *Politics & Society* 21 (2): 133–67.

Nowak, P. (2010) 'What More Can We Do to Grow?' in A. Bryson, P. Nowak, C. Roper, and M. Smith, *Resilient Unions*. London: Unions 21, 11–4.

Nuti, D. M. (2011) 'Industrial relations at FIAT: Dr Marchionne's class war', *Transfer* 17(2): 251–4.

O'Brien-Smith, F. and Rigby, M. (2010) 'The work-life balance strategies of USDAW', *Industrial Relations Journal* 41 (3): 206–17.

O'Donnell, R., Adshead, M., and Thomas, D. (2011) Ireland: Two Trajectories of Institutionalisation' in S. Avdagic, M. Rhodes and J. Visser (eds) *Social Pacts in Europe*. Oxford: OUP, 89–117.

O'Donnell, R. and O'Reardon, C. (2000) 'Social partnership in Ireland's Economic Transformation' in G. Fajertag and P. Pochet (eds) *Social Pacts in Europe*. Brussels: ETUI/OSE, 237–56.

OECD (2012) *Employment Outlook 2012*. Paris: OECD.

Offe, C. and Wiesenthal, H. (1985) 'Two Logics of Collective Action', in C. Offe, *Disorganized Capitalism*. Cambridge: Polity, 170–220.

Olson, M. (1965) *The Logic of Collective Action*, Cambridge: Harvard UP.

Olson, M. (1982) *The Rise and Decline of Nations*. New Haven: Yale UP. Palier, B. and Thelen, K. (2010) 'Institutionalizing Dualism: Complementarities and Change in France and Germany', *Politics and Society* 38 (1): 119–48.

Panitch, L. (1980) 'Recent theorizations of corporatism', *British Journal of Sociology* 31 (2):159–87.

Parent-Thirion, A., Vermeylen, G., van Houten, G., Lyly-Yrjänäinen, M., Biletta, I., and Cabrita, J. (2012) *Fifth European Working Conditions Survey*. Luxembourg: Publications Office of the European Union.

Parker, J. (2008) 'The Trades Union Congress and civil alliance building', *Employee Relations* 30 (5): 562–83.

Pasture, P. (1994) *Christian Trade Unionism in Europe Since 1968*. Aldershot: Avebury.

Pasture, P. (1996) 'Conclusion: Reflections on the Fate of Ideologies and Trade Unions' in P. Pasture, J. Verberckmoes, and H. De Witte (eds) *The Lost Perspective?*, Vol. 2. Aldershot: Avebury, 377–403.

Pedersini, R. and Leonardi, S. (2018) 'Breaking through the crisis with decentralisation? Collective bargaining in the EU after the great recession', 72–106 in S Leonardi and R Pedersini (eds), *Multi-employer bargaining under pressure: Decentralization trends in five European Countries*. Brussels: ETUI.

References

Perlman, S. (1928). *The Theory of the Labor Movement*. New York: Macmillan.

Pernicka, S. and Aust, A. (eds) (2007) *Die Unorganisier ten gewinnen: Gewerkschaftliche Rekrutierung und Interessenvertretung für atypisch Beschäftigte*. Berlin: Edition Sigma.

Pernicka, S. and Glassner, V. (2014), 'Transnational Trade Union Strategies towards European Wage Policy: A Neoinstitutional Framework', *European Journal of Industrial Relations* 20(4): 317–34.

Peters, J. (2011) 'The Rise of Finance and the Decline of Organised Labour in the Advanced Capitalist Countries', *New Political Economy* 16 (1): 73–99.

Petersen, K. F. V. (1997) 'LO launches an intensive campaign on the Amsterdam Treaty', *EIROnline* http://www.eurofound.europa.eu/eiro/1997/09/feature/dk9709128f.htm.

Peterson A., Wahlström, M., and Wennerhag, M. (2011) 'Swedish Trade Unionism: A Renewed Social Movement?', *Economic and Industrial Democracy* 33 (1): 621–47.

Peterson, L. (1981) 'The One Big Union in International Perspective', *Labour/Le Travail* 7: 41–66.

Piazza, J. (2001) 'De-Linking Labor: Labor Unions and Social Democratic Parties under Globalization', *Party Politics* 7 (4): 413–35.

Pierson, P. (2004) *Politics in Time*. Princeton: Princeton UP.

Piotet, F. (2009) 'La CGT, une anarchie (plus ou moins) organisée?', *Politix* 85: 9–30.

Pizzorno, A. (1978) 'Political Exchange and Collective Identity' in C. Crouch and A. Pizzorno (eds) *The Resurgence of Class Conflict in Western Europe Since 1968: Volume 2*. London: Macmillan, 277–98.

Pocock, B. (2011) 'Rethinking Unionism in a Changing World of Work, Family and Community Life', *Relations Industrielles/Industrial Relations* 66 (4): 562–83.

Prausmüller, O. and Sauer, W. (2007) *Internationale Gewerkschaftsbewegung*. Vienna: VÖGB.

Price, R. and Bain, G. (1983) 'Union growth in Britain', *British Journal of Industrial Relations* 21 (1): 46–68.

Pulignano, V., Meardi, G., and Doerflinger, N. (2015) 'Trade unions and labour market dualisation: A comparison of policies and attitudes towards agency and migrant workers in Germany and Belgium', *Work, Employment and Society* 29(5):808–25.

Putnam, R. D. (1993) *Making Democracy Work*. Princeton: Princeton UP.

Putnam, R. D. (1995) 'Bowling Alone', *Journal of Democracy* 6 (1): 65–78.

Regalia, I. (1988) 'Democracy and Unions', *Economic and Industrial Democracy* 9 (3): 345–71.

Regalia, I. and Regini, M. (1998) 'Italy: The Dual Character of Industrial Relations' in A. Ferner and R. Hyman (eds) *Changing Industrial Relations in Europe*. Oxford: Blackwell, 459–503.

Regan, A. (2010) 'Does discourse matter in the formation and consolidation of social pacts?', *Critical Policy Studies* 4 (3): 250–77.

Regan, A. (2012) 'The Political Economy of Social Pacts in the EMU', *New Political Economy* 17 (4): 465–91.

Regini, M. (1984) 'The Conditions for Political Exchange' in J.H. Goldthorpe (ed.) *Order and Conflict in Contemporary Capitalism*. Oxford: Clarendon Press, 124–42.

Regini, M. (1995) *Uncertain Boundaries*. Cambridge: Cambridge UP.

References

Regini, M. (1997) 'Still Engaging in Corporatism?', *European Journal of Industrial Relations* 3 (3): 259–78.

Regini, M. and Colombo, S. (2011) 'Italy: The Rise and Decline of Social Pacts' in S. Avdagic, M.

Regini, M. and Regalia, I. (1997) 'Employers, unions and the state', *West European Politics* 20 (1): 201–30.

Rego, R., Sprenger, W., Kirov, V., Thomson, G., and Di Nunzio, D. (2016) 'The use of new ICTs in trade union protests: Five European cases', *Transfer* 22(3): 315–29.

Rehder, B. (2008) 'Revitalisierung der Gewerkschaften?', *Berliner Journal für Soziologie* 18 (3): 432–56.

Rehfeldt, U. (2009) 'European Works Councils in France' in M. Hertwig, L. Pries, and L.

Rehfeldt, U and Vincent, C (2018) 'The decentralisation of collective bargaining in France: An escalating process' in S Leonardi and R Pedersini (eds), *Multi-employer bargaining under pressure: Decentralization trends in five European Countries*. Brussels: ETUI.

Rampeltshammer (eds) *European Works Councils in Complementary Perspectives*. Brussels: ETUI, 153–85.

Rhodes, and J. Visser (eds) *Social Pacts in Europen*. Oxford: OUP, 118–46.

Rhodes, M. (2001) 'The Political Economy of Social Pacts' in P. Pierson, ed., *The New Politics of the Welfare State*. Oxford: OUP, 165–94.

Richards, A. J. (2001) 'The Crisis of Union Representation', in G. Van Guyes, H. De Witte, and P. Pasture (eds) *Can Class Still Unite?* Aldershot: Ashgate, 13–36.

Rickens, C. (2006) 'Verdi und die Veganer', *managermagazin* 3/2006: 126–33.

Roche, W. K. (2007) 'Social Partnership in Ireland and New Social Pacts', *Industrial Relations* 46 (3): 395–425.

Ross, G. (1998) 'The Euro, the "French Model of Society" and French Politics', *French Politics and Society* 16 (4): 1–16.

Ross, G. and Martin, A. (1999) 'European Unions Face the Millennium' in A. Martin and G.

Ross (eds) *The Brave New World of European Labor*. New York: Berghahn, 1–25.

Rüb, S. (2009) *Die Transnationalisierung der Gewerkschaften*. Berlin: edition sigma.

Rychly, L. (2009) *Social Dialogue in Times of Crisis*. Industrial and Employment Relations Working Paper 1. Geneva: ILO.

Sainsaulieu, I. (2006) 'Syndicalisme critique et défiinstitutionnel', *Relations industrielles/Industrial Relations* 61 (4): 684–707.

Scharpf, F. W. (1999) *Governing in Europe*. Oxford: OUP.

Schelkle, W. (2011) 'Reconfiguring welfare states in the post-industrial age', *European Journal of Industrial Relations* 17 (4): 301–14.

Scherrer, P. (2011) 'Unions still a Long Way from a Truly European Position' in W. Kowalsky and P. Scherrer (eds), *Trade Unions for a Change of Course in Europe*. Brussels: ETUI, 29–38.

Scheuer, S. (1998) 'Denmark: A Less Regulated Model' in A. Ferner and R. Hyman (eds) *Changing Industrial Relations in Europe*. Oxford: Blackwell, 146–70.

Scheuer, S. (2006) 'A Novel Calculus?', *European Journal of Industrial Relations* 12 (2): 143–65.

References

Scheuer, S. (2007) 'Dilemmas of Collectivism', *Journal of Labor Research* 28 (2): 233–54.
Scheuer, S. (2008) *The Individual's Right to Choose*. Bristol: CESR Review.
Schmalz, S. and Dörre, K. (2014) 'Der Machtressourcenansatz: Ein Instrument zur Analyse gewerkschaftlichen Handlungsvermögens', *Industrielle Beziehungen* 21(3): 217–37.
Schmalz, S. and Thiel, M. (2017) 'IG Metall's comeback: Trade union renewal in times of crisis', *Journal of Industrial Relations* 59(4): 465–86.
Schmidt, V. A. (2002) *The Futures of European Capitalism*. Oxford: Oxford UP.
Schmidt, V. A. (2009) 'Re-Envisioning the European Union', *Journal of Common Market Studies* 47 (s1): 17–42.
Schmidt, V. A. (2010) Democracy and Legitimacy in the European Union Revisited. FU Berlin: KFG Working Paper 21.
Schmitter, P. and Streeck, W. (1981) *The organization of business interests*. Berlin: WZB.
Schoefer, S. (2000) *Strategie statt Notwehr*. Münster: Westfälisches Dampfboot.
Schömann, I., Jagodzinski, R., Boni, G., Clauwaert, S., Glassner, V., Kepler, J., and Jaspers, T. (2012) *Transnational collective bargaining at company level*. Brussels: ETUI.
Schreieder, A. (2007) 'Die Lidl-Kampagne' in P. Bremme, U. Fürniß and U. Meinecke (eds) *Never Work Alone*. Hamburg: VSA Verlag, 153–74.
Schroeder, W. (2007) *Soziale Demokratie und Gewerkschaften*. Bonn: Friedrich-Ebert-Stiftung. http://www.fes-online-akademie.de/download.php?d=wolfgang_schroeder.pdf.
Schulten, T. (2004) *Solidarische Lohnpolitik in Europa*. Hamburg: VSA. Scruggs, L. (2002) 'The Ghent System and Union Membership in Europe, 1970–1996', *Political Research Quarterly* 55 (2): 275–97.
Schulten, T. and Bispinck, R. (2018) 'Varieties of decentralisation in German collective bargaining', 72–106 in S Leonardi and R Pedersini (eds), *Multi-employer bargaining under pressure: Decentralization trends in five European Countries*. Brussels: ETUI.
Schulze-Cleven, T. (2017) 'A Continent in Crisis: European Labor and the Fate of Social Democracy', *Labor Studies Journal*. https://doi.org/10.1177/0160449X17747395
Sechi, C. (2007) *Women in Trade Unions in Europe*. Brussels: ETUC.
Seibring, A. (2010) 'Die Gewerkschaften im Fünf-Parteien-System der Bundesrepublik', *Aus Politik und Zeitgeschichte* 13–14: 29–35.
Serafin, E. and van Kaldenkerken, C. (2004) 'Einführung von Supervision, Coaching und Teamentwicklung bei der Vereinten Dienstleistungsgesellschaft', *Supervision* 3: 51–7.
Serroyen, C. (2016) Contribution ACV-CSC to the Meeting of the European Commission with the Belgian Social Partners: 'European Pillar of Social Rights'. Brussels, 13 July.
Shonfield, A. (1965) *Modern Capitalism*. Oxford: OUP.
Shorter, E. and Tilly, C. (1974) *Strikes in France 1830–1968*. Cambridge: Cambridge University Press.
Silver, B. J. (2003) *Forces of Labor*. Cambridge: Cambridge UP.
Simms, M. (2010) *Trade Union Strategies to Recruit New Groups of Workers: United Kingdom*. Dublin: European Foundation. http://www.eurofound.europa.eu/eiro/studies/tn0901028s/uk0901029q.htm.

References

Simms, M. (2012) 'Imagined solidarities', *Capital & Class* 36 (1): 97–115.

Simms, M. and Holgate, J. (2010a) 'TUC Organising Academy 10 years on', *International Journal of Human Resource Management* 21 (3): 355–70.

Simms, M. and Holgate, J. (2010b) 'Organising for what?', *Work, Employment & Society* 24 (1): 157–68.

Simms, M., Holgate, J., and Heery, E. (2013) *Union Voices: Tactics and Tensions in UK Organizing*. Ithaca: Cornell UP.

Simonazzi, A. (2012) 'Italy: Chronicle of a crisis foretold' in S. Lehndorff (ed.) *A triumph of failed ideas*. Brussels: ETUI, 183–97.

Sisson, K., Freyssinet, J., Krieger, H., O' Kelly, K., Schnabel, C., and Seifert, H. (1999) *Pacts for Employment and Competitiveness* http://www.eurofound.eu.int/publications/files/EF9960EN.pdf.

Smith, P. (2009) 'New Labour and the commonsense of neoliberalism', *Industrial Relations Journal* 40 (4): 337–55.

Snow, D. A., Rochford, E. B., Worden, S. K., and Benford, R. D. (1986) 'Frame alignment processes, micromobilization, and movement participation', *American Sociological Review* 51 (4): 464–81.

Stanley, N., Mercer, L., Ferns, S. Richards, P., Goldberg, J., Harris, M., Ivory, B., Stanistreet, M., and Finch, T. (2011) *The Future forUnion Image*. London: Unions 21.

Stern, S. (2010) Mitgliedergewinnungsstrategien österreichischer Gewerkschaften. M.Phil. thesis, Universität Wien.

Stierle, S. and Haar, K. (2012) *Troika for Everyone, Forever*. https://corporateeurope.org/eu-crisis/2012/11/troika-everyone-forever

Stokke, T. A. (2008) 'The Anatomy of Two-tier Bargaining Models', *European Journal of Industrial Relations* 14 (1): 7–24.

Storey, A. (2008) 'The Ambiguity of Resistance', *Capital and Class* 96: 55–85.

Streeck, W. (1988) 'Editorial Introduction', *Economic and Industrial Democracy* 9 (3): 307–18.

Streeck, W. (1992) *Social Institutions and Economic Performance*. London: Sage.

Streeck, W. (1997) 'Neither European nor Works Councils', *Economic and Industrial Democracy* 18 (2): 325–37. Streeck, W. (1999) Competitive Solidarity. MPIfG Working Paper 99/8.

Streeck, W. (2009) *Re-Forming Capitalism*. Oxford: OUP.

Streeck, W. and Visser, J. (1997) 'The Rise of the Conglomerate Union', *European Journal of Industrial Relations* 3 (3): 305–32.

Stuart, M. and Martínez Lucio, M. (eds) (2005) *Partnership and Modernisation in Employment Relations*. London: Routledge.

Stuart, M., Martínez Lucio, M., and Charlwood, A. (2009) *Union Modernisation Fund: Round one*. London: BIS.

Sturmthal, A. (1972) *Comparative Labor Movements*. Belmont: Wadsworth.

Suschnigg, P. (1998) 'Worker Representation in the Era of Free Trade and Deregulation', *Proceedings of the 12th AIRAANZ Conference*: 344–51.

Svensson, P. (2002) 'Five Danish Referendums on the European Community and European Union', *European Journal of Political Research* 41 (6): 733–50.

References

Swenson, P. (1989) *Fair Shares*. Ithaca: Cornell UP.

Tarrow, S. (1998) *Power in Movement* (2nd edn). Cambridge: Cambridge UP.

Taylor, A. J. (1989) *Trade Unions and Politics*. Basingstoke: Macmillan.

Telljohann, V. (2005) 'The Operation of European Works Councils' in V. Telljohann (ed.) *Quality Inventories on the Operation and Results of European Works Councils*. Bologna: IpL, 29–50.

Telljohann, V., da Costa, I., Mü ller, T., Rehfeldt, U., and Zimmer, R. (2009) *European and international framework agreements*. Dublin: Eurofound.

Terry, M. (ed.) (2001) *Redefining Public Sector Unionism*. London: Routledge.

Terry, M. (2004) 'Partnership: A Serious Strategy for UK Unions?' in A. Verma and T. A. Kochan (eds) *Unions in the 21st Century*. Basingstoke: Palgrave Macmillan, 205–19.

Thelen, K. A. (2004) *How Institutions Evolve*. Cambridge: Cambridge University Press.

Thelen, K. A. (2012) 'Varieties of Capitalism', *Annual Review of Political Science* 15: 137–59. Thomas, A. (2013) 'Towards the Managerialization of Trade Unions?', *European Journal of Industrial Relations* 19 (1): 21–36.

Thomas, A. (2016) 'The transnational circulation of the "organizing model" and its reception in Germany and France', *European Journal of Industrial Relations* 22(4): 317–33.

Thompson, E. P. (1968) *The Making of the English Working Class*. Harmondsworth: Penguin.

Thompson, E. P. (1971) 'The Moral Economy of the English Crowd in the Eighteenth Century', *Past and Present* 50: 76–136.

Thomson, D. and Larson, R. (1978) *Where Were You Brother?* London: War on Want.

Tilly, C. (2006) *Regimes and Repertoires*. Chicago: University of Chicago Press.

Touraine, A. (1966) *La conscience ouvrière*. Paris: Seuil.

TUC (1999) *Meeting the Millennial Challenge* London: TUC.

TUC (2001) *Reaching the Missing Millions*. London: TUC.

TUC (2008) *Hard Work, Hidden Lives*. London: TUC.

TUC (2012) *General Council Report*. London: TUC.

TUC (2014) *Young Workers and Unions*. London: TUC.

Trampusch, C. (2006) 'Industrial Relations and Welfare States', *Journal of European Social Policy* 16 (2): 121–33.

Traxler, F. (1995) 'Farewell to Labour Market Associations?', in C. Crouch and F. Traxler (eds) *Organized Industrial Relations in Europe*. Aldershot: Avebury, 23–44.

Traxler, F. (1998) 'Austria: Still the Country of Corporatism' in A. Ferner and R. Hyman (eds) *Changing Industrial Relations in Europe*. Oxford: Blackwell, 239–61.

Traxler, F. (2004) 'The metamorphoses of corporatism', *European Journal of Political Research* 43 (4): 571–98.

Traxler, F. and Brandl, B. (2009) 'Towards Europeanization of Wage Policy', European Union Politics June 10: 177–201.

Traxler, F., Brandl, B., Glassner, V., and Ludvig, A. (2008) 'Can Cross-Border Bargaining Coordination Work?', *European Journal of Industrial Relations* 14 (2): 217–37.

Traxler, F. and Pernicka, S. (2007) 'The State of Unions: Austria', *Journal of Labor Research* 28 (2): 207–32.

Tsarouhas, D. (2011) 'Frame Extension, Trade Union Identities, and Wage Politics', *Social Politics* 18 (3): 419–40.

References

Tu, N. (2008) Les conceptions européennes des syndicats CFDT et CGT à travers leurs stages de formation Europe. Master's thesis, Université Robert Schuman, Strasbourg.

Turnbull, P. (2010) 'From social conflict to social dialogue', *European Journal of Industrial Relations* 16 (4): 333–49.

Turner, H. A. (1962) *Trade Union Growth, Structure and Policy.* London: Allen and Unwin.

Unison (2002) *Stress at work.* London: Unison.

Unite (2010) *Guide to work-related Stress.* London: Unite.

Unite the Union (2014) *Our time is now. Young workers and unions: Lessons from overseas.* http://www.unitetheunion.org/uploaded/documents/InternationalYoung-Workers201411-19078.pdf

Upchurch, M., Taylor, G., and Mathers, A. (2009) *The Crisis of Social Democratic Trade Unionism in Western Europe.* Farnham: Ashgate.

Urban, H.-J. (2005) 'Gewerkschaften als konstruktive Veto-Spieler?', *Forschungsjournal Neue Soziale Bewegungen* 18 (2): 44–60.

Urban, H.-J. (2009) 'Zeit für eine politische Neuorientierung', *Internationale Politik und Gesellschaft* 4/2009: 11–25.

Urban, H.-J. (2012) 'Crisis corporatism and trade union revitalisation in Europe' in S. Lehndorff (ed.) *A triumph of failed ideas.* Brussels: ETUI, 219–41.

USDAW (2010) *Developing competent and confident managers.* London: BIS.

van Apeldoorn, B. (2000) 'Transnational Class Agency and European Governance', *New Political Economy* 5 (2): 157–81.

Vandaele, K. (2006) 'A report from the homeland of the Ghent system', *Transfer* 12 (4): 647–57.

Vandaele, K. (2011) *Sustaining or abandoning 'social peace'?* Brussels: ETUI Working Paper 2011/05.

Vandaele, K. (2012) 'Youth representatives' opinions on recruiting and representing young workers', *European Journal of Industrial Relations* 18 (3): 203–18.

Vandaele, K. (2013) 'Union responses to young workers since the Great Recession in Ireland, the Netherlands and Sweden: are youth structures reorienting the union agenda?', *Transfer* 19(3): 381–97.

Vandaele, K. (2015) 'Trade unions' "deliberative vitality" towards young workers: Survey evidence across Europe' in A. Hodder and L. Kretsos (eds), *Young Workers and Trade Unions: A Global View.* Basingstoke: Palgrave Macmillan, 16–36.

Vandaele, K. (2016) 'Interpreting strike activity in western Europe in the past 20 years: The labour repertoire under pressure', *Transfer* 22(3): 277–94.

Vandaele, K. (2017) 'Belgique. Les syndicats sur le qui-vive pour soutenir les travailleurs des plateformes: l'exemple des livreurs de repas', *Chronique internationale de l'IRES* 160: 85–100.

Vandaele, K. and Leschke, J. (2010) *Following the 'Organising Model' of British Unions?* Brussels: ETUI Working Paper 2010/02.

Vandenberg, A. (2006) 'Social Movement Unionism in Theory and in Sweden', *Social Movement Studies* 5 (2): 171–91.

Vandekerckhove, S., Van Peteghem, J., and Van Gyes, G. (2012) *Wages and working conditions in the crisis.* Dublin: Eurofound.

References

van der Meer, M. J. S. M., van Os van den Abeelen, R., and Visser, J. (2009) 'The focus of the new trade union', *Transfer* 15 (3–4): 439–60.

van der Meer, M. and Visser, J. (2010) 'Doing together what Is Possible' in P. Pochet, M. Keune, and D. Natali (eds) *After the euro and enlargement*. Brussels: ETUI/OSE, 251–79.

Van Gyes, G. and Schulten, T. (eds) (2015) *Wage bargaining under the new European Economic Governance: Alternative strategies for inclusive growth*. Brussels: ETUI.

Van Gyes, G., Van Herreweghe, D., Smits, I., and Vandekerckhove, S. (2018) 'Opposites attract? Decentralisation tendencies in the most organised collective bargaining system in Europe: Belgium in the period 2012–2016' in S Leonardi and R Pedersini (eds), *Multi-employer*.

van het Kaar, R. and Smit, E. (eds) (2006) *Vier scenario's voor de toekomst van de medezeggenschap*. http://docs.szw.nl/pdf/129/2006/129_2006_3_9664.pdf.

van Klaveren, M. and Tijdens, K. (2011) *Collective bargaining in the Dutch metal and electrical engineering industry*. Amsterdam: AIAS.

Van Rie, T., Marx, I., and Horemans, J. (2011) 'Ghent revisited', *European Journal of Industrial Relations* 17 (2): 125–39.

van Wijnbergen, C. (1994) 'Ireland and the Ratification of the Maastricht Treaty' in F. Laursen and S. Vanhoonacker (eds) *The Ratification of the Maastricht Treaty*. Dordrecht: Nijhoff, 181–93.

Vilrokx, J. and Van Leemput, J. (1992) 'Belgium: A New Stability in Industrial Relations?' in A. Ferner and R. Hyman (eds) *Industrial Relations in the New Europe*. Oxford: Blackwell, 357–92.

Visser, J. (1992) 'The End of an Era and the End of a System', in A. Ferner and R. Hyman (eds) *Industrial Relations in the New Europe*. Oxford: Blackwell, 323–57.

Visser, J. (1995) 'The Netherlands' in J. Rogers and W. Streeck (eds) *Works Councils*. Chicago: University of Chicago Press, 79–114.

Visser, J. (1998a) 'The Netherlands' in A. Ferner and R. Hyman (eds) *Changing Industrial Relations in Europe*. Oxford: Blackwell, 283–314.

Visser, J. (1998b) 'Learning to Play: The Europeanisation of Trade Unions' in P. Pasture and J. Verberckmoes (eds) *Working-Class Internationalism and the Appeal of National Identity*. Oxford: Berg, 231–56.

Visser, J. (2002) 'Why Fewer Workers Join Unions in Europe', *British Journal of Industrial Relations* 40 (3): 403–30.

Visser, J. (2006) 'Union Membership Statistics in 24 Countries', *Monthly Labor Review* 129 (1): 38–49.

Visser, J. (2007) 'Trade Union Decline and What Next', *Industrielle Beziehungen* 14 (2): 97–117.

Visser, J. (2009) 'The Quality of Industrial Relations and the Lisbon Strategy' in European Commission, *Industrial Relations in Europe 2008*. Luxembourg: Office for Official Publications, 45–72.

Visser, J. (2011) ICTWSS: Database on Institutional Characteristics of Trade Unions, Wage Setting, State Intervention and Social Pacts. http://www.uva-aias.net/208.

Visser, J. (2012) 'The Rise and Fall of Industrial Unionism', *Transfer* 18 (2): 129–41.

Visser, J. (2015) ICTWSS database. http://uva-aias.net/nl/ictwss

References

Visser, J. (2016) 'What happened to collective bargaining during the great recession?' *IZA Journal of Labor Policy* 5(9): 1–35.
Visser, J. and Hemerijck, A. (1997) *'A Dutch Miracle'*. Amsterdam: Amsterdam UP.
Visser, J. and Rhodes, M. (2011) 'The Evolution of Pacts' in S. Avdagic, M. Rhodes, and J. Visser (eds) *Social Pacts in Europe*. Oxford: OUP, 61–85. Visser, J. and van der Meer, M. (2011) 'Netherlands: Social Pacts in a Concertation Economy' in S. Avdagic, M. Rhodes, and J. Visser (eds) *Social Pacts in Europe*. Oxford: OUP, 203–31.
von Alemann, U. and Schmid, J. (1993) 'Organisations-Reform in der Gewerkschaft ÖTV', *Gewerkschaftliche Monatshefte* 5/93: 293–302.
von Prondzynski, F. (1998) 'Ireland: Corporation Revived' in A. Ferner and R. Hyman (eds) *Changing Industrial Relations in Europe*. Oxford: Blackwell, 55–73.
Waddington, J. (2000) 'Towards a Reform Agenda?', *Industrial Relations Journal* 31 (4): 317–30.
Waddington, J. (2005) 'What Difference has the Merger Process Made?' in J. Waddington (ed.) *Restructuring Representation*. Brussels: P.I.E.-Peter Lang, 375–92.
Waddington, J. (2006) 'The trade union merger process in Europe', *Industrial Relations Journal* 37 (6): 630–51.
Waddington, J. (2011) *European Works Councils*. London: Routledge.
Waddington, J. and Kerr, A. (2009) 'Transforming a Trade Union?', *British Journal of Industrial Relations* 47 (1): 27–54.
Waddington, J., Kahmann, M., and Hoffmann, J. (2005) *A Comparison of the Trade Union Merger Process in Britain and Germany*. London: Routledge.
Waddington J., Pulignano V., Turk J., and Swerts, T. (2016) *Managers, BusinessEurope and the development of European Works Councils*. Brussels: ETUI Working Paper 2016.06.
Ward, S. and Lusoli, W. (2003) 'Dinosaurs in Cyberspace?', *European Journal of Communication* 18: 147–79.
Walton, R. E. and McKersie, R. B. (1965) *A behavioral theory of labor negotiations*. New York: McGraw Hill.
Waterman, P. (2001) *Globalization, Social Movements and the New Internationalism*. London: Continuum.
Webb, S. and Webb, B. (1894) *History of Trade Unionism*. London: Longmans.
Webb, S. and Webb, B. (1897) *Industrial Democracy*. London: Longmans.
Webster, E., Lambert, R., and Bezuidenhout, A. (2008) *Grounding Globalization*. Oxford: Blackwell.
Western, B. (1997) *Between Class and Market*. Princeton: Princeton UP.
Wetzel, D., Weigand, J., Niemann-Findeisen, S., and Lankau, T. (2008) *Organizing. Die mitgliederorientierte Offensivstrategie für die IG Metall*. Frankfurt: IG Metall.
Whittall, M. and Kotthoff, H. (2012) 'Les comités d'entreprise européens, des zones libres de syndicats?', *Revue de l'IRES* 68: 111–40.
Whittall, M., Knudsen, H., and Huijngen, F. (eds) (2007) *Towards a European Labour Identity*. London: Routledge.
Wierink, M. (2017) '2012 à 2017, cinq ans de reconstruction de la FNV, première organisation syndicale néerlandaise', *Chronique internationale de l'IRES* 159: 37–57.

Wills, J. and Simms, M. (2004) 'Building reciprocal community unionism in the UK', *Capital & Class* 28 (1): 59–84.

Wilson, T. (2007) *The Future for Unions*. London: Unions 21.

Windolf, P. (1989) 'Productivity Coalitions and the Future of European Corporatism', *Industrial Relations* 28 (1): 1–20.

Woolfson, C., Thörnqvist, C., and Sommers, J. (2010) 'The Swedish Model and the Future of Labour Standards after Laval', *Industrial Relations Journal* 41 (4): 333–50.

Worre, T. (1995) 'The Danish Referendums on the Maastricht Treaty 1992 and 1993', *Journal of Common Market Studies* 33 (2): 503–17.

Wright, C. (2010) *Swords of Justice and Civic Pillars*. London: TUC.

Wright, E. O. (2000) 'Working Class Power, Capitalist-Class Interests and Class Compromise', *American Journal of Sociology* 105 (4): 957–1002.

Zoll, R. (1991) 'Gewerkschaften als Diskurs-Organisationen', *Gewerkschaftliche Monatshefte* 6/1991: 390–9.

Index

AbvaKabo (FNV public services union) 18, 41, 89, 164
ABVV/FGTB *(Algemeen Belgisch Vakverbond/ Fédération Générale du Travail de Belgique)* 19, 84, 89, 124, 128, 142, 150, 165, 181
AC *(Akademikernes Centralorganisation)* 12
ACLVB/CGSLB *(Algemene Centrale der Liberale Vakbonden van België/Centrale Générale des Syndicats Libéraux de Belgique)* 19
ACV/CSC *(Algemeen Christelijk Vakverbond/ Confédération des Syndicats Chrétiens)* 19, 72, 84, 89, 128, 137, 141, 148, 149–50, 154, 164–5
ACW *(Algemeen Christelijk Werknemersverbond)* 141–2
Africa 163, 164, 165, 166
agency workers 57, 61, 64, 65, 68, 126, 178
airlines 60, 66
AK *(Arbeiterkammer)* 15–16, 61, 149, 163
amalgamation *see* mergers
Amicus union (now Unite) 88, 89, 177
Amsterdam Treaty (1998) 76, 174, 178
Anner et al. 160
anti-capitalist parties 143
anti-discrimination campaigns 61, 147
anti-immigrant parties 41
Anxo, D. and Niklasson, H. 12
apprentices 14, 59, 61
Ardura, A. and Silvera, R. 73, 75
Arlt, H.-J. 152
Asia 164, 166
associational power 30, 31, 37, 39–40, 52, 53, 56, 90, 105, 134, 145, 148, 189
ATTAC *(Association pour la taxation des transactions pour l'aide aux citoyens)* 149, 176
atypical employment 29, 33, 37, 47, 55, 56–7, 60, 64–5, 67, 74, 78, 80, 94, 102, *see also* precarious workers
austerity measures 37, 45, 86, 104, 121, 123, 124, 128, 129, 131, 141, 155–6, 171, 183, 204

Austria 4, 15–17
  BAWAG scandal in 41, 92
  and European integration 175
  female representation in 72
  free movement of workers and 180
  gender equality in 76
  global financial crisis and 123, 126, 127
  institutional framework of industrial relations in 14–15, 16
  membership density in 5, 39–40, 53, 54–5, 59, 60
  migrant workers and 61–2
  political parties and unions in 139, 140–1
  recruitment in 60–1, 69, 70
  strike data in 105
  trade union structure in 83
  tripartism and 116, 127
  union mergers in 89, 92
  union-NGO cooperation in 149
  work-life balance in 114

Baccaro, L. 99
Bacon, N. and Blyton, P. 106
Bahnmüller, R. 109
ballots 99, 115
banking sector 41, 92, 109, 110, 122–3, 124, 125, 127
Barker et al. 193
Barthélemy et al. 91
BASTUN (Baltic Sea Trade Union Network) 162, 184
Batstone et al. 201
Beamte (German civil servants) 15, 83, 84
Beccalli, B. and Meardi, G. 74
Behrens et al. 47
Belgium 4, 6, 18–19
  anti-stress agreements in 113
  equal opportunities in 76
  female representation in 72
  free movement of workers and 181
  global financial crisis and 123, 124, 125, 127–8

263

Index

Belgium (*Cont.*)
  international trade union involvement 164, 165
  membership density in 5, 39–40, 42, 54–5, 62
  political parties and unions in 139, 141–2
  recruitment in 57, 69
  strike data in 105
  tripartism in 116, 119, 128
  union mergers in 89
  union-NGO cooperation in 149–50
  vocational training in 113
Bercusson, B. and Weiler, A. 76
Berlusconi government (Italy) 22, 43–4, 111, 121, 129, 144, 150, 181
bipartite agreements 103, 104, 141
blue-collar workers 10, 58, 59, 109, 173, *see also* manual workers
Blüm, Norbert 140
BNP Paribas (French bank) 124
Bolkestein directive on service liberalization 148, 177, 183
Bondgenoten (FNV general union) 18, 41, 62, 63, 79, 89, 149, 164
Bourdieu, Pierre 200
Britain 4, 24–6, 57, 68, 94, 99, 108
  anti-stress agreements in 113
  'battle of ideas' in 155–6
  coalitional power in 146
  and European integration 177
  Euroscepticism in 179
  female representation in 74, 146
  free movement of workers and 180, 181
  global financial crisis and 123, 131
  international trade union involvement 166–7
  managerial unionism in 96–7
  membership density in 5, 52, 53, 54–5, 65, 94
  partnerships in 48–9
  political parties and unions in 136, 139, 144
  'popular bossdoms' 98
  post-war consensus challenges for 44–5
  recruitment in 65–7
  strikes in 100–1, 105
  sustainable energy projects in 147–8
  trade union structure in 81–2, 83
  union attitudes to EWCs 187
  union mergers in 88–9, 91, 151
British Empire 25
Bulgaria 180, 181
Busemeyer et al. 185

call centres 60, 61, 63
Camusso, Susanna 73, 130
capitalism 3–4, 25, 28, 35–6, 69, 115–16, 134

Catholic Church 20
Catholic conservatism 27, 151
Catholic movements 84, 165
Catholic trade unions 18, 19, 141, 143, 144, 202
CDA (*Christlich-Demokratische Arbeitnehmerschaft*) 140
CDU (*Christlich Demokratische Union*) 140, 157
CD&V (*Christen-Democratisch en Vlaams*) 142
CEE (Central and Eastern Europe) countries 35, 65, 164, 168
CEE (Central and Eastern Europe) migrant workers 41, 54, 62, 68, 180
'Celtic tiger' phenomenon 27, 122, *see also* Ireland
Central Economic Council (Belgium) 18
CFDT (*Confédération française démocratique du travail*) 21–2, 43, 63, 64, 73, 85, 90, 91, 94, 97, 99, 124, 126, 129, 143, 165, 166, 176
CFE-CGC (*Confédération générale des cadres*) 22
CFTC (*Confédération française des travailleurs chrétiens*) 22, 43
CGB (*Christlicher Gewerkschaftsbund*) 15, 84
CGIL (*Confederazione generale italiana del lavoro*) 23, 43–4, 64–5, 73, 84, 85, 90, 100, 101, 111, 120–1, 129–30, 134, 136, 143, 144, 150, 166, 169
CGT (*Confédération générale du travail*) 22, 23, 43, 63–4, 73, 79, 85, 86, 91, 110, 125, 129, 134, 143, 147, 148, 150, 165–6, 167, 172, 176, 181
Charter of Fundamental Rights 176, 177
Checchi, D. and Visser, J. 5
chemicals sector 156, 186, 187
child labour 164, 165
Christian-democratic parties 13, 14, 16, 19, 22, 23, 41, 49, 134, 136, 137, 140–1
Christian trade unions 38, 83, 136, 141, 159
CISC (*Confédération internationale des syndicats chrétiens*) 159
CISL (*Confederazione italiana sindacati lavoratori*) 23, 64, 73, 85, 90, 111, 121, 129, 143, 166
civil society 2, 146, 166, 200–1
cleaners 33–4, 62–3, 66, 79, 146
CMEs (coordinated market economies) 3, 4, 39
CNV (*Christelijk Nationaal Vakverbond*) 18, 19, 62, 128, 137, 141, 164, 165, 181
CNV Jongeren 62
coal mining unions 105
coalitional power resources 31, 145–51, 190
codetermination rights 14, 40
collective agreements 2, 8, 14, 16, 17, 19, 21, 25, 38–40, 47, 76, 84, 99, 102, 107, 114–15, 120, 142, 154, 156, 182–3

264

Index

collective bargaining 3, 5, 20, 24, 26, 29, 36, 55, 102–4, 133, 134, 135, 194
  anti-stress agreements 113–14
  austerity and 122–31
  Austria 16, 109–10, 114, 118, 185
  Belgium 19, 110, 113, 118, 119, 142, 185
  Britain 25, 26, 44, 111, 113, 114, 118
  coordination 184–6
  decentralization of 11, 37, 40, 42, 87–8, 102, 107–11, 120, 185
  Denmark 9, 12, 108, 113, 115, 118, 119, 185–6
  diversity and change 107–12
  France 21, 110, 142, 143, 185
  Germany 14, 15, 40, 109, 113, 114, 118, 119, 185
  innovative strategies and 112–15
  Ireland 112, 121–2
  Italy 43, 110–11, 120–1, 143, 185
  loss of power resources in 104–7
  membership surveys and 115
  Netherlands 17, 110, 115, 118, 119–20
  strategic shifts in 106–7
  Sweden 9, 108, 113, 114, 118, 119, 185–6,
    see also sectoral bargaining/agreements; company bargaining/agreements; concession bargaining
collectivism 15, 32, 33, 34, 154
Commission on Vulnerable Employment (TUC) 67
communications 99–101, 152–3, 189, 203, 205
Communist parties 4, 49, 82, 136, 142, 143
  PCF *(Parti communiste française)* 20–1, 137, 143, 176
  PCI *(Partito comunista italiano)* 22, 23, 120, 137, 143
Communist trade unions 85, 134, 169
company bargaining/agreements 8, 12, 21, 24, 43, 64, 107–11, 126, 158, 166, 188–9
competitive corporatism 103, 117, 118, 131, 184
competitiveness 11, 15, 35, 36, 44, 48, 49, 86, 103, 109, 116, 117, 118, 122, 125, 135, 138, 160, 204
concession bargaining 35, 49, 102, 104, 109, 120, 121, 126, 131
confederations 83, 116
  Austria 83, 85
  Belgium 19, 84, 86, 128, 141–2, 149–50
  bilateral solidarity 161
  Denmark 12, 84, 85, 162
  France 21–2, 42, 63, 84, 85, 86, 165, 166
  Germany 15, 83–4, 85, 92
  Ireland 85
  Italy 23, 64, 85, 129–30, 165, 166
  Netherlands 18, 84, 86, 92, 141, 165

  sectoral 65, 112, 162
  Sweden 10, 84, 85, 162
  women's representation 71, 73, *see also* ETUC; ITUC; TUC
Conservative governments (UK) 26, 44, 177
Conservative-Liberal coalition government (UK) 45, 131, 156
construction sector 32, 68, 90, 165, 182
corruption 22, 41, 143
Cortebeeck, Luc 165
CPE *(contrat première embauche)* 155
Crosby, Mike 68, 94
cross-sectoral bargaining 12, 112, 159, 160
CSR (corporate social responsibility) 150, 162, 164, 165, 166, 188
Culpepper, P. D. 196

Daley, A. 135
Dansk Metal 58
D'Art, D. and Turner, T. 34
Darwin, Charles 6
DBB *(dbb beamtenbund und tarifunion)* 15
De Leeuw, Rudy 165
Dean, H. 75
Decaillon, Joël 176
decentralization of collective bargaining 11, 37, 40, 42, 87–8, 102, 107–11, 120, 185
decolonization 166–7
Dehaene, Jean-Luc 142
Delors, Jacques 171
democracy 1, 2, 7–8, 18, 30, 31, 81, 95, 136, 146, 149, 152–3, 190–3, 195, 197–205
  internal 87–8, 98–9, 101
demonstrations 130, 131, 155, 156, 177
Denmark 4, 8–9, 12–13, 37–8, 177
  anti-stress agreements in 113
  early retirement scheme in 39
  and European integration 174
  female representation in 71–2
  free movement of workers and 181
  global financial crisis in 123, 126
  international trade union involvement 162–3
  membership density in 5, 54–5, 58, 139
  membership surveys in 99
  political parties and unions in 139–40
  recruitment in 59, 69
  strategic reviews in 93, 95
  strike data in 105
  trade union structure in 82
  tripartism in 116, 118, 119
  unemployment insurance in 9, 38
  union mergers in 92
  union-NGO cooperation in 149
  voluntary collective bargaining in 39

265

Index

deregulation 21, 35, 36, 43, 118, 171, 177
DGB *(Deutscher Gewerkschaftsbund)* 15, 82, 84, 85, 86, 89, 93, 113, 147, 149, 152, 156, 163, 183
dock workers 32, 100–1, 105
Dølvik, J.-E. 173
Dølvik, J.-E. and Visser, J. 182
Donaghey, J. and Teague, P. 122
Doorn group 185
Dörre et al. 56
Dufour, C. and Hege, A. 124, 201

early retirement schemes 39, 41, 120
Ebbinghaus, B. 118, 136
ECB (European Central Bank) 44, 123
ECJ (European Court of Justice) 38, 127, 171, 179, 180, 181–4
education and training 14, 36, 59, 98, 112–13, 163, 164, 165, 189
Edwards, P. K. and Hyman, R. 104
EEA (European Economic Area) 168, 186
EEC (European Economic Community) 168, 169, 172, 175, 177
EFAs (European framework agreements) 188
efficacy 29, 48, 193, 194
'efficiency *versus* democracy' thesis 88, 197
EMF (European Metalworkers' Federation) (now IndustriALL) 185, 187
employers' organizations 7, 9, 10, 40, 44, 76, 83, 113, 121, 171
employment protection legislation 12, 14, 44, 125–6, 181–4, 203
EMU (economic and monetary union) 103, 118, 119, 173, 174, 177
Engels, Friedrich 134
environmental issues 147–50
equal opportunities 61, 71, 72, 73, 74–6, 77, 155, 170, 182
Erne, R. 185
ESFs (European Social Fora) 148, 150, 151, 178
Esping-Andersen, G. 3, 13, 26
ethnic minority workers 59, 61, 64, 67, 72, 145, 146, 147, *see also* migrant workers; foreign–born workers
ETUC (European Trade Union Confederation) 71, 75, 76, 113, 127, 158, 159, 160–2, 164–7, 169–70, 171, 173, 174, 175, 176–7, 180, 182, 183–5, 186
ETUFs (European Trade Union Federations) 158, 162, 164, 166, 169, 185, 187, 188
ETUI (European Trade Union Institute) 160, 169
EU (European Union) 167
    Bolkestein directive on service liberalization 148, 177, 183

democratic deficit 198
Denmark 12
deregulation 36, 177
enlargement of 50, 135, 168, 178, 179–80
equal opportunities 76, 77
free movement policy 38–9, 41, 54, 68, 125, 170, 179–81, 183
institutional imbalance in 171
Irish bailout 45, 123, 130
labour law 3
sovereign debt crisis 37, 44, 123
trade unions and 170–84
Eucob@n 185
European Commission 44, 67, 169, 170, 171, 177, 181, 182, 183
European Council 171
European Parliament 137, 139, 171, 183
European Quality of Work Surveys 113
European Social Survey 53
European Transport Workers' Federation 183
EWCs (European Works Councils) 158, 167, 184, 186–9
Ewing, K. D. 2

Fantasia, R. 201
far-right parties 41, 141, 180
farm workers 193
Feltrin, P. 54
female workers 80
    Denmark 13, 58
    equal pay 61, 76–7, 170
    France 63
    Germany 69
    'ghettoizing' risk to 75
    Italy 63
    as negotiators 77
    Netherlands 62, 69
    quotas 71
    recruitment 65
    representation 52, 70–1, 147
    unionization rates 53–4
feminism 74, 87
feminization of work 33, 55
FES *(Friedrich Ebert-Stifung)* 163
Fiat 44, 111
Finland 9, 182
FIOM-CGIL (Italian metalworking union) 99, 124, 148
Fire Brigades Union (UK) 144
fixed-term contracts 4, 34, 45, 54, 57, 59, 65, 66
flexibility 33, 37, 48, 170
FNV *(Federatie Nederlandse Vakbeweging)* 18, 33, 41–2, 62, 63, 73, 79, 84, 86, 89, 99, 120, 128–9, 141, 149, 164, 175, 181
FNV Jong 62
FNV Mondiaal 164

Index

FNV Vrouw 72
FO *(CGT-Force ouvrière)* 22, 43, 64, 73, 143, 165–6, 176
FOA (Danish public sector union) 76, 99, 113
food-processing sector 66, 68
Fordism 32, 37
foreign-born workers 33–4, 54–5, 59, 62, 65, 125, *see also* ethnic minority workers; migrant workers
Fortis (Belgian bank) 124
FPÖ *(Freiheitliche Partei Österreichs)* 41, 180
framework agreements 76, 113, 120, 150, 162, 164, 165, 184, 188–9
France 4, 20–2, 42–3, 79, 94
　anti-stress agreements in 113–14
　'boss-napping' incidents in 125
　and European integration 175–7, 178
　and EWCs 187
　female representation in 73, 75
　free movement of workers and 181
　gender equality in 77
　global financial crisis and 123, 124, 125, 126, 127, 129
　international trade union involvement 165–6
　introduction of CPE 155
　membership density in 5, 6, 21, 22, 42, 52, 53, 54–5, 63
　membership surveys in 99
　nationalization in 36, 43
　political parties and unions in 137, 138–9, 142–3
　recruitment in 63–4, 70
　strikes in 105, 127
　trade union politics in 134, 135
　transnational company agreements in 188
　union mergers in 90, 91, 147
　union-NGO cooperation in 150
'freelance unionism' 58
freelance workers 61, *see also* self–employed workers
Freeman, R. B. 100
Frege, C. M. and Kelly, J. 46, 47
Frege et al. 145
Freyssinet, J. 129
Friends of the Earth 148
FSU *(Fédération syndicale unitaire)* 22
FTF (Danish white-collar confederation) 12, 90, 119

gangmasters 66
Ganz, M. 193, 196
gender issues 10, 11, 53–4, 60, 61, 69, 71, 72, 75–7
Germany 4, 13–15, 46, 127, 135, 161, 182, 184
　anti-stress agreements in 113

debt ratio in 123, 131
　EWCs in 186, 187
　female representation in 72
　free movement of workers and 180, 181
　gender issues in 53, 60, 76
　global financial crisis and 123, 125–6, 127
　institutional framework of industrial relations 14
　international trade union involvement 163–4
　managerial unionism in 96
　membership density in 5, 39, 54–5, 59–60
　membership surveys in 99
　political parties and unions in 136, 138–9, 140
　precarious workers in 57
　recruitment in 60, 61, 70
　Standortsicherung 48
　statutory minimum wage in 156–7
　strategic planning in 93–4
　strike data in 105
　sustainable development 147
　Tarifautonomie principle 14, 156
　trade union structure in 82–3
　transnational company agreements in 188
　unification of 40, 109
　union mergers in 89, 91
　union-NGO cooperation in 149
　unions and confederations in 83–4
　vocational training in 14, 112
　wage moderation in 119
GEW *(Gewerkschaft Erziehung und Wissenschaft)* 149
Ghent system 9, 10, 19, 38, 40, 53, 58, 62, 69
Gläser, C. 169–70
Glassner, V. 127
Glassner, V. and Galgóczi, B. 125
global financial crisis 37, 44, 45, 49, 121, 122–31, 135, 138
globalization 3, 29, 35, 37, 47, 50, 106, 149, 154, 160, 190
GMB (UK general union) 66, 96
Golden, M. and Pontusson, J. 8
'good work' concept 113–14, 115
Goyer, M. and Hancké, B. 43
GPA *(Gewerkschaft der Privatangestellten)* 16–17, 60–1, 69, 72, 76, 83, 98, 114, 164
Gramsci, Antonio 193
Greece 180
Greene, A. M. and Kirton, G. 100
Greene et al. 100
Greenpeace 147, 149, 150
Greens 138–9, 176
GUFs (Global Union Federations) 158, 159, 160, 161, 162, 163, 167, 169, 188–9
Guillaume, C. and Pochic, S. 97

267

Index

Haipeter, T. 109
Haipeter, T. and Lehndorff, S. 126
Hall, P. A. 197
Hall, P. A. and Soskice, D. 3
Hancké, R. and Rhodes, M. 118
Handels (Swedish retail workers' union) 148, 173
Hansen, L. L. 71
Hartmann, H. and Lau, C. 85
Haworth, N. and Ramsay, H. 160
Hayward, J. 136
Heery, E. 67, 96, 193
Heery, E. and Abbott, B. 151
Heery, E. and Adler, A. 56
Heery, E. and Kelly, J. 77, 95, 96
Heery, E. and Simms, M. 67
HK (Danish retail and clerical union) 59, 90, 93, 95, 99
Hoffmann, J. and Hoffmann, R. 3–4, 39
Hotell- och restaurangfacket (Swedish Hotel and Restaurant Workers' Union) 58
HTF (Swedish retail and commercial union) 90
Huber, Berthold 61, 196
human resource management 20, 43, 76, 95
human rights 78, 153
'humanization' of work 113–14
Hundstorfer, Rudolf 141
Hungarian unions 62
Huzzard, T. and Östergren, K. 196
Hyman, R. 160

ICFTU (International Confederation of Free Trade Unions) 159, 161, 162, 163, 164, 165, 166, 167, 169, 172, 188
ICTU (Irish Congress of Trade Unions) 27, 69, 74–5, 83, 85, 94, 130, 151, 167, 177–9, 181
ICTWSS database 53
identity 146, 147, 152, 204
ideology 7, 82, 84, 85, 106, 134, 137, 146, 152, 165, 173, 203
IFAs (International Framework Agreements) 162, 164, 165, 188
IG BAU (German construction union) 61
IG BCE (German chemical workers' union) 147, 156
IG Metall (Industriegewerkschaft Metall) 15, 57, 60, 61, 78, 89, 92, 93, 97, 99, 107, 109, 112, 113, 115, 123–4, 140, 147, 149, 156, 163, 187
ILO (International Labour Organization) 149, 159, 166, 168, 188, 189
IMF (International Monetary Fund) 123
individualism 29, 34, 47, 154
industrial militancy *see* militancy
Industribond (now *Bondgenoten*) 164
inflation 117, 129

informal economy 164, 165
information technology 35, 58, 99–101
institutional power resources 31, 32, 36, 37, 39–40, 90, 189
integrative bargaining 106, 107
international trade unions 125, 158–68
  bargaining coordination 184–6
  European dimension and 168–84
  European works councils 186–7
  motives for involvement 159–60
  power resources and 160–1, 189–90
  transnational company agreements 188–9
Internet 35, 58, 99–101, 146, 151, 185, 189, 203
Ireland 4, 24, 26–7, 45
  Croke Park Agreement (2010) 130
  and European integration 177–9
  female representation 74–5
  free movement of workers and 180, 181
  Gay and Lesbian Equality Network 151
  global financial crisis and 45, 123, 130
  institutional framework of industrial relations 27
  international trade union involvement 167
  membership density in 5, 53, 54–5, 65, 68
  political parties and unions in 139, 144–5
  recruitment in 68–9
  strategic reviews in 68, 94–5
  strike data 105
  trade union structure in 82
  tripartism 121–2
  union-NGO cooperation in 151
Irish Ferries 68, 178
Italy 4, 22–4, 43–4, 46, 57
  and European integration 175
  female representation in 73
  free movement of workers and 181
  global financial crisis and 123, 124, 126, 127, 129–30
  information technology and 100, 101
  international trade union involvement 165, 166
  membership density in 5, 54–5
  nationalization in 36
  political exchange in 117, 120–1, 144
  political parties and unions in 136, 137, 139, 143–4
  recruitment in 64–5, 70
  strikes in 105, 127
  tripartism in 120–1
  union mergers in 90
  union-NGO cooperation in 150
ITUC (International Trade Union Confederation) 130, 159, 160, 161, 162, 163–4, 165, 166, 167, 168
IWW (Industrial Workers of the World) 81, 82

Index

Japan 161
Jarley, P. 201–2
job creation strategies 11, 103
job losses 11, 123, 124, 125–6
Jongerius, Agnes 72

KAD *(Kvindeligt Arbejderforbund i Danmark)* 71, 90
Kammer system 15
Katzenstein, P. J. 116
Kelly, J. 77–8, 79, 204
Keynesianism 36, 115, 133, 137
Kjellberg, A. 88, 199
Kommunal (Swedish municipal workers' union) 71, 148
Korpi, W. and Shalev, M. 116
Kröck, H. 149

labour courts 12, 14, 27
labour markets 3, 4, 9–10, 11–12, 25, 33, 34, 36, 83, 116, 122, 129
  deregulation 21, 43, 171
  flexibility 119
  opening up of 65, 68, 135, 154, 178, 179–81
  regulation 42, 117, 132, 133, 174, 183
  two-tier 40
Labour Party (Ireland) 27, 130, 144
Labour Party (UK) 26, 96, 113, 136, 144, 156, 177
Latin America 163, 165, 166
Latvia 183–4
Laval case (2007) 182, 183–4
leadership 192–5, 195, 198–9, 201, 203
  'tendency to oligarchy' 7, 87, 98, 192
Lecher et al. 186
left-wing politics 5, 138–9, 141, 157, 174, 176
Lévesque, C. and Murray, G. 30, 199
Lévesque et al. 199
LGBT (lesbian, gay, bisexual and transgender) workers 70, 72, 74, 98, 147, 150, 151
Liberal Party (Belgium) 142
Lidl (cut-price retailer) 78, 146, 149
Lind, J. 119
Lindsey oil refinery dispute (2009) 125, 183
Lisbon Treaty (2007) 177, 178, 179
LMEs (liberal market economies) 3, 4, 24
LO (Denmark) *(Landsorganisationen i Danmark)* 12, 13, 39, 71, 84, 90, 100, 139, 149, 152, 154, 162, 174
LO (Sweden) *(Landsorganisationen i Sverige)* 10, 11, 38, 58, 82, 84, 93, 99, 108, 119, 138–9, 148, 152, 162, 163, 173–4, 180, 183, 189
Locke, R. and Thelen, K. 28, 46
logistical (strategic) power resources 31, 66, 90, 97, 106, 190, 191
Logue, J. 160

Lundby-Wedin, Wanja 71, 162, 173
Luxembourg case (2008) 182

Maastricht Treaty (1991) 119, 122, 171, 174, 175–6, 177, 178
McIlroy, J. 145
'magic triangle' model 198–9
managerial unilateralism 21, 43, 110
managerial unionism 95–7
Mandate (Irish retail union) 68–9, 94–5
manual workers 9, 10, 12, 33, 40, 54, 58, 59, 71, 82, 83, 109, 110, 117, 137, 140, 163, 173, 174, 178
manufacturing industries 10, 26, 29, 36, 40, 69, 137, 197
manufacturing unions 89, 116, 117, 173
Margherita party 144
Marks, G. and Wilson, C. J. 172
Martin, A. and Ross, G. 8, 170
Meardi, G. 2, 44, 180, 181
MEDEF *(Mouvement des Entreprises de France)* 20
'mega-unions' 92, 98, 101
membership/membership density 2, 5, 32, 33, 36, 53
  activism 6, 42, 199–202
  age and 34–5, 38, 52, 54, 55, 59
  in Austria 5, 39–40, 40–1, 53, 54–5, 59, 60
  in Belgium 5, 39–40, 42, 54–5, 62
  in Britain 5, 52, 53, 54–5, 65, 94
  cut-price 38, 83
  declining 29, 47, 52, 53, 56, 90, 135, 160–1, 194
  in Denmark 5, 9, 10, 54–5, 58, 139
  female 13, 52, 53–4, 58, 62, 63, 65, 69, 71–7, 90
  in France 5, 6, 21, 22, 42, 52, 53, 54–5, 63
  in Germany 5, 39, 54–5, 59–60
  in Ireland 5, 53, 54–5, 65, 68
  in Italy 5, 23–4, 54–5
  in Netherlands 5, 39, 54–5, 62
  online 100
  resources 30, 31
  in Sweden 5, 6, 9, 10, 38, 52, 54–5, 58, 199
membership surveys 99, 115, 163, 165, 177, 179, 199
mergers 13, 15, 16, 18, 25–6, 27, 47, 48, 72, 83, 88–92, 101, 151, 195
merit pay systems 108, 110
metalworking unions 105, 109, 115, 185–6
MHP *(Vakcentrale voor Middengroepen en Hoger Personeel)* 18, 84, 128
Michels, R. 7, 87, 98, 192
microcorporatism 23
migrant workers 60, 61–2, 65, 68, 73, 82, 150, 178
  in Britain 66–7

269

Index

migrant workers (*Cont.*)
  from CEE countries 41, 54, 62, 68, 180
  exploitation of 68, 178
  in Italy 73–4, *see also* ethnic minority workers; foreign-born workers
militancy 2, 23, 24, 26, 32, 79, 103, 106, 144, 196
Milkman, R. 193, 197
minimum wage 21, 26, 38, 107, 130, 135, 142, 156–7, 182
Mitterrand, François 143, 175
MNCs (multinational corporations) 3, 35, 49, 68, 102, 106, 109, 164, 172, 184, 186, 187, 188, 189
mobilization 52, 77–9, 80, 106, 112, 134
MOC *(Mouvement ouvrier chrétien)* 141–2
Moissonnier, L. 148
Monks, John 167, 177
Monti government (Italy) 44, 129
moral power resources 31, 132, 152, 189–90, 200
Moss, B. H. 176
Müller-Jentsch, W. 6, 37
multi-employer bargaining 8, 25, 29, 102, 107–8, 111

national industrial relations systems 3, 35–7, 49, 76, 102, 172, 186
national pay bargaining 44, 76, 107, 128
nationalism 27, 144
nationalization 36, 43
neoliberalism 36, 37, 38, 49–50, 123, 137, 142, 148, 153, 170, 171, 175, 176, 189, 205
Netherlands 4, 17–18, 41–2, 54, 68, 161
  cleaners' strike in 33–4, 62–3, 66, 79, 146
  and European integration 175
  female representation in 71, 72, 146
  free movement of workers and 181
  global financial crisis and 123, 126, 128–9
  institutional framework of industrial relations 17
  international trade union involvement 164–5
  membership density in 5, 39, 54–5, 62
  membership surveys in 99
  political parties and unions in 138–9, 141
  recruitment in 62–3
  strikes in 33–4, 62–3, 66, 79, 105, 146
  tripartism in 17, 116, 119–20
  union mergers in 89
  union-NGO cooperation in 149
New Labour (UK) 44, 144
NFS *(Nordens Fackliga Samorganisation)* 162
NGG *(Gewerkschaft Nahrung-Genuss-Gaststätten)* 156

NGOs (non-governmental organizations) 2, 50, 78, 145, 146, 147
  independent monitoring by 188
  international trade unions and 162–6
  national trade unions and 148–51, 203
Nice Treaty (2001) 178
NKV *(Nederlands Katholiek Vakverbond)* 18, 141
'non-accommodating monetary regimes' 118
North America 35, 47, 48, 52, 55, *see also* United States
Northern Ireland 24, 27
Norway 9
Notat, Nicole 73
nuclear energy 147
NVV *(Nederlands Verbond van Vakverenigingen)* 18, 120, 141

OA (Organising Academy) 65, 94, 96
Offe, C. and Wiesenthal, H. 30, 203
ÖGB *(Österreichische Gewerkschaftsbund)* 16, 41, 61, 72, 76, 83, 85, 89, 92, 140–1, 164, 172, 175, 180
O'Grady, Frances 74
Olson, M. 47
'One Big Union' concept 81–2
organizational learning 196–7
organizational power resources 30, 31, 37, 39–40, 52, 53, 90, 105, 109, 134, 145, 148, 157, 189
'organizing model' of trade unionism 47, 49, 52, 55–6, 60, 62, 65–70, 85, 95, 96, 97, 146, 151, 197, 198, 202
ÖVP *(Österreichische Volkspartei)* 16, 41, 140–1

part-time workers 4, 33, 54, 74
partnership agreements 45, 111–12, 121, 130, *see also* social partnership
pattern bargaining 15, 16, 109, 185
PCF *(Parti communiste française)* 20–1, 137, 143, 176
PCI *(Partito comunista italiano)* 22, 23, 120, 137, 143
PCS (Public and Commercial Services Union) 79, 131
PD *(Partito democratico)* 137, 144
peak-level tripartite agreements *see* tripartite agreements
pensions/pensioners 14, 24, 36, 39, 43, 45, 52, 63, 70, 100, 105, 115, 121, 124, 127, 128, 129, 130, 131, 136, 144, 150
performance-related pay 108, 110, 115
Perlman, S. 133, 135
Peters, J. 36
Peterson et al. 148
Pforzheim agreement (2004) 109
pillarization 17–18, 19, 42, 141, 149
Poland 65, 180, 184

Index

polder model 16, 141
political exchange 24, 44, 103, 116–22, 133, 144
politics 27, 145–57, 160
   parties and trade unions 136–45
Portugal 20, 180
postal workers 60, 91, 182
power resources 152, 191
   'borrowed resources' 78, 170, 189
   internationalism and 160, 189–90
   loss of 104–7, 120, 145
   and trade union politics 134; *see also* structural; associational; organizational; institutional; moral; coalitional and strategic power resources
precarious employment 56–7, 58–9, 61, 62, 64–5, 78, 79, 109, 147, 150, *see also* atypical workers
Price, R. and Bain, G. 8
Prigent, Nadine 73
private sector 6, 134, 137
   Austria 16, 69, 83
   France 22, 42
   Germany 60
   Ireland 130
   Netherlands 18, 89
   Nordic countries 58
   UK 44, 108, 111, 114
privatization 29, 43, 45, 90, 144
proactive strategy 20, 48, 50, 65, 191, 199, *see also* recruitment
Prodi government (Italy) 144
professional unions 7, 9, 12, 15, 27, 71, 82, 83, 84, 89, 92, 108, 137, *see also* white-collar workers
proportional representation 13, 21, 72, 73, 87
PS *(Parti Socialiste)* (Belgium) 142
PS *(Parti Socialiste)* (France) 142–3
PSI *(Partito socialista italiano)* 143
public opinion 2, 15, 146, 156
public sector 6, 10, 69, 86, 116, 133
   alliances 146
   austerity cuts 123, 129, 130, 131, 135, 144, 155–6
   Austria 60
   Belgium 57, 62, 84, 128
   Britain 26, 45, 88, 96, 114, 131, 144, 155–6
   collective bargaining 106
   Denmark 12, 76, 99
   female workers and 53–4
   France 22, 42
   Germany 40
   international solidarity 148
   Ireland 45, 130
   Netherlands 89
   recruitment 57
   strikes 106, 134
Sweden 11
Putnam, R. D. 200, 201
PvdA *(Partij van de Arbeid)* 18, 41, 120, 141
PWD (Posted Workers directive) 182

QMV (qualified majority voting) 171
Québec union survey 199

railway unions 105
recruitment 2, 22, 26, 30, 32, 47–8, 55–70, 79, 80, 94, 145, 146
referendums 173, 174, 175, 176, 177, 178–9
regulation of labour markets 42, 117, 132, 133, 174, 183
Rehder, B. 40, 97
Rehfeldt, U. 187
Rehn-Meidner model, *see* Sweden
representatives of trade unions 42
   Italy 23
   managerial unionism 96–7
   paid release from work 22
   shop stewards 9, 10, 26, 44, 96, 108, 201
   'tendency to oligarchy' 7, 87, 98, 192
   training 96
retail unions 59, 60, 76, 78, 90, 93, 95, 99, 148, 173
retirement age 36, 41, 128, 129
Richards, A. J. 200
right-wing politics 9, 20, 22, 38, 39, 61, 84, 131, 138, 139, 147, 171, 174, 181
RILU (Red International of Labour Unions) 159
RMT (National Union of Rail, Maritime and Transport Workers) 78–9, 144
Romania 180, 181
RSU *(rappresentanza sindacale unitaria)* 23
Rüffert case (2008) 182
Rychly, L. 126
Ryder, Guy 167

SACO (Sveriges Akademikers Centralorganisation) 10, 11, 38, 59, 89
SAF (Svenska Arbetsgivareföreningen) 10, 11
SAP *(Sveriges socialdemokratiska arbetareparti)* 10, 11, 138–9
scala mobile (Italian wage indexation system) 24, 46, 99, 121
scandals in banking sector 41, 92
Scharpf, F. W. 197
Schmidt, V. A. 198
Schulten, T. 185
SEA (Single European Act) 174, 177
Sechi, C. 71
sectoral bargaining/agreements 12, 15–16, 19, 21, 24, 29, 43, 44, 64, 69, 76–7, 99, 108–11, 113, 114, 118, 119, 129
sectoral unions 64, 72, 86, 160, 164–5, 167

271

Index

self-employed workers 2, 20, 57–8, 60–1, 63, 181
SER (Sociaal-Economische Raad) 17, 119
servicing model of trade unionism 55, 56, 186, 198, 201
SF *(Socialistisk Folkeparti)* 174
shareholder value 39, 102
Shonfield, A. 115–16
shop stewards 9, 10, 26, 44, 96, 108, 201
Shorter, E. and Tilly, C. 134
SiD *(Specialarbejderforbundet i Danmark)* 72, 90, 174
SIF *(Svenska industritjänstemannaförbundet)* 89, 196
Simms, M. and Holgate, J. 65
SIPTU (Services, Industrial, Professional and Technical Union) 27, 68–9, 74, 89, 94, 145, 178, 179
'SMART' management approach 97
SMTs (senior management teams) 96–7
SN (Svenskt Näringsliv) 10
social capital 30, 198, 200–2, 203
Social-democratic parties 4, 9, 10, 11, 13, 16, 37–9, 41, 49, 134, 136–41, 172, 173, 174, 175
social dialogue 76, 103, 124, 127, 130, 171, 183
social dumping 49, 170, 180, 183, 184
social movements 50, 148, 151, 203
social networking 35, 100, 101, 205
social pacts 18, 49, 85, 103, 117, 119, 120, 122
social partnership 4, 13, 14, 49, 115–22, 146, 171, 189
  Austria 16, 41, 85, 103, 141
  Belgium 18, 103
  France 43
  Germany 103
  Ireland 45, 103, 121–2, 130, 145
  Italy 103, 120–1
  Netherlands 17, 42, 103
Socialdemokraterne 139, 154, 174
Socialist parties 6, 19, 21, 22, 26, 81, 82, 142
solidarity 33–4, 79, 108, 154, 165, 189, 199, 200, 202
  international 148, 159, 160, 164
Sommer, Michael 163
South African unions 163
Soviet Union, collapse of 36–7
Spain 20, 180
SPD *(Sozialdemokratische Partei Deutschlands)* 14–15, 136, 138, 140, 157, 163
special committees 71, 72, 75, 80, 98–9
SPÖ *(Sozialdemokratische Partei Österreichs)* 16, 41, 140–1, 175
steelworkers 135, 151, 167
Storti, Bruno 166

strategic capacity 46–50, 96, 192–205
strategic power resources 31, 66, 90, 97, 106, 190, 191
strategic reviews 68, 93–5
strategy/strategic choices 8, 69, 70, 91, 93, 114–18, 122, 125, 144, 154–5, 157, 172, 187
Streeck, W. 14, 40, 186, 192
Streeck, W. and Visser, J. 92
stress at work 113–14
strikes 80, 146, 182
  in Belgium 128
  in Britain 79, 100–1, 125, 183
  declining 42, 103, 104–7
  in Denmark 76
  in France 42, 134, 155
  global financial crisis and 127
  in Italy 129
  legality of 2
  in Netherlands 33–4, 62–3, 66, 79, 128, 146
  payment of benefits 86
  and plant closures 135
  in United States 135
  'virtual' 106
students 59, 64, 155
STvdA *(Stichting van de Arbeid)* 17, 115, 119
SUD *(Union syndicale solidaires)* 22, 84, 110, 143, 150, 176
'supply side trade unionism' 44
sustainable development 145, 147–8
Sweden 4, 8–12, 46, 161
  anti-stress agreements in 113
  Codetermination Act (MBL) (1976) 11
  and European integration 173–4
  female representation in 71
  free movement of workers and 180, 181
  global financial crisis and 123, 126
  international trade union involvement 162–3
  Laval judgment in 182, 183–4
  managerial unionism in 97
  membership density in 5, 6, 52, 54–5, 58, 199
  membership surveys in 99
  political parties and unions in 138–9
  recruitment in 59, 69
  Rehn-Meidner model 10–11, 103
  strategic reviews in 93
  strike data in 105
  tripartism in 116
  unemployment insurance in 9, 38
  union mergers in 88–90, 92
  union-NGO cooperation in 148
  voluntary collective bargaining in 38–9
Swenson, P. 86
'sword of justice' 31, 32, 132, 203, 204

Index

Tarifautonomie, principle of 14, 156
taxation 36, 130
Taylor, A. J. 133
Taylorism 20
TCE (Constitutional Treaty 2005) 175, 176, 177
TCO *(Tjänstemännens Centralorganisation)* 10, 11, 38, 59, 71, 89–90, 93, 97, 108, 113, 148, 162, 173–4, 176
teachers' unions 59, 149
TELCO (The East London Communities Organization) 146
Telljohann, V. 187
temporary workers 57, 60, 61, 63, 64
TGWU (Transport and General Workers' Union) 66, 88–9, 177, *see also* Unite
Thatcher government (UK) 171, 177
Thelen, K. A. 40
3F *(Fagligt Fælles Forbund)* 13, 59, 72, 90
TIB *(Forbundet Træ-Industri-Byg)* 90
Tilly, C. 204
Touraine, A. 79
Toys R Us 148
transport unions 66, 78–9, 88–9, 106, 144, 148, 173, 177, 183
Traxler, F. 108
Traxler, F. and Brandl, B. 185
Traxler et al. 185
Treaty of Rome (1957) 170, 179
Trentin, Bruno 121
tripartite agreements 23–4, 45, 99, 110, 111, 112, 113, 117–20, 122, 127–8, 131, 133, 141, 142
tripartite institutions 11, 14, 17, 27, 31, 103, 116
Tu, N. 189
TUC (Trades Union Congress) 25, 26, 49, 65, 67, 81, 83, 85, 86, 88, 144
   alliances 146–7, 151
   'battle of ideas' 155–6
   equal opportunities initiatives 74
   and European integration 177
   free movement of workers 181
   international influence of 166–7
   managerial unionism 96, 97
   'New Unionism' project 94, 99–100
   partnership 111
   response to austerity measures 131, 155–6
   workplace learning agenda 113
Turner, H. A. 83, 98

UIL *(Unione italiana del lavoro)* 23, 64, 111, 121, 129, 143, 166
UMF (Union Modernisation Fund) 96–7
unemployment 33, 34, 37, 78, 90, 117
   Denmark 9, 10, 12
   former East Germany 40

France 155
Ghent system 62
insurance 6, 9, 38, 128
Sweden 9, 10, 11, 38
and union membership 58
UNI (Union Network International) 94
Unionen (merger of SIF/HTF unions) 59, 90, 196
Unison (UK public sector union) 66, 74, 88, 91, 100, 114, 167
Unite (UK's largest union) 67, 131, 151, 167
United States 56, 81, 201, 202
   'corporate campaign' model and 78
   housing bubble in 122
   'membership-orientated offensive strategy' 60
   opportunity structures in 135
   Steelworkers' Union in 167
   unionization of farm workers in 193
   work rules and job classifications in 46
'Unity is strength' motto 30, 82
UNSA *(Union nationale des syndicats autonomes)* 22
Urban, H.-J. 127
USDAW (Union of Shop, Distributive and Allied Workers) 66, 69

Vandaele, K. 75
VENRO (umbrella body of development NGOs) 149
ver.di (Vereinte Dienstleistungsgewerkschaft) 15, 60, 69, 72, 76, 78, 83, 89, 91, 92, 93–4, 96, 113, 114, 140, 146, 147, 149, 156, 163, 198
Verzetnitsch, Fritz 41, 175
Viking Line case (2007) 182
Visser, J. 29, 160
Visser, J. and Rhodes, M. 122
Visser, J. and van der Meer, M. 128
vocational training 14, 59, 112–13
Vodafone 39
Volkswagen 163
voluntarism 9, 11–12, 18, 24, 25, 26, 119, 182, 185
voluntary sector 150–1, 200

Waddington, J. 46
wage(s) 8, 10–11, 133
   cross-national disparities 179–80
   cuts 124, 130
   gender equality 61, 76–7, 170
   indexation system 24, 46, 99, 121, 128
   performance-related 108, 110, 115
   restraint 103, 116–22, 126, 128, 131, 184
Walton, R. E. and McKersie, R. B. 106
Wassenaar agreement (1982) 119

273

Index

WCL (World Confederation of Labour) 159, 161, 163, 164, 165, 169, 172
Webb, Sidney and Webb, Beatrice 1, 31, 81–2, 91, 114, 200, 201, 202
Webster et al. 31
welfare states 31, 36, 49, 154, 203
   Britain 26
   cutbacks 117, 141
   Denmark 9, 10, 12
   France 21
   Germany 14
   Netherlands 17, 141
   Sweden 9, 10, 173
   'three worlds' of 3–4, 13, 26
WFTU (World Federation of Trade Unions) 159, 161, 166, 169, 172
white-collar workers 10, 16–17, 33, 60–1, 69, 72, 76, 83, 98, 114, 116, 164
   Belgium 19
   Britain 26
   Denmark 12, 90, 119, 137, 163

Netherlands 18, 84
Sweden 89, 137
trade union structure and 82–3, *see also* professional unions
Whittall, M. and Kotthoff, H. 187
WKÖ *(Wirtschaftskammer Österreich)* 15–16
work-life balance 114, 153
working class 25, 32–3, 87, 134, 138, 176–7
working hours 57, 114, 121, 129
works councils 3, 14, 16, 17, 18–19, 31, 42, 61, 109, 197
   EWCs (European Works Councils) 158, 167, 184, 186–9
World Social Fora 150

young workers 40, 58–9, 61, 62, 63–4, 65, 69, 75
youth unemployment 43

Zoll, R. 200

Printed and bound by CPI Group (UK) Ltd, Croydon, CR0 4YY